FRAGMENT

MW01278384

CREATION BOOKS

London • San Francisco

CREDITS

Fragments Of Fear
An Illustrated History Of British Horror Films
By:
Andy Boot
ISBN 1 84068 055 5
CREATION CINEMA COLLECTION, VOLUME 4
© Andy Boot 1995, 1999
First published 1996 by:
CREATION BOOKS
This new updated edition published 1999
Design/layout/typesetting:
PCP International
Design technician:
Bradley Davis
Photographs:
From the Jack Hunter Collection, by courtesy of the film distributors.

CONTENTS

Introduction

There has never really been a book that covers the whole range of British horror movies. There have been plenty of weighty tomes that cover Hammer – and quite rightly, as their output does take up over a fifth of the films covered in this book – and many that mention British movies in amongst the American and European efforts but none that concentrate solely on those produced and made in Britain.

This book is an attempt to redress that balance.

Films chosen for this book had one other criterion: that they must, in some way, have a pretence towards showing their audiences horror. That is why there are seemingly odd choices such as *The Caretaker* (1964), *The Bed Sitting Room* (1969), or Samuel Beckett's *Film* (1979), as all three are attempts by the original authors to show some horrific aspect of the human condition, and are thus just as applicable to this book as any Hammer *Dracula* or *Frankenstein* vehicle, and perhaps more valid.

Speaking of Hammer, the casual browser may notice from the filmography that there is no place for the likes of that company's *Rasputin The Mad Monk* (1966), or indeed that the list includes some efforts by the Baker-Berman team, but stops short at their presentations of *The Hellfire Club* (1960), or *Dr Crippen* (1962). This is because there is a fine line between the horror these producers peddled and such historical melodramas.

In much the same way, there are some sci-fi movies, such as *Night Of The Big Heat* (1967) or *The Projected Man* (1966), yet no room for the likes of Aaru Productions' (aka Amicus) versions of *Dr Who* which were produced in the 1960's. Again, there was a fine line to draw as in the late 1950's and early 1960's, horror moved away from its Gothic and supernatural roots and into the arena of science. Post A- and H-Bomb, most people were terrified of the men in white coats who had given the world powers the means with which to destroy the globe. This is a perfectly reasonable terror, and one which the film-makers of the day exploited with a series of pictures in which the scientists tampered with nature to catastrophic results. Like the mad doctor movies of the 1930's and 1940's, these were just a pseudo-scientific excuse for horror to appease an audience whose credibility for the supernatural and paranormal – the previous hooks on which horror was hung – was beginning to wear thin.

It is interesting to note that, as we draw near the millennium, the past fifteen years has seen a rise once more in the popularity of paranormal based horror. I cannot help but think that the rise of New Age philosophies, and a general disillusionment with a science that has given us nothing but disease and warfare – and even more interesting ways to wipe each other out – instead of improving the general quality of life as was claimed in the golden age of the 1950's and 1960's, is at least in part responsible for this.

In many ways, this is a return to the roots of horror, based on terror and fear of the unknown. Ghosts, ghoulies, and monsters have always been the staple of horror. Unfortunately, the idea of evil forces coming from another realm and taking us over, or ghosts stalking for revenge, is not something that this writer has ever found that scary. The more one researches into the paranormal, as I have for previous books and works in progress, the more one finds that the paranormal did not ever hurt anyone. Most ghosts are lonely spirits who have not realised they have died, or are nothing more than recordings of people or events impressed upon a particular landscape, replaying forever like a video-loop.

There are entities and forces that are malign, but these could only really be termed evil when their energies are directed by human hosts or magicians who have no morality, the forces themselves do not possess a sense of morality. It is the people who are really horrific, and the people who are scared of such things who usually end up hurting themselves...

Perhaps this is why the so-called supernatural (this writer believes that all is natural, just not yet explained) has been an excellent vehicle for writers and artists to express the dark sides of their souls over the years. Along the way, there have been some truly chilling moments produced. For me, the calm way in which M R James can describe a happening, or Stephen King can illuminate the feelings of a character trapped in a weird situation, is much more frightening than a host of gore movies or novels by the likes of Shaun Hutson. Having said that, the latter are wonderful for their revelling in the baser instinct of disgust.

Ultimately, the most horrifying film I have ever seen was *The Animals Film*, a 1980 exposition of animal experimentation and torture in both science and farming. Set to low key commentary and music, the inhumanity displayed in the treatment of animals by man was truly repulsive and horrific. So-called horror movies are just reflections of fears, and are a safe release for tensions. This was the real thing...

Horror movies are primarily entertainment, an entertainment that plays on primal fears lurking just below the surface, perhaps, but entertainment nonetheless. They are intended to make money for the producers, and are a source of income for the cast and crew. I sometimes think that it would be as well for critics to remember this when dissecting the horror film. There are practitioners who have an artistic vision, but even they must pay the gas and electric bill at the end of the day. Too much gore, too much violence, and the film will not get a general release. A string of financial disasters of this order, and even the most dedicated auteur may think again.

Money is why the British horror film got off to a slow start, and why it developed in a slightly more refined manner than its European and transatlantic cousins, and why it suddenly passed them in full flower in the 1950's. Money is also why it died slowly, being absorbed as most culture has been into the global melting pot of the information highway and mass communications. This melting pot has not been the colourful clash and exposition of different cultures that the idealist would have wished for (although this is happening at the fringes), rather it is a pot in which all individual cultures are being subsumed to that which promises the most money. For the last fifty years this has been the USA, particularly in film-making, and so the British horror movie, with its own characteristics, died out in the late 1970's and 1980's until even the few good examples that were being made were undeniably more transatlantic in tone.

Is this a good thing? That depends entirely on what you like. To me, it is sad that the British horror movie has died – but at least Clive Barker still gets to make movies, right?

This book aims to look at the history of the British horror movie. Mostly it is about the films themselves because when they are good, they are very good, but I make no apologies for finding unintentional humour in some films, or even parts of films. It is perfectly possible for a movie to be both genuinely scary and also unintentionally funny at the same time. The one quality does not have to detract from the other. A film may very well be a reflection of deep and dark fears, a mirror to the times – but it can also be extremely stupid and crass because of conscious attempts to exploit those qualities.

This history cannot be complete as there are some films lost forever because of the disintegration of old nitrate stock, and some films that are forever lost because of legal tie-ups and long-dead production companies for whom no-one is responsible. What I have attempted to do is gather together as many British horror movies as I could find, see as many as possible, and research details on those that I have not so far tracked down. If any have been missed, then contact me c/o the publishers, and there will be amendments to any future editions.

It may be noticed that the earlier the film, the more coverage it gets. This is not because of any particular bias, indeed, most of my favourite British horrors stem from the early 1970's. However, the earlier movies have always been neglected, and have not necessarily received that much coverage in the past. It will also be noticed that the sections on Hammer and Amicus are perhaps somewhat briefer in detail than other chapters. Again, these movies have been covered in great detail by other people, and although incredibly important to the development of the British horror movie, limitations of space prevent me giving equal weight to all movies.

Do not expect this book to be hyper-critical, as I'm the type of person who can find something interesting in any film, however ridiculous. After all, there has to be some way of justifying wasting ninety minutes of your life in front of a film or TV screen...

So there you have it, a brief introduction to what you will find in the following pages. These movies sometimes said something, sometimes reflected something, but all of them (with the possible exception of *Film*, financed by the British Film Institute) were made primarily as a vehicle for printing money. Often they say things by accident. Just don't take it too seriously, and enjoy the ride...

VARNEY THE VAMPIRE;
OR, THE FEAST OF BLOOD.

A ROMANCE OF EXCITING INTEREST.

1. The Birth...Kicking And Screaming

Maria Marten was murdered by her would-be lover, Squire Corder, who buried her in his barn and was caught when a dog sniffed out the body. He was made to dig up the body himself, and the hangman for his execution was none other than Maria's one true love.

This old tale, handed down from the early eighteenth century in broadsheet ballad, penny dreadful novel form, and later in stage plays, was the basis on which the first real star of British horror, Tod Slaughter, built his reputation. An actor-manager who toured music halls as well as reputable theatres, his string of terror melodramas in the 1930's and 1940's were uninhibited in their gusto for blood and thunder, and represented one side of the coin on which British horror is based. The flip-side was repressed Victorian sexuality and prim morality. This flip was so strong that Slaughter almost single-handedly forms the core of British horror pre-World War II.

Slaughter's career will be dealt with in the next chapter. First, a brief look at why he was the only consistent horror maker, and at the other contenders.

American horror movies had a vast wealth of written and oral stories to draw on, as vast as the emigré population that peopled the industry and the land. European film-makers, from the earliest days, have been obsessed with the image of film as much as the story. But with the English the play was the thing. Having William Shakespeare, the alleged greatest playwright of all time, born in your country puts a great onus on an audience to be concerned with the literary qualities of any acting performance. Therefore, the cinema was always somewhat frowned upon. Legitimate actors didn't like the fact that a full-length play would be compressed to ten or twenty minutes, the length of one or two reels, or that their gloriously intoned lines could not be recorded. It says a lot about theatre culture that excerpts from plays were as often recorded onto cylinder or record as they were filmed in the early days of the cinema.

With most of the map coloured red for the British Empire (and, presumably, the blood spilt in gaining the Empire), the notion of Shakespeare as being the greatest playwright ever, and English being the pre-eminent language in the world, grew in strength until the figure of Shakespeare loomed over drama like a forbidding ghost. Hence, by the time British film-makers really got going, the only way to gain respectability was to make films as though they were actually plays. And when sound arrived, allowing actors to moonlight from the stage and intone their lines as though they were projecting to the gods (cheap theatre seats, up in the roof of an auditorium) instead of a camera less than ten yards away, the pattern for British cinema was set for some years to come.

Interestingly, the one good British horror film to come out of the silent era was made by Alfred Hitchcock. *The Lodger* (US title *The Case Of Jonathan Drew*), staring matinée idol Ivor Novello was made for Gaumont British in 1926, and re-made with the same star as a talkie in 1932 – with a new US title *The Phantom Fiend*. Although it had a literary source (a novel by Marie Belloc-Lowndes), it also had the freewheeling and imaginative use of the camera that Hitchcock was to make his trademark. All this, and only his third film. *The Lodger* was made by one of the big three studios (the other being, Gainsborough, and Ealing) during the early years of English cinema. It is interesting to note that these three, who controlled distribution and production for the majority of the period from 1920-1949, produced only a handful of horror vehicles, and most of these horror comedies, vehicles for popular stage or radio comics. Rank, who began in the late 1930's and rose to pre-eminence in the 1950's, always fought shy of the supernatural, possibly as a result of J Arthur Rank's religious beliefs.

So, we have the strong stage tradition and snobbishness towards cinema counting against the growth of the British film in general. This resulted in the market being swamped by American movies. Even in the days before sound and the common language uniting the two countries, the Americans had a strong grip on the British market. The simple fact is that they made more films, and better films. Eventually, the distribution arms of the American studios had a stranglehold on British cinemas, using a block booking system that ensured play dates for even the lowliest of their product. What usually happened was that a dud film would be packaged with a good film, or a vehicle for new talent packaged with an established star vehicle. In this way, the cinema manager would have to agree to take the dud or non-star vehicle to ensure gaining the bigger film and filling his house.

The answer was in the quota system. The Cinematograph Films Act of 1927 ensured that a proportion of films shown in British cinemas would have to be English-made. This could be enforced via the licensing act for cinemas – the Cinematograph Act of 1909, which was basically a safety law but had the effect of introducing the first strains of censorship.

The new act should have opened the floodgates to a wealth of English talent. Unfortunately, it didn't work like this, as instead, small-time producers vied with each other to make the cheapest movies possible, in order to make a quick financial killing from bookings.

British movies were generally pretty poor, both technically and artistically. Film was still a poor relation. This was surprising, as some of the early film pioneers had been British, most notably George Albert Smith, who filmed a ghost for the Society Of Psychical Research in 1898. Like his more illustrious French counterpart, Méliès, Smith was an illusionist who loved to work tricks into his films. Walter Booth was likewise influenced by the Frenchman, and films like *The Magic Sword*, *The Haunted Curiosity Shop*, and *The Cheese Mites* (all 1901) featured fighting skeletons, homunculi, and living mummies.

1902 saw the compression of *Maria Marten, Or Murder In The Red Barn*, into five minutes by Dicky Winslow, who cranked his camera at a passing theatre company. Could this be the first English horror? It certainly tapped into the literary vein that was to prove so popular. For English literature, both the highbrow and the pure pulp, has been the basis for much Anglo-American horror over the years.

The British literary horror tradition really began with the Gothic romances and terrors of Matthew Lewis and Horace Walpole. Lewis' *The Monk* and Walpole's *Castle Of Otranto*, published at the end of the eighteenth century, were astonishing for their day. Although both borrowed heavily from European sources, their mix of sex and the supernatural, with horrific results for the protagonist, touched a nerve in the literate populace. The demand for Gothic fiction was such that writers were soon churning books out by the score, often plagiarising each other's work.

Scarcely thirty years later, Mary Shelley wrote *Frankenstein* and Byron's physician John Polidori penned *The Vampyre* as the result of a competition between the Shelley's and Byron over who could write the best chiller. Mary Shelley made horror respectable with a work that is not easy reading after nearly two hundred years, but is still preferable to the convoluted prose of the Gothic writers. Ironically, it could be argued that Polidori, whose work is far less readable than even the worst Gothic (Montague Summers' *A Gothic Bibliography*, published in the 1930's, lists literally hundreds of Gothic novels and part-works published in the period 1764-1864), had the greater influence.

As the Victorian age swung into place, closing the door on the expression of emotion and joy, clamping down the populace with the rigid puritanism of Prince

Albert's personal philosophy, any expressions of fear or lust were forced underground. The Gothics mutated into the penny dreadfuls, cheap and illiterate part works that were spun into years of convoluted plot (the writers were paid by the word, so it was a good move to make a story last as long as possible). The most popular of these was *Varney The Vampire*, an extrapolation of Polidori's stolen themes. *Varney The Vampire* inspired a host of copies, including Bram Stoker's *Dracula*.

Stoker could not write very well; *Dracula* is as hard a read as *The Monk*, with hardly any of the fun. All the sexuality is disguised beneath the veneer of terror. In many ways, this could be said to make it the ultimate Victorian novel.

Certainly, the true inheritors of Shelley were writers like Emily Bronte, who actually has something to say in *Wuthering Heights*, some passages of which touch more primal fears than anything Stoker could dream of.

When film arrived, there were two distinct sides to the British character. The prim and proper public face, and the secret night-stalker who went to see the likes of Tod Slaughter literally slay them in the aisles before retiring to their favourite brothel.

As cinemas were licensed, the prim and proper public side frowned on horror as being low brow, and even the stupidest J.P. had an idea that Dracula was after more than blood... if the threat of an empty house was not enough, the spectre of a lost licence was also looming for the hapless cinema owner who would book horror.

A result of this was that the technically backward British film-makers would not tackle horror. With little chance of getting a booking, even on the quota system, it was a bad move. The number of films that had anything approaching terror could virtually be counted on one hand. All now lost, they were probably toned-down versions of their sources. *The Face At The Window* (1920), *Maria Marten* (again in 1928) and *Sweeney Todd* (1928) were vehicles for penny-dreadful melodrama that Tod Slaughter would later reclaim on film. *The Coughing Horror* (1924) could have been a good pun, but was an adaption of one of Sax Rohmer's Fu Manchu novels. *The Man Without Desire* (1923) had Ivor Novello climbing out of a coffin – which was nothing compared to what Hitchcock would have him doing in his silent version of *The Lodger* (1926), three years later. The only genuine horror stories to be adapted were W W Jacob's *The Monkey's Paw* (1923), and *Esmerelda* (1922), a version of The Hunchback Of Notre Dame story by Victor Hugo.

Despite *The Lodger* and the attempts of these early pioneers, true horror did not arrive until Universal made *Dracula* (1931) with Bela Lugosi. Adapted from a British stage play, based on a British novel, it needed an American company to take the chance (Gaumont had held an option on the play which they swapped with Universal for UK distribution).

It is here that the final obstacle to the growth of the British horror film comes into play. The British Board of Film Censors made every film that could be classed a horror an "A" certificate, which meant that anyone under sixteen was prevented from admission to the see the film. Horrific "A" movies were also reported to the Home Office as being, in the Board's opinion, "horrific in character". In 1937, the "H" certificate was introduced for such films, and some films previously banned were given this certificate. However some US horror movies, like Tod Browning's *Freaks* (1932), remained banned for over thirty years.

In this kind of climate, is it any wonder that British producers were unwilling to make horror movies? Those that did tried to show the horror in an understated way, with implication and use of sound and music instead of outright scenes of horror.

Nearly all the horror films made in this period still carried an "A" or "H" certificate, but they began to carry an undertone of repressed menace that the more overt European and US films did not carry.

This financial consideration, along with the prevailing middle-class attitudes that informed the media and general public, led to British horror developing a strain of repressed emotional terror that infused all British movies, even in the 1950's when Hammer broke new ground with technicolour gore, beating the Americans at their own terror game.

In the same way that H P Lovecraft is a good horror writer because of his limitations (innumerable references to the unnameable leading the reader to imagine the unthinkable), so British horror movies lead the viewer into likewise doing some of the work. And there is nothing so frightening as your own fears and phobias, rather than someone else's.

In the wake of Universal's *Dracula*, British horror movie makers swung into action with a speed quite rare for the British industry, and 1932 saw three horror movies released onto the market.

The first, in 1932, was a sound remake of *The Lodger* for Twickenham Films, with matinée idol and composer Ivor Novello reprising the role he had played for Hitchcock some six years before. Novello plays a mysterious young man who lodges in the upstairs back room of a lodging house, coming and going at odd hours, and always very evasive about his business. Chinese whispers begin around the neighbourhood that he is up to no good. There are a series of murders in which young women are ruthlessly killed, and the general consensus has it that Novello is the ripper.

Marie Belloc-Lowndes (known, as many female novelists of her day, as Mrs. Belloc-Lowndes) was a melodrama queen who had penned the original of *The Lodger* when the series of murders attributed to Jack The Ripper were still fresh in people's memories. In the novel, Jack is the lodger. In the first two film versions, the story was made contemporary to erase all mention of Jack, and the lodger turned out to be innocent. This was not the case in a Hollywood version that reverted to gas-lamps and starred Laird Cregar in the 1940's. There is, however, an unwritten law of casting that stated an idol such as Novello could never be a villain – only mistaken for one.

And so it is in this film, where he is snatched from the jaws of a baying mob by the revelation that the real killer has been found.

To be frank, anyone with any sense would have divined that Novello was not the killer, as his performance is so anaemic as to render him incapable of harming even the commonest house fly. But this only adds to the real horrific element of the film: the way in which a perfectly reasonable young man can become transformed into a monster by the perceptions of other people. The way in which rumours and half-truths are distorted in the re-telling, and the manner in which petty prejudices can grow into damning condemnations is pretty chilling. This aspect of the script is well-presented (Novello co-wrote it with Miles Mander, Paul Rotha, and H Fowler Mear). Perhaps because of the number of people working on the script, it does not really hang together, and although director Maurice Elvey went on to make a series of quite respectable minor movies throughout the 1930's, his handling here is clumsy, possibly because the technology for sound movies in the UK was still lagging behind the Americans, and the idea of movement and sound recording was a little alien.

Novello may have been happier singing on stage than acting on film (he was never as good as Hitchcock made him), but the supporting cast buoys him up, led by a young Jack Hawkins, the reliable Peter Gawthorne (more usually seen as a peppery forces type or police officer, acting as foil to innumerable comics), and Kynaston Reeves, who even at this relatively young age could play crusty old men as though it were second nature.

Castle Sinister (1932) was a cheap, low-rent movie now long since lost, made by a company called Delta, notable for little else other than giving Vernon Sewell the first crack at his life-long quest to make a perfect version of *The Medium* (1934). Coming out of Bushey studios, one of several low rent studios in the Home Counties (another of which was the British Lion studios in Beaconsfield, owned and run by crime novelist Edgar Wallace, who formed the company to film his books "properly",

The Lodger

believing other companies ruined the plots – though two of his books, filmed by those other companies, gave some terrifying moments on the British screen later in the decade), the plot was an early example of the mad doctor school, as actor Eric Adeney tries to transplant the brain of a beautiful girl into the skull of an apeman? It was directed by one Widgney Newman, who seemed to be quite content to let the action unfold without too much effort on his part.

Not a man to be deterred by making a bad film, or even one that failed to make a profit (only those British films that were able to play to full houses – not those restricted by certification – could do more than break even), Newman promoted himself to producer for the even more obscure *The Unholy Quest*.

The last horror movie of 1932 was Hiscott's production of *The Face At The Window*. Like the silent version – and unlike the much more interesting Tod Slaughter version of seven years later – this production down-played the chill for more of a detective story approach. Raymond Massey, a Canadian actor who spent some time in Britain before graduating to Hollywood stardom, took on the role that C Aubrey Smith had played in the silent version. With the name actors taking the role of the detective who solves a series of murders and robberies, the onus was taken away from the horrifying behaviour of the chief villain, one Lucio Degradoff, a banker by day and the sinister thief Le Loup by night. Degradoff's last victim is in the act of writing "I was murdered by Luc..." when he dies.

The police, like all good film police, immediately arrest the innocent Lucien Cartwright, a bank clerk who is in love with a girl Le Loup has designs upon. Naturally, the villain of the piece is not above a little deception in pointing the finger at Cartwright.

One Dr Le Blanc (the setting is France, even if the accents and moralities are pure British) is at work on galvanism, and believes that the last thing a dead person sees is imprinted upon them. If he can get the corpse to revive briefly with electric shocks, then it will finish the sentence.

Of course, Le Loup is none too pleased by this, and sends the character of the title of the film – actually his disfigured brother, who he keeps in a cage and uses on his burglaries – after the Doctor, the Inspector, and everyone in sight.

Naturally, the revived corpse writes Lucio when shocked, and Le Loup gives himself away... just as well, really, as it's not the corpse under the sheet, but Lucien himself.

Pure blood and thunder melodrama under usual circumstances, the Hiscott production is caught between going for the jugular and going for the box office, with the result that it seemed to please no-one.

So far, then, the British horror movie had got off to a tentative start. Although the idea that restraint and distance may be able to add chills by suggestion may have occurred to the producers so far in operation, none had the resources or talent to really attempt this.

As for the big studios; Gainsborough had made a tentative stab at the successful comedy-horror stage-play *The Ghost Train* (1931), in which the laughs were played up at the expense of the horrors; Ealing was still to be pulled together by Michael Balcon, their guiding light; and Gaumont British, the company with whom he was still embroiled, had shied away from horror after their brush with Hitchcock and *The Lodger.*

This all changed in 1933, when Boris Karloff – at the peak of his success – decided to return home to Britain for a holiday. Gaumont offered him the chance to make it a working one, and *The Ghoul* (1933) became the first true British horror. A landmark film, and one which was really a standard for all British horror until the success of Hammer, it will be dealt with in greater detail in the chapter on the larger studios. Suffice to say that Gaumont were pleased enough to follow it up the next year with a version of Edgar Allan Poe's *The Tell-Tale Heart* (1934).

It also spurred a couple of smaller producers to make a further attempt at solving the problem of horror versus bookings.

Delta were back in action with Vernon Sewell's *The Medium* (1934). Brisk, competent and workmanlike, it used a grand guignol play entitled *L'Angoisse* by Pierre Mills and C Vylars as its inspiration. Sewell had bought the rights to this with an idea to establishing himself in movies.

It did not work. There does not appear to be a print extant, but Sewell did use the play several times during his career, most notably as the basis for his film *House Of Mystery* (1960). He also filmed it as *The Latin Quarter* (1945), the *Ghosts Of Berkely Square*, and *Ghost Ship* (1951). The original version may have been low budget and now lost, but it did start him on a career that kept him in work directing film and TV for the rest of his life – interestingly, handling more thrillers than horrors.

The other cheap-jack horror effort of 1934 also came from the Delta stable, if indirectly. Widgney Newman, non-director of *Castle Sinister*, promoted himself to producer with former star Eric Adeney (and I use the term "star" loosely). Deciding that a director would be a good idea, they recruited the hapless R W Lottinga, whose later career in light comedy and musicals seems hardly the sort of thing to inspire terror. The result, *The Unholy Quest* (1934), was reputedly a bit of a mess. Another lost film, it seems to have been a variant on the mad doctor theme, whereby actor Claude Bailey tries to resuscitate an embalmed crusader as part of a search for the Holy Grail. Based in part on Charles Williams' 1931 novel *War In Heaven*, it would have been perhaps better for Newman and Adeney to stick to the book (which I consider a lost classic of restrained horror).

The next year there was little activity from the small studios, except for the entry into the arena of that titan of terror, Tod Slaughter. However, his work will be dealt with as one body. It also saw a small distribution company called Hammer import Bela Lugosi for a film about the ghostly Marie Celeste.

1936 saw *The Terror* from Gaumont, as Edgar Wallace's horrifying crime melodrama was successfully filmed for the first time. It also saw Gainsborough try their hand at straight horror when Boris Karloff returned to Britain and made the excellent *The Man Who Changed His Mind* (1936, US title *The Man Who Lived Again*), in many ways the ultimate mad doctor movie.

Perhaps spurred by this, a small-time producer called Joe Rock got together enough of a budget to shoot his own mad doctor picture, which he called *The Man Behind The Mask* (1936). The plot was simple enough, a mad doctor kidnaps a nobleman's daughter because he is besotted with her, and the hero has to face a number of scientifically-devised terrors to try and recapture her in a series of cliffhanging climaxes that effectively build tension throughout the picture.

Despite a storyline that seems more at home in a Republic or Monogram serial of the 1940's, the film rises above this. The script hangs together well despite being written by four people, Syd Courtnay, Jack Byrd, Stanley Haynes, and Ian Hay. The latter was a former best-selling novelist whose initial success had been with a novel about his wartime exploits. He had then abruptly switched to humour, and written for the gentleman's magazine *Punch*, as well as collaborating on plays with P G Wodehouse and writing a string of strong-selling humorous novels. Perhaps it was his light touch that just leavened the seriousness enough to accentuate the chills when they came.

In the cast was Donald Calthrop, who had been so impressive in *The Man Who Changed His Mind*, and whose speciality was treacherous and weaselish little men. Odd, really, as he was stage actor of some repute, type-cast in films after his appearance as the blackmailer in Hitchcock's seminal *Blackmail* (1929). Cast against him was Hugh Williams, a dour-faced leading man whose urbanity had a hard edge. He was as impressive here as he was in *The Dark Eyes Of London*, three years later – and that's impressive.

It's a surprise to see Michael Powell directing such a project, as his previous films had been straight dramas, and he was later to be one half of the Archers team with Emeric Pressburger, turning out some of the most stylish and impressive British films of all. His skill and sense of pace overcomes the flaws in budget and material, showing the ability to blend horror into the everyday that was to come to fruition over twenty years later in *Peeping Tom* (1959).

Overall, a film that deserves to be resurrected on late night TV as prints do still exist.

One film that would perhaps be better buried is *Juggernaut*, the only independent horror movie to emerge in 1937. This lack of product only serves to show how the certification system defied British producers to make horror. US horror films were either being blocked, or going out a year behind to small runs, so what chance did a British movie have of recouping costs?

Juggernaut is not a bad film per se, but rather like the curate's egg: good only in parts. And like that egg, parts of it are runny and parts congeal horribly. Directed by Henry Edwards with an almost awe-inspiring lack of pacing, the tedious script takes over half of the one hour running time to reach any kind of point. The guilty men are H Fowler Mear (who should have known better), H Frankael, and Cyril Campion. Campion was a novelist, and would have been advised to stick to prose.

The plot concerns yet another mad doctor. This particular doctor plans some outrageous experiments, and can only gain finance for them by committing a series of murders. The actual executions are chilling, as are the scenes where the doctor outlines his plans. This, however, has more to do with the acting that with anything else. For the mad doctor is none other than Boris Karloff, on yet another trip home. Two out of three was not bad, but this was the first time that Karloff had not been given a good vehicle in his home land. Having said that, it should be noted that Karloff always gave of his best, and this is still no worse than many of the mad doctor vehicles he starred in for Columbia in the 1940's.

The last independent horror movie of the 1930's was not released until 1939, and it was also the first British movie to be graced with the new "H" certificate.

The Dark Eyes Of London (1939, US title *The Human Monster*), saw Bela Lugosi return to Britain for the first time since Hammer's tentative toe in the water some four years before. In a dual role, he was pitted against the steely Hugh Williams in a crime melodrama that was shot through with threads of pure horror.

The script, from a novel by Edgar Wallace, is by producer John Argyle (in association with Pathe), Patrick Kirwan, and Walter Summers (who also directed) who keep all the basic elements of the original plot while compressing it into a taut seventy-five minutes.

Lugosi plays an exiled doctor who was drummed out of medicine ("brilliant... but insane"), who has set up a small insurance brokers in London's docklands. Here, a string of his clients, all heavily insured, have mysteriously drowned. The recipients of the claims have all mysteriously "gone away", and policeman Williams is unable to trace them. Which is not good for him, as his superiors are none too happy at the amount of unsolved deaths on his patch. Especially as the dead, who have supposedly drowned in the Thames, have clean water in their lungs...

Things come to a head when the latest victim turns his policy over to Lugosi in return for a loan. What Lugosi does no know is that the man has a daughter, and she is returning from America at the same time as her father is killed. Another thing he does not know is that a clue is in the dead man's pockets...

Lugosi also runs a home for the blind, in dark glasses and white wig, as the Reverend Dearborn. His latest victim has visited there, and a speechless blind violinist called Lew has thrust a warning into his pocket – a warning written in Braille.

Williams puzzles over the piece of paper, but things begin to fall into place as the dead man's daughter is offered a job as Dearborn's secretary – recommended by the doctor. Meanwhile, a forger who the doctor used to fake signatures on policies has been returned from the US by detective Edmon Ryan, who joins forces with Williams to trap the killer. Things get serious when the engine of Lugosi's destruction, the blind giant Jake (brilliantly played with menace by Wilfred Walter), kills the forger and tries to kill Greta Gynt (playing the secretary).

The doctor discovers that Lew has betrayed him, and to stop him being questioned by the police ruptures his eardrums with an electric shock (in the novel, Wallace adopted the less scientific expedient of having the doctor fire blanks in Lew's ear). When Jake discovers this, he goes berserk.

Dearborn has given himself away as not being blind, and Lugosi unmasks Greta Gynt as he is about to kill her. This must have been genuinely shocking for those who did not know that Lugosi was taking a double role, as not only was his disguise excellent, but his voice was dubbed as Dearborn by the actor O B Clarence. Jake, who has been shot by the doctor, rouses his immense strength for a last fight with the man who hurt his only friend, and as the police burst into the room where Lugosi drowned his victims, Jake throws him out into the river, where he dies in the swamp-mud of low tide.

The film moves at a cracking pace, with Williams steely and hard as the policeman under pressure. Ryan is the light relief to William's dour character, and Gynt fulfils the Wallace premise that all heroines must be plucky and get themselves into danger. Lugosi keeps his usual ham tendencies under control, and turns in one of his best performances. There is only one classic hilarious Lugosi moment, where his accent makes "are you accusing me of foul play?" sound more like "are you accusing me of foreplay?".

The true horror lies in the callous way in which the murders and Lugosi's motivations are exposed. Especially noteworthy is the sequence in which Williams and

The Dark Eyes Of London

a pathologist unflinchingly talk about a man drowning, in front of a slide of the corpse floating in a low tide pool of water, mouth agape, eyes staring in death.

Harder-edged than any comparable American film, it is worthy of the master writer himself. Wallace died in Hollywood in 1932, working on the script for *King Kong* (1933), and having written over two hundred novels, the majority of which were thrillers with chilling edges (from the masked monk in *The Terror* to the insanity of the master criminal in *The India Rubber Men*), and a good romantic interest for contrast – this usually enables the heroine to get into danger and enables the hero to battle through even greater disasters.

I confess, *The Dark Eyes Of London* still chills me in places, and is one of my favourite films. Argyle returned to Wallace in 1940 to make *The Door With Seven Locks*. The book has one truly chilling passage where twins, one of whom has been locked up since birth, bond by chanting nursery rhymes under a full moon. The film, however, sacrifices chills for action.

The Dark Eyes Of London was the last British independent horror film before World War II. During the war period, the big studios only tackled the supernatural a few times, mostly in comedy. Most films were directed towards comedy, or hard-edged propaganda.

Post-war, there were only two independent horror movies made during a time when resources were at a premium. These will be dealt with in a later chapter, as will the few wartime horrors.

But first, the king of grand guignol...

2. Tod Slaughter, The Titan Of Terror

There was one man who bestrode the British horror movie each side of World War II, beginning his film career in 1935 and all but ending it in 1948. He missed the boom time of the 1950's, when horror became a good box office bet after the abolition of the "H" certificate and the introduction of the "X" certificate (held for films of such awfulness that you had to be over 18 to enter), along with the relaxation of the "A" rating. But without him, there would have been no such boom.

That one man was Tod Slaughter – an apt name (and entirely genuine) for the king of Grand Guignol.

Born Norman Carter Slaughter in 1885, the Newcastle-Upon-Tyne born actor-manager alleged to be a descendant of Captain Cook, spent most of his career in the fleapit theatres and music halls of the land. For Slaughter's stock in trade was never to be the classics or the farces of Arthur Wing Pinero, the playwright whose delicate comedies of manners were so popular at the turn of the century when Slaughter began to act. Quite the opposite. While Pinero was the public, prim face of the late Victorian and Edwardian eras, Slaughter mined the underbelly of the times. He drew his inspiration from the *Police Gazette* and the *Newgate Calender*, true crime spiced up by penny-a-word writers who also churned out the penny-dreadfuls and broadsheets that told folk tales like that of Maria Marten, or the mysterious Spring Heeled Jack, a monster who leapt tall buildings breathing fire (these two folk tales would bookend Slaughter's film career). In fact, the only creditable literary source that Slaughter ever tapped during his long career was that of Wilkie Collins, whose *The Woman In White* he used as the basis for *Crimes At The Dark House* (1939), accentuating the bloody horror and throwing away the delicate writing. This was just as well, as Collins was one of the dreariest of Victorian writers, notable only for allegedly creating the first real British detective story in *The Moonstone* (and that's yet another dreary book that could have done with the Slaughter touch).

Relentlessly popular in an age when the theatre and music hall were becoming sharply divided, Slaughter married his leading lady, Jenny Lynn, and pulled together a company of actors whose talents were – to judge by their performances in his films – always of a low standard. In fact, the only actor of any note to emerge from the Slaughter stable was Eric Portman, who later went on to make some excellent wartime dramas such as *Forty Ninth Parallel* (1941, US title *The Invaders*), *Millions Like Us* (1943), and *A Canterbury Tale* (1944)

This lack of talent did not matter, like his legitimate theatre counterpart, Donald Wolfit (later Sir Donald – noticeably there was no Sir Tod...), Slaughter was arrogant, vain, and a heavy drinker. He overacted and mugged shamelessly at the audience, upstaging anyone else on the stage. It was his show, and no-one was allowed to forget it, and all the other actors had to do was remember their cues and feed him the necessary lines.

This worked with Slaughter as the audiences had paid to see him, and the material needed all the overplaying possible to cover its poor writing. But Wolfit did the same thing to Shakespeare and Sheridan, and it was only late in his career did his true vocation show, when he starred in Baker-Berman's *Blood Of The Vampire*, in 1958. It was a perfect Slaughter vehicle, and Wolfit carried it off with aplomb.

Because of the nature of his material, and the paucity of his productions, Slaughter was barred from ever gaining true legitimate theatre status, so he spent his career perusing railway time-tables and spending Sundays changing at Crewe (a tradition arose from artistes always meeting at this northern railway junction on Sundays, when there were no theatrical presentations by law, and everyone switched engagements), joining the lowlier music hall artistes in a never-ending trek through the fleapit halls of Britain.

In some ways, Slaughter was before his time. Like the exploitation kings of cinema in the 1930's and 1950's, Slaughter was a barnstorming Barnum of ideas. Just as William Castle had the frightbreak, and gimmicks like electric shocks and flying skeletons for the punters in the auditorium, so Slaughter had a few little tricks of his own when playing the halls. Chief amongst these was the dressing up of members of the company not required on stage in nurses and St John's Ambulance uniforms, and placing them around the auditorium in case anyone fainted. Thus the audience expected to see blood and thunder. They got the thunder, but the blood was mostly in their minds.

Another of Slaughter's favourite stunts could only be carried out while he was playing Sweeney Todd, the demon barber whose forte was throat, rather than hair, cutting. During the interval, Slaughter would stride from the wings into the bar, still dressed in his blood-stained apron, and monopolise one end of the bar, drinking steadily and quietly, daring anyone to come near him. Such was his projection that no-one ever did.

So while it was no surprise that Slaughter should try and transfer his brand of grand guignol to the screen, it does seem a little odd that it took him until 1935. There are many possible reasons for this.

Firstly, Slaughter may have played the halls rather than the legitimate theatre, but he was still an actor, and so felt misgivings about film (he was not, however, above emoting on disc, as there exist two 78's upon which his company haltingly present highlights from *Sweeney Todd* over four 3-minute sides).

Secondly, there was his reputation as a low-brow purveyor of blood and guts on stage. Although the Lord Chamberlain's Office regulated censorship in the theatre, they had surprising blind spots with melodrama, enabling the likes of Slaughter to do things on stage that a film censor would have balked at; remember, there were problems getting a certificate for Universal's *Dracula* (1931), which had played live theatres virtually unchanged.

Thirdly, with the coming of sound, a number of small time film producers started up shop, particularly in the north of England. Their stock in trade was to film northern comics whose acts were verbally based, and so could not have been exploited during the silent era. The likes of Sandy Powell and Frank Randall spent the 1930's, 1940's and 1950's making a string of ultra-low budget movies that grossed a lot of money in the north but hardly ever played down south. The two biggest film comics of the day – George Formby and Will Hay – began their careers with cheapjack producers before graduating to the superior production values of Ealing and Gainsborough. Like these comics, Slaughter was spurned by the legitimate theatre and the southern-based film industry. It was partly class-consciousness, and partly an economic decision. Southern film companies based their projection on country-wide distribution, whereas the cheapjack northern producers had only to keep grinding them out for the Lancashire and Yorkshire fleapits. And, like the aforesaid comics, Slaughter's work was primarily based on verbal exchanges, and without the words, his gestures were empty.

This brings us neatly to the fourth reason why Tod Slaughter had to wait for sound film to be really effective; his looks. Although a giant of a man, with a barrel chest and broad physique that drink was turning flabby, Slaughter did not have a naturally filmic villain's face. Huge, jug ears were offset by marvellously expressive eyes, but it was the lower face that let him down. Aptly described by critic Kim Newman as a "mooncalf's smile", his slightly receding lower chin gave him the look of a village idiot when he tried to be nice... although this was not very often.

It was Slaughter's voice that was his great weapon, a bellowing roar that could rasp pure hatred or sweeten into an oily unctuousness that would make even Uriah Heep seem harsh. Tod used it to great effect in the split-character roles that became his stock in trade. For in almost every play and film, he played the same character with a different name. Always he was vain, arrogant, greedy, lustful, cruel and spiteful – but hiding these traits under a sometimes prim and always polite and mild-mannered exterior.

It became a stereotype, but nobody did it better.

Under the auspices of producer George King, Slaughter began his screen career in 1935 with *Maria Marten, Or The Murder In The Red Barn*. This was one of his most popular vehicles, based on the true story, distorted in folk tale, of Squire Corder, who lusts after the sweet Maria Marten. Corder – typically for a Slaughter character – is oily and unctuous in public, but a heartless villain concerned only with his own well-being and satiation in private.

Corder becomes a friend of the Marten's, and schemes a way to put Maria's father in debt to him. To call in that debt, he uses her father to bring Maria to him, where he has his wicked way with her. The inexorable way in which Slaughter draws people into his net is truly shocking, as is the blacked-out scene where it is implied that he rapes Maria.

Soon, Corder has a double problem. He is now deeply in debt, and marries an ugly but rich spinster that he has been wooing, sharing aside-glances of disgust with the audience when he kisses her (Slaughter was one of the few stage or halls stars to ignore cinema convention and break the fourth wall, sharing with the viewer). The marriage is threatened when Maria comes to him, revealing that she is pregnant.

Faced with social and financial ruin, Slaughter does just what any reasonable early nineteenth century gentleman would have done, and kills Maria, hiding her body in a red barn, trying to lay the blame on her gypsy lover, played with conviction by Eric Portman. Of course, Corder being a squire and the other man only a common gypsy, the forces of law and order are soon after Portman... who leads them straight to the barn, where Maria's dog sniffs out her body.

The climax is wonderful: lit from underneath, a sweating and terrified Corder is forced to dig for the body himself, and cracks up when he uncovers it, claiming that her dead eyes are accusing him of the murder. Ham acting it may be, but the over-the-top quality fits the madness totally.

Corder is led to the gallows on the day of his execution by a masked hangman. Corder jeers the crowd, calling them curs up until the last, but his nerve totally cracks when the hangman reveals himself to be... Maria's gypsy lover.

In many ways the quintessential Slaughter story, most of the other movies are just variations on this theme. Director Milton Rosmer was, as the credits claim, loaned from Gaumont-British. They must have wanted to get rid of him, as his work is truly awful. The camera is static for most for the time, and close-ups are taken at ludicrously apposite moments. It actually resembles the type of film made five years before, when the introduction of sound led to a period of static cameras.

No matter, Slaughter's grand-standing carries the whole production through threadbare costumes and cardboard sets. He milks the character for every drop of moral bankruptcy he can, giving him the chilling air of a psychopath.

George King must have watched Rosmer carefully, as he took over direction as well as production duties from here on in, using exactly the same technique for each successive film and even cutting corners on such extravagances as outside shooting. The few exteriors used in *Maria Marten* were superseded by entirely set-based pieces.

One last word on Squire Corder. The murder and execution occurred in 1827, and the scalp of the real Corder can still be seen in Bury St Edmunds Museum...

The next year, King and Slaughter immortalised on celluloid another of the great warhorse's most popular vehicles, *Sweeney Todd, The Demon Barber Of Fleet Street* (1936). Adapted for the screen from the Victorian melodrama by George Dibdin-Pitt, it had remained unchanged in the seventy or so years since it was first penned.

The story was, once again, a folk tale distortion of a historical event. Sweeney Todd owned a barber's shop in Fleet Street, in the City Of London. He made a habit of killing his customers with his large, cut-throat razor, and stealing their purses. In legend, he disposed of the bodies by dumping them in the cellar, where they were dismembered by Mrs Lovatt, Sweeney's grotesque paramour, who had the most popular pie shop in London. No prizes for guessing what was supposed to be in the pies...

In this movie, there's no real lust interest for the great man, and most of the screen time spent with the equally grotesque Mrs Lovatt is spent in a bickering feud and simmering mutual hatred. The enmity is truly terrifying in an old couple whose only link is now their mutual guilt.

Sweeney Todd presented King and Slaughter with a problem. On stage, the blood would flow freely as Todd went about his dastardly business. On film, however, such processes would lead to an "H" certificate or even a ban. So the gruesome twosome changed the legend slightly, and Todd merely rendered his victims unconscious with a sharp blow to the head before tipping them into the basement, there to render the razor off-screen, with a few accompanying howls. The point is made partly by this, and partly by Slaughter keeping in the lines where he lovingly strops his razor and examines his customers, purring "what a lovely throat for a razor," and "that's the way I polish them off," as he dispatches them to the dank cellar.

This, of course, made the film much more frightening in some ways, and enabled King to show one genuine piece of imagination. Cutting directly from the dispatch of one victim, two punters come out of Mrs Lovatt's shop, happily munching on one of her pies and musing on just what it was that made them the best in England... the imagination does all the work, admittedly, but the restraint was admirable for grand guignol.

In Slaughter's cardboard world, Fleet Street moves a couple of miles down the road to docklands, and a lot of his trade comes from passing sailors, who nobody will miss. One of these sailors is Bruce Seton, a British B-movie lead who had a brief post-Slaughter career of which this still remains the highlight. Seton escapes the infamous chair in which Todd kills his victims, and then catapulting them into the basement. Only stunned, he manages to make good his escape and tell of the nefarious happenings in Fleet Street.

Eventually, fate catches up with Todd and Lovatt, and Todd is trapped in a burning shop, falling through his own trap door into the flaming cellar and thus, by inference, into the very pit of hell.

Like *Maria Marten,* a quintessential piece of Slaughter, and these are the two films that anyone interested in the man must see. Though it would be best to ignore the terrible framing device in *Sweeney Todd* where a man in 1930's Fleet Street enters a barbers and asks the razor-stropper about a picture of Sweeney's shop on the wall. "Ah, thereby lies a tale..." begins the barber and the film... ending with the frightened punter leaving the chair, shaving lather and all, and running full pelt down Fleet Street and onto a bus, totally ruining the atmosphere Slaughter had built up at the story's climax. King needed shooting for that little addition.

The Crimes Of Stephen Hawke (1936) followed hot on the heels of *Sweeney Todd* and featured Slaughter as a mild-mannered money lender who also doubles as a murderer and robber who is terrorising London, and has been nicknamed The Spine-Breaker. The film starts in wonderful fashion as Hawke tries to break into a house and is caught in the undergrowth by a precocious brat who berates him, telling him that "my father did not make this garden for the likes of you to look at." With relish, the child's back is broken, and the viewer is frankly on Slaughter's side at this point...

The story develops along familiar lines, with the police on Hawke's tail, and The Spine-Breaker in fine cackling form. The only jarring factor is that Hawke actually cares for someone other than himself, his adopted daughter, to whom he leaves all his wealth when he dies at the end. His spine is broken in a fall, a nice bit of irony or an accident? Writer H F Maltby, who worked on the adaption of *Sweeney Todd*, had tried to add another dimension to the Slaughter persona, so perhaps it is as well to give him the benefit of the doubt. There is little doubt that the film is less horrific melodrama than crime melodrama, and was perhaps an attempt to give a breadth to Slaughter's film career.

Having said that, The Spine-Breaker going about his work is worthy of the best moments in his first two films, and the police do not intrude too much on the rampant horror of what must be one of the earliest serial killers on film.

As with *Maria Marten* and *Sweeney Todd*, the direction is stilted in the extreme, and the supporting cast just run through their lines in a perfunctory manner. However, the real appeal is to see Slaughter striding through the cardboard sets and cardboard people, the only three dimensional character in sight. In a sense, this adds another layer of unintentional chills to the film, as Slaughter appears as an almost Ubu Roi-like figure, laying waste to all around him until he is the king of nothing but a barren land.

Of course, that's all in retrospect. At the time, Slaughter was as close to horror as the British public could get on screen and stage, and they lapped him up. Which makes it all the more surprising that Slaughter and King chose to spend 1937 making two dreadful sentimental musicals, *Song Of The Road* and *Darby And Joan*. Perhaps they both realised that the screen used up material in a way that the theatre never could. Like the music hall comics whose careers had more in common with Slaughter's than any conventional actor, the screen could use up a routine or act that they had spent years peddling around the halls, refining it as they went. Suddenly, instead of returning to the same hall a year later with the same sketch, they found that the cinema audiences wanted something different when they next stepped in front of the camera.

Like these comics, Slaughter possessed only a small repertoire with which he had toured. Frightened of running out of material too quickly, perhaps he had opted to try and broaden his palette.

It did not work, and Slaughter was quickly back to the villains both he and the audience loved so well.

George King tried to hand the direction over to one David MacDonald for the first Slaughter vehicle of the next year, *It's Never Too Late To Mend* (1938), which had Slaughter doubling as his usual wicked squire, and the governor of a prison in which brutality was the norm. Cackling wildly at the degradations of his prisoners, the evil Slaughter spends half his time reaching for the cat-o'-nine-tails and murmuring delightedly about a "little relaxation", and the other half chasing the love of the obligatory girl who would rather die than be Slaughter's lover.

H F Maltby again wrote the script, basing it on another old blood and thunder play by Charles Reade and Arthur Shirley. The twin-personality aspect of Tod Slaughter was never again quite as accentuated as here, where he seems almost to be two characters, so perfectly does he disguise aspects of his personality. It became, almost by accident, a telling allegory on the times in which it was written, so great was the division between the public primness and the private perversions.

Following the usual morality play pattern, Slaughter is found out and ends up on his own punishment wheel, insanely cackling and bellowing the title phrase over and over again.

MacDonald and King were interchangeable directorially, perhaps it was the paucity of the budgets, but it seemed that no-one at this time was able to film Slaughter vehicles in anything other than a static manner. Ironically, although in a purely cinematic sense this jars, it does make it easier for the viewer to sit back and imagine themselves in a sweaty flea-pit of a music hall, watching the great man bestride the boards.

In the same way that William Beaudine's mis-direction of the comic Will Hay and foil Gordon Harker in sequences of *Boys Will Be Boys* (1935) enables the viewer to imagine the men on stage (the camera is as static as though it were squarely in the front row of the stalls) and capture a flavour of the era, so perhaps the static camera techniques and ineptitude of King and his flunkies enable the viewer to gain some insight into the full power of Slaughter on stage.

Ticket Of Leave Man (1937) was heading back into traditional Slaughter territory. Originally a vehicle for the character of Hawkshaw the Detective (an earlier Victorian prototype of Sherlock Holmes, Hawkshaw was a penny-dreadful policeman), Slaughter takes it over to the point where Hawkshaw is left with only a few walk-on sequences, while the villain he hunts takes centre stage once again.

A mysterious criminal called The Tiger is haunting London's underworld. Using his gang, he is perpetrating a series of robberies that have gone unsolved. The odd thing for the police is that they are unable to trace to any of the gang. Of course, some of the methods used fit known criminals, but these are ticket-of-leave men (an early system of paroling prisoners), many of whom have left the country to start a new life abroad... so what's going on?

Once you know that the ticket-of-leave men are being sent to a kindly social reformer played by Slaughter, I think you may guess the answer. Once again, it's the double-role ploy. By day, Tod is a kind Victorian gentleman who is a social reformer, pledged to help these men start new lives either in this country or abroad. By night he is The Tiger, using his position to have the pick of the newly released criminals. If they co-operate he will use them, then send them off to new lives in order to avoid crimes being traced to them – and so, by inference, to him. If, however, they should refuse to co-operate, then he will have them violate their ticket, and so condemn them back to prison... and nobody gets a second chance for a ticket.

Again, this is more of a crime melodrama than outright horror, but there are genuinely chilling elements. All of them, of course, in the performance of Slaughter, who was getting so used to such roles that it may have been tempting to surmise he was like this off stage, as well. The manner in which he can switch from kindly upper-class gentleman to a scheming arbiter of evil is a little frightening, suggesting as it does a long stint in the psychiatrists chair. And again, it's the Victorian theme of moral bankruptcy masquerading under false piety that is so horrible. This was supposed to be a glorious period in British history, yet all art (both high and low-brow) reflects a knowledge and revulsion for the double standards that took place.

The Tiger is, of course, undone by the love he cultivates for a convict's girlfriend. Throwing his usual caution to the wind he makes sure this particular convict is caught and, knowing that he will therefore be unmasked, he attempts to escape, pursued by Hawkshaw in a chase scene that is pure farce. Both Hawkshaw and The Tiger have beer-fed pot-bellies, and to see them wobbling and straining over the cardboard scenery is not a pretty sight. It will come as no surprise to find out that The Tiger dies proclaiming his love for the girl.

The next movie that Slaughter made was the best of his attempts to combine crime and horror into one melodramatic package. Ironic, therefore, that it was not a typical Slaughter vehicle, was not based on any of his stage work, was contemporary rather than historical, and was in fact George King's attempt to combine two of the seams of low budget movie-making he was mining.

Sexton Blake And The Hooded Terror (1938) saw the dashing detective played by George Blake, pitted against The Snake, hooded leader of the gang known as the Black Quorum. Alert readers will have no trouble in guessing who was cast as the Snake...

George Curzon had already played Blake in two previous King excursions, *Sexton Blake And The Bearded Doctor*, and *Sexton Blake And The Mademoiselle*, both in 1935. It was King's success with Slaughter that had diverted his attention away from a series that had the same ability to tap into the public unconscious.

Despite its contemporary setting, the story was as old as the plays Slaughter himself had mined. Indeed, the character of Blake himself derives from late Victorian pulps. Sexton Blake was the invention of a group of writers who worked for the Harmsworth Press, instructed by their boss to create an office-boys rival for the great Sherlock Holmes. So it was that Blake was born, along with his trusty sidekick Tinker (aka Edward Carter, a teenage boy for the readers to identify with), the great brindled bloodhound Pedro, and Mrs Bardell, the token "lawks luv a duck!" cockney housekeeper.

During the 1920's and 1930's, Blake was at the height of his popularity, having graduated from Union Jack magazine through Detective magazine to his own Sexton Blake Library, which ran until 1963. Even then, after being closed down by Fleetway (as the comics/fiction arm of Harmsworth had become), the last Blake editor and doyen of British pulp W Howard Baker resurrected him for a string of forty-nine paperbacks before the last original Blake adventure was played out. Even after this, Baker used his own imprint to re-publish old Blake stories until his death in 1991.

Blake was the epitome of British courage and daring, with his hawk nose and widow's peak framing an intense gaze. Lean, mean, and a fighting machine, he was more inclined to punch his way out of trouble than use his intelligence, as Holmes would do; but this can be put down to overwork on the hacks who toiled over the Fleetway benches churning out nearly a thousand Blake pulps throughout his seventy-seven years of original publishing.

It was no surprise for Blake to come up against master villains and secret societies, especially in the era of Edgar Wallace, the master of the evil genius – *The Crimson Circle*, *The Fellowship Of The Frog*, and especially *The Terror*. Even in his last phase, Martin Thomas ranged him against *The Sorcerers Of Set* and *The Mind Killers* – worshippers of Egyptian gods and mad doctors performing brain experiments with mind-altering drugs. Other graduates of the Fleetway Blake treadmill include surreal fabulist Jack Trevor Story and the one-man industry that is Michael Moorcock.

Given this vein of horror, and the previous history of Blake on screen (there had also been six two-reelers in the late 1920's), the viewer could be entitled to sit back and expect a thrill-a-minute chiller.

Not so. The film has all the requisite elements from Slaughter. A kindly stamp dealer and collector by day (it is, in fact, a rare stamp that gives away his identity near the end), but by night he becomes The Snake donning the black hood and cloak of the Black Quorum (looking suspiciously like a reversed Ku Klux Klan outfit), planning daring robberies and kidnappings. He also has designs on heroine Greta Gynt, the beauty who would later grace The Dark Eyes Of London. At last Slaughter has a heroine worthy of lust, and one who can return his bug-eyed leering with a degree of revulsion and terror that actually seems real.

Initially allied to the gang, she falls for George Curzon's Blake when he enters the scene, and soon ends up giving away all her secrets. Blake is still captured by the gang, however, and is saved by Granite Grant, an adventurer chum who happens to be around at the time. This was David Farrar in a bit part, and he in fact went on to play Blake in two 1943 movies, *Meet Sexton Blake* and *The Echo Murders*. Despite the paucity of production values, he is actually closer to the spirit of Blake than Curzon, his may be because he is a better actor.

The ultimate showdown and unmasking is actually full of tension, and George King in the director's chair shows that he is gradually learning something about pace, suspense, and the use of camera. Although no great talent, he does allow some kind of dynamic that increases the atmosphere when Blake confronts and finally unmasks The Snake in the underground cellar that the Quorum use as their meeting place (I suspect that it's supposed to be a catacomb, but the budget would not stretch that far). Another chase ensues before The Snake finally meets a sticky end.

Being a big fan of Blake and Slaughter, I was at first disappointed with the film, but this was more due to my expectations than anything else. There are some genuinely creepy moments worthy of any Universal horror from the period, and writer A R Rawlinson gives the cast plenty to work with in the way of thrills and chills. Ultimately, it is the budget that prevents this film from really opening out and becoming the full throttle sub-Wallace horror-thriller that it should have been. (The reader may have noticed the constant references to Edgar Wallace – ft should be noted that his influence has been even greater on European horror than on British, as the Germans and Italians have adapted and used elements of his work for over sixty years in their thrillers and horror movies.)

The only bad thing about the film is that Slaughter is surprisingly subdued. Could this have been because he was so used to dealing with the poor acting of his own cast and company that the skills of Gynt and Farrar perplexed him? Maybe, certainly he was back in full flight on the last film of an extremely busy year when he appeared in *The Face At The Window* (1939).

Whereas previous versions of this old melodrama had concentrated on the policeman investigating the possible guilt of Lucien and the identity of Le Loup (as in the silent versions), Slaughter turned the play on its head in the same way that he had with *The Ticket Of Leave Man*. A Rawlinson joined hack Randall Faye (a long-time Slaughter writer) in adapting the vehicle into another barnstormer for Slaughter to run through his double-identity shtick.

By now, it should have become a tired cliché, but the fact is that King was continuing to show the improvements as a film-maker that he had shown on the *Sexton Blake And the Hooded Terror* movie, and the production budget was slightly up from the poverty-row excesses of earlier Slaughter. The sets actually look solid, and there is even Aubrey Mallieu in the cast to act as a foil to Slaughter. Knowing when to play down to the master ham, he adds just a little touch of class over the usual ragbag of ham and wood that comprises the rest of the cast.

Slaughter goes to town as Le Loup, seething with pent-up rage as Lucien's girl turns him down, oozing oily unction as he offers to help, all the while twisting the knife in Lucien's back and making him look guilty. In between, he retreats to the cellar of his house and confides in his maid and deformed half-brother, the face of the title, who is caged and treated like a wild animal. It really is chilling to see this poor man, reduced by brutality to a wild and primitive state, trying to understand what his brother is saying as Le Loup rants and raves with his face to the bars, hair greasily falling over his staring eyes.

The end is particularly worthy of note: killing his brother before he can give him away, Le Loup falls into a sobbing wreck as the fake corpse writes his name, confessing all as the great criminal is reduced to a blubbering wreck of self-pity.

The Face At The Window is Slaughter's finest hour in terms of production, and he turns in a performance to match. Perhaps if *Todd Sweeney* or *Maria Marten* had been made in 1938 instead of 1935 and 1936, then Slaughter would be better remembered.

From here, the only way forward was into self-parody, and this is what *Crimes At The Dark House* (1939) comes across as. Slaughter's only film of 1939, it takes Wilkie

Crimes At The Dark House

Collins' interminably boring *The Woman In White*, throws away most of the book and keeps the basic idea of Slaughter as a wicked Victorian land-owner who kills his wife and hides the fact by using a lunatic as her double. With more suggested blood and violence than Collins would ever have dreamed, writers H F Maltby, Edward Dryhurst, and Frederick Heyward use this premise as a vehicle to replay the best of Tod Slaughter, as all the elements that made Slaughter the only genuine British film frightener of the 1930's are trotted out revue style, directed with relish by the rapidly improving King.

Slaughter, of course, is in his element, striding the set like a man possessed, he runs through every trick he ever learnt on the halls, barnstorming his way through material that seems meaty, but is in fact a thin gruel. For someone whose grand guignol style forever teetered on the edge of self-parody, the chance to guy himself was something that Slaughter should never have been offered. Overplaying even by his standards, the film ends up falling flat. There are none of the occasional chills up the spine that even the cheapest Slaughter film had produced, only knowing smiles as the viewer recalls from which movie each line is taken.

The coming of the Second World War was disastrous for the British film industry, although in retrospect it enabled the larger studios to produce a stream of war-time dramas that were the height of British film quality for the period. George King moved into propaganda dramas, dropping Slaughter. Unable to find anyone who could put money into him, Tod returned to the halls, where in many ways he was always happiest.

The war and post-war periods were dreadful for film-makers. The silver nitrate stock was at a premium, and there were two taxes which destroyed independent production. The first was on cinemas, a tax on admission prices lead to an increase at a time when people had less money in their pocket. Thus the cinema managers were very careful in choosing their programmes, and anything that risked an "A" or "H" certificate would be bad business. Secondly, there was an Entertainment Tax on producers, this was to discourage the waste of stock, and also to raise revenue from the most popular form of entertainment at that time. In many ways, it had the opposite of this effect, small producers, unable to pay the tax, either stopped producing or went for anodyne product that was assured a booking.

Like all taxes, these continued long after the reason for which they were levied had retreated into history, and so there were only four horror movies independently produced between 1945 and 1950 (and none during wartime itself). Two of these were the twin swan song of Tod Slaughter – the other two will be dealt with in a later chapter.

The Curse Of The Wraydons was produced by Bushey in 1946. Written by Michael Barringer and directed (after a fashion) by Victor M Gover, it was one of the shoddiest vehicles yet given to Slaughter. Even the return of Bruce Seton, from *Sweeney Todd*, to play the hero opposite the great man could not revive the old magic.

Slaughter played Spring-Heeled Jack. In late Victorian times, Jack was a mythical folk monster who was allegedly eight feet tall, breathed fire, and sprung over tall buildings. There were numerous sightings of him in the 1880's and a wave of hysteria swept Britain. Not slow to cash in, penny-dreadfuls appeared by the score, some proclaiming Jack a hero, others the devil's pawn. Eventually, an eccentric Victorian nobleman confessed to creating the whole hoax for a prank, but the legend lived on.

The *Curse Of The Wraydons* drew on this tradition, and Slaughter was cast as nobleman out for revenge. Quite for what is another matter.

A confused vehicle, with a muddled script that gives Slaughter little chance to barnstorm, there is too much Seton and romantic interest to make it chilling in any way. Besides which, Slaughter was now 61, and his barrel chest had dropped to around his belly. The idea of him being able to leap tall buildings may have worked on stage, but the camera was too cruelly honest to make any suspension of disbelief possible.

Slaughter was now ensconced on the boards, and Bushey only tempted him in front of the cameras one more time, to make *The Greed Of William Hart* (1948). Sporting a strange Irish accent that seemed to slip into Scottish from time to time, Slaughter was one half of Moore and Hart, grave robbers who were obviously based on Burke and Hare. John Gilling's script was without interest, and Oswald Mitchell's direction was less than perfunctory. There is even a fight scene at the end that is speeded up on the finished print to almost ludicrous extremes.

Slaughter tries hard, but in this movie he has to be unremittingly rotten, with no oily unctuousness for contrast. He is also playing a working class idler instead of one of the upper or merchant classes. This may be a fault in the viewer, but after his previous roles it seems to jar.

Finally, the film is ruined by the censor. The British have always had a thing about grave robbing, and the exploits of Burke and Hare. On film, it is impossible to show the horror of their activities by implication, thus making it a sore subject for the censor and also for the kind of horror shorthand at which the British film-makers came to excel.

The British Board Of Film Censors (BBFC) had a real problem with Burke and Hare, snipping a scene out of Val Lewton's production of *The Body Snatcher* (1946) where Boris Karloff sings a nursery rhyme mentioning their names, and they also butchered the rest of the print. They forced Dylan Thomas to change the names in his play *The Doctor And The Devils*, which was unfilmed until 1985.

In *The Greed Of William Hart* they do something even worse. After the film was made, they made the producers dub in "Moore" and "Hart" for every mention of

The Greed Of William Hart

Burke and Hare. Often, this is done in different voices to the actors speaking, so it stands out ludicrously.

Gilling remade this screenplay, directing himself, for Baker and Berman in 1958, this time using the genuine names. It still was not that hot a movie, though.

With his film career petering out like this, Slaughter only appeared in a few two-reel shorts of a crime/terror nature, most of which appeared on TV or were put into compendium movies for theatre release in the US. This was a common practise in the early days of TV, when low-rent British producers like the Danzigers made series like *Sabre Of London,* or Anglo-Amalgamated's *Scotland Yard*, which were sold in Britain and in the US to TV networks and also for movie release as supports or B-pictures.

Otherwise, Slaughter returned to the boards, and was still playing in *Maria Marten* when he succumbed to a heart attack in 1956, at the age of 71.

In many ways, his horror was different to that of Hammer, who would take up the horror banner in the 1950's. Yet his influence is discernable in some elements of their period pictures, and also in the wealth of low budget shockers that relied on grand guignol techniques to overcome production paucity.

Tod Slaughter was the first British horror star. He would not be the last...

3.   The Major Studios: From Beginning To End

When talking about the major studios in British films, it should be noted that this does not refer to any British outposts of the likes of MGM, 20th Century Fox, Warner Brothers, etc. Although, at various times throughout the history of British film-making there have been offices for production in this country of movies by any of the US majors, this involvement has been at best intermittent. Apart from a brief heyday in the 1960's, such involvement has been patchy, dependent on UK Government taxes and levies on film production and distribution.

Instead, when talking about the majors, one is referring to Gaumont, Gainsborough, Ealing and Rank. All of these had their own distribution network as well as production facilities. In this way they differ from the likes of Anglo-Amalgamated (a distributor who occasionally produced, but used outside production facilities) or Independent Artists (who were producers, using mostly Anglo as a distributor). The only comparable outfit were Exclusive, a distributor who made a few films pre-World War II as Hammer, and post-war ran their own distribution in tandem with production for a while. The distribution arm of the company, Exclusive, fell into disuse as the production side, Hammer, grew larger.

By the time this happened, Rank was the pre-eminent producer/distributor in the UK. Formed in the late 1930's by J Arthur Rank, a mill tycoon who wanted to make religious movies, it had soon grown into a large concern that made mostly comedies and light drama, modelling itself heavily on the US giants with such things as the Rank Charm School, where starlets of both sexes were groomed for success. As mentioned before, they made no horror movies at all, possibly a reflection of Rank's religious beliefs, possibly his hard-headed business sense (and that of senior producers like Earl St. John) that horror and Rank combined would not be good box office, so at odds were the two images. It seems that as long as Hammer did not make comedies – or at least, not good ones – Rank were content to let each company have their own side of the fence.

Gaumont, Gainsborough and Ealing have long since disappeared. Ealing was the last, ceasing production in the late 1950's when the costs of running studio and distribution together came to more than their productions made. Famed for their "Ealing Comedies" (a name strong enough to define a genre for humour critics), the sad truth is that they simply ran out of steam, and were unable to diversify in a changing economic climate. Their Lime Grove studios were sold to the BBC and used for TV production. Whereas you could not get the mild sauce of Rank's *Doctor* series or the blood of Hammer on the small screen, Ealing's family entertainment blueprint had been so strong that it was used almost wholesale for sit-com and drama on television.

Gainsborough had disappeared years before that, their studios along Eagle Wharf in Islington disposed of and their company moved to Ealing's Lime Grove in the immediate post-war period, when they were bought-out by Ealing. Best known in the 1930's for their string of music-hall comedies (the most successful featuring Will Hay), they ended their career with a string of Gothic romances featuring James Mason and Margaret Lockwood. It was not so far from the likes of *The Monk* and *Castle Of Otranto* to *The Man In Grey* (1943) and *The Wicked Lady* (1945). Although wildly popular, and occasionally still thrilling, they fall outside the scope of this book.

The name of Gaumont lasted a little longer, finally being phased out in 1958 when their chain of cinemas were merged with the Odeon group. Gaumont had been the first of the producers, running their cinemas to show their product, and was in fact both the parent company of Gainsborough and the original owners of Ealing's Lime Grove site, which they opened in 1915. They had, however, ceased production years before the other companies.

Gaumont stopped making films because they made more money showing them, but it was the war which really killed Gainsborough, with the end of the quota system and the crippling taxes on both admission prices and production. Ealing kept going partly because they produced a series of fine wartime propaganda dramas, and partly because they had the maverick genius of Michael Balcon to guide them. Balcon had worked for all three majors at one time, and had been a co-founder of Ealing.

Born in 1896, Balcon first entered film production in 1922, forming a small production company with Graham Cutts. Their first film was a success, but their second flopped and their company folded. However, Balcon had caught the attention of Gaumont-British (the parent was French, although the two had separated by this time). The two men tried again, and formed Gainsborough, selling its product exclusively to Gaumont in return for cash injections. They took up studios in Islington and went into production. The company was soon successful, and Balcon was invited to join Gaumont, which he did as head of production.

When the company ceased production to concentrate on the cinema chain in 1937, Balcon joined the UK arm of MGM, but soon found himself stifled by directives from overseas. He left, and the following year formed Balford films with Reginald Baker, in order to make good quality programmers (the successor of the quota quickie, churned out to meet the gaps in cinema programming and fill the still extant quota system) at the old Gaumont studios on Ealing. Shortly after, the name was changed to Ealing.

It is Balcon's mind that informs major studio product in Britain through the 1920's, 1930's and 1940's. A naturalized Hungarian, like his more flamboyant colleague Alexander Korda (whose London Films tried to ape David Selznick and work as an independent with major backing: possible for a maverick in the US, but in a British system still at the mercy of block booking through the 1920's and 1930's almost impossible), Balcon had very middle-class and cultivated tastes, which made horror a big no as such films were considered too common and vulgar. It is notable that Max Miller, the bluest and most popular comic of the day, had to make his films under the auspices of Warner's UK office, rather than the more cerebral twists of Will Hay (whose use of ignorance in humour depended on the viewer first knowing what the character was being ignorant about!) or the anodyne (if still funny) antics of Arthur Askey.

The last two comics are not named by accident, they featured in the only type of horror film that Balcon felt at ease producing, the horror comedy, a strange hybrid that is as rare in US horror as in the UK. Apart from Bob Hope – *The Cat And The Canary* (1939) and *The Ghost Breakers* (1940), and Abbot and Costello, it was left to B-production and no-hopers like Wheeler and Woolsey, who usually dropped it after one attempt.

However, this collapse came in the 1950's. During the 1920's, 1930's, and the war, all three studios did produce a handful of both horror comedy and straight horror, including two pictures that still stand as classics of their kind.

Gaumont were the first on the block to have a horror picture released by a major company although, confusingly, it was produced by Michael Balcon for Gainsborough. So close were the two companies at the time that it eventually went out as a Gaumont film, even though histories sometimes credit Gainsborough.

As befits a Balcon picture, *The Lodger* (1926) is a classic of its kind. Alfred Hitchcock's third film, it was the most successful adaption of Mrs Belloc-Lowndes pseudo-penny dreadful, based on Jack The Ripper. Starring Ivor Novello, it followed the story faithfully up until the end, where the ending was switched so that idol of millions Novello was not the real killer, but rather the victim of mistaken identity.

The plot of this film has already been discussed when talking about the 1932 re-make. What can be said about this version is mostly to do with the brilliance of the director, and the wisdom of Balcon (himself still only thirty) in allowing the young Hitchcock to direct.

In later interviews, Hitchcock would refer to this as his third film, but his first real picture, the first time he had really exercised his style. It is often said that Hitchcock would have every move planned in his head before the crew even stood on the studio floor, and making a movie with the director was like following an electronics blueprint with everything exactly mapped out in advance. This was a skill he was still developing, as instead, Hitchcock had everything mapped out on paper with scriptwriter Eliot Stannard. Between them, the two men fashioned a film of contrasting shade and light that reflected everything Hitchcock had picked up on a trip to Germany's UFA studios in a very English light.

When in Germany, Hitchcock had been both impressed and fascinated by the use of light and camera work in German fantasy and expressionist movies, from Robert Wiene to Fritz Lang, from *The Cabinet Of Dr Caligari* (1919) to *Doctor Mabuse The Gambler* (1922). This usage he translated into an English milieu, as fogbound streets and dimly-lit backrooms became the playground for fear and suspicion. The camera moves as a silent observer in a way that had not previously been done in British movies, using angles and lighting to create atmosphere that had previously been attempted by ham acting. If anything, Novello underplays in this film.

Artistic as well as frightening, it did well at the box office, but not well enough to encourage Balcon into any more productions, either under Gainsborough or Gaumont auspices. It would be five years before he let one of his companies try even a horror comedy, and seven years before his first true horror film.

Gaumont were almost as reticent. They held the option to produce a film of the stage version of *Dracula*, which was pulling in crowds in the London's West End. If they had made it, then perhaps the world would never have heard of Bela Lugosi, and British character stalwart Raymond Huntley – who was at this time the handsome young actor playing Count Dracula in the theatre – would have become Britain's first horror star. Instead, Gaumont worried about certification and profit margins, were relieved to take the money Universal offered them to release the option and launch Bela Lugosi on his downward spiral of a career.

It was only when Boris Karloff returned home from his late success – he was in his forties when he made *Frankenstein* (1931) – that Gaumont decided to risk their hand at another horror vehicle. Noting Karloff's success in James Whale's *The Old Dark House* (1932) (adapted from the novel *Benighted* written by that quintessential Englishman J B Priestley), and his work in *The Mummy* (1932) Gaumont fashioned a vehicle that took in elements of both, and added an English Gothic element that could not have been carried off anywhere else. *The Ghoul* (1933) is a genuine classic that still has the ability to send a chill up the spine if watched late at night.

Balcon, now at Gaumont full-time, decided that a quality vehicle could be made if the right amount of work was put in, so he assembled a team of writers including Leonard Hines, L DuGarde Peach, John Hastings Turner, Rupert Downing, and noted novelist and short story writer Roland Pertwee, to work on a script from a novel *The Ghoul* by Frank King. Each writer, or combination of writers, reworked the script until Balcon was happy, and all were credited on screen no matter how much of their work was used.

Director T Hayes Hunter was assigned to the film, and photographer Gunther Krampf was brought over from Germany to work on some suitably expressionist camera work. Supporting Karloff in the cast were respected stage actors such as Cedric Hardwicke and Ralph Richardson – at the beginning of a brief flirtation with movies

The Ghoul

that would see him corner the market in urbane, eccentric villains, as personified by his role as a Mabuse-like character in *Bulldog Jack* (1935), the black comic touch of Ernest Thesiger – who had played with Karloff in *The Old Dark House* (1932), and would again join him as Dr Praetorius in *The Bride Of Frankenstein* (1935), and the straight romantic leads of Dorothy Hyson and Anthony Bushell. Playing Hyson's scared and skittish friend was Kathleen Harrison, who actually outshines the romantic lead with her coquettish behaviour – this despite the fact that the actress was playing a character nearly twenty years younger than her true age (as I write, Ms Harrison still lives in happy retirement at the age of 103).

The plot of *The Ghoul* is a strong compendium of modern Gothic and horror elements. Karloff is an Egyptologist near death. His riches – stolen treasures from the pyramids – are hidden somewhere in his house and grounds. Before he dies, he begs his butler to perform a ceremony to the Ancient Gods he now worships.

Morning comes, and Karloff is seemingly dead. After a short period, he is buried in a tomb modelled closely on the pyramids, and his few legatees are invited to the hearing of his will. Amongst them are Hyson and Bushell, who after a bumpy start decide to get along, despite their families not liking each other (a plot line used in one of Karloff's last movies, *The Ghost In The Invisible Bikini* [1966], where he is once again the dead man whose will everyone has assembled to hear!). Hyson has brought her friend with her, and she wastes no time in shrilly proclaiming how scary the old house is...

A wandering clergyman turns up, stays a while, then departs, this is Ralph Richardson in disguise. He knows there are hidden treasures in the house, and means to gain them one way or another. Harrison, of course, falls for his charms... such people are always, of dramatic necessity, poor judges of character.

As the sun sets, and the legatees start to search for the treasure, Karloff is awoken. Was he in suspended animation, or is he one of the walking dead? That question is never really addressed, and becomes rapidly irrelevant as he reveals super-human strength in an attempt to stop anyone gaining his treasures.

Karloff has some superbly subtle make-up in this film, with padding added to his jowls to give his face a puffy distortion, and his hair combed forward to accentuate a built-up brow that shadows his menacing eyes.

Richardson and Bushell fight in the tomb, as Hyson looks on, and all are temporarily trapped before all comes out right – as it must.

The film is genuinely creepy as Boris rises from the dead and stalks the house, and the lighting and direction ensure some shocking moments, sometimes for excellent comic effect. For, in the character of Harrison this film has a light relief that was lacking in the Universal product that it seeks to emulate. However, this occasional leavening of the grim situation with humour is something that is typical of British horror. Perhaps it is an attempt to remind the audience that it is all a fantasy, and not real... the intended and actual effects are awry, as all it does is to accentuate the moments of terror.

The basic elements of this film were combined with a little of *The Old Dark House* and used by Baker-Berman for their 1961 horror-comedy *What A Carve-Up!*, which has its own fair share of chills.

Despite gaining an "A" certificate, and being the first British film to be notified to the Home Office as "horrific", the film was successful enough for Gaumont to attempt another horror vehicle the next year.

The Tell-Tale Heart (1934) was directed by Brian Desmond Hurst, and was also notified to the Home Office. More of a low budget affair (*The Ghoul* was slow in making back its money, despite rave notices, because of its certification), no prints are known to survive. This is a shame, as I for one would like to have seen how Edgar Allen Poe's tale of a walled-up body whose heartbeat haunts the killer could possibly be translated to the British screen, given the strictures of the time. The lack of star quality, however, meant that even the meagre budget was not recouped. Enough adults could be pulled in to see Karloff, it seemed, but not horror per se.

Balcon had washed his hands of horror by this time, and the last horror made by Gaumont before they folded was virtually a horror by default. But horrific it certainly was.

The Terror (1938) was another of Edgar Wallace's crime melodramas with horror overtones, except that this time there was more of an accent on the horror element. The story had already been filmed several times in the US, most notably in 1928, and continued to be filmed, both officially and unofficially, for several decades in Europe.

Another of Wallace's thrillers *The Ringer*, had been filmed as *The Gaunt Stranger* (1937, US title *The Phantom Strikes*) and had been a small budget success for Gaumont the year before with Wilfred Lawson, a craggy faced stage actor with a penchant for oily voices and suppressed menace, as lawyer Maurice Meister, around whom the plot revolved. For *The Terror*, Lawson was brought back to play the title role.

I do not know what it is about Lawson, but he seems perfect for the British horror, everything is suppressed and suggested, with a bland veneer covering a seething cauldron of menace. He always seems on the brink of breaking out into utter madness. Of course, this could be because he was a heavy drinker, and so made all his films in an intoxicated condition. To illustrate the man, consider the following. An actor friend met Lawson in a pub one lunchtime, and after several drinks Lawson invited him to watch the matinée of a play in the theatre across the road. Once seated, they drunkenly giggled their way through the first act until Lawson turned to his friend and said; "see that door over there? When that speech finishes, that's where I come in."

Lawson is at his heavy breathing best in a story that begins with an audacious robbery masterminded by a man seen only in a gas mask. His accomplices are rounded up after a tip-off, and serve time in prison, vowing to get him when they are released, but refusing to co-operate with the police.

The story moves forward ten years... the pretty heroine is returning to a hotel owned by her ex-Army father. There are vague threats towards him from Lawson, a long-term resident who is suitably oily towards the heroine when she returns. He wants to marry her, despite being more than twice her age.

There are a mixed-bag of residents in the hotel, including an irritating middle-aged woman with a scrap-book of true crime cases who claims to know Scotland Yard's leading detective, and also a drunk – played by Bernard Lee – who is seeking shelter. The two released prisoners turn up, one posing as a tramp looking for work, and the other – an early Alastair Sim performance – posing as a vicar.

Then the first murder takes place, and a mysterious monk is seen walking across the grounds of the house before disappearing into a crypt. Lee is revealed to be the Yard's leading detective, calling the bluff of the irritating old woman, to his cost, however, as Lawson sneaks a look at her scrapbook and discovers Lee's true identity.

Lee and Lawson's true love are captured via a series of secret passages, and end up tied together in the crypt where Lawson, now wildly staring and smiling in benign insanity, sits playing the organ in his monk's robes, revealing his true identity. He gleefully tells them how he will kill them too, just as he killed the two convicts who came after him...

Except that Sim is not dead, and emerges dusty and wild-eyed from his coffin to grapple with Lawson as the police try to dynamite their way into the tomb.

Being Edgar Wallace, Lawson and Sim die in the explosion, the hiding place of the long-lost stolen money is revealed, and Lee gets the girl. A good, and typical, ending for a melodrama. However, there have been some genuinely creepy moments along the way, such as the first time Lawson's cowled figure is seen walking across the lawn, or the way in which people disappear in the blink of an eye while going from one room to another.

Another plus is the bit-part performance from comic and actor Richard Murdoch (later to play in the 1941 version of *The Ghost Train*) as a bumbling but dashing CID man, knowing exactly the right level of levity to bring to his part as a contrast to the heavy-duty madness of Lawson. This makes up for the perfunctory direction and the clumsy handling of the fight at the end. Once again, it looks unconvincing partly because the camera is speeded up in the final print, and partly because it is so poorly choreographed and shot. For some reason, it seems to me that British film-makers were totally incapable of filming a convincing fight scene pre-war.

The horrific moments make this a genuine contender as a British fright movie – and one of the last Gaumont would produce.

Over at Gainsborough, things were even thinner on the ground for horror. Balcon's distaste after the Gaumont/Gainsborough production of *The Lodger* meant that no such projects were considered until something special came along. Though that something special came in the chance to get a leading light comedy duo in front of a camera, and also to resurrect a stage success that had been silently filmed three years before, with little to credit it.

The Ghost Train (1931) is a comedy-thriller with a supernatural theme. A group of people are stranded at a remote railway station in Cornwall when their rail connection goes awry. After being told by a lugubrious porter that there are no other trains for the night, they try their best to bed down in the waiting room. However, they are also told that the station is haunted, and that a swing bridge on the branch line had given way some fifty years before, depositing the train and its occupants into the river. The ghost of that train still comes through at night, and the ghost of the station-master, who died attempting to right the crank that closed the bridge, still stalks the platform...

Advised to lock themselves in, the passengers vacillate between bravado and fear. Amongst their number is a prim old lady with a parrot, and a typical upper-class silly ass. The latter were played by Cicely Courtneidge and Jack Hulbert respectively, the stars for whom the vehicle was designed.

Both were long-time stars of the London West End stage, specialising in light comedy and musical comedy. At first glance, this would seem to be a strange vehicle for them, a more typical movie being *Under Your Hat*, a 1941 version of their breezy stage success. However, they were having money problems at this time. Hulbert's business partner had mismanaged their money, and left them virtually bankrupt. At a public meeting of their creditors, Hulbert had asked for a year in which to earn the money to pay off the debts his partner had incurred. Accepting an offer from Balcon to make movies by day, and play the stage by night, was a big part of his plan.

Although Courtneidge was a pleasing comedienne, she did not shine on film like her lantern jawed husband, whose ability to look incredibly stupid seemed made for comedy. Starting with this film, where his silly-ass role is really a cover for a Scotland Yard detective on the lookout for smugglers, Hulbert developed a line in comedy thrillers that peaked with *Bulldog Jack* (1935, US title *Alias Bulldog Drummond*), where he played a silly-ass cricketer who stands in for pulp hero Bulldog Drummond. It was a pleasing departure from his stage persona, as the silly-ass exterior hid a heart of pure steel.

Of course, being a stage success and a Balcon film, there has to be a rational end, and the smugglers are using the story of the ghost train to disguise their activities, and Hulbert uncovers them after noticing that the previously chained crank for the bridge has changed position...

Hulbert and Courtneidge were well supported by another West End player, Angela Baddeley, and also by that doyen of film villains, Donald Calthrop. Not surprisingly, he plays the member of the party who is in league with the smugglers. Later Ealing director and writer Angus MacPhail adapted the play (with Lajos Biro), and it was directed by stalwart British film director Walter Forde. Sad to say, only fractional prints are believed to still exist, as time and silver nitrate have wreaked havoc.

Calthrop also featured heavily in the next Gainsborough horror, and the only straight horror they made during their production life.

The Man Who Changed His Mind (1936, US title *The Man Who Lived Again*) was scripted by L DuGarde Peach with John L Balderston and Sidney Gilliat (the latter at the beginning of his career, and before his long partnership with Frank Launder). It starred Boris Karloff on one of his long trips home, and was directed by Robert Stevenson.

In many ways, this surpassed *The Ghoul*. The pacing was swifter, the plot more coherent, and the effects more startling. Where it failed to score over the earlier film was in terms of the plot. The epitome of mad doctor movies, it may perhaps have seemed a little tame after the dark house Gothic of *The Ghoul*.

Karloff plays a scientist who, as always, has been drummed out of his profession for his experiments with thought and personality transference. Now he lives in isolation, helped only by the beautiful Anna Lee, an ex-student he is in love with, and Donald Calthrop as a misanthropic, bitter wheelchair user. Karloff has promised to help Calthrop when his experiments are successful, and one of the creepy things about the movie is the unspoken, almost Faustian bond between the two outcasts.

Lee has a paramour, British leading man John Loder (a hearthrob in his day). He is a journalist who tracks her down to the isolated house, and wants to write a story about the scientist. It just so happens that this cub reporter is the son of a newspaper magnate played by Frank Cellier, who suddenly falls in love with the ideas of Karloff, and promotes him to front page news in an attempt to win the ratings war. This was a topical reference: the major newspapers spent the 1930's trying to out-do

The Man Who Changed His Mind

each other in insurance schemes, free gifts, and other inducements to win readers, including sponsoring things like callisthenics. So although it may seem strange now, it was a touch of vérité when the film was made.

Karloff, Lee and Calthrop are brought to London after Karloff has successfully transplanted the personalities of two chimps in the old house. Ensconced in a sparkling new art deco lab (the sets are wonderful), he continues his experiments until Cellier forces him into the first great publicity stunt, a speech and demonstration in front of his peers – the ones who rejected him before...

Not buoyed by Calthrop's cynicism beforehand, Karloff is hesitant in front of an audience, and is soon jeered by his peers. Naturally, Cellier is not impressed, and corners Karloff in his lab, blustering wildly, he threatens him with legal action and – worse – taking away his facilities. This is too much for chain smoking Karloff (I know it's really stupid, but I've often ended up fascinated by how many times he lights up in the movie), who lays out Cellier.

Calthrop, sneaky as ever, reminds Karloff that this will mean the police, unless... the two men conduct an experiment, trying to swap the personalities of Calthrop and Cellier. The experiment is successful, and the newspaper magnate dies as he over-exerts Calthrop's weak body, trying to walk.

Although there have been some creepy moments up to this point – most notably in the personality transfers of the chimps – this is where things really start to get nasty. Cellier turns in a wonderful performance, as his imitation of Calthrop, from the slight narrowing of the eyes to the adoption of the latter's speech patterns, convince the viewer that a transfer has really been effected. The "new" man tries hard to fit into Cellier's life, but the biggest shock of all comes when he realises that Cellier was dying of a heart condition, the brutal irony is that he has swapped one damaged body for another – and this one is so diseased that he will die quickly.

Showing his true persona, he tries to blackmail Karloff, who has declared his love for Lee and been snubbed. Cellier proposes swapping his body for that of Loder, but Karloff has other notions. He strangles Cellier, and plans a swap with Loder, leaving the innocent man to be hanged in his old body...

By this time, the action is racing, and Loder confronts Karloff in his lab while the police search for Cellier's killer. Overpowered, Loder is swapped with Karloff, and the innocent man throws himself out of the window rather than be caught.

It all seems to be over, but...Lee arrives in the nick of time, with fellow scientist Cecil Parker, who helps her convince the police that Karloff is now Loder, and vice versa.

Unwilling to be hanged, the soul of Boris agrees to swap back, and dies in his old body as Loder is restored to Lee.

Although the plot is, in many ways, a standard mad doctor movie of the sort the Americans were always churning out, it had never been done in this country before, and the enthusiasm of both the cast and director give the film a manic pace and believability that lifts it above the norm. Certainly far superior to the independent *Juggernaut* (1937), which pursued similar themes a year later, it still stands as one of the two or three best British horrors from the pre-war period (along with *The Ghoul* and the silent version of *The Lodger*).

Such were the economics of the British film industry that Gainsborough shied away from pure terror, and only produced two more films in a horrific vein, both of these being horror comedies designed for the diminutive comic Arthur Askey.

The first was a 1941 remake of *The Ghost Train*, again directed by Walter Forde, but with the leading role of silly ass detective split into two: the detective was played with aplomb by Richard Murdoch, and the idiot was converted into a tenth rate music hall comic, perfect for Askey to prance and mug about the screen. Askey and Murdoch were teamed in a couple of films during this period, the first of which was *Band Waggon* (1939), which used an old dark house theme as a cover for Nazi spies sending television pictures to Germany. This was used by Askey and Murdoch to mount their own TV spectacular after being thrown out of the BBC.

Band Waggon was taken from the popular BBC radio show, in which the two men allegedly lived in a hut on the roof of the BBC's Broadcasting House. Askey had been a concert party and music halls comic, and Murdoch was an actor. The pairing of the two for the radio show saw the beginning of an intermittent team that would last for the rest of their lives.

The film of *Band Waggon* saw Moore Marriott in a character part. Marriott specialised in playing toothless, bald old idiots with squeaky voices, although earlier in his long and versatile career he had played in early silent horrors like *The Face At The Window*. Along with fat boy Graham Moffatt (whose character was always called Albert, just as Marriott was always Jerry or Harbottle), he spent most of the 1930's playing stooge to comic Will Hay.

Two of the trio's best movies were variants on the ghost train theme, with the chill subsumed beneath the laughs. *Oh Mr Porter* (1937) is possibly the funniest film ever made, and features Hay as an incompetent railway employee who is transferred to the out-of-the-way station of Buggleskelly, in Ireland. When an excursion he runs is entirely populated by Buggleskelly Wednesday, a soccer team that does not exist, the locals think that Hay has gone barmy and seen the ghost of One-Eyed Joe, the miller who haunts the hill. Of course, the hill hides a railway line that takes gun runners through to Northern Ireland from Eire, and Hay and his disbelieving cohorts eventually uncover the plot and catch the runners via a manic train chase.

The next year, they replayed the theme with *Ask A Policeman* (1938), where they are the most incompetent policemen in Britain, unwittingly allowing a lugubrious lighthouse keeper to put a signal in their top floor window proclaiming the health of the lighthouse keeper's grandmother to his brother, still on the lighthouse... it takes two reels for them to realise that there is not a lighthouse off their part of the coast.

The ghost train here is a ghost carriage, a flaming, horse-drawn affair with a headless coachman who turns out to be the local squire. When they follow the carriage into a deserted stable, and the one genuinely creepy moment in either film, when they count the shadows on the wall by the light of a match... and there's one too many!

Both films were directed by Marcel Varnel, a Frenchman with an unrivalled genius for directing English comics (he also got the best out of George Formby and marshalled the anarchic talents of the Crazy Gang onto celluloid). All the horror elements of the ghost train derived plots are subsumed to the comic drive, but both pictures are classics of their type.

Varnel died in the 1940's in freak circumstances when his car ran off a deserted stretch of road, with no other skid marks to indicate a collision. It was summer, and the coroner concluded that a bee had entered the car, distracting Varnel to such a degree that he had crashed. Unlikely? Possibly, but Varnel did have a phobia about bees...

Hay exploited the horrific elements of the horror comedy to better effect when he transferred to Ealing and directed himself, leaving behind his regular writers of Marriott Edgar (by coincidence, the half-brother of Edgar Wallace), J O C Orton, and Val Guest (early in his career and yet to become Britain's premier independent writer/director).

By something less than coincidence, these writers were assigned to re-write *The Ghost Train* for Askey and Murdoch. Faced with a director who knew the piece, and a duo that relied less than Hay on the comic interplay of dialogue, they were fairly faithful to Arnold Ridley's original play, adding only the clowning from Askey that divided the original character into two halves. Murdoch was less an ass than an unassuming man of action.

A nice touch was that the lugubrious porter who warned the passengers about the ghost train, and later turned up dead, was played by the same bit part actor who had been the lighthouse keeper in *Ask A Policeman*.

With ten years more experience and a slightly larger budget, the chase sequences are more exciting, and the roar of the ghost train rattling the windows of the waiting room is genuinely scary. Askey adds just the right note of comic trembling fear to Murdoch's cool detective, and Kathleen Harrison does a nice comic turn as the prim old lady with the parrot who misses all the action through being drunk.

Encouraged by the increased quota of thrills and chills to laughs, producer Edward Black put Askey into another horror comedy the next year. *Back Room Boy* (1942) written by Edgar and Guest without Orton, had to become a solo starring vehicle as Murdoch had joined the RAF (and started a long radio association with Kenneth Horne in the services radio comedy *Much Binding In The Marsh* – comics who had joined the RAF, Army and Navy were all given time off to make their own radio series as a morale booster during wartime). However, to make up for the loss of Murdoch, Askey inherited Moffatt and Marriott from Will Hay.

Not so much an old dark house as an old dark lighthouse chiller, Askey is a meteorologist who plays the pips every hour on the radio. Tied of this, he starts playing them in morse, and is reprimanded for such behaviour. His punishment is to take over a deserted lighthouse and meterological station in the Orkneys, off the north east coast of Scotland.

Before he takes up residence, the local townsfolk warn him about the sirens on the Kelpie Rock, and the strange incidences of madness amongst the lighthouse keepers. When Askey discovers that the Kelpie Rock and his lighthouse just happen to be in the same position, he begins to regret being sent out to the middle of nowhere, an impression that is not improved by a strange journey in which he is informed that he can only be visited every few weeks because of the storm-tossed seas.

No sooner has he arrived than his baggage mysteriously disappears from the quay, piece by piece, as he counts it, turning his back for only a second. When he makes his way to the lighthouse, he finds that his bed has been made, and someone has started to cook for him... a friendly ghost, if nothing else.

The ghost turns out to be little Vera Frances, a hard-voiced cockney kid who was in several comedies during the war. She plays an evacuee who wants to get to the island next door, where her uncle Steve is spending the war ringing birds. She may be flesh and blood, but director Herbert Mason handles the balance between comedy and the unknown beautifully as things happen for no apparent cause.

By now, a nervous Askey has adopted the expedient of talking to himself, calling himself "Arthur" and "Mr Pilbeam" (his character name). This nervousness is made worse when he awakes in the middle of the night to hear a woman calling. Is it the siren of Kelpie Rock? When he eventually plucks up his courage, he sees what appears to be a mermaid on the rocks...

Mermaid? It is Googie Withers, a wonderful statuesque actress who graced British movies of all types throughout the 1930's, 1940's and 1950's – she was in the Ealing horror classic *Dead Of Night* (1945). She plays one of a group of models shipwrecked after an attack by a German U-boat and believes herself to be the only survivor – until, that is, the rest of the girls turn up with the crew of the ship, consisting as it does of Moffatt and Marriott. The old man spreads doom and gloom everywhere, and it seems that *Back Room Boy* is going to be another mildly diverting comedy.

But no, one by one, the girls start to disappear, suddenly and mysteriously, even from locked rooms. The use of lighting on the winding stairs and passages of the lighthouse, combined with peerless acting from all concerned (it really is surprising how good all the comics are at straight fear), give the film an incredibly creepy atmosphere. Is it really a ghost?

Well no, of course not, this is a British movie, and we are in the middle of a war. So there has to be a rational explanation to keep the censor happy, and a lot of

German saboteurs routed by Askey and co. to keep the audience morale high. The film end in a thrilling, but distinctly unspooky, chase.

In this manner, Gainsborough's contribution to the British horror movie ended, not even with a whimper, but with the solid bang of a Nazi battleship being blown up by Arthur Askey, Graham Moffatt, and Moore Marriott.

Over at Ealing, Michael Balcon was busy establishing a company built on solid drama and music hall comedy. There was no room for anything approaching horror. However, he had bargained without the ideas of Will Hay, who was keen to explore the properties of comic horror when he signed to the company from Gainsborough. His first and third movies were straightforward war-time comedies, with Hay the hero bashing the Germans (etc, etc). The second – and especially the fourth – were another matter.

The Ghost Of St Michael's, made in 1941, was directed by Marcel Varnel. The director was the only old colleague Hay carried with him, as he had ditched his writers and stooges in an attempt to re-invent a formula he felt was becoming stale.

An old dark castle variant on the familiar theme, this saw Hay as Lamb, an incompetent schoolmaster called up in war time to replace a drafted colleague. The school has been evacuated to a castle on the Isle Of Skye, off the coast of Scotland, and Hay joins them as they catch the ferry. The kids, led by Charles Hawtrey, soon catch on to what an idiot Lamb is... and one of the other teachers – a marvellous slimy performance from Raymond Huntley – knows for sure, as he was at Lamb's previous school.

The headmaster – a vague turn of some proportion by Felix Aylmer – is found poisoned in his bed after threatening to sack Lamb... who also happens to be chemistry master. Meanwhile, there are phantom pipes to be heard and caretaker John Laurie (one of those wonderful supporting players who never played a duff show) is wandering around proclaiming a curse on the castle.

Hawtrey and co., who have been taught by Lamb (cribbing from a text book kept in his mortar board), know that any attempts at poisoning would be more likely to harm Lamb than any target, so they cannot believe it when he blandly incriminates himself at the inquest (rather being surreally held in a barn which the farmer is still using, so that Lamb ends up in the witness box holding a piglet).

With the help of fellow idiot teacher Claude Hulbert (brother of Jack, and perhaps even funnier as silly-ass characters), Lamb sets out to solve the crime... assisted from behind by Hawtrey and chums.

Very much modelled on *The Cat And The Canary* (1939) and *The Ghost Breakers* (1940), two Bob Hope vehicles that were doing excellent horror comedy box office, the script (by the new Hay team of Angus MacPhail and John Dighton) is full of creepy noises, secret passages, and hints of ghostly goings on. In the end, of course, it's the obligatory Nazi spy story, although in this case it rather surprisingly turns out to be cuddly matron and not the loony caretaker – an excellent red herring.

Not as creepy as either *The Back Room Boy* or *The Ghost Train*, Varnel is not terribly good at the chill factor, preferring to hurry this out of the way so that he can get onto the next gag.

Much better is *My Learned Friend* (1943) which Hay co-directed with Basil Dearden. It was Hay's last movie, as rectal cancer and a series of heart-strokes saw him decrease his workload to a scattering of radio series before his death in 1947. This is a shame, as *My Learned Friend* is the blackest comedy made in Britain up until this point, and with Dearden's talent for suspense, this is a tragi-comic forebear of the psychological horror Hammer churned out in imitation of *Psycho* (1960) some twenty years later.

Not as innocently funny as his 1930's classics, this is almost the work of a different man. Unlike horror comedies where the laughs come between the terror, in this they are the flip sides of the same coin. The audience laughs at the absurdity of a man caught in a horrific situation.

The plot is fairly straightforward. Hay is a seedy barred lawyer who is in court for writing fake begging letters to charities. Claude Hulbert is the prosecuting counsel, who has to win this or else he is out of a job. He fails, as Hay is much too clever for him, and afterwards they meet in a bar. Hay notices in Hulbert's newspaper that a judge has been found dead in the Serpentine river in London's Hyde Park, the same judge who sentenced a mad killer to confinement some years before. Hay was the defence lawyer, and the killer swore to avenge himself on both the judge, Hay, and the principal witnesses.

Who should pop up in the pub but the killer himself, played by Mervyn Johns – an Ealing contract player of no little talent – with manic glee. He has a list, and Hay is seventh on it. He has one chance to save himself, to catch the killer in the act before it gets down to his name.

Enlisting Hulbert's help, Hay tries to stop the murders, assisted by a gleeful series of cryptic clues from Johns, which he leaves on the ceiling of Hulbert's flat, in phone conversations, or shares from the back seat of Hulbert's car, when holding the two men at gunpoint.

Despite their best efforts, the two men are unsuccessful, an actress dies on stage, the judge's death is passed by a coroner as suicide, and a psychiatrist is horribly killed by a spiked tiger trap set by one of the inmates at his asylum (helped, of course, by Johns). While this last killing is going on, Hay and Hulbert are desperately trying to convince an inmate posing as the doctor (a waspish and fey performance from the great Ernest Thesiger) that he is in danger.

The final act before Hay's death is to be the bombing of the House Of Lords, as the Appeal Court has refused Johns clemency. Hay and Hulbert, posing as Beefeaters, search the House of Lords and find the bomb, but not before they are captured by Johns and led at gunpoint to the clock face of Big Ben. He plans to dispatch the pair of them when the bomb goes off...

In a climax that is both thrilling and funny, all three men scale the face of the clock – thus drawing attention to themselves – before the police arrive to capture Johns, while Hay and Hulbert are left hanging by their belts on spikes protruding from the clock tower, a couple of hundred feet above ground with nowhere to go but down...

If it does not sound that funny from the plot alone, rest assured that Hay and Hulbert are masters of drawing out the humour in any situation – which they have to be, as there are very few actual gags. But that is what sets this film apart, the humour is an a very black vein shot through with terror as both men are caught in the spiralling madness of Johns' vendetta.

Dearden's eye for suspense is sure, and co-director Hay has the experience of years on the boards and on film to time the humorous moments. The only thing that really lets the picture down is that same old inability to choreograph fight sequences, and the facility of some editing rooms to speed up the fights on the final print. Something strange happens to the music, as a full score is reduced to a toy town Wurlitzer organ for the last reel.

None of this can take away from a film that is the most remarkable blend of horror and comedy to come out of a British studio. It was a film the like of which had not been seen before, and I for one am sorry that Hay was never again fit enough to follow up on this new direction.

It was not until the following year, 1944, that Ealing felt confident enough to tackle their first serious chiller. Like all Ealing movies, it had a middle-class veneer that was lacking from the more populist terror of Gainsborough and Gaumont, and was that strangest of animals, a polite ghost story. Yet this worked entirely in its favour.

The Halfway House begins with a series of people who are looking for something in their lives, something that is lacking. For Tom Walls and Françoise Rosay it is their marriage falling apart after the death of their son. For Sally Ann Howes it is a last desperate attempt to bring her parents back together before they divorce. Esmond Knight is a brilliant concert pianist who has a terminal illness, and is thinking of taking his own life. Alfred Drayton is a fat-cat war profiteer who is on the verge of being caught. Guy Middleton is an ex-RAF flier, wounded and discharged, who is searching for a living and has followed Drayton in the hope of getting into the black market business.

All arrive at a small hotel in Wales, called The Halfway House. The viewer is given the idea that something is amiss when Middleton, arriving by bike, stares down into the valley and cannot make out the hotel for a strange haze and it only becomes visible as he gets closer.

Running the hotel are a man and his daughter, played by Mervyn Johns and daughter Glynis Johns. They seem distant and other-worldly, but the guests at first put this down to some kind of native Welsh shyness. It is only when Middleton notices that the newspapers on the desk are a year old, and Walls turns on the radio to find that the programmes are a year out of date, that the inhabitants of the hotel realise that something is wrong.

The clincher comes when Glynis Johns is seen by Middleton talking to Knight on the lawn. It is a sunny day, and he is casting a shadow – but she is not.

Before the truth is revealed, the inhabitants of the hotel begin to come to terms with their problems. Knight abandons all thoughts of suicide, realising that he should spend his final months sharing his gift with the public. Walls and Rosay finally overcome the barrier of silence between them, talking about their son and coming to terms with their loss, and the fact that they still have each other. Howes fakes an accident to get her father to save her – both he and her mother see through this deception, but realise how they are hurting their daughter.

The biggest volte-face comes from Drayton, who suddenly realises how his criminal lifestyle is possibly costing lives in a war that is more important than his pocket. Middleton, too, rediscovers the spirit that made him a flier, before his injuries forced him to look elsewhere and made him bitter. He decides to try and rejoin the RAF as an instructor.

All of these lessons are acceptable, with the possible exception of Drayton's, it jars that such a villain should suddenly change his mind. But no matter, this is wartime, and we are getting near the crux of the matter...

The hotel was bombed a year before, and the couple have been allowed to return to give help to those who need it. The film ends with the bombing, and the ghosts of the owner and his daughter assisting the guests out of the flaming wreckage, as bombs rain down, so that they can go and rebuild their lives.

Produced by Alberto Cavalcanti, directed with a deft touch by Basil Dearden, the Angus Macphail and Diana Morgan script is hindered only by the relentless moralising of the Denis Ogden play on which it is based. Otherwise, the growing sense of unease that is built up by the reactions of the guests, slowly coming to terms with what is happening at the hotel, is genuinely creepy, and the revelation that they are replaying a moment in time is shocking the first time you see the film.

Encouraged by the success of this picture, Balcon handed producers Sidney Cole and John Croydon the task of fashioning a horror portmanteau. With writers John Baines, Angus MacpPhail and T E B Clarke (later fêted as the architect of Ealing comedy) adapting both their own original stories and ghostly tales from H G Wells and E F Benson, the producers assigned direction tasks to the cream of their staff, Cavalcanti himself, Basil Dearden, Robert Hamer, and Charles Crichton.

The result was *Dead Of Night* (1945). The inspiration for the series of

Dead Of Night

compendium movies made by Amicus, and possibly for such TV series as Brian Clemens' *Thriller*, it stands alone as being a beast quite unlike anything before or since.

The stories are linked by Mervyn Johns, an architect who visits a country house owned by Roland Culver. He awakes from a nightmare to be greeted by his wife, who has taken a message for him. Someone called about a job, he goes to the house, and finds it all too familiar. Roland Culver is the owner, and the architect tells his strange story to the guests, who are intrigued. They all have a story to tell...

Anthony Baird recalls how, after an accident, he was convalescing in hospital when he awoke, it was bright daylight, and when he lifted the blinds a hearse was waiting in the yard. The driver (played by Miles Malleson) cheerfully looks up: "Just room for one inside, sir!" Baird shakes his head, and it is night once more. Yet, when he leaves hospital a few days later and tries to board a bus, he comes up against Malleson again, the bus conductor, who says "just room for one inside, sir". Shaken, Baird steps back and the bus crashes just a few hundred yards down the road.

Sally Ann Howes relates how she went to a Christmas party at a large old house, and when playing hide-and-seek stumbles on a boy, ill in bed. She befriends him, and promises to help him find his sister. It is not until later, when asking around, that she discovers the room has long been empty, and once belonged to a child who died there.

The most whimsical story involves Basil Radford and Naunton Wayne, two actors who cornered the market in dotty English gentlemen after their performance as Charters and Caldicott in Hitchcock's *The Lady Vanishes* (1938), is H G Wells tale. They play two golfers vying for the hand of a beautiful woman. To decide who gets her, they elect to play a round. Equally matched, Radford only wins by cheating. Wayne strides into the lake to commit suicide, but because he was defeated by dishonesty, he returns to haunt Radford on his wedding and honeymoon.

The stories up until now have been mild shudders, but there are two that are horrific in the quality that only nightmares could contain. Googie Withers recalls a mirror bought by her fiancé, a mirror which seemed to take him over. Sometimes he could look into it and see a strange room, quite unlike his own. Gradually, his personality changes, and he becomes nasty and mistrustful towards her. Worried that he may be going mad, yet unwilling to believe him about the mirror, Googie discovers that it came from an old house, and the original owner spent hours staring into it after a riding accident confined him to his bedroom. He eventually went mad and strangled his wife...

Googie rushes to tell her fiancé, only to find him staring in the mirror. She, too, can see the other room, and seems powerless as her possessed fiancé tries to kill her. The spell is only broken when she manages to smash the glass.

The last story in the film is the most remembered, and stars Michael Redgrave as a ventriloquist called Maxwell who is successful, but troubled. His act is getting out of hand as the dummy seems to be controlling him, ad-libbing lines that make him look stupid, and insulting the audience. It even gets him into a fight in a hotel bar. A fellow ventriloquist offers to help, but instead gets overtures from the dummy about taking over from that poor idiot Maxwell. The story culminates in the murder of the rival, and Maxwell in prison, refusing to talk unless it is to, or through, the dummy. In this, the true malevolence of the blankly grinning dummy's face is exploited to the full.

At the end, the architect finds himself suddenly flung into a surreal farrago as the group gang up on him, and he tries to murder a psychiatrist (Frederick Valk, with the usual cod-Freud accent for the period) who is present. A chase ensues through a nightmare series of passages, ending with the architect awakening as Maxwell's dummy stalks him.

So it was all a dream... the architect's wife comes in, and someone on the telephone has a job for him. As he approaches the house in his car, it seems strangely familiar...

Superb acting and writing is matched by Cavalcanti's inspired direction of the linking sequences, the Christmas party, and the ventriloquist story. Robert Hamer made the mirror sequence taut and frightening, while Charles Crichton brought a light touch to the golfing story. Basil Dearden directed the hearse story with his usual brisk efficiency.

A critical and box office success, it should have signalled a new dawn for British horror. Instead, Balcon took the portmanteau idea and applied it to drama with films such as *Holiday Camp* (1947) and *Train Of Events* (1949), and concentrated on developing T E B Clarke's whimsical comedies, beginning with *Hue And Cry* (1946) and *Passport To Pimlico* (1949).

If Balcon had been more of a horror fan, the story of British horror would have been different. Instead, it was left to what cash the few independent producers could scrape together in post-war austerity.

The end of the 1940's saw only two horror movies produced, and the early 1950's saw not many more. It took the success of imported AIP product, and the popular re-releases of Universal horrors to really inspire British film-makers to take risks, helped in no small part by a slight relaxation in censorship and the end of wartime taxes on production.

4. The Comedy Of Terrors

Comedy and terror are flip sides of the same coin, a laugh is as much a release from anxiety as a scream. Perhaps this is why producers have tried to tap into a vein of horror-comedy that provokes both screams of terror and laughter. A bad idea, as people like to be scared, or they like to laugh, but very rarely do they like both at the same time.

Yet for most of the 1930's and 1940's, that was all the major studios in Britain gave their audiences, a cheap thrill mixed with low comedy from a music hall star. At the same time, over the Atlantic, the Ritz Brothers were tangling with *The Gorilla* (1939) and Bob Hope was stalking old dark houses with *The Cat And The Canary* and *The Ghost Breakers*. The accent here was on comedy rather than chills, and reached rock bottom with the likes of Z-grade vaudeville clowns like Carney and Brown, and their *Zombies On Broadway* (1945). Abbott and Costello I do not even want to mention. Forty years later, this old formula was dusted down and given a new lease of life via special effects for *Ghostbusters* (1984), despite this, the field of horror comedy has always been a little barren.

Why was the pre-war and war period the time when horror comedy had its brief heyday?

Part of this reason lies in the economic situation that the western world found itself in throughout the 1930's. The depression led to a trend in cinema that was escapist, horror takes the audience into another world, away from the everyday, comedy has always been the stock-in-trade of oppressed people – just consider the Jewish comics and Afro-Americans whose talents livened up the entertainment business in both the 1930's and the 1970's, times when booms went bust. I am thinking here of the Marx Brothers, Mel Brooks, Richard Pryor, Eddie Murphy... all American names, but bare with me.

In the States, slumps have seen a burgeoning of both comedies and horrors on the screen. The urge to both escape into fantasy worlds and to laugh at problems, thus making them seem smaller than they are, have led to box office (latterly home video and cable) booms.

In Britain, it was somewhat different. The stringent censorship laws, and local watch committees who handed out licences to cinemas and sat in judgement on movies that had already been passed by the censor, meant that a pursuit of the fantastic was a little difficult. Comedy, however, was another matter. As long as music hall comics kept their more vulgar excesses in check, then they were perfectly permissable on screen.

So what better way to sneak a little horror onto the screen than under the guise of a comedy? The West End stage success of Arnold Ridley's *The Ghost Train* pointed the way, and the rush of horror comedies began.

Post-war, things began to change. As the 1940's blended into the 1950's, censorship began to relax. The horrors of war made anything the silver screen could dream up seem tame, and revivals of *Dracula*, *Frankenstein*, and other Universal horror pictures were as much nostalgia as fear-based. Even when British producers touched the supernatural, it was with a light touch that spurned the horrific. David Lean's version of Noel Coward's *Blithe Spirit* (1945), and Vernon Sewell's *The Ghosts Of Berkeley Square* (1947) were versions of stage successes that used whimsical ghosts to carry comedy.

As time went on, independent US horror, usually aimed at a teenage market via American International Pictures, began to cross the Atlantic, and British producers, encouraged by the certification these films received, began to make their own horror pictures. There was no longer any need for the veneer of comedy. The quota system gradually faded away as the US majors fell into their long decline, and independent studios boomed. With less and less block booking, it was easier for British producers to get their product shown.

So the horror comedy died out, its function more or less fulfilled. Between 1945 and 1990, there were only six movies that attempted to mix and match. For the most part, they were glorious failures... but not without their moments.

In 1952, a young man called Richard Gordon was working in New York, promoting the poverty row pictures of British producer and distributor George Minter, whose company was called Renown. Gordon would later go on to produce numerous British horrors throughout the 1950's, 1960's, and 1970's, and his name will crop up frequently. However, at this time he was 27 and restless.

Always a horror and pulp fan, his biggest thrill had been to meet Bela Lugosi, who was touring the US in a cheapjack production of *Arsenic And Old Lace*, the horror-comedy in which Boris Karloff had first made his name in the theatre.

Lugosi shared his dream with Gordon, to put on a new production of *Dracula* in London's West End, maybe with a transfer to Broadway. It would kick-start a dying career, and Gordon was keen to help. Two London producers called Routledge And White put on the production, and kept costs to a bare minimum, this included poor quality supporting actors who kept fluffing their lines. This would not have mattered, except that Lugosi had a severe hearing impairment by this time in his life, but knew the play well enough to return lines without hearing the cues...

The production was a disaster, and closed before finishing its out-of-town run. Lugosi was stranded in England without even the fare home.

Gordon came up with a wild idea. Comedian Arthur Lucan, whose act consisted of dressing in drag as an old Irish washerwoman called Mother Riley, had starred in a series of ultra-low budget movies for Minter, most of which are unwatchable. Usually paired with his wife Kitty McShane, who played his daughter in the act, Lucan was in decline. His performances were perfunctory, often leaving a stand-in (Roy Rolland) to double for him on stage while he sat drunk in the dressing room. If not this, then he and Kitty would carry their rows onto the stage, and the climax of the act (plate smashing) became a real dogfight. He was an alcoholic, and she a nymphomaniac who taunted him for his impotence. The real horror movie would have been the story of their marriage.

Lucan's movies were doing worse and worse business. However, if Minter could pair Lucan with Lugosi – for a fee of just $5000 (his fare home plus) – then perhaps he would make some money on this...

So was born 1952's *Mother Riley Meets The Vampire* (US title *My Son The Vampire*), with production and direction chores handled by a young John Gilling, and a script by veteran Val Valentine. The plot concerns Mother Riley unmasking a crook called The Vampire (Lugosi, of course, sinister but not particularly supernatural), who has some ridiculous robots under his charge. Most Mother Riley movies entailed him/her catching crooks after first being accused of the crimes, so there was little change in the basic formula.

Gilling tries hard, but the film is relentlessly downbeat from start to finish. Fascinating for all the wrong reasons, it's sad to watch Lugosi play on autopilot, patently baffled by the drag act playing opposite. Lucan, for his part, goes through his shtick with all the enthusiasm of a corpse. Truly horrific, but not scary, it was a horror comedy with no chills and no laughs.

At least it got Lugosi back home, where he met Ed Wood Jnr through Richard's brother Alex, an AIP man who was sharing an apartment with Wood. After

Mother Riley Meets The Vampire

Mother Riley, Ed Wood's transvestite tendencies must have seemed mild to the baffled Bela Lugosi.

Nine years passed before the next attempt at a comic horror. In 1961, Baker and Berman decided to break away from their usual run of grand guignol and melodrama to remake *The Ghoul* as a comedy. It must have seemed like a good idea at the time, but it did not do very well at the box office, discouraging them from further efforts.

Which is a shame, as the renamed *What A Carve-Up!* (1961) is a splendidly funny picture, with an excellent cast, a deft hand from Pat Jackson on the helm, and a script that takes Frank King's original novel, forgets all about the original movie, and mixes in little bits of *The Old Dark House* for fun. Scriptwriter Ray Cooney, assisted by Tony Hilton, later went on to write a series of long-running stage farces with titles like *Run For Your Wife*, and founded the only Theatre Of Comedy in Britain. For that alone, he deserves a cheer, but on this movie he really does turn in an excellent job considering that he was a bit-part actor only just starting to write.

The cast list reads like a who's who of British comedy and horror, with Kenneth Connor and Sid James representing the comics, and Donald Pleasence and Michael Gough the sleaze-horror contingent. In the middle stands Shirley Eaton, the blonde who started in British comedy, got painted gold for a Bond movie, and ended up in Jess Franco movies. A similar fate awaited Dennis Price, another cast member (although he was never painted gold – at least, not on screen).

The plot concerns mild-mannered Connor, a manuscript reader who lives with his friend Sid James, a down-to-earth lad who like nothing better than a pint at the dog racing track (James was obvious for this, as it mirrors the character that brought him fame in the *Hancock's Half Hour*). The opening sequence sets the tone for the whole piece. Connor is proof-reading a horror novel in a semi-darkened room. He reaches a particularly spine-chilling passage as the door begins to creak open behind him. Terrified, he leaps up – to find James arriving home with fish and chips...

No sooner has he calmed down, and told James about the passage where a spooky stranger appears on the doorstep, than he opens the front door to be confronted by sepulchral Donald Pleasence, with a graveyard smile...

Having fully established the tone, the plot then proceeds. Connor has been named in his late uncle's will, but to hear it he has to travel to the uncle's big old, dark

What A Carve-Up!

house in the middle of nowhere. Scared, he asks James (sneering at the idea of fear) to accompany him.

When they get there, they find other family members, Valerie Taylor and Dennis Price are the spongers who hope to get everything, Michael Gough is slimy (no-one can act slimy and sinister like Gough), and Shirley Eaton is an innocent abroad, just like Connor. There is the obligatory butler, and also uncle's deaf sister, who will insist that he is not dead...

Of course, she is dismissed as dotty. And of course, she is right, uncle is not dead at all, but instead intends to kill all his relatives off so that they will not get their hands on his cash. He is, needless to say, quite mad.

Director Pat Jackson (usually, Robert S Baker handled direction himself) uses the camera and lighting to good effect, getting the most out of the black and white stock. Tension is built up through a series of murders and double-blinds, including a village policeman who is not, and an organ on a lift platform that is excellent at hiding bodies.

Eventually, only Sid, Ken and Shirley are left alive, and they come face to face with nutty uncle in a series of hidden passages (shades of *The Cat And The Canary*). He threatens to unleash his pet dogs – Dobermans, starved to savagery – upon them, and it's only Sid's scheming that saves them, as uncle is dispatched by the dogs in a bleak and black finale that does jar slightly against the rest of the film. One of the few horror comedies to match the thrills and laughs well, it was a triumph for those concerned.

Considering Kenneth Connor and Sid James were portraying the character types that were their *Carry On* stock, it comes as a surprise to realise that neither were in *Carry On Screaming* aka *Carry On Vampire*, the next horror comedy to be made, in 1966. The team of producer Peter Rogers and director Gerald Thomas had been making *Carry On* movies for eight years, following fitful careers as comedy and thriller B-movie producers. Using every old music hall and picture postcard gag they could find, Norman Hudis' original series of light comedies had gradually been changed to a Rabelaisian parade of low comedy from the pen of Talbot Rothwell. The floating repertory company of actors were drawn on according to availability, and any subject could be plundered.

Carry On Screaming

Carry On Screaming was an attempt to parody and cash-in on the popularity of Hammer, who at this point were at their commercial and artistic peak. As a parody, it's next to useless. Where it really scores is in its ability to take the usual *Carry On* themes (toilets, lack of sex, bad puns) and put them in a period context. Kenneth Williams shines as Dr Watt (quite literally, when he is plugged in to be recharged), owner of the Bide-A-Wee rest home, whose business is sending out his monster Oddbod (a revived Neanderthal) to kidnap young girls who he then hardens in a wax-like solution and sells as shop-window dummies. He is assisted by his sister Valeria, a sexy Gothic vamp in a low-cut velvet dress and immensely back-combed hair, played by Fenella Fielding. I confess, even if the film was awful, I would watch it just for her...

What little plot there is concerns the efforts of Jim Dale to convince the police that his girlfriend has been taken and turned into a dummy by Watt. As the police are Harry H Corbett (Sgt Bung) and Peter Butterworth (Constable Slowbottham), he is on to a loser from the start. Especially as Bung is besotted by Valeria, and Slowbottham does not even notice that the butler, Sockett, is dead...

There's lots of chasing about, and men dressing in drag, before Bung solves the mystery, reversing the process on Jim Dale's girlfriend (Angela Douglas, with little to do except make like a statue) but not on Mrs Bung. Why? All is revealed at the end when he sets Valeria up as his housekeeper.

Best jokes? The mummy called Rubber-Titi, who finishes off Watt when revived. Valeria asking Bung "do you mind if I smoke?" then bursting into spontaneous combustion, and the music that accompanies Bung – a mix of *Z-Cars* (a popular BBC television police show at the time) and *Steptoe And Son* (Corbett's hit television comedy about a pair of rag-and-bone men).

Lots of laughs, but little horror. Given the series premise, that is not surprising. If you want parody, however, look at the section where Dr Fettle (a pre-*Doctor Who* Jon Pertwee) constructs Oddbod Jnr from Oddbod's severed finger, using electricity... dangerously close to Tigon's *The Creeping Flesh* – except that was not made until 1972. So which is the true parody?

Now that is what I call frightening.

The House In Nightmare Park aka *Nightmare Park* was made in 1973, and was the next in the sparse crop of comic horrors. Starring Frankie Howerd as a failed ham actor (a premise set up by his awful reception in the first scene) who is called to perform for a family in the middle of nowhere, it was produced by EMI in conjunction with Associated London (the agency that handled Howerd) and Extonation (a company formed and named by Terry Nation and Clive Exton). This unwieldy teaming is, in itself, indicative of the parlous state of British movie making in the 1970's, wielding together disparate elements in the hopes of scoring a hit.

This was not. It is 1907, and an axe murderer prowls the house by night. Howerd performs, as asked, but they all seem to be uninterested. Nanny in the attic comes after him with a knife when he pokes around the house, and head of the household Ray Milland is off-hand with Howerd. Even worse is the downright insulting behaviour of Hugh Burden...

Guess what, it is that great comic-horror stand-by, the old dark house meets the ghoul. Howerd is really an illegitimate son, entitled to half the money when the old man in the locked bedroom dies – except that he already has, and they are all pretending he is alive until they find the money. There are poisonous snakes in the cellars, hidden diamonds, and people start to drop dead. All this and lots of references to Indian Gods and curses (the family are Raj remnants).

With Kenneth Griffith, John Bennett, and Rosalie Crutchley in the cast, you know you are going to get quality playing. But when even the pretty young miss that Frankie falls in love with tries to kill him, things have tipped just that bit too far into horror. Trapped in a house of psychos, Howerd the genius comic has nothing to bounce his talent off, and ends up floundering as he is asked to be a serious actor.

The film ends with everybody dead, and Howerd faced with the task of digging up the entire grounds in order to find his inheritance.

Exton and Nation are both fine writers – Exton was later a suspense novelist, and wrote low-budget horrors like *Doomwatch* (1972), while Nation created cult sci-fi television series *Blakes Seven* and *Survivors*, as well as writing for numerous thriller series – and, of course, inventing the Doctor Who and the Daleks – comedy though is not their forte. They work a few laughs early on, but soon revert to type, leaving Howerd with less and less to do as the plot becomes faster and faster.

Yet despite this build-up, the direction of Peter Sykes is strangely static. He and photographer Ian Wilson frame a creepy movie that does anything but move.

Falling between the two stools rather than balancing, this is a flawed film that has a genuine unease to it because of that.

Another variant on the theme was presented in *Bloodbath At The House Of Death* (1983), another EMI collaboration (this time with Wildwood) in 1983. Produced and co-written by Ray Cameron, it was a vehicle for Kenny Everett, a pop music disc-jockey with a sense of humour who somehow believed for a few years that he was actually a comedian. Starting with a series of stock characters and good writers, he became progressively more desperate until jacking it in to go back to spinning discs. But not before he had made this.

If you want one film to show you a) how desperate the British film industry had become, and b) how not to make a comic horror, then this was it.

Self-consciously camp (which rarely works), the plot concerns a group of scientists, led by the wacky Everett, who investigate a haunted house. Mayhem ensues, with buckets of obvious fake blood and some ridiculous overplaying by the lead, with desperate supporting actors who are trying to make it all work.

With a cast of talent that includes John Fortune, Sheila Steafel, and Graham Stark, all comic stalwarts, and floundering then you know it must be bad. Gareth Hunt and Don Warrington try to play it straight but are overwhelmed, and Vincent Price shines as the only one present who can actually caricature this type of thing – why not,

I Bought A Vampire Motorcycle

he had been parodying himself for years. As for Pamela Stephenson – well, I bet she doesn't put this one on her CV.

The few good laughs can be credited to co-writer Barry Cryer, who has spent many a year salvaging other people's material. Ray Cameron also directed – badly – making it a hat-trick of horrors for him.

A disaster area for all concerned, it seemed to close the account for comic horror – but there was one last throw of the dice. *I Bought A Vampire Motorcycle*

(1990) was the first horror comedy for thirty years to be both funny and scary. Centred around a dumb motorcycle courier called Noddy, who buys a cheap old Norton motorbike, it follows his bemusement when the bike refuses to be rolled out of the garage until after dark, and has a distinct aversion to garlic in the take-away food on which he exists.

When you add to this the fact that it sprouts blades from its wheels, and thrives on blood rather petrol, then you know Noddy's got problems.

Neil Morrisey is Noddy, and the film re-unites him with much of the cast, crew and location of the TV series *Boon*, in which he shot to fame. For instance, Michael Elphick is a garlic-crunching police Inspector called Cleaver – when faced with a dead body that he is invited to look at, Noddy tells the Inspector "I'll have a butchers, Cleaver" (boom,boom).

Throw in a dream sequence with a talking turd, a decapitated biker gang called The Road Toads, and an exorcist who says "right – let's kick some bottom", and you know you have the film *Carry On Screaming* should have been. Shot in Birmingham by a group of Central TV production staff who were moonlighting after meeting Sam Raimi, it is a heartening indication that this small and erratic sub-genre still has some life in it.

Having stepped out of chronology in order to cover the art of horror-comedy, let's now backtrack to the end of the 1940's. Austerity meant that only two horror movies – both low-budget independents – were made between 1945 and the turn of the new decade, But when that decade came, the gates were (eventually) unleashed for the Golden Age of British horror movies.

5.   The Calm Before The Storm

Immediately post war, it was difficult to get a film produced and shown independently. A combination of wartime taxes, shortage of film stock, and an overly cautious series of watch committees had dissuaded the smaller entrepreneur from even attempting a horror movie: the British fascination for the macabre would not really arise until almost ten years later.

In such a climate, it is something of a miracle that any movies were made at all. Certainly, the two films that did make it as far as the screen during the latter half of the 1940's were cheap in the extreme.

The Fall Of The House Of Usher (1949) was distributed by Valiant, whose stock-in-trade had been quota quickies pre-war. Produced on something less than a shoestring in Brighton by one George Barnett, it was an attempt to convey the subtle horrors of Poe's story. A young Gwen Watford, on her way to becoming a film and TV support throughout the 1950's, 1960's and 1970's, here made a first tentative appearance on film, playing the cataleptic sister of Roderick Usher, whose premature burial presages the burning of the family home.

Ivan Barnett's direction is stilted, although this may be due to the old equipment he is using, certainly, the sound recalls recordings on wax cylinders. The only other named cast members are Kay Tendeter and Irving Steen – who?

Valiant by name and nature, it was a brave attempt to film Poe for the first time in England since *The Tell-Tale Heart*, some fifteen years before – actually, that is a trifle inaccurate, as legend has it that Barnett's film was actually made in about 1946, but it took him three years to find a distributor.

If Barnett's film looked cheap, then it was not the only one at the time. I recall a surreal afternoon sitting in a hospital visitor's room, watching *Dick Barton, Special Agent* (1948, US title *Dick Barton, Special Detective*), from Hammer that seemed to have been shot silently, with a radio soundtrack added on afterwards. It had that strange quality where the voices sound the same indoors or out, and the actors never mouthed directly at the camera... they also seemed to have trouble matching their actions to the soundtrack.

I mention this not just to share that memory, but because it illustrates perfectly the approach some low budget producers had to the immediate post-war problem. Shooting without sound and post-dubbing it was considerably cheaper. For a start, there was no sound recordist to pay for, and less stock used in re-takes caused by fluffed lines – just keep going, and it will be covered later. If movies could be shot in this way, and still be brought to the screen, then it was possible to scrape a small profit.

It was this approach that informed *The Ghost Of Rashomon Hall*, a 1949 release that starred Valentine Dyall, then popular on the BBC as the host of a series of horror stories. Commonly known as "the man in black", Dyall's sepulchral tones brought an authority to the series that it may not otherwise have had. Like many radio actors of this period, Dyall was a treading the boards man through and through, so the chance to appear on film as a lead must have been a good break... although Dyall does enliven other movies – particularly the early Amicus film *City Of The Dead* (1960, US title *Horror Hospital*), and supports in earlier movies like Brief Encounter (1945), and *The Life And Death Of Colonel Blimp* (1943, US title *Colonel Blimp*), this was not to be the one.

I sometimes wonder if I have dreamed this film. To the best of my knowledge, it appeared only once on TV, in the early hours of the morning. It was videoed twice, once for me, and once on my mother's machine (she is a Valentine Dyall fan). Both tapes were accidentally erased after the film was watched. I can find no mention of it in any film reference book, and even biographical entries on Dyall fail to mention it.

Does it really exist? Only the fact that both my wife and my mother recall it, too, convinces me.

And why not? It was certainly an hallucinatory experience. As far as I can remember, it was produced by Highgate Films, and had an incredibly small cast. Topped and tailed by Dyall as a doctor, the bulk of the film is silent with post-dubbed sound.

The prologue and epilogue are sound-on-vision, featuring a small group of people at a cocktail party. Dyall turns up late, and is asked his opinion on ghosts, a subject they have been discussing with a degree of scepticism. He recalls an interesting tale, and begins...

The plot concerns a young couple who have cheaply bought a run-down old manor house. This is the Rashomon Hall of the title. While they are settling in, strange things begin to happen – odd noises, apparitions, and the mysterious moving subjects of a small painting. Down in the village, the locals discuss the happenings up at the Hall, and show each other old books with the history of the building.

The young couple are being torn apart by the haunting. Enter Dyall, an old friend, who manages to rid the place of the ghost.

Back to sound-on-vision and the cocktail party, the guests are dismissive of Dyall's story, and ask him what makes him think that ghosts are real, he laughs wildly, then disappears in front of their eyes...

By the end of the film, the viewer is probably sitting on the edge of his seat, open-mouthed. Not only is it logically inconsistent that Dyall should be a ghost, but the main section of the film has presented the viewer with an inadvertent set of images that verge on a bad LSD trip.

For a start, the dubbed sound is ludicrously out of synch, and the leaden script has dialogue that consists solely of non-sequiturs. The film looks as though it was hand cranked, as the action is jerky and prone to both speeding up and slowing down. The close-ups are out of focus, and the shots of a laughing ghost are thrust in almost entirely at random.

The strangest thing of all concerns the title of the house: "Rashomon Hall" on the credits, yet everyone refers to it as Rammlesham, and when the local butcher shows someone a history book, an illustration of the house is labelled "Rammlesham Hall". The same butcher and his customers talk to each other under dialogue exchanges in a murmured buzz that is not real conversation at all – rather, it is an attempt to sound like background noise, yet so close to the microphone that you can actually hear them going "hmmmm, hurummmmm..."

It sounds as though it should be absurd, and in some ways it is, yet it is also extremely disturbing, in the same way that a patently absurd nightmare can be. The heavily distorted soundtrack over the endless tracking shots of the oil painting, where a nude figure seems to move closer and closer to the painted house with each shot, is genuinely scary in the sense that the viewer is absolutely bewildered.

An unintentionally strange film, and one that I wish I still had on tape.

The 1950's was a decade of two distinct halves. During the early years, Britain was pulling out of the post-war recession, and Harold MacMillan – Supermac – was rebuilding the economy in what turned out to be the artificial boom of "you've never had it so good". Perhaps not, but it was built on the myth of colonialism and an Empire that was (thankfully) beginning to crumble. It could not last, but while it did new avenues began to open.

The Fall Of The House Of Usher

Television and new communications satellites were the beginning of the global village. Old standards began to change. From America came rock'n'roll and American International's horror exploitation of the new teenager – *I Was A Teenage Frankenstein* (1957), *I Was A Teenage Werewolf* (1958), *Monster On The Campus* (1958) etc. – a trend which culminated in Herman Cohen's attempt to produce *I Was A Teenage Gorilla* in the UK; more on that later.

In the big scheme of things, these films were unimportant, but in terms of this book it was quite the opposite. AIP and its maverick B-king Roger Corman had been producing horror flicks from the early 1950's that had invaded UK cinemas, and when Hammer were the first to cross the Atlantic in 1955 with *The Quatermass X-periment* (US title *The Creeping Terror*), and make inroads into the US horror market, then British producers knew that they could make big bucks with blood. Something British censorship and the block-booking domination of the US majors had previously prevented.

So the on-rush of British blood begins post 1955. Up until then, things were fairly quiet as British producers still battled against the pre-war systems. So quiet, in fact, that only three films were made before the Hammer landmark.

In 1952, there were two attempts to put a horror movie on the screen. The first was *Mother Riley Meets The Vampire* aka *My Son The Vampire* aka *Mother Riley Meets The Vampire Over London* aka *King Robot* aka *Mother Riley Runs Riot* aka *Dracula's Desire*, the sad and tired vehicle for the bewildered Bela Lugosi and the incoherent Arthur Lucan. This was discussed in the chapter on horror comedies, and the only thing to add is that Lucan was a fine performer in his day, but that day had long since gone, his talents eroded by drink and a nightmare marriage. I stick by my opinion that this is an horrific film for all the wrong reasons.

The other film to tackle horror in that year was *The Ghost Ship* (1952), written and directed by Vernon Sewell for Anglo-Amalgamated.

Anglo was a distribution company run by Nat Cohen and Stuart Levy. During the 1950's and 1960's they became one of the leading independent distributors in the country, dipping their toe into production finance during the 1960's with the first *Carry On* movies, and a string of sci-fi and horror movies that warrant a chapter to themselves. After Levy died in the late 1960's, Cohen sold Anglo and went on to run EMI for a brief period. The beauty of their approach was that they trusted their producers and directors to know their job, and concentrated on the process of selling the movie.

At this time, Anglo were still a small distributor, and so their productions were few and far between. When Sewell approached them for financing, they knew that they were on to a sound proposition.

The Ghost Ship is that old Sewell stand-by, another re-write of *The Medium*. Only this time, the gimmick is that instead of a haunted house, you have a haunted boat.

The plot concerns a young couple who buy a motor boat. Recently married, they use it as a houseboat, and strange things start to happen to them. There are weird noises, moving objects, and odd intimations that something is not quite right. Intrigued and frightened (but not necessarily in that order), they decide to look into the history of the boat, and find that the previous owner's wife died in mysterious circumstances.

It soon becomes apparent that the woman was murdered, and it is up to the young couple to prove this.

Sewell, who showed a surprising facility for comedy in *The Ghosts Of Berkeley Square* (1947), directs with his usual brisk efficiency. The film is a standard second feature length at just over seventy minutes, and the script enables him to squeeze the maximum action from a minimum of sets.

The cast, with Hazel Court in her pre-Hammer and AIP scream queen days, Dermot Walsh as her husband, and Hugh Burden as the murderous previous owner of the boat, are all as solid as you would expect from such talent. Sewell, as a director, was never interested in actors per se, preferring them to just get on with things while he concentrated on pacing, and sometimes his films suffer from this.

I think this is one of those occasions. Unlike *House Of Mystery* (his 1960 re-write of *The Medium*, for Independent Artists), the cast seem to forget that they are in a supposed horror film, and the fear that they are supposed to show when the boat is discovered to be haunted is soon forgotten in the hunt for the truth.

Like many of Sewell's horror outings, *The Ghost Ship* seems to forget about halfway through that it is supposed to be a chiller, and Sewell concentrates on the thriller aspect.

In many ways, this is indicative of why it took a new generation of talent to put British horror on the map. Vernon Sewell was in his late forties when he made this film, and all his life he had worked in a British film industry that was hidebound by censorship both moral and financial. For film-makers of his generation, the idea of an out-and-out horror film was something that it was hard to get used to, and he carried with him the baggage of his generation.

The way towards a new type of British horror film was shown by two American producers who came to Britain in the late 1940's and stayed for fifteen years. Brothers Edward J Danziger and Harvey Lee Danziger were American B-movie producers who had made *Jigsaw* (1949) in the States before emigrating. Most film talent took the opposite route, but the Danzigers obviously saw an opportunity to move in on a depressed market, where they would not have to compete with larger poverty row producers like Monogram and PRC.

Setting up the New Elstree studios, they churned out a series of low-budget B-pictures, and made early moves into television with series like *Sabre Of London*

The Ghost Ship

(about a one-armed private detective), which still plays on satellite and cable stations. One of these interminable B-pictures was an adaption of a stage play that mixed horror and science-fiction. It was called *Devil Girl From Mars* (1954).

To cash in on the new sci-fi film boom that was happening in the States, the Danzigers rushed their version onto screen in 1954. The hurry with which it was prepared showed through in the paucity of the special effects, but the quality of writing and acting carried the picture beyond its B origins.

A group of people are gathered at a remote Scottish inn, the inn- keeper and his wife, their young nephew, a barmaid, and a beautiful female model who is running away from a failed relationship. New arrivals include a scientist and a journalist, both in search of a meteor that has landed in the district, and an escaped murderer who is the ex-boyfriend of the barmaid.

The journalist recognises the murderer, and is also attracted to the model. So far, we have the beginnings of an interesting if somewhat clichéd thriller.

But suddenly, the writers (John C Maher and James Eastwood, from the latter's play) throw a spanner into the works, the meteor lands near the inn, but it is no meteor... instead, it is a spaceship from Mars, piloted by a stunning Amazon dressed in black PVC.

Suddenly, minor antagonisms are forgotten in the face of this unknown property. Bestriding the inn with her presence, she reveals that she has only landed here because of a fault in her ship. Her real target is London, where she plans to show the power of her race by destroying vast tracts of land. What does she want? Men, and lots of them. Mars had a series of wars, and the male race was decimated. The women left need good breeding stock. This is a nice reversal of the usual situation, where bug-eyed men come after earth women. And whatever this Devil Girl is, she is no bug-eyed monster. In her tight fitting PVC mini and tunic, with sheer black tights and an uplift bra to add to the high patent leather boots, she is an S&M wet dream, and certainly one of the strongest images to make it onto a mainstream cinema screen during this period.

As played by Patricia Laffan, the alien has a cold beauty and an icy charm, she looks on the humans as though they are fodder, somewhat in the way that we look at beef cattle or stud horses. Her proclamations, uncaring of how they affect the dynamics of the group relationships (and thus, by implication, the whole of humanity), have a callousness that is the true horrific element.

The group stays solid at first, not knowing how to battle against her, but begins to splinter when fear intrudes on shock. She is impervious to both bullets and electricity, and it seems that the only way to stop her is to enter her ship and blow up the nuclear reactor that powers it.

In a less thoughtful film, this action would take precedence, but instead the film concentrates on how each member of the cast handles the idea of dying for such a cause. Eventually, the escaped murderer, realising that he has little to stay on earth for (he knows recapture would be imminent, and also has trouble living with his crime), substitutes himself for the gung-ho journalist.

Ignore the awful special effects (including a cardboard robot that is actually funny where it should be frightening), and concentrate on the acting; Hugh McDermott as the journalist, Hazel Court as the model, Peter Reynolds as the murderer, John Laurie and Sophie Stewart as the inn-keepers), Joseph Tomelty particularly good as the tetchy Professor and Adrienne Corri as the barmaid. Director David MacDonald overcomes the stagey limitations of both set and budget to keep the dynamics of the film within the group of actors rather than the sets, and uses the stage limitations to emphasise the isolation and claustrophobia of the situation.

Although tame by modern standards, there was a shift in attitude in this film that paved the way for the horrors to come. The storm was about to break.

6.   Après Quatermass – Le Déluge

After the success of *The Quatermass X-periment*, Hammer attempted to repeat the formula with *X – The Unknown* (1956), the following year, before stumbling onto their Gothic formula in 1957 with *The Curse Of Frankenstein*. The story of Hammer is deserving of a chapter or two to itself, so for the moment the company from Bray will be flung to one side, like a corpse abandoned at the side of a road.

For now is the time to look at the movies that followed in the wake of *Quatermass*. Between the end of 1955 and the turn of the new decade, fourteen horror movies were made in the UK – as many as in the fifteen years preceding. Certainly, the relaxation of censorship on a local and national level, together with the collapse of the major US studio's stranglehold on cinema bookings was a great contributor to this. The other great contribution was that of TV. With the introduction of a commercial channel in 1955, there were more programmes than ever on the air, and although it may seem strange in these days of channel surfing, the television was hailed as the end of cinema, sending a stream of consistently interesting programmes into the home that would mean never having to go out in the cold November air to a cinema ever again.

At least, that was the theory. In practice, TV was still in its infancy, and much of the entertainment spewed forth was anodyne and of an even lower budget than most B pictures. There were also more stringent standards and moralities at work, leading to less chance of something shocking being shown. For every *1984* (the TV version of George Orwell's fable, with Peter Cushing as Winston Smith, has gone down in history as one of the most powerful productions from early small screen days), there were a dozen anaemic sit-coms and soaps.

The cinema had to hit back. One way was in gimmicks, this was the age of Vistavision, Cinemascope, and 3D. The latter was a useful tool for some horror makers, as shown in Bryan Foy's Warner production of *House Of Wax* (1953), with Vincent Price. However, it was a little unwieldy, calling for hundreds of pairs of special glasses that were always lost and broken at every performance. Another way of hitting back was through more graphic depictions of the subjects TV could not tackle – either because of Government Charter (the BBC are still, at the time of writing, reliant on money given by the Government, raised by the TV licence), or because of commercial pressures (ITV has always been terrified of controversy, and the subsequent withdrawal of advertising revenue).

So it was that horror began to get more graphic, and sex became more prevalent. In the US, this happened earlier than in the UK, partly because of the earlier rise of TV in the States, and partly because of the differing moralities in the two countries. The US has always seemed to be split between libertines and hard-line fundamentalists, whereas in the UK the two parties are not only not so far apart, they are also more discreet about putting across their points of view (this is, of course, a gross generalisation). Subsequently, any changes take longer as both sides are sneakier about getting their own way.

But enough about public morality per se, how did it apply to horror movies in the UK? In the case of Hammer, they scored by taking a TV hit that everybody was talking about, and filming it with a greater emphasis on the horror aspects. Nigel Kneale's original *Quatermass* television had the time (six half-hours, as opposed to a 90-minute maximum for theatrical release) to philosophise as well as put in some action. Hammer, with their slightly bigger budget and brief to pull in punters who may have seen it on TV but wanted more, cut straight to the chase and ladled on more graphic horror as well as using the budget for a better quality of photography, adding light and shade to the terror.

The success of this led producers to believe that there was money in horror. The nature of censorship was still such that much had to be suggested, but there was definitely more scope for on-screen terror.

The true British horror movie, with its mix of the graphic and the sleight of hand, was about to be born in earnest.

The Bespoke Overcoat was produced by the tiny Remus company in 1956, and was designed as a supporting short. It ran at thirty-three minutes, and featured two Jewish character actors of great talent, David Kossoff and Alfie Bass. Both were better known for their comic roles, but here they turned in beautifully judged performances.

Based on a short story by Russian writer Gogol, with a script by award-winning novelist Wolf Mankowitz – also a respected scriptwriter at this time, following the success of his *A Kid For Two Farthings* (1955) – the film was an old fashioned ghost story, with a light yet sinister touch.

Simply, a clerk in a clothing warehouse is refused an overcoat and asks a tailor friend to make him one. Before this happens, he dies of the cold, and his ghost returns to ask the tailor to steal him the coat he deserved. There is little suspense, but a nice feel to Kossoff and Bass' interplay, with an edge to their relationship once one of them is dead that is unnerving.

Produced and directed by Jack Clayton, the film is strong in atmosphere and has the feel for the paranormal that he brings to *The Innocents*, the 1961 version of Henry James' novel *The Turn Of The Screw* which he also directed. Unlike this later film, where horror was mostly eschewed in favour of a trendy psychological approach, this is definitely a tale of the undead, if a minor one.

Ranged against this was the other non-Hammer horror entry for 1956, *Fire Maidens From Outer Space*.

This film was produced by Eros, a bucket-shop distributor who had imported cheap movies from the US and Europe, dabbling in skin flicks, they now hoped to cash in on the trend towards horror. They produced four horror movies before going under at the end of the 1950's, a fate that also awaited Producers Associates, a company with whom they were allied in some of these projects.

While later Eros films got the balance right, this first effort is possibly the worst British movie ever made – and that is saying something if you have ever sat through some of the films I have. If *The Bespoke Overcoat* is all that is best about British horror (atmosphere and story-telling), then *Fire Maidens From Outer Space* represents the worst excesses.

Written and directed by Cy Roth, it tells the story of a bunch of British astronauts (okay, so they are supposed to be American, but as they include cockney actors Sidney Tafler and Harry Fowler putting on the worst accents I have ever heard, they are definitely Brits) who travel to the thirteenth moon of Jupiter after receiving signals. There they find it populated by lots of scantily clad young girls who run around a lot at the behest of their master – the last man left alive, and a descendant of the original races who (get this) flew to the moon from Atlantis before it was destroyed.

He wants earth men to help repopulate his lands, as he has fathered only daughters (just one point – where are the mothers of these girls?). Also, he needs help to fend off a savage mutant who skulks outside the grounds of his own personal Eden. Who this could be is never explained...

The sixteen girls (count 'em) strike poses on the cheap cardboard scenery and look embarrassed. Harry Fowler and Sidney Tafler let their accents slip, and insult the Americans so much that it could explain Dick Van Dyke's cockney accent in Mary

Fire Maidens From Outer Space

Poppins (revenge). Nothing much happens until they fly back to earth as the moon explodes...

The dumbfounded viewer can see that parts of the film are supposed to be horrific – for instance, whenever the savage appears, the girls run around a lot, screaming. Yet Roth is so incompetent, and his budget so small, that everything just looks like a home movie. If his idea was to make a British version of *Queen Of Outer Space*, the schlock sci-fi movie with Zsa Zsa Gabor that this resembles, then he succeeded. I guess the fake American accents are to facilitate a US sale. Hmm...

One of those films that is entertaining for the wrong reasons, it is best remembered for the appalling editing. The most famous sequence is where Harry Fowler looks at his watch. He is wearing short sleeves. The close-up, however, is of a man with a long-sleeved shirt...

If nothing else, this film seemed to make Eros a name to look out for – if only to walk past the cinema with a hurried stride.

In 1957, however, Eros got it right... with the help of Richard Gordon and his further attempts to single-handed start a pulp horror revolution. *The Fiend Without A Face* stands as one of the best sci-fi horrors ever made in Britain, even though it is supposedly set on and around an air-force base in Canada. It has to be said that this little ploy does not work. Actually filmed at Walton Studios, on the banks of the Thames in the Thames Valley, just outside London, the scenery is lush English Home Counties, nothing like the wild Canadian Prairie that it is supposed to be. This becomes even more apparent when the action moves into town, and large Canadian houses are represented by suburban villas and rather nice little 1930's cottages. In fact, there is nothing Canadian about this film at all – even the overseas sale concession, Marshall Thompson, is an American. There is one other genuine American in the cast – bit-part actor Michael Balfour, who has spent most of his life in this country.

The story of *The Fiend Without A Face* is taken from a pulp magazine story *The Thought Monster*, written in the 1930's by Amelia Reynolds Long and passed on to Alex Gordon at AIP by her agent, legendary fan and collector Forrest J Ackerman.

Fiend Without A Face

Although not right for AIP, Alex passed it on to brother Richard, who set up the deal with Eros and Producers Associates. As with all his movies, his name does not appear on screen, that credit going to his long-time collaborator John Croydon.

An aged Professor is working on thought transfer, and the materialisation of thought. Played in a gloriously bad-tempered and vague fashion by Kynaston Reeves, the Professor stumbles on a way of disconnecting thought from the mind, and creates little thought creatures that only attain shape after attacking men at the air-force base, local farmers (Canadians with remarkably English yokel accents) and their animals. In each case, they have sucked the brain and brain stem from the victim.

Marshall Thompson is the chief security officer at the base, and has a nasty feeling the Professor is somehow involved, even though the breaches of security are at first put down to nothing more than spying. He gets to know the Professor's secretary, played by a wasp-waisted Kim Parker, and learns something of the Professor's work. He also falls in love with Kim.

The plot proceeds like a horrific whodunit, with strange activity and death spurring paranoia and an attempt to divine the purpose of the thought monsters. All becomes clear at the climax when the Professor cracks, and reveals what happened to him when the first thought creatures broke away, in a flashback that is creepy and shocking, even now. Given impetus by a lightning strike and power surge, the monsters gain independence and smash up the Professor's lab, preventing him from finding a way to stop them.

While the story is unravelled, the monsters gather outside his house, and mount an attack. At first invisible, they are gaining power all the time from a nuclear power station at the base, forcing it to overload in order to feed them. They gain visible form, and are akin to the brains they have taken, complete with brain stems for tails.

An exciting climax sees them attack the house, while Thompson, Parker, Reeves, and the local mayor and sheriff attempt to protect themselves by boarding up the windows and shooting brains that come down the chimney and through the unprotected gaps. They cling to their victims, sucking out the brain from the back of the neck.

Thompson has to escape and shut down the power station before it overloads, taking his chances with the monsters. Although it may be obvious that he will succeed, the tension is still kept high, and it really does run to the wire whether or not the viewer will be given a happy ending or the kind of apocalyptic gloom that was briefly in vogue during the 1950's.

Despite the incongruity of the alleged location, the cast all turn in underplayed performances that allow director Arthur Crabtree to keep the pace moving. This understatement also makes the moments of terror more horrifying, as the tautness of the film and the mundane atmosphere of the day-to-day base suddenly jumps in intensity. H J Leder turns in a tight script with no room for digression, and the special effects are quite remarkable for the period – especially for such a tightly budgeted movie. Stop-motion models filmed in Munich by model-makers Ruppel and Nordhof (discovered by Croydon), they sent the film over its budget – but even so, it still cost less than £90,000.

The final sequence, where the brains attack the Professor's house, was released as a super-8 reel for home projection. It was one of the few reels to be really scary, and in the context of the film it can still make the viewer cast a glance behind them.

Encouraged, Eros put another horror into production, *The Man Without A Body* (1957) was a co-production with Guido Coen, and concerned a tycoon who owns the head of Nostradamus, which he keeps alive in the hope of having it transplanted for his own. A ludicrous script by William Grote does not help matters. Badly plotted and incoherent, it does not give the director much to work with. Still less the fact that two directors actually worked on the movie. It could be that W Lee Wilder and Charles Saunders were working as a team on this project, but the evidence would suggest otherwise. Parts of the film are flat and banal, yet others make a decent stab at atmosphere, and the one or two genuinely unsettling moments come from the combination of this style of direction and the acting of lead George Coulouris, a British actor who had spent some time in the States – including playing banker Walter Thatcher in *Citizen Kane* (1941) – before returning to bit-part roles in comedy and horror pictures.

One of those pictures that is worth a cursory look, but should not be followed too closely (unless you spot the plot inconsistencies), it closed Eros' account for 1957.

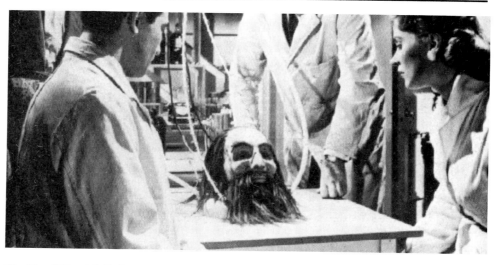

The Man Without A Body

If only for *The Fiend Without A Face*, they were still ahead on points.

There were two other horror movies made in that year (other than Hammer, of course). The first is a minor effort for Insignia Films called *The Cat Girl* (1957) aka *The Cat Woman*, scripted by Lou Rusoff and polished by Alfred Shaugnessy, a jobbing writer who worked on thrillers and comedies and later found his niche on TV as a historical dramatist, it is nothing more than an ultra-low budget rip-off of Val Lewton's *Cat People* (1942). Every writer who has mentioned this film has made the comparison, and I wish I could be different, but the sad fact is that it is so blatant that I am surprised RKO never sued.

Barbara Shelley – a future scream queen and Hammer heroine – was at the start of her horror career in this picture, playing a woman who believes that she is the inheritor of a family curse that will cause her to turn into a marauding leopard. Jack May (later to find fame in long-running radio serial *The Archers*!) plays her husband, who gets a little tired of her neuroses, and starts to dally with Kay Callard, a suitably more forthright other woman.

Anyone who has seen the Lewton/Tourneur movie will be able to guess what is coming next, Shelley starts to mutate, and ends the film quite mad, having ripped hubby to bits. Did she really turn into a leopard, or was she just insane?

This is a question that is never answered. Shaugnessy directs the picture himself, and makes a good job of imbuing the cheap settings and poor lighting with some degree of atmosphere. The script is all over the place, and highly confusing. This is not like Shaugnessy, usually a tight and competent writer. The viewer can only assume that some outside interference prevented him from making the film he really wanted, or else Rusoff's original script was beyond repair. It is just a shame that it is such a blatant rip...

The last horror movie of 1957 to come outside of the Hammer studios was, quite possibly, one of the best of the period. *Night Of The Demon* (US title *Curse Of The Demon*), aka *The Haunted*, was made in Britain by Columbia, in collaboration with the small Sabre company, whose Frank Beviss acted as co-producer with Hal E Chester. Chester was a veteran of the American B-picture scene, and was the man responsible for teaming the ageing Bela Lugosi with the Bowery Boys, his own creation, a group of teenage thugs who had "adventures" and talked with thick Brooklyn accents, they included proto-gangster Leo Gorcey and amiable idiot Huntz Hall.

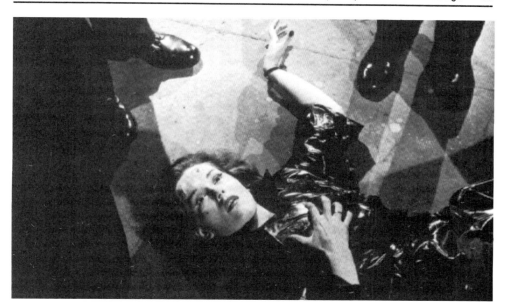

The Cat Girl

Chester's pictures were ultra-low budget, and virtually unwatchable. So it comes as somewhat of a surprise to find him dispatched to the UK by Columbia overlord Harry Cohn with orders to take Dana Andrews and make a horror picture based on a story by that master of understated horror, M R James.

James' story *Casting The Runes* concerns a mild-mannered man who incurs the wrath of a magician and is passed a slip of paper with runic symbols. If these are destroyed, or are still on his person seven days later, he will die. The crux of the story

Night Of The Demon

is the man's gradual realisation that these things are true, and that he must return the runes to the magician to prevent his own death.

Taking these bare bones, Chester and co-writer Charles Bennett take the late Victorian setting of the original and make it contemporary. To establish Andrews' presence in the UK, he becomes a psychology professor attending a conference on witchcraft, at which he intends to expose the sect headed by Karswell (a splendid performance by mild-mannered Niall MacGinnis) as a fraud. However, the co-presenter of the paper, played by Maurice Denham, meets a sticky end just before Andrews arrives, via a very silly looking demon. The death appears to police as an accident, and it takes Denham's niece (Peggy Cummins) to persuade Andrews that something is going on after he is handed the runes by Karswell in the British Museum reading room.

Director Jacques Tourneur turns in one of his best pieces of work. From the beginning, when Denham is pursued by a strange cloud, to the very end when Karswell, knowing the runes have been passed back, tries to escape along railway tracks before being savaged by the demon, the atmosphere is always on the edge of fear. Every scene is loaded with tension, the latent fear of the unknown bubbling below the everyday surface. This is achieved by the performances, and also by the lighting, Ted Scaife's photography complementing Tourneur perfectly.

The secret of the film's success lies in the way that Tourneur and the scriptwriters keep to the spirit of James' original understatement – the appallingly fake model demon was added at the beginning and end of the film at Chester's behest, fearful that Cohn would rail at a horror movie with no monster. Tourneur was known to be unhappy at this, feeling that a stupid monster would detract from the atmosphere he had so carefully built up. Not so, as this intrusion is easily ignored by the viewer, intent on the careful character build-up. Andrews' stubborn persistence in disbelieving that anything supernatural is going on is revealed to be a childhood quirk that started with refusing to walk under ladders, and it is that same stubbornness that now stops him from accepting what is happening to him. Karswell, on the other hand, is gradually revealed as a broken down children's entertainer and mummy's boy whose only insecure grab at independence was to practise magic – to the point where he is more frightened of the powers that wrestle in his grasp than any of his followers could possibly be...

There are too many excellent set pieces to mention. For instance, the séance run by medium Reginald Beckwith, where Karswell's mother (unhappy at her son's activities) asks Denham to come through with a message after the seemingly absurd singing of "Cherry Ripe". Cummins is shocked to hear her uncle's voice, but Andrews, despite looking uncomfortable is too keen to dismiss this as mimicry. Then there is the moment when Andrews confronts the family of farmer Ran Hobart, who is imprisoned for killing a man he claims was killed by the demon. The whole room swims before his eyes, and the runes escape his wallet, seeking to destroy themselves on the open fire.

Also the interrogation under hypnosis of Hobart (played with bug-eyed intensity by a young Brian Wilde), where – instead of the truth Andrews is waiting to hear – an invocation of the demon is yelled across a crowded room before Hobart escapes, plunging to his death from a high window. Or, indeed, Karswell's little demonstration of his powers at a childrens' party, where he conjures up a hurricane from nothing.

Fine support to Andrews, McGinnis and Cummins comes from Athene Seyler as Karswell's doting mother, finally driven too far by his excesses and turning against him, and Liam Redmond as a colleague of Andrews' who is not so keen to dismiss witchcraft out of hand.

It is an indication of the gap between the Americans and the British at this time that a "low budget" movie from Columbia, financed in a foreign country, should cost more than the equivalent from, say, Eros – thus enabling a glossier look. On the other hand, not many British low budget companies had Jacques Tourneur under contract. This highlights another problem for British movies in general, as any truly talented directors moved to the States, or relied on US money. Jack Clayton, who made such an excellent job of *The Bespoke Overcoat*, was financed by 20th Century Fox when next venturing into the horror field with *The Innocents*, and home grown and cultivated talent like Terence Fisher and Freddie Francis were kept busy with Hammer and Amicus, while other directors relied on TV for a living. This problem persisted, Robert Fuest who made his name on TV series *The Avengers*, had to turn to AIP to finance his own British horrors in the shape of *The Abominable Dr Phibes* (1971) and sequel *Dr Phibes Rises Again* (1972) at the turn of the 1970's. Even a recognised UK cinema talent like Charles Crichton, the noted Ealing director, ended up grinding out TV episodes to pay the rent.

So, with no Tourneur to turn to, British horror movie makers had to turn to unknown and untested talent like Quentin Lawrence. He was the man given the chance by Eros to helm *The Trollenberg Terror* (US title *The Crawling Eye*), one of the independent horrors made in 1958.

This was scripted by Jimmy Sangster, the Hammer scriptwriter and later director, and was taken from a BBC TV series written by Peter Key. Like the Hammer adaptations of Nigel Kneale's *Quatermass* series, this compressed a six part half-hour series into less than ninety minutes of screen time, substituting a lot of the more thoughtful elements for biff-bang-pow action.

Despite this, and the presence of Forrest Tucker as the lead, the film is actually quite good. Okay, so Tucker – more at home in Westerns – would not know how to act subtle if it hit him over the head; but he had made several genre movies in Britain by now, having appeared the previous year in Hammer's *The Abominable Snowman* (1957, US title *The Abominable Snowman Of The Himalayas*), and the ultra-low budget *Planet X*, a no-hope sci-fi picture. By this time, he knew enough to just keep his head down and be the token concession to getting US play dates. Janet Munro and Warren Mitchell provided sterling support, with Laurence Payne and Jennifer Jayne as romantic interest and co-leads.

The plot is a little less complicated than Kneale's affairs, revolving around alien landings in Switzerland. The alien monsters are little seen, and Laurence and Sangster fashion a creepy little mystery out of the sci-fi bones. It suffers in comparison to the *Quatermass* pictures, but in its own right it is well worth a look.

The rest of the year seemed to belong to Richard Gordon, having a burst of activity, and his association with Producers Associates, a short-lived company who were, like Eros, shortly to go down the tubes.

Three pictures came out of this deal, two starred Boris Karloff, one not being released until a few years after its completion, the other was an attempt to both cash-in on the US sci-fi boom and also take some of that old *Quatermass* magic.

First Man Into Space (1958) went directly to the States, and had only a very limited release in Britain. It is only in the last year or two that it has been made available in Britain on video, and British audiences at last got a chance to see it. Like all the Gordon movies from this period, the named producer was his colleague John Croydon, and the directorial duties were helmed (as on the year's other two movies) by American Robert Day, who shortly afterwards vanished into the limbo of American TV.

Written originally by Wyatt C Ordung, an American low-budget auteur of crazed sci-fi movies, the original script was passed on by Alex Gordon at AIP, who sent it to brother Richard hoping that he could do something with it. Commissioning a complete re-write by John C Cooper and Lance Z Hargreaves, Gordon followed the *Fiend Without A Face* example by having the film set in the US, but filmed in England

The Trollenberg Terror

with an English supporting cast and crew for an American lead. And that lead was none other than Marshall Thompson, who turned in his usual reliable performance.

The first man into space runs into a cloud of meteor dust, which has a strange effect on him. He returns to earth seemingly normal, but before long starts to exhibit an unusual interest in blood. Before long, he is a vampire, killing to appease his desires.

The re-written film is tightly paced and scripted, with atmospheric shocks at regular intervals combined with convincing playing. A fine example of low-budget movie-making, it is just a shame that it took so long before it was seen in its country of origin. That, in itself, caused a few problems. The nominal setting of the film is

First Man Into Space

Albuquerque, New Mexico, and US distributors MGM decided to première the movie in that particular town. It must have seemed a good publicity angle – but someone should have checked and a triumphant première was turned into farce as local residents laughed it off screen... despite the accents of the cast, the film was actually shot in Boreham Wood, Hertfordshire.

The two Boris Karloff vehicles were on much more familiar ground, being set in nineteenth century London (enabling the same sets to be used to good effect). The first of the pair was titled *Grip Of The Strangler* (1958, US title *The Haunted Strangler*). Again, Robert Day was at the helm, with music from Buxton Orr, fast becoming a Gordon regular.

The plot concerns Karloff as an ageing novelist who begins to research an old murder case for his new book. Twenty years before, a killer known as the Haymarket Strangler stalked that the Haymarket part of London, preying on young girls whom he would strangle in a most unusual manner. It was obvious that only one of his hands was fully functional. Karloff, still a young man at this time, follows the case and has his own ideas about the killer, ideas that he intends to share in his forthcoming book.

His daughter, played by Elizabeth Allan, rarely sees him while he is working, and worries about strain brought on by overwork. She then worries that he will be a target for the killer, who has suddenly returned to action after a twenty year hiatus. As the plot develops, it is revealed that Boris was overworking to a great degree at the time of the initial killings, and suffered periodic black-outs...

It is no great surprise when Boris is revealed to be the strangler, this personality overtaking him during his black-outs. The horror lies not in this sudden revelation or in the killings, but rather in the manner in which a man can be so overtaken by another personality that he does not even realise what he is doing – even to the point where he starts to strangle his own daughter before being stopped by Anthony Dawson, a young writer and friend of Karloff's who is enamoured of the girl.

A small scale horror movie that works because of the way the viewer becomes involved with the characters, Day's direction is strong, and the playing from all concerned is sure. Karloff had nursed a desire to make the film for some time, the screenplay having been submitted directly to him by writer Jan Read some years before. In fact, Gordon had been given the script by Karloff when he was expressing

Grip Of The Strangler

his desire to get into movies, and it was the culmination of a long time ambition when the film was finally completed.

The second Karloff/Gordon movie of the year did not really see its first release until 1962, and was actually trumpeted on the video copy I bought some years ago as "the horror film of 1964"!

Corridors Of Blood (1958), originally titled *Doctor From Seven Dials*, is an uneasy movie to watch, never quite sure if it wants to be a horror movie or a straight historical drama. This is possibly because the subject matter – that of the discovery of anaesthetics – precludes a straight treatment.

Karloff plays Dr Bolton, a doctor who is appalled by the way that patients are strapped down to tables and operated on while still fully conscious. After witnessing an amputation in such a manner, where the patient dies of shock, he decides that there must be an answer, and that he must do anything to find that answer. The only way is to experiment, and to do that he needs corpses...

At this point in the film, the viewer could be forgiven for dreading yet another Burke and Hare rip-off, but no, this is a film of a more serious nature. In search of bodies, Bolton knows that he must search out "resurrectionists", men who will dig up freshly buried bodies for doctors to dissect. In a low tavern, he meets Black Ben and Resurrection Joe – the latter is a top-hatted, silent man played with brooding menace by Christopher Lee. Only just graduated to horror stardom via his roles as Dracula and the Frankenstein monster, Lee has little to do in this film, but his immense presence lends weight nonetheless.

The two grave-robbers supply Bolton with a steady stream of cadavers, and his work progresses well. But they are aware that they are breaking the law, and seek some kind of protection and insurance. This they decide to do by blackmailing Bolton over a fake death certificate that they get him to sign after plying him with drink. The man they have brought to him has been murdered, and if Bolton does not co-operate with them then he will share their gallows.

Unable to live with himself, this kindly man of medicine confronts them in

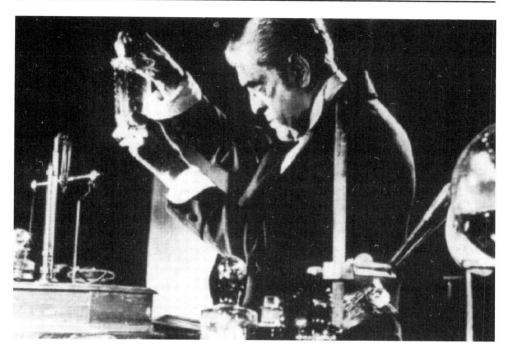

Corridors Of Blood

their tavern haunt. He is stabbed, and lies dying when the tavern is raided. The film ends with Bolton's assistant, played by Francis Matthews, promising to carry on his work. A short epilogue makes the history of anaesthesia clearer.

Again, the horror of the film does not lie in the overt gore of either the operations or the body snatching, although the cold heartlessness of such matters are brought home convincingly. Rather, the horror lies in the interplay of the charters; in the callous disregard of doctors for their patients, as personified by the self-satisfied Frank Pettingell; in the way that the powerless Bolton agonizes when faced with the choice between dying patients and the rape of graves; and in the way that the "resurrectionists" are forced by their lowly circumstances to rob graves and kill for money, but soon become hardened and de-sensitised by their surroundings.

As with *Grip Of The Strangler*, the horror lies in the people and the consequences of their actions rather than in outside agencies such as demons or aliens. The fear is internalised rather than externalised. This is rare in horror of any kind, and particularly in the case of Gordon, whose tastes usually run to pulp horror thrills.

Jean Scott Rogers wrote the thoughtful and intelligent script, and supporting actors Finlay Currie and Adrienne Corri contributed to the good ensemble playing. Quite why it remained unreleased for so long is a little mysterious, possibly it was too close in period and cast to *Grip Of The Strangler*, which was already assured US play dates paired with *Fiend Without A Face*. It did not deserve to languish on the shelf for so long.

The same year – 1958 – saw the entry into the horror field of a production team that was never quite at home with out-and-out horror, preferring melodrama with a tinge of the horrific. This makes their films sometimes quite painful to watch, but when they work they are worth at least a look. That team was Monty Berman and Robert S Baker.

Baker was born in 1916 and founded Tempean Films in 1948 with Berman, having worked in the business as a cameraman and director. In fact, he directed quite a few of their features, including the 1959 horror *Jack The Ripper*, although he was more at home on the likes of *The Siege Of Sidney Street* (1960) about the well known anarchist seige in the East End in 1911, it featured a wonderful performance from Peter Wyngarde as anarchist Peter The Painter, and *The Hellfire Club* (1960). This latter spotlights the problems of trying to figure out a Baker-Berman movie. A film about the witchcraft-practising, hard-drinking, whoring group of noblemen who threatened to undermine British political life should have given ripe opportunities for horror. But no – instead, it peters out into a stodgy historical melodrama. The same is also true of *Dr Crippen* (1960), with Donald Pleasence marvellously twitchy as the wife murderer and those expecting a horror feast were left with a long-winded film and a trial sequence that seems to go on forever.

Monty Berman, Baker's partner, was born in 1913, and had previously worked as a cinematographer before starting up Tempean. The two men worked so closely on their productions that it is hard to know whose taste influenced the overt horror of *Blood Of The Vampire* (1958) or *Jack The Ripper*, but one thing is for sure, both men found their niche much more readily in television.

The 1960's was a boom-time for Baker and Berman. They produced the long-running and successful television series *The Saint*, based on Leslie Charteris' pulp hero, and starring Roger Moore. They also produced series of *Gideon's Way* and *The Baron* (both based on John Creasey characters), and developed Dennis Spooner's series *The Champions* and *Randall And Hopkirk (Deceased)*. Most of these were for ITC, the company run by Sir Lew Grade, a man who knew when to let talent run with the ball.

Given the obvious crime/thriller tendencies of the duo, it is hardly surprising that their mannered and melodramatic horrors border on the absurd. However, the four overtly horrific movies they produced are still worth a second look.

Two of these were released in 1958, *Blood Of The Vampire* and *The Flesh And The Fiends* (US title *Mania*).

Blood Of The Vampire features Sir Donald Wolfit, the noted classical actor and last of the great actor-managers to tread the boards. Always regarded as a ham by most critics, his knighthood probably came for persistence in roles to which he was blatantly unsuited. This particular viewer harbours a nasty suspicion that the loopy Shakespearean ham who fakes his own death and returns to murder his critics in *Theatre Of Blood* (1973) – a marvellous camp performance from Vincent Price – was based on Wolfit, who had not been dead long enough to be forgotten when the movie was made.

A sort of respectable Tod Slaughter – as may be recalled from the chapter on Slaughter – Wolfit here shows that he simply is nt up to the job in grand guignol, although he does turn in an eye-rolling performance.

Jimmy Sangster, enjoying a good year away from Hammer product, wrote the script, and this sceptical viewer wonders how many times he went to see Tod Slaughter vehicles when he was a young man, as the plot is a combination of Hammer horror and Slaughter bravado.

Wolfit is a mysterious doctor, working in a castle. Young girls have been disappearing from a nearby village, and are found dead, drained of their blood. Is he a vampire? When Barbara Shelley goes missing, her boyfriend intends to find out. Here is where the film has its first problem, the boyfriend is played by Vincent Ball.

Ball was an Australian character actor who came to Britain after the war in order to pick up work, much like Bill Kerr. While Kerr found his natural home in comedy, Ball was left stranded in a welter of bit parts and character roles in anything from a war movie to a *Carry On* comedy. As the latter showed – in *Carry On Cruising* (1960) – Ball was a very good light comedy lead, and could also tackle suspense. He had a spell in TV soap that also showed him to best advantage. But horror?

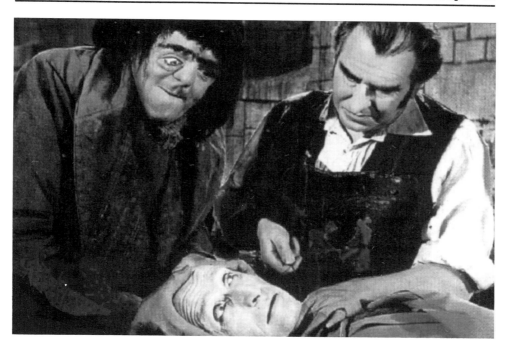

Blood Of The Vampire

No. The athletic and graceful Ball excels at running around the cardboard scenery looking dashing, but when called upon to deliver his lines is a little out of his depth. Heavy melodrama is not his forte, and without a strong male lead to pitch against the onus is on Wolfit to deliver.

As he stalks the cardboard castle, dressed in a stained leather apron, the viewer almost expects Wolfit to cackle wildly at incongruous moments (Tod would have). Instead, despite moments of pure evil when he is with Shelley, he seems a little depressed, as though bemoaning the comedown from his classical fate to this piece of tat.

It need not have been that way, as Sangster's script is a good compendium of grand guignol moments, if a little loose on plot; the cardboard sets and lurid Eastmancolor (everything looks like it has been dipped in bright, primary colours) are ripe for terrifying overacting; and some of the support acting is strong. Particularly of note is Victor Maddern, who plays the obligatory hunchback with a deformed face... remember, these were the days pre-political correctness, and everyone who was a "freak" was of necessity evil.

In this case, Maddern certainly is. With dreadful make-up that push out his face and plants a palpably fake eyeball half-way down one of his cheeks, he opts for the only course open to him. None of the "poor little hunchback who is at the mercy of the wicked doctor" routine, Maddern plays the doctor's assistant as a mute and malevolent elf, unhinged and on the verge of violence. Despite the laughable make-up (not forgetting the fake hump, which looks so uncomfortable that it gives the viewer back-ache half-way through the picture), Maddern has an intensity that is truly frightening. A little more of this, and it would not be such a rag-bag of a picture.

Even the title is a little misleading; Wolfit is not a vampire as such, but rather a mad doctor experimenting with blood, draining his victims into a series of glass jars and interesting looking vacuum pumps. A victim of one of his own experiments, he has a craving for blood, and the young girls partly satisfy this, and partly act as fodder for his experiments to find a cure. It is only at this point that Wolfit really shines, his eyes gleaming as the blood flows. Nonetheless, with a title like *Blood Of The Vampire*, the least you can expect is a real live (or undead) supernatural child of the night...

The last few minutes redeem the picture, as the flaccid pacing by director Henry Cass picks up immeasurably. Wolfit unleashes his hounds, and Ball has to use all his athletic skill to evade them, eventually trapping Wolfit outside with the hungry beasts, for an off screen gory fate.

In many ways, this is a perfect example of what was wrong with British horror movies in the post Hammer world. It had restraint, but also a desire to show blood in glorious colour. The attempts to compromise the two positions just lead to an occasional rush of blood in the midst of the coyness, and the colour does nothing more than show up the stagey sets (not helped by Cass' direction). The best British horrors post 1957 (the year of Hammer's *Curse Of Frankenstein*) were able to keep those M R James elements of restraint, and still let the blood flow. It was a delicate balance.

Baker and Berman never really got it right. Switching their co-production from Artists Alliance (for *Blood Of The Vampire*) to Mid-Century, they produced *Jack The Ripper* in the same year.

With a Sangster script, and the team of Baker and Berman themselves handling the direction and photography, reverting (for the most part) to black and white, the film had a lot of genuinely creepy atmosphere, and an interesting take on the ripper myth.

As the Ripper murders terrorise the whole of East London, there is a palpable tension in the air, with the staff of the Mercy Hospital For Women coming under suspicion. Why? Simply because the locals do not like Dr Trenton, a strong and silent type who seems to always be missing when the murders take place. When he is around, he stalks the streets and the corridors of the hospital dressed in a long black cape – as though he has just come in from out of the night.

A section of the local populace (presumably those who do not realise that all doctors have maniacal Ripper-like tendencies) place their bets on the mute, deformed hunchback who is the hospital porter, and has a liking for playing around with the sharp and nasty surgical instruments. I hate to sound like a political correctness freak, but what was this thing that Baker and Berman had with mute, deformed hunchbacks? Or was it Jimmy Sangster's favourite red herring device? Because that is two such characters in two succeeding films...

Placing such considerations aside, the sinister Dr Trenter has a ward, Ann, who looks a likely candidate for the knife until she befriends a young prostitute called Kitty. Now the story begins to fall into place, as the real Ripper is revealed, and Sir David, the head of the hospital is revealed as the real ripper. As with the later *A Study In Terror* (1965), this is a tale of revenge against prostitutes. In this case, Sir David's son fell in love with Kitty, and killed himself when he found out that she was a prostitute.

Tighter than *Blood Of The Vampire*, *Jack The Ripper* is a fairly fast-moving film, with some genuine scares in the London fog, and the murders are discreet throat cuttings with the mutilation occurring off-screen. This is where the British approach works, as most people are aware of the ripper mutilations through folklore and history, and so the imagination can be far worse than anything Baker and Berman could squeeze past the censor.

In the final analysis, this film is spoilt by only one thing, the gimmick ending. Ann is trying to protect herself against the mad Sir David, and after a taut scene the Ripper ends up trapped beneath the floor of an elevator, which is going down. And so the Ripper meets his grisly end, blood seeping up through the floorboards.

This would have been a good end, if not for the fact that the producers decided to go for an audience-grabbing gimmick, the elevator scene is in colour, to

Jack The Ripper

show the blood in glorious Eastmancolor. This is a similar idea to that used by William Castle in *The Tingler* (1963), where a woman sees a bloodied arm rise from a bath of blood – the only colour segment in a black and white movie.

In *The Tingler*, this works fine, but in *Jack The Ripper*, it totally ruins the atmosphere and tension built up over the rest of the ninety minutes running time. However, it did get the Baker and Berman team a US release via Joseph E Levine, who had just made a killing with the Italian *Hercules* (1957) and *Hercules Unchained* (1959) etc, movies. Unfortunately for Levine, the blood scene at the end had US censors babbling wildly from state to state, with the censor in Memphis wildly declaiming that the film showed heads and hands amputated on screen!

Back in England, encouraged by the success of *Jack The Ripper*, Baker and Berman turned to another fine old English folk-legend for their inspiration; that of Burke and Hare.

The *Flesh And The Fiends* (1959) aka *Mania* aka *The Fiendish Ghouls* aka *Psycho Killers*, is a remake of the Tod Slaughter vehicle *The Greed Of William Hart*. This

The Flesh And The Fiends

time, writer of the original, John Gilling gets to direct, with his script amended by Leon Griffiths. At least, that is what the credits say. Having seen both movies more than once, I would be loathe to point out where the changes come. This is, more or less, a straight re-make without the ridiculous dubbing of names that marred the earlier picture, and with a slightly larger budget.

A better cast too, although that is no disrespect to Tod Slaughter. His role is taken over by the sinister Donald Pleasance, here affecting an accent and a wide-eyed innocent attitude that has sly and cunning undertones. George Rose, as his colleague, is a complete idiot. The viewer just knows that this man will meet his end before the end of the picture. Doctor Knox, the hard-nosed doctor to whom Burke and Hare peddle their wares, is played with suitably aristocratic disdain by Peter Cushing. Knox despises the men who peddle dead bodies, but uses them from sheer necessity for his classes and experiments.

One of his students, played by Dermot Walsh, has a conscience about these things. He also has a girlfriend, Billie Whitelaw, a barmaid at the local tavern. Because of the difference in their social positions, he has to keep her secret; but she has little liking for his studies, knowing all too well what Burke and Hare are up to as she serves them every night.

Burke is discontented with the pay they receive from Knox, who is getting sparing with the silver and moaning over the state of the corpses. So perhaps it is time for Burke and Hare to go into the business of making corpses, and their first victim is Daft Jake, played with blank-eyed innocence by Melvyn Hayes. They kill him and sell the fresh corpse to Knox, who is none too fussy about its origins.

Billie Whitelaw's barmaid seems to show more sense and intelligence that anyone else in the picture, and when Jake goes missing, she has little doubt that she knows where he has gone, and wastes little time in telling Walsh. Faced with his imperious tutor, the quivering student is powerless, and his girlfriend loses all patience with him.

Little does she know that Burke has her lined up for his next victim... When this happens, and Walsh finds her body in the Doctor's cellar, the dénouement is only just around the corner. Knox is arrested, and Burke and Hare are chased through the streets by an irate public, baying vengeance for Daft Jake and the barmaid.

Despite the more obvious violence and gore (not as effective in black and white as Hammer's colour), the true horror of this movie once again lies in the people; in the apathy of Walsh, the willingness of Burke and Hare to do anything for a silver coin, and especially in the arrogance of Doctor Knox. A supposed man of medicine – who should, in theory, care for people – he is quite content to be party to murder so long as he gets a fresh corpse for his experiments. Knox looks on the people of Edinburgh not as human beings but as laboratory animals. It is this attitude that is the most frightening aspect of the film, and is brought out thanks to the same cold aloofness that Cushing gave his Baron Frankenstein.

The cast all turn in good performances (not mentioned yet is a wonderful support from Renée Houston as a lush of a tavern landlady) but the direction is a trifle unsteady, with patches where nothing much seems to happen separating those scenes which are charged with emotion. Was this Gilling, or was it interference from the producers? A point worth pondering, as Gilling – while no genius – is a competent director of fast-moving action, and the pacing problem is something that all Baker-Berman movies suffer. This co-production with Regal/Triad was the last straightforward horror film that Baker and Berman put their name to. The next year's *Dr Crippen* (1962) is a mish-mash of courtroom and melodrama, with the horror elements down played out of existence (despite Donald Pleasence as Crippen). From then on it was straight melodrama and thrillers, graduating into TV, the medium in which their ideas were most at home.

The Giant Behemoth

There was one last Baker-Berman movie that used horror, *What A Carve-Up!* (1962), the horror comedy mentioned in detail in the chapter on this small sub-genre.

But that was two years away, and the beginning of another decade. To end the 1950's, Anglo-Amalgamated gave Michael Powell the money to make *Peeping Tom* (1959), the most controversial film of his career, and one in which the horrors of the human mind were explored to the utmost. And Herman Cohen came from America to make the first of his occasional forays into British horror with *Horrors Of The Black Museum* (1959), a suspense-filled pulp horror that gave Michael Gough one of his juiciest roles in a grand guignol career that is filed with such tempting morsels. Both of these films will be discussed fully in chapters relating to the producers.

That leaves just one film from 1959 up for discussion. Is it a case of leaving the best for last? Maybe not, but it was certainly the biggest...

Artists Alliance were proud to bring to you, *The Giant Behemoth* (1959), aka *Behemoth The Sea Monster*, written and directed by Eugene Lourie, assisted on the helm by Douglas Hickox. The alternative title kind of gives the game away. A radioactive palaeosaurus is awoken in the depths of the sea, and heads for London where it causes mayhem. That, literally, is the plot.

Lourie liked monsters like this, as his *Gorgo* (1960) was so similar (giant sea monster ravages London) as to be almost a re-make! Gene Evans is the nominal lead, but he is almost as plastic as the terrible model. André Morrell and Jack MacGowran, actors of a far better hue (Morrell was TV's Quatermass, and later made some excellent Hammer appearances, while MacGowran was brilliant in Samuel Beckett's TV exposition of a tortured mind *Eh, Joe*?), try to make what they can of the material, but it is a hopeless task.

Not even fun in a mindless way, *The Giant Behemoth* is bad in every way that a film can be bad; no imagination, no budget, no talent in the writing or direction. *King Kong* (1933) is still the ultimate big monster movie, and Toho's *Godzilla* (1955 onwards) movies (which this was presumably intended to emulate) were better made and had more sense of fun and imagination.

Not the best way to end a chapter on the 1950's, this was the worst horror of the period bar none – at least *Fire Maidens From Outer Space* was funny! However, from this low point things can only get better.

The turn of the new decade saw the birth of Amicus as a horror company, and the boom in independent production continued via Planet and Gala amongst others. There were also great features from Anglo and Independent Artists. So let us forget about crap like *The Giant Behemoth* and get on to the good stuff.

7.   Hammer: The House Of Horror

Dreadful cliché, that title. But the fact remains that Hammer not only gave British horror a brand name with which it could be identified around the world, they also changed the face of that horror. Under the sound business sense and exploitation sensibilities of Sir James Carreras (knighted for services to the British export industry), Hammer grew from a tiny cottage industry to an expansive and profitable company.

Here was one of the dichotomies about Hammer, for while they stayed a family concern, both in the sense of proprietors (the Carreras and Hinds family held sway throughout most of their successes) and staff (the same faces and names working on each project in front of and behind the camera), they also became the most successful British film company of their period. Of course, the established critics ignored them, in Alexander Walker's numerous books about the resurgence of British film in the 1960's, and then its 1970's decline, there was no mention of Hammer; again, in George Perry's *The Great British Picture Show*, the best history of British film from day one to its publication in the mid-1970's (before the decline of Hammer), the company merits but one or two brief lines. Like a cinematic equivalent to Trotsky, the company that did not toe accepted lines was expunged from the record.

This is because horror has always been looked upon by serious critics as a sick joke. Perhaps it is, but what is wrong with that? If not, then it really is a way of facing primal fears in a symbolic form, in which case the critics find it too scary to handle... actually, I think that the truth about horror movies lies between the two, and that is what serious film critics cannot get their heads around. They do not know whether or not to take the film seriously or just enjoy the ride. By unconsciously straddling both viewpoints and just doing what pulled in the punters, Hammer confused critics – and a confused critic only knows how to lash out.

Dichotomy number two, Hammer brought more sex and blood into the British horror film. Yes, this is undeniably true. However, something struck me as I sat through endless video re-runs to pick up points I may have missed. The sex is there, but it is still terribly prim and English. This is not really due to the censor, an expanse of female flesh in the UK may have been increased to a fuller nude for re-shot continental prints, but the attitude underlying it remained unchanged from previous standards, where the sexual awakenings in women were usually followed by them coming to a sticky end, either at the hands of a mad killer or as a result of meeting a monster. In the case of *The Gorgon* (1964) or *The Reptile* (1966), sexual awakening and the onset of adolescence actually creates a monster... this is not so far from the "if you screw you'll get killed" message of early slasher movies like *Halloween* (1978), where I still feel uncomfortable that the only virgin in the bunch escapes the killer's knife.

The more sex Hammer brought into their movies, the more bloodily the sexually awakened woman met her end, culminating with the decapitation of vampire Ingrid Pitt in *The Vampire Lovers* (1970). A strange mix of exploitation and morality, this sub-text will probably be self-evident as we whiz through the glory days of Hammer.

Dichotomy number three: Hammer was the face and name of British horror. It still is, in many senses, even non-horror fans have heard of Hammer, whereas they may not have heard of Amicus unless pushed, let alone Tyburn, or Peter Walker, or Eros (and until recently very few people had heard of Richard Gordon, whose pulp sensibilities make him something of a hero to me, recidivist that I am...). Yet despite their reputation, Hammer and Exclusive (one of their early names) made their early reputation on a varied roster of B and programmer movies, with everything from fantasy to comedy, taking in war and a decent stab at British film noire. You want names? Okay, they adapted radio serials like *Dick Barton, Special Agent* (1948) and *Life With The Lyons* (1954) in the immediate post-war period. *The Quatermass X-periment*, the film that changed their destiny, was nothing more than another TV adaption to begin with. And while they developed horror, they also made war movies like *The Camp On Blood Island* (1958) and thrillers like *Hell Is A City* (1959) a film that has hard edges marking it as close to film noir as British film-makers ever achieved.

In the 1960's, there were fantasies like *She* (1965) and the abominable cave-girl movies *One Million Years BC* (1966) – great box office for Raquel Welch and her fur bikini but boring to watch, *Slave Girls* (1968, US title *Prehistoric Women*), made just watchable by Martine Beswick, and *When Dinosaurs Ruled The Earth* (1969), in which Victoria Vetri's career took a nosedive. Historical pictures like *Rasputin The Mad Monk* (1966) got mixed in with the horror, and there was even a crack at straight sci-fi with the space opera *Moon Zero Two* (1962).

And in the 1970's, when all seemed to be falling apart – the reasons for which will be apparent later – the biggest grossing film of 1972 was a Hammer picture. Not a horror, but a return to TV and radio spin-offs, it was a movie version of the popular sit-com *On The Buses*. Oddly enough, it was very close to a *Carry On* movie in humour and style, which draws a fascinating parallel, the *Carry On* films are hardly ever mentioned in "serious" histories of British film, either... yet it was Frankenstein and Sid James who kept punters rolling through the doors of the local Odeon and ABC when prestigious British movies like *The Charge Of The Light Brigade* (1966) and *Accident* (1967) kept them away in droves.

So there you have it, encapsulated as neatly as possible; a company who became the face of British horror yet changed it; who brought sex and blood into movies yet were still prudish; who remained small while becoming big; and who made non-horror movies more successful than their stock-in-trade.

Built on a foundation of such contradictions, it is no wonder that they eventually collapsed. Yet the legend lives on, and Roy Skeggs – who bought the company out of bankruptcy and turned it around – is now beginning to make pictures for the big screen again.

Hammer as a name is bigger than anything or anyone connected with it. Why? Because for a twelve year period, they were the most consistent and the most productive of British horror producers. There are other single movies that stand out above those of Hammer, but no other company can match their consistency.

There have been numerous books, the best being *House Of Horror* by Jack Hunter, and magazines about Hammer over the years, so a mammoth survey would be ridiculous and a waste of space which could be devoted to other, lesser-known pictures. Therefore, this run-down may seem a little brief compared to some other chapters.

But hey – you can always catch at least one Hammer per night on cable and satellite, or down the local video hire shop, right?

Hammer is the story of the Carreras and Hinds families. Enrique Carreras was a Spanish immigrant who settled in the UK and ran a small chain of theatres and cinemas. William Hinds was a businessman, occasional semi-pro comic and music hall performer who wanted to be in the entertainment game once more. The two men therefore set up a film distributor called Exclusive in the 1930's, and made a small string of movies using Hinds' stage name – Hammer – before the war curtailed activities. One of these was *Song Of Freedom* (1936), which starred the phenomenal singer and civil rights campaigner Paul Robeson as a black London docker who becomes a professional singer and travels to Africa in search of his roots. An unusual film to make, it hinted that here could be a company which may produce interesting movies.

The year before, Hammer had brought Bela Lugosi to England to make *The Mystery Of The Marie Celeste* (1935, US title *Phantom Ship*). Just as Boris Karloff enlivened a few British horrors of this period, so Lugosi was used as a name to bring in the audiences and ensure a US sale.

It is tempting to report that this is a lost gem, pointing the way for Hammer. That, however, is not the case. Written and directed by Dennison Clift, it does have a few creepy moments. These are outweighed by stretches where nothing much happens at all in the story of what really (allegedly) occurred on the Marie Celeste. The ghost ship was populated by a fairly rancid crew, one of whom is the venerable Lugosi. So when one of the crew goes mad and starts to kill the others one by one, it does not take long to guess who is behind it all.

Bela Lugosi shamelessly overacts, as usual. Clift's script is full of holes and dull patches that his direction cannot quite gloss over, and the rest of the cast are perfunctory. Yet there is something that keeps you watching. Perhaps it is just the fact that it is the first Hammer horror, and it stars Lugosi. The patina of nostalgia and hindsight enabling the viewer to ignore gross defects, perhaps? Whatever, it can be viewed fondly – and the scene where the last two men on board face each other is genuinely gripping.

After the war, Exclusive returned to the business of making programmers alongside their distribution activities. The Hammer name fell into abeyance, but Exclusive had all the staff in place, and Enrique's son James took over the running of the company, and his son Michael joined to learn the ropes. William Hinds' son Tony joined as producer. A studious, quiet man, Tony Hinds later turned out to be the creative force behind Hammer. If James Carreras was the business head, then Tony Hinds was the man who shaped the Hammer Gothic image by turning away from producing towards his first love, writing. Michael Carreras left Hammer for a while in the 1960's, making a musical *What A Crazy World* (1963) with Joe Brown) before returning. It was after Tony Hinds left, and Michael took over from his father, that the company lost direction. No surprise to learn that Michael – though a gifted film-maker

The Mystery Of The Marie Celeste

– was no fan of Gothic.

Alongside the family members were director Terence Fisher and production assistant Jimmy Sangster. Fisher was a programmer director of average talent. By all accounts a thoroughly nice man, he was able to get the best out of his actors simply be being there, although his skills on pacing were always ropey. Sangster was an ideas man who was told one day to write a script... and he was so good at it that he ended up becoming the best known British horror movie writer of them all.

So everything was in place, waiting for an event. That was not to happen until 1955. In the meantime, three films with a horrific flavour were made...

Room To Let (1949) was produced by Tony Hinds, and was an adaption of a BBC radio play by Margery Allingham, the thriller writer and creator of Albert Campion. A Jack The Ripper story, it was directed in a creaky fashion by Godfrey Grayson from a script he wrote with John Gilling. It starred the sinister-voiced Valentine Dyall as Dr Fell, with juvenile lead Jimmy Hanley, fresh from his role as policeman Andy Crawford in the smash-hit *The Blue Lamp* (1949) – the movie in which PC George Dixon of *Dixon Of Dock Green* TV fame made his first appearance, and got shot by a twitchy Dirk Bogarde), playing the part of Curly, a journalist.

Fell arrives at the house of Mrs Musgrave the same night a local asylum catches fire. There are rumours that an inmate has escaped, although the management refute this. However, Fell soon dominates the house, refusing to let the curtains be opened during the day, and showing a distinct interest in his landlady's niece Molly. It is up to family friend Curly to reveal Fell as the escapee and murderer Jack...

Brief at fifty-four minutes, it still seems to drag, and betrays its radio roots by being too talky. However, it does have a nice Victorian Gothic atmosphere, and Dyall is wonderful. Art director, by the way, was a certain Jimmy Sangster, who may have been taking notes for the Baker-Berman *Jack The Ripper* movie he wrote ten years later...

In 1952, Terence Fisher helmed two minor B-movies that had a vaguely psychotic edge. *Four Sided Triangle* was a sci-fi movie written by Fisher and Paul Tabori, adapted from a novel by William F Temple. Tabori was an Hungarian who had worked with fellow emigré Alexander Korda. He had a genuine interest in the paranormal, and wrote a fascinating biography of ghost-hunter Harry Price during this period. This film is carried by the script and performances, as Fisher directs at a lazy pace, and with a minimal budget.

John Van Eyssen and Stephen Murray are two chums who happen to be working on a matter replicator in their barn during a vacation from an Oxbridge college. Avuncular scientist James Hayter is keeping an eye on them. The problem comes in the shape of Barbara Peyton, who pals around with both of them, but soon falls in love with Van Eyssen, and marries him.

This is a bit of a problem, as Murray is besotted by her, and grows insane with jealousy – until he decides to reproduce her in the machine he and Van Eyssen have perfected. Of course, the replica falls in love with Van Eyssen, and Murray really goes over the edge. In a performance that stays just (but only just) on the right side of ham, Murray tries to kill his friends and eventually sets fire to the barn, killing himself and destroying the machine.

An interesting rather than gripping movie, it showed that there were some fascinating ideas kicking around Exclusive, who were now beginning to use the Hammer name for production again, keeping Exclusive for distribution. Eventually, both this side of the business and the name would fall away.

Stolen Face (1952) is a psycho-drama that hints at better things. Produced in association with Robert Lippert, it features Hollywood players Paul Henreid and Lizabeth Scott in the leads. Lippert was instrumental in getting US players into early Hammer films, which helped him to sell them in the US. It was an invaluable link, as his son went on to work for giant US studios who pumped money into later Hammer horrors.

Henreid is a plastic surgeon in love with Lizabeth Scott, a pianist he meets by chance in a Scottish inn. After a week together, during which he declares his love, she has to go off on tour, where she is jealously guarded by her fiancé and manager André Morell. Henreid becomes resigned to never seeing her again...

To say he is heartbroken would be an understatement. He is almost unhinged by grief, which worries his staff. Now comes the plot twist that lifts this out of melodrama and into something a little stranger. As the world's greatest plastic surgeon, he does "charity" work on the side. In this capacity he goes to Holloway prison where he meets a prisoner whose face was disfigured and scarred by a bomb blast when she was a child. Both he and the Governor are convinced that her life of crime is due to her bitterness... ah, the "all cripples are bitter" line favoured by movie makers.

Henreid agrees to re-build her face, and she is suitably grateful, promising to go straight, etc. Except that he has a hidden agenda, and he rebuilds her face as a replica of his lost love, then marries her.

Of course, this is still mostly melodrama, and she is soon milking him dry, having her fellow crooks in for wild parties, and shop-lifting in between picking up men. When Lizabeth Scott as pianist returns (she handles the dual role extremely well, by the way), she is mistaken for her double, and things are a little confusing. However, Henreid eventually plans to run away with his first love, and they are on a train when his drunken wife confronts them. There is a struggle, and she dies plunging from a train, leaving them free to marry.

This is a strange film to watch, uncertain of whether to be psychodrama or melodrama, it veers uneasily between the two. Fisher gets an excellent performance from Scott, and Henreid is suitably tortured as the surgeon. However, the script by Martin Berkeley and Richard H Landau is stodgy, and the cast have to work hard on some of the dialogue. Not a film to treasure, but it does have a few spine-tingling moments – such as the scene where Scott takes off her bandages – that marks Fisher down as having more talent than might have previously been suspected.

Nigel Kneale was a staff BBC writer, and as such had worked on anything from plays to childrens puppet shows. Unlike today, where writers are hired for a specific project, a contract writer in the early days of TV had to tackle almost anything that was flung at him. But he still had time to pitch his own projects.

Kneale had a project; a story about the British Rocket Group, and their head scientist, Professor Bernard Quatermass. When a rocket sent into space returns with only one of the three crew left, and when this man starts to mutate into something less than human, Quatermass has to step in and avert disaster.

The Quatermass X-periment was a landmark TV series, mixing science and horror with philosophy. Astronaut Victor Carroon, infected with a space virus, has absorbed the remains of the other two crew members and is mutating into a walking mass of vegetation which eventually takes refuge in Westminster Abbey before being destroyed.

Tony Hinds thrust a pile of scripts at writer/director Val Guest when the latter was just about to fly off on holiday with an instruction to read them and turn them into a film.

Guest took the bones of the story, and gave the ending more dynamism. In Kneale's original, Quatermass reasoned with the creature, appealing to the remnants of its humanity to let its life slip away. His impassioned reasoning worked, and the creature simply died.

On film this would not work, so Guest has Quatermass electrocute the monster in a shower of sparks and fire. Bang (literally) goes the philosophy, but boy did it pull

The Quatermass X-periment

in the punters. Kneale was not happy with this, and neither was he happy with American hard-man Brian Donleavy as Quatermass. Not surprising, Donleavy was used to playing two-fisted heroes and villains, and found a thinking man hard to portray. His B-movie stardom ensured US bookings (under the title *The Creeping Unknown*), but harmed the movie. Permanently drunk, he would lace his black coffee when no-one was looking. His Quatermass is hard and unreasoning.

Jack Warner buoys this up as Inspector Lomax, the Scotland Yard man who must help Quatermass track Carroon. As always, Warner has a humanity about his performance that contrasts nicely with Donleavy. The real stars of the movie, however, are Richard Wordsworth and Leslie Bowie. Wordsworth is Carroon, and portrays anguish and terror without a single line of dialogue and while changing into a plant. Especially effective is a scene where he is hiding out, and is discovered by a little girl. In an echo of an earlier Frankenstein (and Carroon is, by circumstance, a man-made monster of Quatermass' making), he manages to dredge up part of his humanity and chase the girl away before he can drain her of all her life energy and fluid – the way the creature feeds.

Leslie Bowie is the special effects man, who achieves great results on Wordsworth, and also manages to construct a half-way decent monster with literally no more than a bucket of tripe.

Guest keeps things moving, to gloss over holes where Kneale's story was compressed (Richard Landau assisted on the script, and they did a good job of compression), using hand-held cameras and a vérité style to disguise the lack of budget, and a taut score by James Bernard – soon a Hammer stalwart – helped make the film even scarier. Art direction was by one J Elder Wills – notable for lending part of his name to Tony Hinds, who began to write scripts as John Elder after this.

Re-titled *The Quatermass X-periment*, with the emphasis on the certificate they hoped to get (and did), the film was a tremendous success, beyond all expectation. It made James Carreras think about the company's direction…

Sci-fi horror was the order of the day for the follow-up movie, *X – The Unknown* (1956). In a meeting for ideas, Jimmy Sangster contributed most, and was given the job of writing the script. He turned out a passable first effort. *X – The Unknown* has none of the tension of *The Quatermass X-periment*, and is carried by the traditional thriller-pacing and style of director Leslie Norman, a toiler in the B-movie and TV fields. Unlike many of his contemporaries, Norman had a good eye and a talent for adding pace where the script was lacking, so any low points of Sangster's first script are glossed over.

American name Dean Jagger plays a nuclear scientist – Dr Adam Royston – who is too busy messing around with a sonic device for detecting and neutralising radiation to bother with his real work at a nuclear power plant. He is assisted by William Lucas, the son of station boss Edward Chapman.

While soldiers are on manoeuvre, radioactive sludge oozes from the ground, killing some of them. It is also an intelligent sludge, and polishes off a young Anthony Newley while he is on patrol.

Because of the nature of the radiation burns, Royston is called in. Government investigator Leo McKern is also on hand, and he acts as the "so you mean to say, Professor…" foil through which the plot is explained.

The sludge careers through a village, kills several boys in the woods, and is a right nuisance. Yet, although the film is taut, it is not really threatening enough, the sludge being too impersonal. In fact, the scariest moment comes when William Lucus is trying to lure the sludge out of the fissure it has created, by driving a Landrover full of atomic material close enough tempt it between the poles of the Professor's sonic device. The wheels get stuck in mud, and it seems as though Lucus will die. By contrast, the moment when the sludge is neutralised is a complete anti-climax.

Again a success at the box office, it was not enough for Carreras. While Hammer made *Quatermass II* (1957), and also filmed Kneale's *The Abominable Snowman* (1957), Carreras was hatching plans to make a more universal horror movie (ha-ha), and in colour.

Quatermass II centres around a deserted village, a bombardment of meteorites, and the way in which people who come into contact with the meteorites are affected. An acidic gas, which leaves a scar, links the humans to an alien intelligence that is manipulating Governments to build complexes – allegedly for artificial foodstuffs – that are actually incubators for the alien creatures to get acclimatised to earths atmosphere.

Quatermass stumbles on this by accident, when his rocket group track the path of these meteorites. Following up, one of his colleagues (a young Bryan Forbes) is taken over by the aliens, and he discovers that the workers at the factory – labourers not infected – are happy as long as they are fed and can buy subsidised beer. Here is a none too subtle allegory on Nazism and the mass herd instinct...

Quatermass eventually teams up with Lomax (this time played by ex-matinée idol John Longden) and reporter Sid James (the "so you mean to say, Professor..." role), after MP Vincent Broadhead (a good, bluff performance from Tom Chatto) is killed by immersion at the food plant – a wonderfully chilling scene as he stumbles, covered in black goo, down the side of a large storage tank.

Lomax and Quatermass are on their own, the Commissioner of Police is taken over by the aliens, and a near-riot at the plant brings things to a head. Quatermass has his staff fire their rocket at the creatures' hidden ship, and he incites a riot which leads to the monsters being unleashed, to writhe and die in an atmosphere they cannot take...

There are wonderful touches; the controlled humans use workers flesh to stuff the pipes carrying destructive oxygen to their master's tanks; John Van Eyssen, giving a guided tour of the plant, makes your flesh creep; and William Franklyn is heroic as the scientist who dies launching the rocket.

The real star is the location, the outdoor shots were filmed at the Shell Oil Refinery in Canvey Island, Essex. Flat country and super-science construction blend in an uneasy landscape. It is also very windy, and Donleavy was forever losing his toupee, demanding retakes... Val Guest wrote the script with Nigel Kneale, and directed in a more conventional manner than the first movie, aided by James Bernard's third excellent score in a row. It whips along at lightning pace, and is less successful only because it is the second Quatermass...

Quatermass And The Pit (1967, US title *Five Millions Years To Earth*), the third of Kneale's trilogy was optioned. However, Kneale wanted to stick out for sole screenplay credit (no doubt tired of his work being changed in intent – viz the ending to the first movies, and an important subtext removed from the second), and it was ten years before the film was finally made.

One Kneale project which did get made was *The Abominable Snowman* (1957), based on the BBC play. Val Guest directed Kneale's script, which was a trifle slow-moving but nonetheless enthralling. A scientist and a trapper are both in the Himalayas, in search of the Yeti. The scientist wants to study the creature, and the trapper wants to kill it and bring it back to civilization, making a pile of money on the back of his discovery. That, in a nutshell, is the plot. The tension of the film lies in the conflict between the two men, and the horror is in the attitude that would wantonly kill a fellow creature for a few pounds or dollars. A supernatural chill is added by Kusang, the Lhama at the monastery where the party are camped, he is in contact telepathically with the creatures, who protect themselves by luring members of the party to their death in a fair imitation of dead men's voices. Interestingly, in the final showdown between the two parties, the scientist tries to protect the Yeti, and after finally seeing one (and passing out), he finds himself returned to the monastery, spared because of his bravery in trying to disarm the trapper.

Wisely, Guest keeps a view of the Yeti to a minimum, as it is a pretty poor monster. Some location shooting by a second unit adds scenic spice, and the real joys are in the performances. Peter Cushing, in his first Hammer horror, is wonderful as Dr Rollason, pottering around his makeshift lab with his pipe and enthusing about the prospects of finding a new species. Forrest Tucker, the token American and never the most subtle of actors, is in his element as Tom Friend, whose hunting attitude belies his name. Belligerent and thoroughly nasty, he is the real monster of the picture, not the gentle Yeti.

Able support comes from Maureen Connell as Rollason's wife, Richard Wattis as the dithering and homesick Peter Fox, and Wolk Morris – not very oriental but suitably inscrutable – as Kusang. A fine picture, but restrained, and not what James Carreras had in mind...

A priest listens to a madman, about to be hanged for murder, tell a story of how, from an early age, he had experimented with building new life, and how he had finally built a man. A man whose brain had been damaged, and who ran amok. A man who had committed the murders for which he was about to be hanged. Ironic, when his own murders had been undetected. More ironic that the man-made man had fallen into an acid bath, and all that work had come to naught...

Sound familiar? It is *The Curse Of Frankenstein* (1957), the landmark British horror. Under James Carreras' eye, son Michael and Tony Hinds fashioned a movie that had more gore than before, and more sex, Baron Frankenstein is having an affair with a maid, while his fiancée swans around in period gowns that show a lot of bosom. Rejecting a script they were shown by Milton Subotsky as being too close to the original, Carreras and Hinds gave Jimmy Sangster the job of refashioning the Frankenstein myth. He took equal parts Universal and Shelley, making an eighteenth century costume drama with blood.

Cushing began his long tenure as the Baron, and bit-part actor Christopher Lee got his break as the monster. Constrained by lawsuits from using the familiar make-up, Hammer make-up man Phil Leakey fashioned a road-crash victim that was probably a more accurate reflection of a real monster, but less of a trademark. Lee made the most of his wordless role with excellent mime. Robert Urquhart was excellent in his only Hammer (he hated horror movies) as Paul, the Baron's tutor and eventual lab assistant, and Hazel Court secured scream queen status as the Baron's fiancée, Elizabeth.

Terence Fisher directed his first true Hammer horror, and made the most of colour, drawing visceral images and excellent performances into a taut script that did not leave him the usual pacing problems. Panned by the critics, it made a fortune, and set the Hammer agenda for the next few years...

Columbia, keen to get a slice of the profits, signed up for co-production, and the inevitable sequel appeared. *The Revenge Of Frankenstein* (1958) saw the Baron mysteriously escape the noose and turn up practising under a pseudonym. The idea of keeping the Baron as the focal figure instead of the monster was tough on Lee, but a wise move as it enabled the company to search for ever more outlandish monster ideas. In this version of the story (only the trappings ever really change), hunch-back dwarf Karl assists the Baron in his work with the proviso that he is given a new body. Victor Stein (the Baron's pseudonym) complies, and the handsome Michael Gwynn is a wow on the local party scene – until brain degeneracy sets in, and he becomes a slavering cannibal, murdering and feeding at will. Before finally being killed, he reveals the Baron's true identity and we are set for another town, another sequel...

Fisher again directed a tight Sangster script (it had to be – the hunchback dwarf is a dead giveaway!), with no room for his slack pacing. Leonard Salzedo contributed the score, but he is not as good as James Bernard (the master of this kind of Gothic). Francis Matthews – as Doctor Hans Kleve – takes over the Urquhart role, and Cushing is wonderful. Oscar Quitak is Karl pre-operation, and Michael Gwynne is the real star, with a bravura performance. Good support from Lionel Jeffries and Eunice Gayson, and the inevitable Michael Ripper. Where would British horror movies be without Ripper lurking in the credits?

Another success, but one with nowhere near the impact of the other Hammer horror for 1958...

The Curse Of Frankenstein

Sangster was given the task of refashioning the Dracula story to Hammer standards. Universal eventually granted permission to film in return for US distribution, a wise move. They had signed up Bram Stoker's estate for a huge fee in order to secure their sole rights to the property during the 1930's. It would not be public domain until fifty years after Stoker's death, in 1962. Carreras did not want to wait.

Sangster returned more to the book, and fashioned a taut, blood-riddled thriller that kept the suggestion of supernatural powers but confined the Count to on-screen bloodletting only – there was no wall-scaling or turning into a bat on camera.

In *Dracula* (1958, US title *Horror Of Dracula*), Fisher again contributes a fast

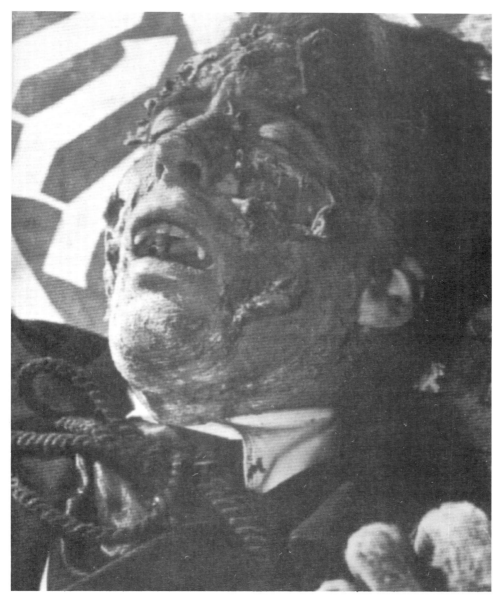

Dracula

pace – something that dropped off after the initial adrenalin rush of these three movies. The plot was the standard Transylvania to London jaunt that everyone knows about – the difference here was in the transition from vague menace to a very real, fearsome monster. Christopher Lee quite literally got his teeth into the role, using his height and imperious stare to make the Count an awe-inspiring figure, aloof from man yet needing its blood to survive.

Along with the blood, there was plenty of sexual suggestion, with milky white bosoms and throats exposed for biting, and lots of orgasmic gasping at the moment of penetration. Subtle it was not, but it pulled in the punters and had some genuine scares. It also had wonderful supporting performances from Melissa Stribling and Carol Marsh (Mina and Lucy), and Michael Gough and – particularly – John Van Eyssen (Arthur and Jonathan). James Bernard contributed another great score to heighten tension.

But it was Cushing and Lee, matching talents and wits, who were the true stand outs. Cushing's Van Helsing was an avenging angel who had more in common with Sherlock Holmes than the loopy Dutchman of the book, but it worked: good versus evil writ large, and the climax, where Van Helsing sprints across a room and slides along a table to rip down the heavy drapes and expose the Count to sunlight, is still breathtaking.

Like the first *Frankenstein*, this was a landmark British horror. After it, things were never quite the same. Like *Frankenstein*, it was the beginning of a cycle which eventually led to the law of diminishing returns, obscuring more interesting Hammer pictures in favour of another scrappy character vehicle.

That was still some years away, though...

8.   Hammer: The Glory Years

1959 and 1960 were the years when Hammer consolidated their success with some sturdy but not spectacular films. It is interesting to look back and see that not only were they still heavily into producing non-horror, but that the horrors they did produce during this period were not as memorable as either the early films, or later 1960's efforts.

The Stranglers Of Bombay (1959) aka The Strangler Of Bombay, and The Terror Of The Tongs (1960) aka Terror Of The Hatchet Men, are a case in point. To be honest, I am not even that sure if they are really horror movies, being historical dramas with horrific edges.

The former was produced by Tony Hinds and written by David Z Goodman, who presents the viewer with a story in which travellers in India are waylaid by a religious cult of Thugees and ritually killed. There are attempts at escape, and some stalking through obvious sets. Terence Fisher tries to get things going, but his problem with pacing returns with a vengeance, and the script is dull, giving him or the actors little to work with. The costumes (it is 1826, and the Raj has not really got going yet) are good, as always, and James Bernard's score injects some tension, but Guy Rolfe and Allan Cuthbertson are left struggling with wooden dialogue, and even the usually reliable Andrew Cruickshank seems to be mentally counting the days until his pay-cheque is in the bank.

The Terror Of The Tongs is better, if only because it has Christopher Lee rehearsing for his Fu Manchu movies and a Jimmy Sangster script, which ensures a rapid chain of events if nothing else. It is 1910, and a wealthy Hong Kong merchant sets out to avenge the death of his daughter at the hands of the Tongs. Directed with gusto by Anthony Bushell, and with another Bernard score (did they chain him to a piano?), it is let down only by some tight production values and ropey acting by leads Geoffrey Toone and Yvonne Monlaur. But is it really a horror picture? I think not, despite the odd orgy of a blood-letting and sexual variety.

The same could be said of The Hound Of The Baskervilles, a 1959 production in which Peter Cushing thoroughly enjoys himself as Holmes, with Lee opposite him as Sir Henry Baskerville and André Morell as a vague but willing Watson. A straightforward adaption of the Sir Arthur Conan Doyle story, this does not pit Holmes against a true horror villain like the later "Holmes vs The Ripper" movies mentioned in this book. However, it does have an extremely spooky air to the scenes on the moors, and the hints of the supernatural are maintained up until the very end.

Peter Bryan's screenplay condenses the story well, the acting is superb (particularly cherishable is Miles Malleson's mild-mannered arachnid-loving Bishop), and Terence Fisher's rather stately pacing fits the feel of the whole piece, enhanced by a score from that man Bernard again.

During this period, Hammer were also trying to set up a Frankenstein TV series, to be produced in America. In b & w, the pilot was an unhappy amalgam of Hammer and Universal, with Anton Diffring struggling to make something of the Baron out of the godawful script he was saddled with. Michael Carreras flew out to the States, but the show was soon scuppered, leaving Diffring to return to the UK and star in a wonderful piece of Hammer period, The Man Who Could Cheat Death (1959).

Taken from Barré Lyndon's play The Man In Half Moon Street (under which title it was filmed in the 1944, with Nils Asher), Diffring stars as a brilliant surgeon who has appeared over the last seventy years in a variety of towns, always apparently the same age. His secret is a series of gland transplants from beautiful women. He is now one hundred and four years old, and due for another transplant, the only thing keeping him alive being a rapidly diminishing elixir.

Hazel Court is attracted to Diffring, but he has a rival in the shape of sculptor Christopher Lee. Lee becomes suspicious when an old (literally) colleague of Diffring's meets him at a party and remarks on his youth. This ageing surgeon is soon taken into Diffring's confidence, and is to help him with the operation – but not before Lee has made some enquiries. The giveaway is a series of busts that Diffring collects, each one being a missing woman – a woman who has given him more than her love...

In an exciting climax, Lee and the police break into a warehouse where the rapidly ageing Diffring is pleading with Court, having kidnapped her. He truly loves her, and wants to offer her the chance to join him. As he begins to age she screams the house down, and a fire starts in her struggle to escape. Lee rescues her as Diffring dies in the flames.

Icy and brittle, Diffring plays this role to perfection. Lee is a gay artist, the opposite of the roles he was beginning to be known for, and all the better for playing against type. Hazel Court is the consummate professional as the girl in the middle. Terence Fisher's direction is a trifle leaden, but its stately pace suits the age of the material, from which Jimmy Sangster trimmed all excess.

Lee played against type again in the next year's *The Two Faces Of Dr Jekyll* (1960, US title *House Of Fright*), aka *Jekyll's Inferno*, where he was wonderful as the alleged friend of Paul Massie's austere Dr Jekyll, bearded and boring. Secretly he laughs at Jekyll as he beds the good doctor's wife (Dawn Addams). However, Jekyll's serum turns him into the handsome and debonair Hyde. In this guise he wins back Kitty and arranges her murder (a spectacular piece of killing involving shattering stained glass) and lays the blame on Lee's Paul Allen, and subsequently on his other self – Jekyll. Hyde also becomes infatuated with a snake dancer, which gives the director (Fisher again) the chance to put in some sexy cabaret shots.

Hyde comes undone when giving evidence at Kitty's inquest. Jekyll keeps breaking through again, despite Hyde's attempts to suppress him, even going so far as to fake Jekyll's death. However, the good doctor will not let his evil side win out, and the films ends with a descent into madness.

On paper it sounds like a good chiller, but in fact it is overlong and boring. Writer Wolf Mankowitz was an acclaimed playwright who used this as a vehicle for his ideas about psychology, proving in the process that he knew nothing about structuring a good thriller. Dull dialogue gives the actors little to work with, and a snail's pace script leaves Fisher floundering in a slew of long takes that leave the viewer falling asleep. Paul Massie – usually a good actor (he was in Tony Hancock's *The Rebel* [US title *Call Me Genius*], the same year, and was wonderful) – is fine as Hyde, but his Jekyll has the most irritating and monotonous voice ever heard on screen. David Kossoff does his usual excellent turn as Jekyll's friend Litauer, and Dawn Addams gets to wear a fetching basque before dying, but otherwise it is all a bit ropey.

The same could not be said of *The Mummy*, Lee's 1959 return to monsters. Starring as Kharis, an Egyptian priest whose tongue is gorily torn out at the beginning of the movie, and who is condemned to eternal life as guardian of the tombs, Lee gets to play most of the movie wrapped in bandages. Even so, he brings a solemn sadness to the role matched only by Karloff's initial 1932 Universal performance.

Peter Cushing is John Banning, who opens the tomb with his father (Felix Aylmer) and uncle (Raymond Huntley) on an expedition. Alone in the tomb, Aylmer is attacked by the Mummy. No-one really believes him, and four years later he is in an asylum, desperate to convince Cushing that the Mummy is real.

Why? Because it is being transported to Britain, and Aylmer is convinced that the Mummy will want to kill them all. Under the direction of Mehmet Bey (George

The Mummy

Pastell), a member of the cult that Kharis belonged to, this is exactly what happens – Aylmer being the first to go in a wonderful attack on his padded cell.

Cushing's wife Isobel (Yvonne Furneaux) bears a striking resemblance to Ananka, Kharis' queen and lost love, and it is only by her commands that Banning is saved. After several deaths, Bey gets his when ordering Kharis to kill Isobel. Kharis is less than impressed, and ends up kidnapping Isobel and taking her to a swamp. She commands him to put her down, and he does so, walking to his death in the swamp as bullets fly through him.

Jimmy Sangster's script is an amalgam of every Universal mummy picture ever made, and the players treat it with the right attitude: fast-moving pulp that only lags in a few "let's explain the plot" scenes featuring Eddie Byrne's Inspector Mulrooney. Terence Fisher keeps it moving as well as could be expected, and draws a fine mute performance from Lee.

The Brides Of Dracula (1960) should have been another Lee triumph, but he was unwilling to return to the Count after seeing the script, so a hasty piece of re-writing was in order. Jimmy Sangster's script was re-written by Peter Bryan and Edward Percy, and it shows. David Peel takes over the vampire role as Baron Meinster, a disciple of Dracula, and his boyish good looks actually make him rather more sinister in this context than the Count would have been. The original ending (hordes of bats destroying the vampire) was changed, and later used for *Kiss Of The Vampire* (1964).

The plot centres around Yvonne Monlaur's Marianne, whose journey to the Lang Academy, where she is to become a teacher, is interrupted by the Baroness Meinster, who rides abroad seeking young girls for her son. She leaves him chained up in their castle. Why is he chained? Because he's a vampire, and his mother cannot bear to have him killed. Instead, she goes out on the prowl.

Poor foolish Marianne releases him, falling for his boyish charm, and he immediately bites his mother in a distasteful but highly appropriate piece of vampiric incest. He later turns up at the Academy, following Marianne. As a bat, he gains entrance at night and starts to drain the pupils of their blood. He also wants to marry Marianne and have her as his bride.

Enter Van Helsing, who hears from vague doctor Miles Malleson about strange goings-on at the Academy. He visits Baroness Meinster, and at her behest kills her (a wonderful scene from Martita Hunt, who makes you weep for what her son has done to her) before confronting the Baron in an old mill. Splashing the Baron with holy water, a fight ensues, and Van Helsing is bitten. In an excruciating moment, he has to immediately cauterise the wound using a blacksmith's fire iron before dispatching the Baron in a climactic fire.

There is one big hole in all this that really grates, if the Baron could turn into a bat, why did chaining him up keep him captive at the beginning? Something that must have been over-looked in the re-writes, it does not stop this from being a pretty good movie. The action scenes are handled well, Peel is suitably slimy, and Cushing *is* Van Helsing, with all the authority that implies. Terence Fisher has problems with the talky middle-section, centred around the Academy, but makes up for this with the frenetic pace of the climax.

There were no Gothic horrors released in 1961, partly because a planned film about the Inquisition would have proved too gory for the censor, so Tony Hinds was put to work on dreaming up a movie that would use the sets already built. By changing the location of Guy Endore's novel *The Werewolf Of Paris*, and using Oliver Reed in his first starring role, Hinds was able to fulfil this task.

In the meantime, Jimmy Sangster was given the chance to develop a pet project: influenced by Hitchcock's *Psycho* and *Les Diaboliques* (1954), a contemporary French chiller, Sangster wanted to develop a strain of psychological horror that did not need period dress or monster suits. He was also influenced by the fact that Eros billed him as Jimmy "Frankenstein" Sangster on *The Trollenberg Terror*...

Taste Of Fear (1961, US title *Scream Of Fear*), was the first fruit of this idea. It told the story of Penny Appleby, a wheelchair user who is invited to her father's house in the South of France by her stepmother. Daddy is away on business, and Penny (his heir) has not seen him since her mother died. She soon starts to see him – all over the house, and very dead.

Of course, everyone thinks she is cracking up, except Ronald Lewis as her stepmother's chauffeur. He is on her side, and wants to help her find out what is going on...

After a series of torturous plot twists and taut scenes, it transpires that daddy is dead, and step-mummy and the chauffeur are in it together. The local police are confused, and Lewis plans to kill off Penny in a faked car crash. It is only when he returns to the house and mistakes his lover, sitting in her step-daughter's wheelchair, for Penny, that he sees red and tips her over the edge of a cliff before realising his mistake. By which time Penny has returned on foot, with the police. She is not the real Penny, who died, but rather a friend who wanted to fulfil the dying Penny's last wish and get to the bottom of this mystery.

Confused? You will be. Seth Holt directs in grainy black and white, matching Sangster's every gleeful plot twist with visual invention. Lewis is brilliant, matched by Susan Strasberg as Penny and Ann Todd as her stepmother. A wonderful, low-key series of frights, it started an occasional ten year cycle of such movies.

The Curse Of The Werewolf aka *The Wolfman* was back on familiar territory for 1962, with Hinds writing under his John Elder pseudonym, and Terence Fisher directing at a too-stately pace.

In an over-long prologue, a mute serving girl at the court of the Marques of Santa Vera is raped in the dungeons by a mad beggar (Richard Wordsworth) after spurning the advances of the Marques. Managing to escape, and killing the old man,

Curse Of The Werewolf

she is found in the woods by Don Alfredo Cortello, who takes her home and looks after her. Her son, Léon, is born on Christmas day – an affront to God (novel way of inducing lycanthrope – no bites here). At his christening, the water boils and the church shakes.

Léon grows up, turning into a wolf every full moon and going hunting – even collecting buckshot after savaging sheep. A priest explains to the Don that love can stop this happening, while vice, greed and anger will bring it out.

Oliver Reed plays the adult Léon, sent on an apprenticeship to the vineyards of Don Enrique (Peter Sallis) where he falls in love with the Don's daughter Christina (Yvonne Romain). She is meant for another, despite also falling for him, and frustration leads Léon to begin changing.

A series of set-piece deaths follows, resulting in a fiery climax as Léon is chased around the rooftops of the village before being killed by his father, who has fashioned a silver bullet from a cross. Reed is magnificent, capturing all the pathos of a man pushed beyond his limits by something happening to him that he cannot control or understand. Clifford Evans, as Don Alfredo, matches him with a display of torn love. He knows the that only way to truly help the son he loves is to kill him.

Good performances make up for a script that has several troughs, and a lack of pace that slows the film to a halt in places. Acclaimed as a "classic", I would have to differ. It has plenty of great moments, but overall leaves the viewer frustrated.

Evans was also brilliant in *Kiss Of The Vampire* (1964) aka *Kiss Of Evil*, another rapidly re-written Dracula project that ended up without either Lee or Cushing. Instead, the Van Helsing savant role was taken by Evans as Professor Zimmer, a cranky old man with little time for people who does not appreciate the evil he was fighting. Compared to the suave Dr Ravna (Noel Willman) and his charming children Carl and Sabena, who are the leaders of a cult of vampires, most people would chose the family of evil.

In fact, this is what happens to Marianne and Gerald Harcourt (Edward de Souza and Jennifer Daniel), newly-weds whose car runs out of petrol while on their honeymoon. Staying at a small hotel, they are glad to accept Ravna's invitation to dinner, and fall under the sexual allure of the Ravna children. It is only with some difficulty that Gerald breaks the spell and returns to the hotel, where Zimmer warns him not to go back.

Phantom Of The Opera

But they do and the Ravnas hold a ball, attended by the cult devotees. It is a ruse to entrap the Harcourts, and although Gerald escapes, Marianne is initiated. Zimmer reveals that his daughter was also a victim of the cult, and begins an incantation from an old manuscript while Gerald ventures to recapture Marianne.

A horde of bats descend on the castle, killing the cult devotees and the Ravnas and with them dead, Marianne is released.

Effects man Les Bowie does wonders on a small budget, and although some of the bats are palpably fake, the majority seem genuine. De Souza is a good, honest hero, and Noel Willman is suave beyond belief. Director Don Sharp handles his first feature (his next was a Tommy Steele musical!) with style and grace, while the John Elder script is tight and exciting. There is more implied decadence than before, and Evans is almost an anti-hero, making this unusual for a Hammer horror, but one of the best of an uncertain period.

De Souza is also cast in *The Phantom Of The Opera* (1962), where he is the lover of opera singer Christine, trained by the Phantom (played by Herbert Lom, who struggles with a terrible mask). Cary Grant was originally interested in the role, but would not be seen killing people, so a dwarf was written in to be the murderer. Surprisingly, evil dwarf spotters will be amazed to learn that it was not a Sangster script! This time, John Elder (Anthony Hines) took up the dwarf-battering baton.

Perhaps because it was originally intended as a Hollywood star vehicle, it is strangely anaemic. Hardly a horror at all, it has more in common with the Andrew Lloyd-Webber musical, turning Gaston LeRoux's grand guignol epic into a tragic romance. No thrills, no chills...

Even worse was *The Old Dark House* (1962), a co-production with the king of US horror gimmicks, William Castle. Castle was great in his own backyard, but lost with a re-make of James Whale's 1932 movie of the same name. Based on J B Priestley's *Benighted*, it is a dark horrific comedy, with a knowing smirk. However, Whale was English, and understood the humorous side. Castle did not, and Robert Dillon's script is terrible. Tom Poston tries hard as Tom Penderell, who arrives in England to visit his

The Damned

friend Caspar Femm, only to discover Caspar is dead, but not his twin Jasper. There is some talk of a plot revolving around treasure, but the film soon degenerates into a bunch of British character actors trying to come out of this mess looking good.

Mervyn Johns, Joyce Grenfell, Janette Scott, Peter Bull, Danny Green, Robert Morley and Fenella Fielding all overact as though their lives depend on it. But no good, Castle is heavy-handed, the script is too far away from the source, and the colour film stock just takes away from any atmosphere. The fact that Bull and Morley used to trade their best lines with each other over smoked salmon for lunch gives you an idea of the sort of film it was...

A horror in the wrong sense.

An attempt at diversification that was a little more successful came in 1963 with *The Damned* (US title *These Are The Damned*), directed by Joseph Losey, who had travelled to Britain to escape Hollywood blacklisting. This sense of paranoia and alienation that was a natural corollary of the Communist witch-hunts managed to communicate itself in all the early 1960's films he made – *The Servant* (1963), with Dirk Bogarde as the servant who enslaves and disempowers his master James Fox, covers much the same territory and only missed out on inclusion in this book because it is not quite terrifying enough. It does show that the true monsters have human form, however...

A theme that was developed a little further in this movie. Macdonald Carey is Simon, an American visitor who is picked up by Joanie (Shirley Anne Field). She is luring him into the clutches of her brother's motorcycle gang (Oliver Reed is brilliant as King, her brother). Saved by scientist Bernard and his girlfriend Freya, Simon later comes across Joanie again, this time on the run from her brother. Together, they escape on a boat to a cove where they discover Bernard's secret project, a group of children sealed off from the world and monitored by giant TV screens.

Simon and Joanie want to help them escape but realise too late that they are radioactive, the children of parents exposed to radiation, and a controlled experiment to forge a post-nuclear society. Simon and Joanie escape to die of radiation exposure, King is driven off the cliffs by security men when he tries to break in, and Bernard shoots his girlfriend before returning to his project...

A thoroughly bleak but fascinating movie, the harsh Dorset coast is a good counterpoint to the unnatural goings-on. The performances are solid, Losey has a definite message, and Evan Jones' script leaves little of the original novel (*Children Of Light*, by H L Lawrence), but adds much of its own. However, the film was ruthlessly pruned for a double-bill slot at the expense of some of the story. Scary it still is – but do not expect it to make too much sense.

The other entries for 1963 were both in Jimmy Sangster's psychological series, and met a mixed reaction. *Maniac* was written and produced by Sangster, with Michael Carreras handling direction, and what an under-rated director he was. Donald Houston is George, an escapee from a French asylum (obviously *Les Diaboliques* had a big effect on Sangster, who also set *Taste Of Fear* in France) who wants to kill his wife's lover. The wife is Nadia Gray, and the lover is Kerwin Matthews. Houston underplays, and also has a fetish for oxy-acetylene torches, with which he causes much panic.

A brief eighty-six minutes and full of little twists and "who's-behind-the-door" shocks, it really works first time you see it, but is not a film to watch repeatedly.

Paranoiac

There's less reliance on shock effect in *Paranoiac* (1963), which is handled by Freddie Francis in a manner more befitting a thriller. And this is really what it is, Sangster's script relies heavily on Josephine Tey's *Brat Farrar*, a novel which is not credited but which Hammer had at one time optioned.

Oliver Reed is wonderful as Simon, an organ playing psychopath who keeps his brother's body in an outhouse. Then Alexander Davion turns up, claiming to be Tony (the dead brother)... how can Simon reveal the imposter without giving himself away? Easy, he will just try and kill him – and anyone else who gets in the way.

Set in England, it was almost a country house thriller of the traditional English school, except that Reed was psychotic beyond belief, and there was more blood than in an average Agatha Christie. Janette Scott plays the love interest, and turns in one of her best performances, while Maurice Denham is the eternal supporting actor turning in a good show. It also benefits from a good score by Elizabeth Lutyens, one of many English composers who go slumming it in low-grade movies. She also did some great Amicus scores.

Francis and Sangster stayed together for the next two entries in the psychological series, *Nightmare* and *Hysteria*, both 1964 productions. The former was a retread of *Taste Of Fear*, with David Knight and Moira Redmond trying to send Jennie Linden mad with a now-you-see-it, now-you-don't approach to hiding a body. Although it did not have the impact of the first film, it was still fun in a mindless kind of way, and supporting actors Brenda Bruce, Timothy Bateson and George A Cooper made it worth watching.

Hysteria is another matter, eighty-five minutes of complex plot twists that leave you confused if you so much as look away for a second. Robert Webber is Christopher Smith, an American who has lost his memory. He is set up in a flat by the kindly Doctor Keller (Anthony Newlands), who has been caring for him. Smith does not know Keller is behind this, only that an anonymous benefactor wants to help him.

Keller has a hidden agenda, he has murdered his wife in order to marry his mistress (Lelia Goldoni – a bit-part scream queen who did some Tigon pictures), and wants to leave the body on Smith's bathroom floor. A nice, simple frame... except that Smith has regained his memory, and now knows why he lost it in the first place...

Maurice Denham lurks in the background, giving character to the somewhat bland leading actors. However, they are little more than ciphers anyway, as Francis and Sangster whip the viewer through the complex film at a lightning fast pace, leaving little room for breath, Don Banks' score blaring across the dialogue and making it even more of a nightmare ride.

Three Gothic horrors were also made in 1964, beginning with Michael Carreras' pet project, *The Curse Of The Mummy's Tomb*. In this entry to the short *Mummy* series, Dickie Owen played the Mummy, unearthed by John Bray (Ronald Howard) and Alexander King (Fred Clark). The latter is an American showman, who financed the expedition in order to make a fortune travelling the Mummy around the world. Bray, who is in love with his boss' daughter Annette (Jeanne Roland), is unsure of this. He is also a little annoyed at the attention shown Annette by wealthy playboy Adam (Terence Morgan), who met them on the boat home.

This was no accidental meeting, as Adam planned it, because he wants the Mummy. Annette innocently explains the legend of the sons of Ramases VIII to Adam: there were two sons, Ra and Be. Ra dedicated his life to the search for immortality. Be sent assassins to kill Ra, but the medallion containing the secret of raising the dead is lost. She now has that medallion.

Shortly afterwards, the medallion is stolen, and the Mummy revived, going on the rampage. Adam reveals – after a series of suitably graphic deaths – that he is Be, condemned by his father to eternal life, and only Ra can kill him, ending his misery. He is behind the revivification of the Mummy.

The police, with Bray in the lead, arrive, and Adam retreats to the sewers, where his long-dead brother finally kills him, as Bray rescues Annette.

Henry Younger's screenplay is hardly a classic, but the director handles it well – so he should, as Younger was a pseudonym for Carreras. There are a series of set piece deaths, and although Morgan hardly has the angst you would expect of a man waiting for death, Fred Clark does a lovely comic turn as showman King before being bumped off, and the whole thing is an animated horror comic that rips along splendidly.

Better still was *The Evil Of Frankenstein* (1964) with Cushing returning as the Baron, and Sandor Eles in tow as his servant Hans. Freddie Francis had his first crack at directing a *Frankenstein* when Terence Fisher fell ill, and the John Elder screenplay kept up the high standard of the first two movies.

On the run, Cushing's cold Baron is using a water mill to continue his experiments. The local priest bursts in (a brief but excellent show from James Maxwell) and breaks up the laboratory. The Baron has to flee... He and Hans return to the Baron's deserted Château, previously broken up by a mob of angry peasants. Together, the two men set to work rebuilding the lab, working in secret. They find the monster encased in ice, and cannot revive it.

All this is a little familiar, Universal were now pumping money into Hammer, and Hinds borrowed liberally from the Universal *Frankenstein* movies for his trappings.

The Evil Of Frankenstein

The next twist is totally against the Cushing character, as the Baron resorts to using a drunken stage hypnotist, "Professor" Zoltan, to bring the monster back to life.

It works – but the creature is now under Zoltan's control. As Zoltan is a drunken lecher, the monster goes woman hunting, and is also used to settle a few old scores. The peasants start to revolt again, and send a lynching party to the Château. Meanwhile, Zoltan and the Baron are having a little disagreement, which results in Zoltan ordering the creature to kill its creator. The Baron repels it with fire, and Zoltan is killed. The creature has drunk brandy, and now tries chloroform. Running amok, it sets fire to the Château, and the film ends with the Baron caught between an angry mob and a burning Château.

Francis moves this at a rapid pace, glossing over any character changes in the Baron – he seems a bit panicky compared to the cold scientist of old, even though Cushing gives him the usual calm authority. Eles is good as Hans, and Peter Woodthorpe is wonderful as the drunken idiot Zoltan. Not so good is Kiwi Kingston, who plays the monster. Freddie Francis wanted him because of his size (he was a wrestler), but even without dialogue he just looks wooden. He also resembles Karloff as Universal surrendered make-up rights and Roy Ashton's original designs went out of the window for a quick Universal fit-up.

Overall, this matches up to the earlier films, but the seeds of the series' decline were already there.

The Gorgon (1964) was the last of the three Gothics for this year, and also the best. Terence Fisher directed a John Gilling script, based on a story by J Llewellyn Devine. Gilling was at his scripting best, and Fisher's stately approach to pacing benefitted a movie that was as much about character as action.

Professor Heitz visits the village of Vandorf, in Transylvania, to investigate the death of his son Bruno. In a deserted castle, he glimpses something that is slowly killing him, but not before he can write to his son Paul.

Paul (Richard Pasco) arrives in the village, and falls in love with Carla Hoffman (it is Barbara Shelley, so who wouldn't?), assistant to Doctor Namaroff (Peter Cushing). What he does not realise is that Carla is really Magaera, last of the Gorgons. Even though she has lapses of memory that coincide with deaths and the appearance of the creature, Paul still refuses to believe. Enter Christopher Lee as the hard-headed Professor Meister, who is investigating the deaths.

The Gorgon

Namaroff hides records that would reveal Carla's secret, and it is a joy to see the two actors sparring with each other. When Paul asks Carla to come to Leipzig she agrees, but then disappears to the castle, where Namaroff is waiting to put her out of her misery. Paul fights him, and they both fall to the gaze of the Gorgon. Meister arrives in time to cut off the Gorgon's head and see it change back to Carla...

Stately until the climax, it suddenly ups a gear or two and gets tense. Gilling also broke contemporary conventions by killing off the hero, heroine and savant in one fell swoop at the end. Pre-figuring George Romero in this bleakness, it does give the film an edge over other horrors of this period.

Prudence Hyman played the Gorgon – the gorgeous Barbara had wanted to wear a headdress full of live snakes for the Gorgon role, but was forbidden by producer Anthony Nelson Keys. Despite this, the film is still the best of the period from Hammer.

Gilling turned to direction for 1965's *Plague Of The Zombies* aka *The Zombie* aka *The Zombies*, which was scripted by Peter Bryan (an occasional writer, Bryan had worked for Hammer in various capacities since the days of *Dick Barton*). André Morell was the bad tempered savant Sir James Forbes, who travels to Cornwall at the request of his former pupil, Dr Peter Thompson (Brook Williams). Thompson is at the end of his tether as villagers are dropping dead, and he cannot find the cause. He hopes Sir James will help.

Sir James finds more than he bargained for. Squire Clive Hamilton has recently returned from the West Indies, and is practising voodoo, creating zombies as slave labour for his run-down tin mine. Sir James discovers this when he tries to exhume a body and finds a grave empty.

The Squire is after Sylvia, Sir James' daughter, and also has a hold on Alice, the doctor's wife. Things come to a head when Sir James breaks into the Squire's house, and ends up caught in a fire. Escaping to the mine, he burns the place down, escaping with his daughter only just in time, as the Squire and his cronies are condemned to a fiery underground death.

Moving from action to dream-sequence in the blink of an eye, the stand-out scene is where Dr Thompson is attacked by zombies rising from their graves. John Carson as the Squire hams it up shamelessly, but it works in this context. Jacqueline

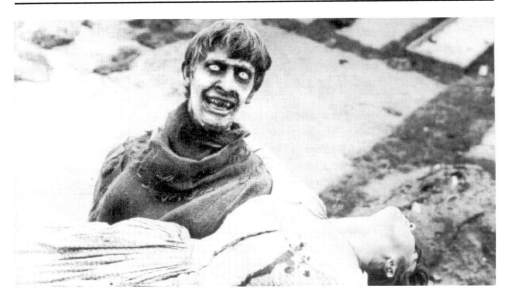

Plague Of The Zombies

Pearce (Alice) and Diane Clare (Sylvia) swoon about prettily, but sadly are not required to do very much. Never mind, there's enough going on elsewhere, and Morell is the best grumpy old man to be a hero since Professor Zimmer in *Kiss Of The Vampire*.

Speaking of vampires, Christopher Lee was back as Dracula, after seven years, in *Dracula, Prince Of Darkness* (1966), aka *Disciple Of Dracula* aka *Revenge Of Dracula* aka *The Bloody Scream Of Dracula*. A pseudonymous script revealed Jimmy Sangster (as John Sansom) writing from a Tony Hinds (John Elder) idea. Terence Fisher was in the directors chair, and Andrew Keir was in fine form as gun toting priest Father Sandor. Sadly, no Peter Cushing – Keir's role was a fine replacement.

Charles and Diana (Francis Matthews and Suzan Farmer) are holidaying in Carpathia with Alan and Helen (Charles Tingwell and Barbara Shelley). Their car breaks down, and a mysterious carriage transports them to Castle Dracula, where the sinister Klove (Philip Latham) lays on dinner, and tells them his master was expecting them – even though he is dead...

Dracula, Prince Of Darkness

Alan is used to revive Dracula, his throat cut as he is suspended over the empty tomb of Dracula. Originally this was to be a decapitation, but the BBFC refused to pass this. This version, however, is more sadistic than any mere beheading, as Klove relishes every drop of blood.

Helen is bitten by Dracula, and turned from a prim prig into a wanton woman who tries to seduce Charles. He manages to escape to the monastery of Sandor with Helen, but Dracula is after her. Using his slave Ludwig (a Renfield clone who eats flies, played with humour by Thorley Walters), Dracula gains access to the monastery and takes Helen.

The climax comes on the ice outside Castle Dracula, as Charles and the Count fight. Sandor breaks the ice with gunshot, and the Count plunges to his death in the purity of running water.

Lee refused to speak the few lines given him, and played the role silent, and his Dracula this time is no suave Count, but a hissing, spitting wild animal. This reflects the sexual angle much better, and is appropriate in view of Shelley's character change. Even when she is staked by a group of monks, she writhes and screams orgasmically in some strange group-sex parody. Was it unconscious that this occurred? Who knows, it does however, help the picture over the few dragging moments.

Not quite up to the strength of the original, this showed that Lee had been right to hold out on a sequel.

There were also two psychological horrors in 1965. *The Nanny* is an acknowledged classic, as Hammer tempted Bette Davis over from Hollywood to play in a low budget movie as the children's nurse from hell. Only her charge – Joey (William Dix) – knows how evil she is as she rules him with a rod of iron and arranges the deaths of those adults she does not like, such as Penelope (Jill Bennet) who has a heart attack. Others are reduced to "suicide".

Ms Davis is grand guignol personified, with Wendy Craig (as Joey's mother) at her mercy. James Villiers, Alfred Burke, and the ubiquitous Maurice Denham are also on fine form. Jimmy Sangster's script is a study in character, and Seth Holt directs with a fly-on-the-wall approach that is suited by his grainy black and white photography.

One of the best of the series, it was matched by *Fanatic* (1965, US title *Die! Die! My Darling*), which was a contrast made in hell. In colour, with a blood strewn script from Richard Matheson (adapted from Anne Blaisdell's *Nightmare* novel), it was directed with kinetic relish by Silvio Narizzano.

Tallulah Bankhead, the veteran US star, played Mrs Trefoil, the lunatic mother of Stefanie Powers' dead fiancé. A religious maniac, she persuades Powers to go through a religious ceremony "marrying" her to the dead son – and then she will make sure they are reunited in paradise...

Donald Sutherland steals the show as a lunatic odd-job man with a penchant for large knives matched only by Bankhead's, and the whole film actually proceeds without a single plot twist, and the entire story is relayed in a linear fashion, but with a bloody relish.

These two films were definitely the high point of the psychological series, and it was downhill from here...

1966 was the year in which the company made only four horrors, all of them Gothic. There was a *Frankenstein* that tried to break new ground, a modern-Gothic, and the last of the *Mummy* cycle. There was also the ultimate sexual bad trip...

The Reptile (1966) saw Jacqueline Pearce as Anne Franklyn, a distant girl who periodically sheds her skin and turns into a snake monster, killing for food. This is the result of her initiation into a snake cult when she and her father were in Borneo. It seems that the onset of adolescence and sexuality are equated in this cult with the ability to turn one into a snake. So when she gets excited, the venom really flies...

These facts come to light when Harry and Valerie Spalding (Ray Barrett and

Jennifer Daniel) travel to Cornwall in order to find out how Harry's brother died. When local village idiot Mad Peter (John Laurie, wasted in a bit part) is also found dead in the same way, local Tom Bailey (the ubiquitous Michael Ripper) recognises the marks on his neck as a snake-bite.

Valerie tries to befriend Anna, but finds her terrified of her father (Noel Willman), who is himself terrified of his Malay manservant (Marne Maitland). Harry is lured into a trap by Anna, and attacked. He is saved only by the prompt action of Valerie. The outraged wife confronts Franklyn, who reveals the truth. Under prompting, he kills the Malay and starts a fire – the fate of his daughter is left open.

The make-up from Roy Ashton is excellent, and John Gilling directs John Elder's script with pace and fire. Jacqueline Pearce is cold and distant here in a way that she did not exploit again until her role as Servilan, the leather dominatrix of TV's *Blakes Seven*. Interestingly, this film was shot back-to-back with *The Plague Of The Zombies*, using the patented Hammer money-saving technique (they also shot *Dracula, Prince Of Darkness* back-to-back with the historical drama *Rasputin The Mad Monk*), but not released until a year later. Even more interestingly, Elder nicked some of the plot ideas for his Tyburn script for *The Ghoul*, filmed in 1975. *The Reptile* was also liberally used for Tigon's *The Blood Beast Terror*, made a year later – although, being perverse, I actually prefer the Tigon movie!

Gilling was also back in action for the last of Hammer's *Mummy* movies, *The Mummy's Shroud* (1966), which he wrote and directed. "Beware the beat of the cloth-wrapped feet" ran the tag line, and that just about sums it up. A horror comic with tongue-in-cheek, Gilling unravels (ahem) the story of Paul Preston (David Buck) who exhumes a Mummy along with Sir Basil Walden (André Morell) and assistants Clare and Harry (Maggie Kimberley and Tom Barrett). Preston wants the credit for himself, and has the exhausted Sir Basil confined to an asylum. Sir Basil escapes and is killed by the Mummy, re-activated by Egyptian fanatic Hasmid Ali, who has sworn death to all who defile the tomb. This also includes Preston, his wife Barbara (Elizabeth Sellars), and father Stanley (John Phillips).

Stuntman Eddie Powell plays the Mummy with the requisite muscle (come on, it hardly requires much skill in a plot like this), and Roger Delgado (better known as the Master in Doctor Who) is in fine declaiming form. Michael Ripper is there, too, as the Prestons' agent Longbarrow.

The finale sees the Mummy rip itself to shreds after Claire recites an ancient spell commanding it to kill itself. After this, where could the Mummy series go? Gilling's rip-roaring pulp, with blaring Don Banks soundtrack, was the natural end.

Not so natural was what the Baron was doing in *Frankenstein Created Woman* (1966) aka *Frankenstein Made Woman*, where Peter Cushing takes the corpse of "crippled" Christina and turns her into the beautiful Susan Denberg. Interestingly, she also goes from mousey to blonde at the same time...

Christina tries to kill herself after seeing her lover Hans (Robert Morris) guillotined for the alleged murder of her father. In fact, he was framed by three rich young men who used to taunt Christina – Peter Blythe, Barry Warren, and Derek Fowlds. Unfortunately for them, Hans was the assistant of the Baron, and Frankenstein is working on trapping the soul, assisted by Thorley Walters as a dotty doctor.

Putting Hans' soul into his monsters body, he creates a woman who uses her wiles to trap the three young men, killing them in revenge while keeping his/her head (Hans', that is) on her dressing table.

A screwball mix of psychology and transsexual imagery pervade the film, giving it a bizarre and kinky edge. John Elder has a script full of set pieces rather than a developed plot, and Terence Fisher builds tension at the expense of pace while Peter Cushing is relegated to almost a supporting role, watching the action from the sidelines. Not perhaps a great *Frankenstein* movie, but interesting if treated as a separate project.

The last film of the year saw Nigel Kneale return to Hammer, scripting *The Witches* (1966, US title *The Devil's Own*) making a taut movie of Peter Curtis' turgid novel *The Devil's Own*.

Joan Fontaine is Gwen, a teacher who has a nervous breakdown while teaching at a mission school in Africa (an excellent opening sequence sees her menaced by the local Witchdoctor). Back in England, she is employed by Alan Bax (Alec McGowen), whom she believes to be a priest. He runs the village school, and Gwen is shocked to learn from his sister Stephanie (a wonderfully arch Kay Walsh) that he is not a priest, but merely wears a dog collar because he wanted to be one but failed... Stephanie is no slouch at eccentricity herself, being a writer with a penchant for the occult.

The Witches

Gwen sees evidence of witchcraft when her star pupil Ronnie is mysteriously taken ill and dies. She lays the blame at the door of Gwen Ffrangcon-Davies, the grandmother of Ronnie's sweetheart. After this, things start to go wrong, and Gwen suffers a nervous breakdown.

In an institution, she at first has no memories of her time in the village, but in an atmosphere of paranoia she begins to recall events, and returns to the village, where she finds that Stephanie is the leader of a witches coven that wanted Gwen out of the way. Stephanie wanted Ronnie dead as his sweetheart, Linda, is marked to be a virgin sacrifice, restoring her to youth.

Gwen is forcibly initiated into the cult, but turns the spells against Stephanie by spilling her own blood in the circle. With Stephanie dead, Alan is free to come into his own, and he and Gwen run the school together.

Director Cyril Frankel was more at home on TV, directing many episodes of

The Champions and *Randall And Hopkirk (Deceased)*. He uses his small screen skills to keep the story as low key as Kneale's script, which allows tension and paranoia to develop through the characters. To do this, you need good acting, and Fontaine and Walsh are superb. The true stand-out, however, is Alec McGowen as Alan, who is under the spell of his sister and retreats into his fantasy world of religion. Without her occult interests, he no longer needs his religion to balance him, and he emerges under Gwen's eye as a fully-fledged character. Twitchy and nervous, he is shy and subdued at the beginning of the film, and only really comes to life when Gwen shows an interest in him.

With all this going for it, it is surprising that the film was not successful, however, it is hardly the average Hammer horror, and was perhaps buried under the welter of Gothic and psychology. One thing it did achieve, though, was to pave the way (at last) for the third Quatermass movie.

9. Hammer: To The Death

During excavations for a new underground extension at Hobbs End station, the skeletons of prehistoric men are unearthed. Unusual for their time, they are carefully preserved by a scientific team led by Doctor Roney and his assistant Miss Judd. Then something else is unearthed. Is it the biggest unexploded bomb of all time?

Colonel Breen, an expert in such matters, is pulled away from a meeting with Professor Quatermass, with whose rocket group Breen has just been placed. Accompanying the Colonel out of interest, Quatermass stumbles on an aborted mission from a dying planet. Martians, resembling giant locusts, genetically tampered with early man to try and preserve remnants of their dying race.

Now, unearthed after thousands of years, the sentient ship is active again, causing those people who carry some of the altered genes to become aware of the Martian hive instinct. Tracing strange events at the station through old archives and eyewitness reports (a nervous policeman standing in the empty houses opposite the station recalls their haunted reputation when a child), Quatermass realises that to try and remove the object would be disastrous, when a disbelieving Breen convinces a Member of Parliament that the ship is a harmless propaganda weapon, and TV cameras are taken down to film it, then the unleashed power threatens to enslave London.

It is only the ingenuity of Roney, unaffected by the ship, that enables him to earth the power of the ship by sacrificing his life and turning a large crane into the Martian power surge that dominates the landscape ("mass into energy – iron, the Devil's enemy", Roney supposes).

This is *Quatermass And The Pit* (US title *Five Millions Years To Earth*). Nigel Kneale compacts his original television story into ninety minutes, and Roy Ward Baker expertly marshals his resources and actors. Despite cutting great chunks of plot (again, the original serial ran for three hours in total), nothing is lost, and the pace is electric. Andrew Keir is Quatermass – a more humane, thinking Quatermass – and despite not getting on with Baker still pulls out a stupendous performance, ably assisted by Julian Glover as Breen – unable to face the truth, and pig-headedly resorting to the thinnest rationalisation when faced with the Martian ship. Barbara Shelley is wonderful as Miss Judd, especially when she telepathically sees the cleansing of the Martian hives, floating around a glowing ship with aborted objects careering about. James Donald is the perfectly rational and urbane Roney, keeping his head when chaos hits.

Les Bowie works wonders on a small budget, with collapsing London streets, energy force Martians, and gigantic explosions. Tristram Cary's music is tense, with the high taut strings of the Martian theme jangling the nerve ends.

A "must-see", this is the best of the Quatermass movies (retitled in the US, where Quatermass meant nothing), and one of the best Hammers.

The other Hammer horror of 1967 was equally as good. *The Devil Rides Out* (US title *The Devil's Bride*), was a pet project of Christopher Lee, a Dennis Wheatley fan who badgered Tony Hinds into reading the book. Hinds loved it, and optioned the project. Richard Matheson condensed the pan-European action into a few miles of the home counties, and Terence Fisher was given an action-packed script with which to work. James Bernard returned to the score, and contributed one of his best.

Lee took the lead role, as occult expert the Duc de Richleau, with Leon Greene as Rex Van Ryn, his sidekick and friend. The Duc and Rex had met young Simon Aron in a previous novel, and the three had become firm friends. Lee was really too young for Wheatley's Duc, but his dynamism is such that if you read the novel after seeing

Quatermass And The Pit

the movie, you ignore the author's description and see Lee in your mind.

Simon (a young Patrick Mower, with one of his best performances) has become involved with Mocata (a sinister Charles Gray) and his black magic group. Shunning his old friends, Simon hosts a party for his new cronies. It is the anniversary of their meeting, and Rex and the Duc turn up at Simon's house. The Duc knows what is happening almost immediately, and warns Simon. Later, they kidnap him and take him to the house of the Duc's niece, and her husband. There he is to stay until he is safe – after the date for his Satanic baptism. Mocata has other ideas, and magically attacks the house, taking Peggy (the Duc's great-niece) as a sacrifice in revenge. Rex has by now become besotted with Tanith, another convert who wants to escape Mocata. The sorcerer magically kills Tanith, and it is only when the Duc tracks Mocata to his lair that the sacrifice is prevented. The Duc attempts to speak an incantation that can only be used once, but the spirit of Tanith uses his niece's body, and her mother's pure love for Peggy, to save the child and turn back time. Tanith lives again, her life restored and that of Mocata taken in its place.

With action that does not let up for a minute, the goat of Mendes and the horseman of death making appearances at regular intervals, and a giant spider effect that does not quite work, the film barely has room for performances. But Fisher, who always prefers acting over action, draws great things from his players. Lee, obviously thoroughly enjoying himself, gives one of his most committed performances as the Duc, and Charles Gray's Mocata is a worthy adversary.

Pulp compared to the thoughtful sub-text of the Quatermass movie, both films nonetheless express the action and chills at which Hammer could excel. A vintage year, and vintage movies. Hammer filmed Wheatley's novel *Uncharted Seas* next as *The Lost Continent* (1968) – a sea-born romance – the next year. It was the author's favourite film of his work, but the next Wheatley horror – *To The Devil... A Daughter* – would not get made for another eleven years.

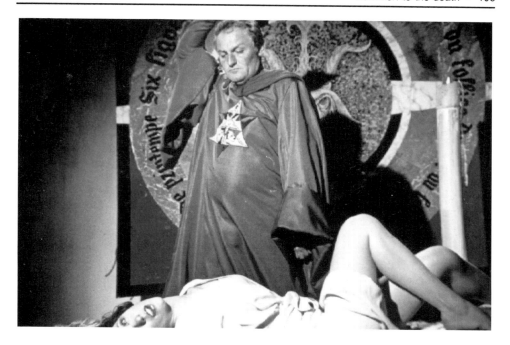

The Devil Rides Out

If these two movies were Hammer at their best, then the next year was when the rot began to set in.

The Anniversary (1968), was an attempt to fit black comedy into the psychological horror formula. Written by Jimmy Sangster, and directed by Roy Ward Baker from a play by Bill MacIlwraith, it featured Bette Davis on her return to Hammer, getting her teeth into the role of a malevolent widow who has her family come round each year on the anniversary of her husband's death for a little family get-together. The fact that all the family seem to hate the dead man is neither here nor there. The occasion is ripe with suppressed hates and grudges, full of elliptical dialogue.

This film should, by rights, fit into the Harold Pinter school – the horror of English pettiness. However, Sangster is a plot man, not a great dialogue writer. There is no way he is able to match Pinter for elliptic chills, and the black humour that runs mordant through both Pinter and Samuel Beckett fall flat on its face here. The piece betrays its theatrical origin, and whereas this does not matter with Pinter – the focus is always on the finely honed dialogue – here the eye begins to wander.

A noble failure. Sheila Hancock, Jack Hedley and James Cossins buoy up Davis' grand guignol hamming, but between them they just about fail to save the movie.

Dracula Has Risen From The Grave (1968) aka *Dracula's Revenge* was a sign that things were going wrong. It was Tony Hind's last movie before retiring as a producer – only in his forties, he had enough of the low-budget treadmill – and his John Elder script does betray some of this tiredness. Monsignor Muller (a fine show from Rupert Davies, making a name away from TV's *Maigret* as a horror player) arrives in a village near Castle Dracula where the local priest has become a drunken sot. The drunken priest leads him to Castle Dracula, where he bars the door with a giant cross. The Count is outraged, and uses waitress Zena (the lovely Barbara Ewing) to trap Maria, the niece of Muller and girlfriend of nominal heroic lead Paul (Barry Andrews).

Maria is rescued, but Zena is killed. Dracula tries again, biting Maria. She

Dracula Has Risen From The Grave

becomes enslaved, as does the drunken priest, who kills Muller under the Count's direction. Maria removes the cross from the door of Castle Dracula, and Paul confronts the Count. In a fight, the vampire falls over the parapet of the castle, and is impaled on the cross.

A film of no substance, but much style, there are great shots from Freddie Francis of priests hanging from bell ropes, and from the climactic fight and destruction of the vampire. In places, it actually has the feel of a spaghetti western. Veronica Carlson was in her first movie (plucked from a tabloid picture by James Carreras), and she is not very good – although it would be hard to shine on a movie where most of your part ends up on the cutting room floor. Francis played up the love interest, and this was chopped.

Lee was also less than happy – no lines again, and at one point he actually pulls a stake out of his chest because it "wasn't religiously motivated". This breaks continuity with previous movies and was a bad idea, it might have worked in a non-Dracula vampire picture, but here the lore and rules were already established.

James Bernard's score is hacked as much as Francis' kinetic action scenes, and overall it is a bit of a farrago.

Taste The Blood Of Dracula

New producer Aida Young (one of the first women in the industry besides Betty Box to produce, and the first at Hammer) followed this with an attempt to make a Dracula picture without Lee...or the Count! It may sound odd, but *Taste The Blood Of Dracula* (1970) is actually a great idea, and a better film than *Dracula Has Risen From The Grave*, but it was interference that spoiled it yet again.

Geoffrey Keen, Peter Sallis, and John Carson are three upstanding Victorian business men who like to go to "business meetings" once a week that are excuses for visits to bordellos. Here they meet Lord Courtley (Ralph Bates) who promises them a bigger thrill – black magic.

At their black mass in a deconsecrated church, Courtley drinks his blood mixed with the powdered blood of the vampire. He goes into a fit, and the three scared gentlemen beat him to death with their canes...Swearing each other to secrecy, they leave the body.

When they are gone, it reconstitutes into Dracula, who swears revenge. Keen's daughter (Linda Hayden) beheads him with a spade, Carson's son (Martin Jarvis) becomes a vampire and kills his father. But Sallis' son (Anthony Corlan) is forewarned, and confronts Dracula with holy relics in his church hideaway. Pushed back into the light of a stained glass window, the Count crumbles to dust over an altar cross.

Lee was brought back at the last minute, and spends much of the film lurking in shadows – his fate for the remaining *Dracula* movies. Apart from his almost incongruous presence, the film is actually a good shot at Victorian hypocrisy, with first time movie director Peter Sasdy (whose later career is a history of blown chances) getting some good images onto celluloid, matching his cast's excellent performances.

I think it would have worked without Lee, Dracula being used as an allegory. However, the punters were worrying Sir James Carreras (as he now was). The company had received the Queens Award For Industry in 1968, and now audiences for non-horror pictures were nose diving. *Moon Zero Two* (1969), the big budget space opera to cash-in on the success of *2001: A Space Odyssey* (1968), had gone belly-up. Something had to be done...

Frankenstein Must Be Destroyed

Send for Peter Cushing! *Frankenstein Must Be Destroyed* (1969) is a fine pulp adventure, with Veronica Carlson getting the chance to show that she can act. The Baron is up to his old tricks, fleeing London to Altenberg, where he lodges with Anna

Spengler (Carlson). Her fiancé Dr Holst (Simon Ward) works at the local asylum, and has been stealing drugs. The Baron uses this knowledge to blackmail them and gain admittance, his old colleague Dr Brandt (now insane) is there, and the Baron wants him free.

Brandt is released, and his brain is transferred to the body of Professor Richter (Holst's superior) when Brandt dies of a heart attack. He holds a secret which the Baron desperately needs to continue his work.

Unfortunately, Brandt/Richter (played with mad aplomb by Freddie Jones) escapes Holst and goes on the rampage, visiting Brandt's wife to condemn the Baron before trapping him in a blazing inferno.

That James Carreras was losing his grip is confirmed by the rape scene where Cushing and Carlson grunt uncomfortably. Both they and director Terence Fisher were embarrassed by this inclusion and tried to get it out of the way. It does not fit the Baron's ascetic image, as despite his mistress in the first movie, he had spent subsequent films celibate, with a maniacal devotion to his work. This sudden change is even out of character with the rest of the film!

Despite this, the script is excellent, Bert Batt (a cameraman friend of Anthony Nelson Keys, who wrote the story with him) turns in a good first time job, and Fisher injects more pace than is usual. Thorley Walters and Geoffrey Bayldon are on hand as able support, and the picture moves at a lightning speed.

It was a step in the right direction, but only glossed over a few cracks.

The last 1969 horror was a psychological entry. *Crescendo* looked like a left-over Sangster script into which Alfred Shaugnessy injected some drug abuse and nudity. More "now-you-see-it-now-you-don't" dead body activity, with Stefanie Powers overacting shamelessly on drugs and showing an awful lot of flesh. Director Alan Gibson tries to keep things moving, but it all looks sadly dated. Even talent like Jane Lapotaire and Joss Ackland down in the credits cannot pull anything out for this one.

1970, the start of a new decade, and an attempt to re-tell the Frankenstein myth from the beginning. The Baron kills his father in order to get the money to go to university, where he befriends a fellow kook called Wilhelm. On their way home from Vienna, they rescue Elizabeth Weiss and her father from highwaymen. The Baron steals her father's pet tortoise, kills it, and experiments with bringing it back to life. He also has one of the highwaymen's heads locked up in his lab.

Professor Weiss is bumped off, and so is a grave robber who supplies the body for the Professor's brain and the highwayman's head. Wilhelm is electrocuted for getting frightened and wanting to pull out. The monster is activated in a burst of thunderstorm, and is sent out on killing missions. The police get onto him, and he is accidentally dissolved in acid...

Sounds a bit flat put like that, eh? Quite right, too, as the movie is extremely flat. *The Horror Of Frankenstein* has a tongue-in-cheek mordancy running through it that just does not work. Original scriptwriter Jeremy Burnham is better known for his comic work, and Jimmy Sangster, returning to Hammer after a brief period writing novels (his *Touchfeather* series, about a female spy, are wonderful spy-era spoofs and deserve digging out), was given the task of making something out of the movie. Coming in late, he took over production and direction, re-writing parts of the script.

Ralph Bates takes over as Frankenstein, the idea being to build a whole new series with him as Baron. Maybe it would have worked at another studio, but the punters wanted Cushing from Hammer, and so there was initial resistance to the idea. Bates, however, is extremely good, as is Veronica Carlson, who was improving all the time. Dennis Price makes an excellent grave robber, despite looking too pickled to be able to dig his own grave, let alone anyone else's, and Kate O'Mara makes her first Hammer appearance as a voluptuous serving wench (hey, this is Kate O'Mara – anything she does would be voluptuous). David Prowse seems to go through the film

The Horror Of Frankenstein

in an oversized diaper, being the geekiest monster of them all.

This is not a bad movie per se, it has its faults in direction and pacing, but if Freddie Francis could have directed, and Sangster had written the script from scratch, they might have succeeded in reconstituting the Baron. As it is, Cushing would return one last time...

Scars Of Dracula (1970), was also an attempt at reconstitution. In many ways it resembles the *Dracula, Prince Of Darkness* (1965). The John Elder (Anthony Hinds) script was directed by Roy Ward Baker and produced by Aida Young, and between them they attempted to keep the *Dracula* ship on a more even keel. Lee appeared more in this picture than in the last two put together, though paradoxically, there was less for him to actually do.

The plot concerns Paul Carson (Christopher Matthews), who escapes the wrath of his fiancée's father by hiding in Castle Dracula. He is almost bitten by vampire Tania (Anouska Hempel), and escapes by fleeing down the castle walls in a hair-raising scene. Once down, he finds himself trapped in Dracula's tomb.

Many years before, the villagers had set fire to Dracula's castle, and he had unleashed a swarm of bats to kill them all, especially those who took refuge in the churchyard. This has very little to do with the actual story, but is loosely tied-in as an excuse for a good effects scene and for Baker to get his teeth into Dracula (ahem). Now, there is an attempt to rationalise this as Paul's brother Simon (Dennis Waterman) and his girlfriend Sarah (Jenny Hanley – suffering the ignominy of dubbing because her voice was not "little girlie" enough) follow in search of the missing man. They escape the castle the first time only because Klove (Patrick Troughton this time) falls for Sarah, and releases them, and in some nasty scenes, he feels the wrath of Dracula with a good flogging.

Simon returns alone to find his brother impaled, and sees Dracula scale the castle walls like a fly (Baker's pride and joy, and something no Hammer Dracula had ever done before). In a fight, Dracula is impaled on a metal rod, then struck by lightning, burning to death.

A return to a more action-oriented approach, this is an entertaining movie without the subtext that makes *Taste The Blood Of Dracula* so interesting, but with more coherence than *Dracula Has Risen From The Grave*...

However, the era of Gothic was coming to an end, and with the more liberated 1970's, sex and blood needed to be writ ever larger. Hammer were useless at the sex, and the blood still looked phoney in Gothic. New avenues had to be found, and a period of floundering began.

Countess Dracula

The first fruit of this was *Countess Dracula* (1971), the first outside production handled by Hammer. Alexander Paal brought it to the company, with a story by himself and Peter Sasdy, based on research by vampire historian Gabriel Ronay. It was to be a serious picture depicting the life and times of Elizabeth Bathory, who bathed in virgins blood to keep her youth, and was responsible for atrocities galore.

With Ingrid Pitt in the lead, and the promise of historical vérité for nudity and violence, Hammer could not resist. Unfortunately, Jeremy Paul's script plodded, with little sex or violence, and Peter Sasdy suddenly went static. Nigel Greene and Sandor Eles floundered with some terrible dialogue, almost casting despairing glances at the camera, and the glorious Ingrid, despite acting her heart out, could not bring the boring Bathory to life. Frankly, on this evidence she must have bored her virgins to death rather than put them to the sword...

A complete disaster area, Hammer lurched into a deal with Fantale that fared little better. Three films were mooted; *The Vampire Lovers*, *Lust For A Vampire*, and *Vampire Virgins*. All three were to be soft-core lesbian and horror flicks, scripted by Tudor Gates, and produced by Harry Fine and Michael Style (the trio that comprised Fantale).

In Europe, the likes of Jean Rollin and Jess Franco were making this kind of movie with aplomb, but Hammer were too English and too stiff-necked to compete. Their movies turned out to be prudish, the lesbians getting their heads chopped off for their sins. Great message, eh?

Gates was a good jobbing scriptwriter, but his attempts at soft-core were appalling. Michael Carreras nixed *Vampire Virgins* as being too much of the same thing, but the other two still got made.

The Vampire Lovers (1970) has Ingrid Pitt as Carmilla, with Dawn Addams in an all-too brief bit-part as her "guardian". Carmilla travels from house to house, vamping the daughters of great families. George Cole and Peter Cushing do their best with a turgid script as the savants who must put an end to this, and Jon Finch is wasted with cardboard lines as dashing romantic lead Carl. The movie ends with Cushing lopping off Pitt's head in slow-motion – and slow-motion is what director Roy Ward Baker seems to use all the time.

The Vampire Lovers

Kate O'Mara, Madeline Smith and Pippa Steele join Ingrid in a display of flashing bosom, which redeems the film somewhat – but, let us be frank, this is all most unfair. My complaint with soft-core like this is why are there no chaps dangling their members for the delectation of the female fans, eh? An equality in nudity would have made these soft-core horrors more fun for everyone.

Lust For A Vampire (1970) aka To Love A Vampire, shifts the action to a school run by Countess Herritzen (Barbara Jefford), with Mike Raven being appallingly over-the-top as Count Karnstein, and Yutte Stensgaard as Mircalla ("but isn't that an anagram of..."). Ralph Bates is savant Giles Barton, a schoolmaster that was originally to have been played by Peter Cushing (who dropped out because of his wife's illness). Bates acquits himself well, and director Jimmy Sangster keeps enough tongue in cheek to overcome the fact that Stensgaard is no Ingrid Pitt – at least Ingrid could act. Stensgaard is now a born again Christian, and refuses to discuss these movies – can you honestly blame her?

As if that was not bad enough, editing was taken out of Sangster's hands by Harry Fine and Michael Style, and this included the dubbing of a terrible song by someone called Tracy, which was totally out of place in a Gothic milieu. Sangster recalls seeing the movie with Bates in a Hammersmith cinema, and both men slinking out when the song began to blare over an incongruous scene.

Failing with *Vampire Virgins*, and *Vampire Hunters* (another un-optioned project), Fantale tried to double their money with *Twins Of Evil* (1971) aka *The Gemini Twins* aka *Virgin Vampires* aka *Twins Of Dracula*, moving slightly away from Carmilla and starring Maria and Madeleine Collinson, identical twins who had been Playboy centrefolds. Director John Hough had to cope with the fact that neither could act, but

Lust For A Vampire

with the help of talent like Peter Cushing, Dennis Price, and David Warbeck he was able to work round them.

Maria and Freida Gelhorn are orphaned and sent to live with their puritanical uncle Gustav Weill in the village of Karnstein (Gates just cannot get away from that completely, can he?). There they are treated with a rod of iron, and when libertine Count Karnstein argues openly with Weill (leader of a witch-hunting sect called The Brotherhood), Freida is fascinated. She slips away from her good sister to join the Count, and becomes his lover. Unfortunately for her, he has resurrected the spirit of his ancestor Mircalla who has turned him into a vampire.

Now the fun starts, as Freida gets naughty with members of The Brotherhood and starts biting a few necks, all the while blaming it on innocent and stupid Maria. When Freida is arrested, Karnstein switches her for Maria. Only Anton Hoffer (David

Twins Of Evil

Warbeck) knows what is going on, and he persuades The Brotherhood to invade the Castle Karnstein, where he impales the vampire Count, proving Maria's innocence.

There is actually a good subtext to this film about fanaticism of any hue, as Cushing's Gustav is a blinkered fanatic who is cruel in his own home, and harbours barely suppressed desires for his nieces. His wife (the sadly underused Kathleen Byron) is a drudge, and he lives a pathetically joyless life that pushes fun-loving Freida into the hands of the Count.

More interesting on any level that their two soft-core efforts, this showed that Fantale could produce a decent movie if they tried.

Shot partly on sets for *Twins Of Evil*, *Vampire Circus* (1971) was another step in the right direction. Tightly paced by director Robert Young (who later forged a TV drama career) and written with genuine affection by Judson Kinberg, this movie centres around the village of Schtettel. Fifteen years after the villagers staked vampire Count Mitterhaus, the Circus Of Nights comes to the village.

Cut off by a mysterious plague, there are many deaths, and Dr Kersh (Richard Owens) and his son Anton (John Moulder Brown) investigate. They soon find that the Circus is led by Emil (Anthony Corlan), a descendant of the Count, and that the Circus itself is full of shape-shifting vampires who are out for revenge, carrying the plague with them via a collection of rabid bats.

The finale takes place in the crypt of the Castle (of course) where the vampires are staked, and the revived Mitterhaus is decapitated by a crossbow wielded like a crucifix – his head being taken off by the string of the bow.

The movie suffered at the box-office because of a lack of recognisable names. Adrienne Corri and Thorley Walters both turn in good performances, but they are hardly horror stars...

All these vampires were beginning to get monotonous, but Hammer did have other ideas. A nice line in psychological Gothic was evolved then left to wither with *Hands Of The Ripper* (1971) and *Demons Of The Mind* (1972).

Hands Of The Ripper was written by L W Davidson, from an Edward Spencer Shew story, and produced by Aida Young. Peter Sasdy was in the director's chair, and atoned for his appalling *Countess Dracula* with a much pacier handling of this story.

Dr Pritchard and Member of Parliament Dysart (Eric Porter and Derek Godfrey) are attending a séance held by Mrs Golding (the wonderful Dora Bryan). It is a fake, and the voices of spirits are supplied by Anna (Angharad Rees), an orphan that Golding has in her charge. In a prologue, the viewer has seen Anna's father, Jack The Ripper, return from a killing spree and murder her mother. The flashing of bright objects becomes associated with murder.

When Dysart pays Golding for the pleasure of Anna, he is shocked by her change of character when she catches sight of his flashing watch chain. When Mrs Golding tries to pacify her, and touches her, Anna impales her to the bedroom door with a poker.

Dysart is in trouble and turns to Pritchard for help. Although the men dislike each other, Pritchard is fascinated by the girl, and takes her into his home. His son Michael (Keith Bell) introduces her to his blind fiancée Laura (Jane Merrow), who offers to help her adjust to her new life. Unfortunately, things start to go wrong, and a maid has her jugular severed in the bath, and the Queen's favourite medium is stabbed when Anna is taken to see her. She also stabs prostitute Long Liz (a great cameo from Lynda Baron) when she tries to make love to her. Pritchard is reduced to rapidly hiding bodies and covering up for Anna while he tries to get to the root of her problem. There is a potential for black humour here which is never exploited to the full, though perhaps this is as well, as it may have detracted from the films other assets.

At the climax of the picture, Anna stabs Pritchard (who has fallen in love with

Vampire Circus

her) and takes Laura to the whispering gallery at St Pauls Cathedral in London. Possessed by the spirit of her father – either supernaturally or psychologically – she intends to kill the girl. Mustering his strength, and bleeding profusely, Pritchard follows, and begs Anna to spare Laura from the floor of the Cathedral.

Demons Of The Mind

Laura is confused by hearing the voice of the Ripper (leaving the supernatural element nicely open), and is spared when Anna plunges to her death, landing on the dying Pritchard. Flawed, and so close to the fag end of Gothic that it could almost be a parody, this is nonetheless a film well worth watching.

None of these faults are shared by *Demons Of The Mind* (1971) aka *Blood Will*

Have Blood, where Peter Sykes handles Chris Wicking's excellent screenplay with aplomb. Wicking really was one of the best horror movie writers of this period, and this is one of his best efforts.

Elizabeth Zorn escapes from her Aunt Hilda whilst on her way home from Vienna, where she has been a patient of the psychoanalyst Falkenburg. She takes refuge with student Richter, but is recaptured and returned to the family home, where her loopy father, Baron Zorn, keeps the entire family prisoner, believing them to be victims of hereditary insanity. She has a brother, Emil.

Falkenberg travels to the home, in order to continue his research. Hypnotising the Baron, he realises that the children are sane, but the sadistic Baron is tortured by his past ill-treatment of his wife, which led to her suicide in front of the children. There are a series of murders taking place in the nearby village, where young girls are strangled and their corpses covered in rose petals. Emil is committing these, under the influence of his father.

Falkenberg takes a chance, and re-enacts the suicide using a serving girl called Inge, dressed in the dead wife's clothes. Coming so soon after Richter has arrived to take Elizabeth away, it is all too much, and Emil kills Inge, and runs off to the woods with his sister. The Baron shoots Falkenberg, and follows them. Meanwhile, the outraged villagers follow, and stake the Baron with a burning cross. Emil is shot, and Richter saves Elizabeth.

Breathless, with excellent exposition of early psychoanalytic techniques, this is one of the best horrors of the period because it manages to be both thrilling and thought-provoking at the same time. Harry Robinson's score is suitably schizophrenic, and is the best of the many scores he composed for the company during this period. Sykes has a great eye and excellent pacing, and the actors are superb. Patrick Magee is a sinister Falkenberg, Robert Hardy a palpably barmy Baron, and Gillian Hills a vulnerable Elizabeth. Shane Briant is superb as Emil, and went on to other Hammer movies.

Lower down the cast list is British character actor Kenneth J Warren, Michael Hordern as a priest, and singer/actor Paul Jones as Richter. Inge was played by Virginia Wetherell, who was really more at home in Tigon tat...

Chris Wicking also wrote the script for *Blood From The Mummy's Tomb* (1971), an adaption of Bram Stoker's novel *Jewel Of The Seven Stars* that was ill-fated – director Seth Holt died from a heart attack during shooting, replaced by Michael Carreras, and Peter Cushing had to pull out after filming a few scenes due to the death of his wife. Andrew Keir replaced him as the archaeologist Fuchs, who opens the tomb of Egyptian Queen Tera, to find her body perfectly preserved. Influenced by the dead Queen, he orders her relics to be shipped to England. His wife dies giving birth to their daughter Margaret at the exact moment he enters the tomb.

Margaret is given Tera's ring on her twenty-first birthday, and the spirit of the dead queen takes her over, preparing for her return to life. Margaret spurns her boyfriend Tod Browning (surely an in-joke referring to the vintage horror director?), who then dies in a mysterious crash. She befriends the sinister Corbeck, a member of her father's Egyptian expedition who has the scroll of life in his possession. One by one the party members die, until only Corbeck and Fuchs are left.

Fuchs stops the ceremony to revive Tera, starting a fire and mutilating his daughter, and she loses the same hand that was severed from Tera centuries before.

There is one survivor of the fire, a dark-eyed girl swathed in bandages...is it Margaret or Tera?

The actors are uniformly excellent (although Mark Edwards as Browning is a little bland). Keir has an authority as Fuchs that belies the circumstances in which he was hired, while James Villiers is a wonderfully slimy Corbeck. Hugh Burden, Aubrey Morris, Rosalie Crutchley and George Colouris are all good, but the stand-out is Valerie

Leon as Margaret/Tera. A statuesque beauty of unusual handsomeness, Leon was an early 1970's icon in TV advertising and bit part acting. This was one of the few opportunities she was given to shine, and she made the most of it.

The last two films from Hammer in 1971 both sprang from the fertile mind of Brian Clemens, and were produced by Clemens and long-time collaborator Albert Fennell.

Dr Jekyll And Sister Hyde (1971) was the result of a lunch-time joke: but Clemens, the man behind the wackier exploits of television series *The Avengers*, went away and thought about it before coming up with a script where Henry Jekyll (Ralph Bates) discovers that the secret of longevity lies in female hormones, when a long-lived fruit fly is found to have changed sex. Experimenting on himself, Jekyll turns into a beautiful woman (Martine Beswick). Disgusted but fascinated, he continues to experiment on himself and also on corpses supplied by Burke and Hare (who obviously fled Edinburgh in a hurry). When they are caught by a mob, Burke (Ivor Dean) is hanged and Hare (Tony Calvin) is blinded by being thrown into a lime pit.

Jekyll is conducting an affair with Susan Spencer, the girl upstairs – and Hyde is having a fling with her brother (Lewis Fiander, on his way to Italian horror epics). Meanwhile, in order to get experimental subjects Hyde is luring prostitutes into dark corners and carving them up, thus leading to the stories of Jack The Ripper...

Clemens throws everything gleefully into the plot bar the kitchen sink, and Jekyll is discovered when Hyde escapes the scene of a crime and the blind Hare recognises the footsteps as Jekyll's. Colleague Professor Robertson (Gerald Sim) has suspected something for a long while, and the police come to him for assistance.

Jekyll is forced to escape over the rooftops, but changes into Hyde, who has not the strength to support herself, plunging to her death. In repose, the face of Jekyll/Hyde is a mixture of their characteristics.

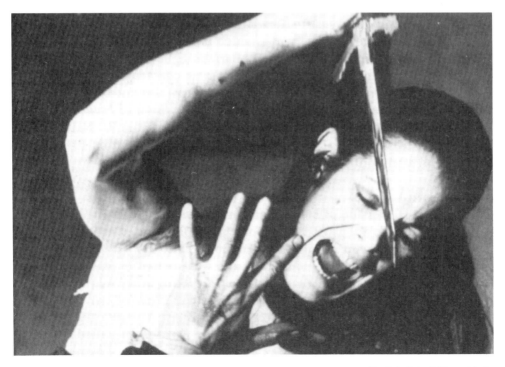

Dr Jekyll And Sister Hyde

With more of a knowing wink than a tongue in cheek, this is a romp that is more thrilling than chilling, and tremendous fun. The resemblance between Beswick and Bates is uncanny (and accidental – Martine was not first choice for the role), and both play their roles with relish. Director Roy Ward Baker creates a good atmosphere on fog-shrouded sets, and this is a bit of a late-flowering Hammer triumph.

I wish the same could be said for *Captain Kronos – Vampire Hunter* (1973) aka *Kronos* aka *Vampire Castle* aka *Captain Kronus, Vampire Hunter*, Clemens' other brainchild, which he also directed. However, it is too deeply flawed to be a success, though its not without fun moments. Basically the pilot for a feature series, it attempts to re-invent *The Avengers* in a Gothic context, with ace swordsman and vampire hunter Kronos as Steed, assistant Carla as Mrs Peel/Cathy Gale (but more like Tara King, actually), and hunchback Professor Hieronymous Grost as Mother. This would work if the plot had been strong enough for ninety minutes, but it is better suited to an hour series format.

Captain Kronos – Vampire Hunter

The team travel to a village where several girls have been killed by vampires. The local doctor (ably played by John Carson) has also been infected, and Kronos kills him with a cross. As his reward, the idiot peasants attempt to kill Kronos.

Our intrepid hero knows that the Durward estate is behind this. Paul and Sara Durward (Shane Briant and Lois Daine) live there with their aged mother (Wanda Ventham). Kronos is suspicious, and uses Carla as bait to draw out the vampire – who turns out to be none other than Lady Durward, who is not so old and ill as she pretends. After a lot of sword play, Kronos despatches the vampires.

Caroline Munro is not given much to do as Carla except look sultry, and she manages this with ease. John Cater is also quirkily eccentric as Grost, with a fine supporting performance from Ian Hendry as Kerro. The big problem is Horst Janson as Kronos, as he just does not have the charisma – despite his blonde good looks – to carry off the leading role, and Clemens seems unable to draw a good performance from him.

A film that is good in parts, it splutters to a halt after sixty minutes only to revive in the last ten. A noble failure.

Shane Briant was back in the Hammer studios the next year, in one of two psychological terrors that finished the irregular series. Along with this, there was a disastrous attempt to update Dracula. 1972 was not a good year for Hammer horror, although paradoxically they began to be the biggest success in British films with their weak-kneed TV sit-com spin-offs. This confusion could account for the fact that only seven more horror movies were made before they temporarily folded, only one of which could be classed as a classic.

Shane Briant was the only good thing about *Straight On Till Morning* (1972), which was written by Michael Peacock from his stage play. It was satisfactorily opened out, but lost all sense of tension and suspense in the meantime. Rita Tushingham plays Brenda, who leaves her Liverpool home and travels to London in order to find someone to make her pregnant(!). At the same time, Peter (Briant) is calmly murdering his tawdry and ageing girlfriend (a brief flash of inspiration from Annie Ross).

Once in London, Brenda gets a job at a terrible clothes shop run by Tom Bell, and lodges with his girlfriend (Katya Wyeth). She works in the back room with James Bolam, in the same year that he made *Crucible Of Terror* (1971), and before his career re-started, Bolam shows little of his true quality as he sleep walks through the film.

Actually, that is a fair reflection of all the performances bar Briant's, and the brief appearance of both Ross and Claire Kelly (who plays Brenda's worried mother in the first and last five minutes). Director Peter Collinson opts for a cinema vérité approach, and when I first read reviews slagging this movie for that very reason, I wondered...it seemed like a good idea to try something different in a film of this type.

Unfortunately, I then got to see the movie, and knew that every other reviewer was right. The kitchen sink approach sucks in this context, making the film devoid of tension and atmosphere. Brenda goes to live with Peter, and calls herself Wendy. Ross' dog is called Tinker, so you have a vague Peter Pan analogy set up that goes nowhere...then Peter kills the dog, and Wyeth when she comes looking for Brenda.

In essence, this is more a thriller like *Deadly Strangers* (1974) than a horror film. This film scripted by Philip Levene, covers similar territory to *And Soon The Darkness* (1970). But whereas Brian Clemens uses the story of a psychopath threatening women as a hook for suspense and horror, Levene takes a different tack and pursues the thriller element. In *Straight On Till Morning*, Collinson and Peacock seem to be pulling in opposite directions, with the result that nothing gets achieved. In the end, Peter plays Brenda the tape recording of him killing Tinker, and she breaks down, trying to escape the house. The final, bungled shot shows Peter alone in the house. Did Brenda escape? Is she dead?

Who cares...

Straight On Till Morning was released by Michael Carreras on a double bill with *Fear In The Night* (1972), the other psychological horror. Although contrived, it was much more the sort of thing the viewer wanted...Produced, directed and written by Jimmy Sangster, he took an old script called *The Claw*, written in the mid-1960's and unfilmed, and changed the location from a houseboat to a school in the middle of nowhere.

Judy Geeson is married to Ralph Bates, and is recovering from a nervous breakdown. When he gets a job as assistant master at a private school in the country, she is pleased, especially as she is being followed and has been attacked by a man with an artificial arm.

Because of her medical history, Bates does not really believe her, and does not call the police. They go to the school, and Geeson finds it hard to understand why there are so few pupils...well, none actually. Then she notices that the headmaster (Peter Cushing) has an artificial arm. His wife (Joan Collins – shamelessly overdoing it, but still poutingly good) shoots wildlife too near to Geeson for comfort, and the attacks begin again.

It is revealed to the viewer that Bates is actually nurse to Cushing, who is recovering from a nervous breakdown himself, following a fire at the school some five years before. Bates and Collins are lovers, and want to kill Geeson, fake Cushing's suicide, and run off together. They think they have killed Cushing when the school bell goes...

In a confused and too-fast ending, Geeson is the only one left alive, carrying a shotgun and mute with shock when the police arrive. As she is led away, there is the sound of boys singing coming from the old school.

This complex plot is more of the same from Sangster in many ways – but face it, who did it better? Fast, thrilling, genuinely shocking in some moments, this was the perfect counterpoint to Collinson's dull movie, and a master showing how it should be done.

They may have needed him on *Dracula AD 1972* (1972 would you believe?) aka *Dracula Chelsea 72* aka *Dracula Chases The Mini Girls* aka *Dracula Today*, which attempted to bring Dracula into the twentieth century. Director Alan Gibson did a fairly good job with Don Houghton's dodgy script, as the Count (buried just outside a London churchyard after a nineteenth century prologue) is revived by modern day follower Johnny Alucard ("But isn't that a backward spelling of..."), played by Christopher Neame. Alucard is the leader of a group of (overage) teens that includes Jessica Van Helsing (Stephanie Beacham), the granddaughter of Peter Cushing's Lorrimer Van Helsing, occult expert, anthropologist and descendent of you-know-who.

Dracula AD 1972

A desperate attempt to both ride the death of Gothic and cash in on the success of AIP's *Count Yorga Vampire* (1970) and *The Return Of Count Yorga* (1971) movies, which were contemporary vampire movies with Robert Quarry as the testy Count; this has none of the latter two movies' humour. In a ridiculous party scene, the San Francisco band Stoneground get to play a couple of numbers, and it is somehow very Hammer to pick the worst of the San Francisco bands for their hip movie.

Neame's Alucard becomes Dracula's slave and is vamped. He then has to get food and Jessica – in that order – for the Count. The baffled police call in Van Helsing after a few murders, and he runs Neame to earth and kills him with a reflection of daylight and pure running water from a shower (come on...have you tasted London tap water?).

Jessica is under the Count's power, and he wants to take her for his bride and kill Van Helsing at the same time. He has already had Marsha Hunt (terrible performance) and Caroline Munro (not much for her here, either), so why not Jessica?

The climactic fight is well-staged, and Dracula plunges into a pit of stakes to die writhing, but really it is not too impressive. Fun in a "look at those flares!" way, and not too bad if you check in your brain before watching, it was hardly the future.

Gibson and Houghton were given another chance the next year, with *The Satanic Rites Of Dracula* (1973, US title *Count Dracula And His Vampire Bride*), aka *Dracula Is Dead...And Well And Living In London*. If Lee had little enough to do in *Dracula AD 1972*, being barely in the picture, here he was reduced to sitting in shadows and talking with a dreadful fake "mittel European" accent before having a 5-minute fling in his cape at the end.

A dying spy gives his boss (William Franklyn) film of businessmen and scientists attending a secret meeting. The last shot is blank, yet a man came out of the door...Inspector Murray (Michael Coles in another good performance reprising his *Dracula AD 1972* role) consults Lorrimer Van Helsing, who recognises his old colleague Julian Keeley in the photographs. Keeley (Freddie Jones) is developing a new strain of bacteria, and is depressed when Van Helsing visits him. Next thing you know, he is dead.

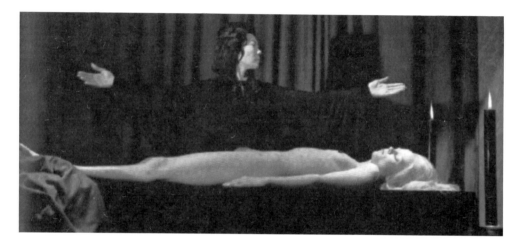

The Satanic Rites Of Dracula

Jessica (this time the much better Joanna Lumley) is getting in the way a lot, and ends up in a cellar full of vampires in a house owned by businessman D D Denham. Only the sprinkler system and psychedelic filters on the camera prevent her being vamped. Van Helsing, meanwhile, has traced Denham's office to a building erected over the spot where Dracula met his end in the last movie.

Surely some coincidence? No, for Denham is none other than Dracula, using the businessmen and scientists to create a super-weapon. While they believe they are worshipping Satan and are about to receive great power, the Count is plotting the end of mankind and thus his own death.

A pretty major death wish, and in the climax, Van Helsing and the Count fight, with the bacteria being loosed on Patrick Barr's Lord Carradine, one of the worshippers, then consumed in fire. The Count gets his when he is entangled in a hawthorn edge.

Without Lee, this would have been an updated Dennis Wheatley, or an episode of an ITC action series with added horror. As it is, the *Dracula* mythos sits uneasily. I like the movie, but can see why it flopped – in the US it was unreleased for several years before gaining the generic title *Count Dracula And His Vampire Bride*. It was no the answer, and coming in the same year as *The Exorcist* (1973), it was virtually the end for Hammer. They were out of time, and did not have the resources to compete with bigger US studios.

The last gasp was *Frankenstein And The Monster From Hell* (1973) with Cushing's last appearance as the Baron, Terence Fisher's last movie, and a John Elder script. Shane Briant (once again excellent) is Simon Helder, flung into Carlsbad Asylum for using corpses in his experiments. He knows that Frankenstein died in the asylum some years before, but the director is secretive about details. Not surprising, as the asylum is effectively run by the Baron under the name Dr Victor. He is still conducting experiments, and Simon is all too keen to assist.

The Baron is unable to use his hands to operate since an accident, and Simon helps him bring his creature to life. The Baron has an idea to mate the creature (David Prowse under a ridiculous but pretty repulsive make-up) with his other assistant Angel (Madeleine Smith). The other inmates, however, have other ideas and rip the creature to pieces. The last shots are of the Baron pottering around his cell, muttering and sweeping up, quite barmy.

With James Bernard on board to score the picture, it was a fitting end for the Baron. Cushing is as committed as ever (despite an awful bouffant wig), and Fisher stumbles on the talkier scenes but handles character well. Elder's script reduces the Baron, for all his noble ideals, to the level of a failed butcher, the natural conclusion to a series in which his experiments got more and more outlandish.

At least Frankenstein got a last movie that fitted the continuity. Not so poor old Dracula...

James Carreras sold the company. Michael, unwilling to see it fall into outside hands, bought it. But he was never in tune with Gothic, and made some bad calls about bringing it up to date. Amidst unfulfilled projects (a film about the Loch Ness Monster, and one on Vlad Tepes) and disastrous attempts at going outside the genre such as *The Lady Vanishes* (1979, after which the company went bankrupt), there were two horror movies left.

Ironically, neither was really Hammer. They were attempts to copy other countries' styles, although one did turn out to be a genuine classic. It is also ironic that the two TV series Hammer turned out over the next fifteen years had more in common with Brian Clemens' *Thriller* series, and traditional British suspense and ghost stories, than the bloody product that had made the Hammer name.

That is all Hammer was: a name. Carreras had no real understanding of what made the company's product tick, although he is to be admired for trying to find a way out of their financial mess – by the mid-1970's, the TV spin-off racket that had kept them afloat was also a dying form.

Carreras admired the Shaw Brothers of Hong Kong, makers of exploitation *Kung-Fu* movies. So he agreed a co-production deal for two movies. One was the execrable *Shatter* (1974, US title *Call Him Mr Shatter*), a terrible thriller, and the other was *The Legend Of The Seven Golden Vampires* (1974, US title *The Seven Brothers Meet Dracula*), aka *Dracula And The Seven Golden Vampires*, which would pit Dracula against the martial arts.

Don Houghton wrote the script and co-produced with Vee King Shaw, who gave director Roy Ward Baker headaches by having non-soundproofed sound stages and a local crew ready to direct the martial arts sequences for later insertion. If this was not enough, Christopher Lee refused the role of Dracula, so bit-part actor John Forbes-Robertson made a brief appearance as the Count (in green face make-up!) before changing into the form of Kah, oriental disciple of the vampire.

Van Helsing is delivering a lecture in 1904 at Chungking. Scoffed at by the locals for his belief in Dracula, he is confronted by Hsi Chiang (David Chiang – the

Frankenstein And The Monster From Hell

Shaw's answer to Bruce Lee), who wants him to help destroy the vampires that are decimating his village. Van Helsing refuses, but relents after Hsi and his brothers and sister save Leyland Van Helsing – Robin Stewart, fresh from sit-coms but a horror veteran after *The Haunted House Of Horror* (1969) – and Vanessa Beren (a rich widow played by the awful Julie Ege) from the local Tongs.

The vampires wear golden masks, and have desiccated faces. They also keep semi-naked virgins chained up around a pit of boiling blood. There are some neat schlock horror sets in this, and despite the lack of plot there are some great action scenes before Van Helsing despatches Dracula.

Not a thoughtful or well-written movie, it nonetheless has a lot of action, and Cushing is excellent as always. He and Chiang work well together, and the Hong Kong actor shines. Robin Stewart also puts in a good performance, despite having little to do. Roy Ward Baker keeps it all moving so quickly you do not have time to notice the holes in the script or the budget. Nothing much to do with Hammer or British horror,

Legend Of The Seven Golden Vampires

it is nonetheless as much fun as a Jackie Chan movie, and well worth a look.

There were other Dracula ventures mooted, but without Lee there was little response, and the fact that this movie was not released in the US until 1979 killed off any further revivals.

And that seemed to be that for Hammer...except for one last throw of the dice, and a genuine classic. Christopher Lee's Charlemagne Productions had optioned Dennis Wheatley's *To The Devil... A Daughter* some years before, and this option had been sold to Hammer, but nothing was done until 1976 when producer Roy Skeggs put writer Chris Wicking and director Peter Sykes to work. The result was an excellent movie that managed to out-do *The Exorcist* for thrills despite the low budget. Poor US distribution may have killed its commercial chances, but it was a fine way for Hammer horror to end.

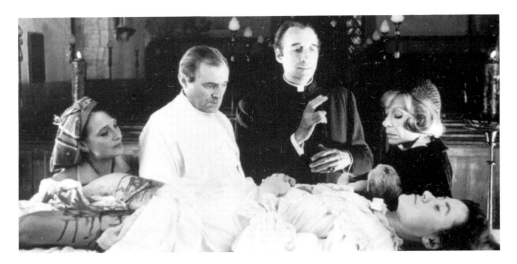

To The Devil... A Daughter

Henry Beddows (Denholm Elliott) approaches occult novelist John Verney (Richard Widmark – not a horror name, but turning in a great performance), asking him to look after his daughter Catherine (a young Nastassia Kinski) when she arrives in London from her Bavarian school. She is under the control of a group of Satanists run by excommunicated priest Father Michael (Lee), and has been chosen to become the incarnation of the dark god Astaroth. Verney enlists the help of his agent Anna (Honor Blackman) and her partner David (Anthony Valentine). Father Michael tries to kill Verney magically but only gets David (in a ball of fire – nice effect). Meanwhile, Verney is investigating the methods of the cult with the help of the Bishop who excommunicated Father Michael (a nice cameo from Derek Francis).

The climax occurs in an old church, where Catherine is to be baptised and transmuted into Astaroth. In the magic circle, Michael directs Catherine to kill Verney, but it is turned back against him, destroying him and freeing the girl.

A good, solid pulp plot (Wheatley's strength) enhanced by the literate Wicking script, and given an imaginative eye by Sykes, this has pacing, chills, and an excitement that Hammer had not seen for many a year. All the performances are excellent, with Lee committed to a project he loves and Widmark stretching himself in a new genre.

A little gem of a film, it may have been the final Hammer horror, but what a way to go!

10.   Initial Problems: IA & AA

The 1960's were another "up" in the boom/bust cycle for the British Cinema. The 1960's were an artificial boom for many branches of the entertainment industry, but for cinema it was the last great gasp.

The American studios, intent on keeping a hold on the money machine they had grasped for so long, developed the concept of the blockbuster. This usually meant that a whole lot of stars were brought together in a big budget spectacular, and the production credit was shared between the studio and the entrepreneur who kept the whole show on the road. In the early 1960's, with the likes of *Lawrence Of Arabia* (1962) and *Doctor Zhivago* (1965), this kept audiences pouring into the cinemas. Later in the decade, when the Beatles had made London and England swing, and the British pop machine was beating all-comers in the American charts, the major US studios all established London offices, and went into production in the UK.

This very rarely led to horror movie production, but it did have an effect on the amount of horror movies produced in Britain. With the move towards blockbusters, costing vast amounts of money, more people were drawn to the cinemas, but there was less product for them to see. The majors scaled down A-movie production, and the B-picture all but disappeared, replaced by a new wave of independent production.

Cinema-going became a habit, and there was less product for people to see. In the States, the rise of the drive-in led to a demand for cheap pictures.

Companies like AIP had it sewn up in America (in fact, AIP were the only American independent to establish a London office, working with Tigon and Amicus on pictures, as well sole productions), but there was still a gap, so enter the Brits.

Late night Saturday shows for the teenagers here, and drive-ins in the States (drive-ins always failed in the UK; mainly because of the appalling British weather, and partly – I like to think – because of British shyness, snogging in a darkened cinema is more discrete than at a drive-in), brought a demand for the type of cheap picture turn-over that the majors could no longer produce.

Hammer and Amicus made big money Stateside, and also went into the black in the UK (something almost unheard of pre-1950's for horror). A whole lot of other British independents followed suit – as, indeed, did the Italians and Germans, and roving producers like Harry Alan Towers (of whom a little more later).

Two of those UK indies were Anglo-Amalgamated and Independent Artists. Between them, they produced some of the most intriguing low-budget British horror of the 1960's.

Nat Cohen and Stuart Levy of Anglo have already been mentioned. Their first foray into the world of the supernatural as producers was Vernon Sewell's *The Ghost Ship* (1952), already discussed in a previous chapter. The picture made a little money, but it was too early in the 1950's for horror to really pay, so it was seven years before they approached the genre again. But when they did, it was to make one of the most controversial films of 1959.

Peeping Tom is simply one of the best suspense movies made about a psycho-path, better than *Psycho* (1960) with Norman Bates, and better than anything that came after. Ironically, it is not the writing or direction that give it the edge: Hitchcock and Powell are equally matched in skill and distinctive style, while Joseph Stefano adapts Robert Bloch well, and Leo Marks turns in a taut script for *Peeping Tom*. What gives Powell's movie the edge is simply that it is in glorious Eastmancolor. *Psycho* was in black and white because Hitchcock could not get the budget for colour, so convinced were its producers of the film's probable failure.

As must be obvious by now, I have a love of black and white movies, but even so the vibrant colour of *Peeping Tom* with art direction that pushes everything into a kaleidoscopic riot of colours, gives the viewer the eyes of Mark, the central character. Eyes that look out on a world that is larger than life, and bursting at the edges with hidden colours so bright as to be painful, and a brightness that his drab little soul is too frightened to enter. Powell used colour to brilliant effect in earlier movies like *A Matter Of Life And Death* (1946, US title *Stairway To Heaven*), and – particularly – *The Red Shoes* (1948), where the vibrant use of red in the ballet contrasted with the smeared blood on the legs of the suicidal ballerina at the finish.

In this film, the urgent washes of colour, relieved only when Mark retreats into the dark and black of his own room, are like a constant assault on the eyes, reflecting the constant assault of everyday life on Mark's fragile persona.

Mark (played with admirable restraint for a man on the edge of breakdown by Carl Boehm) is a stills photographer at a film studio, where he is known as a quiet man. He lodges in a large house with Anna Massey and her mother, played by Maxine Audley. Anna is a young teacher and writer of children's books, who wants Mark to take photographs for her, to illustrate her books. She has an ulterior motive, as she has fallen for Mark, and wants to draw him into a relationship.

This can never be, as Mark is incapable of relationships. In a coldly terrifying scene towards the end of the film, he tells her about his life. His father was an anthropologist who used his own son as a subject for study. Mark shows her some of the films of his childhood. In one, he is woken in the middle of the night, a torch shone into his eyes until he starts to cry. The object? A study of human fear. There are thousands of photographs of Mark, but not one with his father. Daddy spent his whole life with a camera, taking pictures of his son for later study.

The result of this is that Mark, also, is never without a camera. The heavy bag of camera equipment is always hanging from his shoulder, or within easy reach. On the one occasion when Massey tempts him out to dinner, and persuades him to leave the camera behind, he spends the whole evening in a state of barely disguised anxiety.

Anxiety barely disguised is actually the way that he spends most of his life, for Mark has suppressed sexual desires, and the only way he can relieve them is to kill – and in a way that mirrors his own experiences.

There are actually few murders in the film; the first is that of Shirley Anne Field, in an early role, as a bit-part actress at the studio where Mark works. He offers to take some photographs of her, for her portfolio... as she cavorts to loud pop music, Mark becomes more and more excited, until the only way to satiate his desires is to move in for the kill.

Mark's camera is a large, unwieldy affair on a tripod. Mark lifts the camera to close in for a close-up, lifting the tripod legs to a ninety degree angle, at the same time sliding a razor sharp bayonet from the bottom of one of the legs. With this, he pierces his victim in the throat, the light reflector on the camera showing her a reflection of her own fear as she dies – photographed in the death throes, of course.

Mark is caught at the end of the film by the police, just as he is about to close in on Anna Massey. This is his terrible dilemma, on the one hand, his desires need satiating, and he is stained by the murders he has already committed; on the other, he knows that Anna is offering him a chance to find out what a normal relationship would be like.

Perhaps, in the hands of a lesser film-maker, he would take this chance, and she would love him until he is hung for his crimes (this was pre-abolition of capital punishment). Not exactly a happy ending, but still close enough. Powell is unflinching throughout, pushed towards the edge, Mark moves towards Anna with the tripod up. She sees her face reflected – the only time in the film we have the victim's eye view,

Peeping Tom

and all the more chilling for that.

As the police close in, hammering at the door, Mark takes the camera away from her, and runs the bayonet through his own neck. What does this mean? Is it that Mark has decided to kill himself rather than the only woman for whom he has ever felt anything approaching love (his mother is conspicuous by her absence in the old films and photographs, a mere cipher for his father to gain an experimental subject)? Or is that he cannot face arrest, and decides to kill himself with the biggest sexual thrill of all, impaled, with his own fearful face reflected in the camera? Powell leaves it up to the viewer to decide.

The film is low key, with little in the way of sensational elements. Yet despite this, it nearly finished Powell's career. Condemned at the time as immoral and disgusting, the work of a pervert, it is now recognised for what it is; one of the first attempts to portray a psychosis on screen without recourse to melodrama.

As the film is about cameras, Powell uses his skills freely. One of the most chilling moments in the film is also one of the most incongruous. Following a prostitute he has importuned back to her flat, Mark uses his movie camera (sometimes stills, sometimes movies – as long as he records their death, he is happy) to film her climbing the stairs, the camera tight on her wiggling bottom. Then it pans to catch full in the face an old woman who is passing them on the stairs. She stares into the lens, and her expression seems to eat right though to the soul, and it is almost as if she knows what he is thinking.

Images are very important to Mark. It is notable that the one woman of whom he is outwardly scared, and in whose presence he finds it impossible to disguise his disquiet, is Maxine Audley, as Anna Massey's mother. She is blind, and so can detect things in his voice that are hidden by his demeanour, a demeanour that means nothing to her. She is also the only woman he cannot kill. He attempts to, but cannot bring himself as she shows no visible fear. Unable to see herself in the reflector, she cannot give him the fear on which his passions thrive.

Inadvertently, *Peeping Tom* also helped the boom in Britain's skin flick industry, as model Pamela Green has a small part in this film. Britain's answer to Betty Page, Green was at this time living with Harrison Marks, a photographer and film-maker who hung around the set, picking up tips from photographer Otto Heller.

Following this, Marks set up the most successful skin-flick business in the UK, utilising techniques learnt from Heller.

Anglo's next horror flick, in 1960, teamed them with Independent Artists for a grand guignol feast called *Circus Of Horrors*.

Independent Artists was formed in 1958 by Leslie Parkyn and Julian Wintle, producers who had been working in movies since the end of the war. Wintle was born in 1913, and Parkyn's birth date was never revealed. Some would say that this was not important, but in some ways it was. The elder statesmen of Hammer were exceptional in their desire to put blood and sex on the screen for profit. Those that followed whole-heartedly in their footsteps were either Americans domiciled in the UK (like Milton Subotsky and Max Rosenberg of Amicus), or younger (like Tony Tenser of Compton and Tigon, and later producers like Anthony Balch and Peter Walker). Men like Wintle and Parkyn, like Baker and Berman, were of a generation who were wary of blood and sex on screen. For too long had they battled the censor and the tail end of the quota and block-booking systems. Thus, their pictures tended to be more diverse in nature, and dipped toes into blood and sex rather than plunging in wholeheartedly.

Wintle and Parkyn's Independent Artists, like Anglo, made a wide variety of films. Some of their best remembered are Lindsay Anderson's dour debut *This Sporting Life* (1963), and breezy comedies like *The Fast Lady* (1963) and *Father Came Too* (1964), the latter two both starring Stanley Baxter and James Robertson Justice. They were also involved with the series of TV/B-picture thrillers turned out by Merton Park under the series title of *Edgar Wallace*. Using a bust of the pulp author as their logo, the movies were all tight B thrillers that had little or nothing to do with original Wallace stories.

Wintle is perhaps best remembered now as executive producer on *The Avengers*, the cult TV series that is, in many ways, the ultimate 1960's show. This carried many of the fantastic and occasionally horrific moments that Wintle brought to the few fantastic films that IA produced.

A gory and insane plot informs the whole of *Circus Of Horrors*. Written by George Baxt, who was also responsible for Amicus' *City Of The Dead* (US title *Horror Hotel*), the same year, and co-wrote IA's *Night Of The Eagle* (US title *Burn, Witch, Burn*), in 1961. It concerns the exploits of a plastic surgeon who has to flee his practice after a dreadful accident. He changes his identity and buys a derelict and run-down circus, where he acts as ringmaster. However, this sudden change of career is not prompted purely by a need to get away from things...

The surgeon has scores to settle, and intends to do this using a group of criminals who have been enticed to the circus with the promise of a change of face. Once there, they find that they are trapped, and heaven help any who try to get away.

The surgeon is played with cold aloofness by Anton Diffring, a German actor of no mean talent who was an excellent lead in Hammer's *The Man Who Could Cheat Death* (1959), and played Baron Frankenstein in the abortive TV series pilot produced by Hammer. I suspect that is not for Peter Cushing, Diffring could have become a British horror icon. As it was, Cushing landed the plum roles, and Diffring was left with little in British horror except a genuinely chilling iciness to lend to second-rate productions like this.

And second rate it is, unfortunately. Despite a cast that includes Donald Pleasence and the great Kenneth Griffith (a character actor capable of the comic and the cunning), director Sidney Hayers insists on taking everything at a funereal pace, and telegraphing the horrific moments from about ten minutes away. It seems that grand guignol in the UK could never escape the long shadow of Tod Slaughter, as the pacing of this film closely resembles the rudimentary efforts of George King.

Diffring loves Erika Remberg, but she rejects him, and he decides to turn starlet Yvonne Monlaur (whose pulchritude enlivened a few duff movies at this time) into a copy of his love using the surgeons knife. It is, naturally, doomed to failure, as

Circus Of Horrors

the police move in, a few criminals get their faces melted, and Diffring dies before he can be captured.

If this sounds perfunctory, that is because it is in many ways. The inept direction spoils what could have been a good film. The cast all play well, and Baxt's script is suitably loopy, mixing elements of *Dr X* (1932), and *Freaks* (1932) into a compendium of loony doctor horror that would probably work on paper, but the stilted shooting leaves all tension and suspense slack. It is still worth a look, but just do not expect to be too scared.

You will not be scared by IA's first solo entry into the horror field, either. It is, however, creepy in parts, and is probably the best effort by Vernon Sewell to make the perfect version of *The Medium*.

Handled by Anglo in distribution, *House Of Mystery* (1960) aka *The Dark*, is a strange little movie. Made in the same 55-minute time slot as the Merton Park *Wallace* thrillers, it seems to be pitched between horror and thriller. As usual, Sewell directs and writes. I know a lot of critics call him a hack, and moan about the numerous versions of *The Medium* he made over the years, but I cannot help having a liking for his films. They are always brisk, and the actors involved usually fill out the gaps left by Sewell's concentration on pace.

Instead of the on-board boat setting he designed for his earlier Anglo movie, this time the action is set in a house. A young couple, one of whom is played by Ronald Hines just before his brief period of TV stardom, visit a cottage which is for sale. The door is opened by a woman who claims to be the housekeeper and offers to show them around. The couple are astounded that such a beautiful property should be available at such a low price, and that it has not been snapped up.

It is then that the flashbacks begin, as the woman tells the story of the house. Nanette Newman and Maurice Kaufman are a young couple who are resident in the cottage. There are unusual power fluctuations in a lamp in the lounge, and Nanette screams as a figure walks towards her. When her husband rushes to her aid, the figure is gone. But not for long, as his face appears on the TV screen as they watch, and still the lights continue to fade...

Eventually, they call in a suave psychic investigator, played by Colin Gordon. Gordon is more usually found playing light comedy as a cynical civil servant or teacher, but his manner here is perfectly pitched as the parapsychologist who must try to convince Kaufman that phenomena really exist before actually solving the case.

Enter the medium, a homely old lady who immediately feels ill at ease in the house. When she goes into a trance, we get a flashback within a flashback. Peter Dyneley was the face that Nanette had seen, an electronics genius with a weak heart, he was found dead in his workshop after his wife and best friend had seemingly run off together. But this is not the case, after discovering by accident that they planned to kill him, Dyneley bugs the house and hears more of their plans. He resolves to do something about this, and sets a trap; the lounge is wired up electrically, and the furniture, curtains and carpets soaked in a conductive solution. He offers them one chance; if they can find a way out by morning, then they can go off together. If they do not find a way, then they will die in the attempt.

These are the tensest moments in the film, as the full import of the situation hits the couple – Jane Hylton and John Merrivale – and they try to escape. He is soon killed, but she seems on the point on escape when...

The film cuts to Dyneley being found dead some time later. Merrivale's body is found buried in the workshop, but Hylton is undiscovered.

The film ends with Hines and his astonished wife asking the housekeeper if she was ever found. "No, some say she was walled up in the house," says the housekeeper – Hylton – as she backs into the wall and vanishes.

An enjoyable if not particularly frightening movie, it moves well and is engrossing. Where it does score is in the matter-of-fact way in which Gordon's parapsychologist conducts his investigation. In many ways, he reminds me of the eminent psychic investigator Robin Furman – except that Furman was still ten years away from his first paranormal experience when this film was made.

Gordon also contributed an excellent support to IA's next horror outing, the far superior and genuinely creepy *Night Of The Eagle* (1961).

Based on a novel (*Conjure Wife* by Fritz Leiber), and given the US title of *Burn, Witch, Burn* (an A A Merritt novel filmed in 1936 as *The Devil Doll* by Tod Browning), it would be easy to mistake this for an American movie, or an attempt to cut into the American market, if not for the fact that everyone is terribly English.

The lead is taken by Peter Wyngarde, that most English of actors who was immortalised in the late 1960's and early 1970's as Jason King in both *Department S* and a spin-off series bearing his name. Here, Wyngarde plays a psychology professor recently returned from the West Indies. Tipped for the top at his University, he has nothing but good luck. This he ascribes to his talents and ability. His wife Tansy (played by Janet Blair) has other ideas, as the house is littered with talismans and good luck charms purchased from a witch doctor. These are her magic, bought to protect her beloved husband from harm and misfortune.

Seeing as his stock-in-trade is a rubbishing of all superstitions, Wyngarde is not too pleased when he discovers one of these talismans and searches the house, eventually unearthing a whole store of them, and much to his wife's horror, he burns them.

Any horror film buff could have told him that it was a bad idea...

Night Of The Eagle

From here, things start to go wrong. One of his female students accuses him of assaulting her after he rebuffs her advances. She runs weeping to her tutor, the wonderfully sinister Margaret Johnston, who assures our hero that it will all amount to nothing. In fact, she is extremely nice to him... so nice that anyone except our self-assured hero would be a little alarmed.

Part of a college clique, our professor is in competition with Colin Gordon's mild-mannered professor for the psychology chair. In an incestuous situation, he is married to Margaret Johnston's character, who has her brother – also a college professor – and his wife (Reginald Beckwith and Kathleen Byron) in her pocket.

With this kind of set-up, it is no wonder that Tansy was nervous, and rightly, as things get worse. Wyngarde is nearly knocked down, mysterious phone-calls start, and the tape of a lecture he receives through the post has some kind of sonic signal that is both hypnotic and disturbing.

The final straw comes when the boyfriend of the female student – also, incidentally, a psychology major – attempts to threaten Wyngarde with a gun. Tansy offers herself in a spell, whereby any harm on her husband will be reflected on her.

This draws fruit when, in a trance, she drives to the sea and tries to drown herself. It is only by driving like a maniac and ignoring his own injuries in a crash that her husband manages to save her.

Like Dana Andrews' similarly disbelieving character in *Night Of The Demon* (1957), Wyngarde is gradually coming to realise that there is something in magic after all, and he goes to the college to find out what is going on, having figured out what the viewer had gathered about an hour before, that it is the wife of his rival who is the problem.

And it is her love for her husband that spells the end for her scheme. While Wyngarde is at the college, his house catches fire in a chain of accidents. Tansy is asleep, recovering from her ordeal. Confronting Johnston in her office, she reveals to him her belief in magic, and how she will crush him. She tells him that his house is on fire as she sets alight a house of cards.

As he rushes from the college, she plays a recording of his speech, complete with sonic overlay, and he finds himself pursued by an eagle – the stone eagle that stands over the door of the college entrance.

Escaping to Tansy – who has been rescued from the burning house, he does not see Johnston's husband come to fetch her home. As she rushes to stop him from entering the college, where her magic is still at work, the stone eagle teeters on its parapet, crashing onto her when she pushes her husband away.

Fast, thrilling, and tightly written by Charles Beaumont and Richard Matheson with George Baxt, the film has excellent performances from the whole of the cast. There are moments of genuine terror as the realisation that magic is real overtakes Wyngarde, and the first time you see this film you really have no idea what will happen next. Producer Albert Fennell was one of the men behind the look and style of *The Avengers*, and that kind of eye shows in this piece. The photography, by Reg Wyer is excellent, and the direction assured and – in places – inspired.

Which is strange, as it was directed by Sidney Hayers, who made such a mess of *Circus Of Horrors* the year before. Either he learnt quickly, or there were things about *Circus Of Horrors* that caused problems in direction and editing. After all, many a well-directed film is ruined under the editors scalpel – a fate that almost befalls *The Night Caller* (US title *Blood Beast From Outer Space*), an Independent Artists co-production from 1965.

Made with the New Art and Armitage companies, *The Night Caller* was written and directed by John Gilling, based on a pulp novel by Frank Crisp. Short and compact for a 55-minute B-slot (although overrunning this slightly), it proceeds well, but shows signs of heavy editing towards the climax, leaving the finale unsatisfying and clumsily realized.

Starring John Saxon and Patricia Haines as two scientists working on a rocket and meteor project, the film begins in a brisk and business-like manner. A meteor lands in Yorkshire, and Saxon, along with his boss Maurice Denham, is dispatched to collect the remains. Except that there are no remains, just a small patch of burnt grass and a metal sphere. Perplexed, the scientists take it back to London under Army guard (a good performance here from John Carson as a Major forever having problems explaining the situation to his Minister over the phone).

The sphere glows in a stock room one night, attracting the attention of Haines, who is working late. When she tries to enter the room, a claw-like hand grabs her... Naturally, when the building is searched, there is no intruder, and the scientists decide to conduct an experiment. Linked by radio, Denham stays in a room with the sphere all night. It glows, and the intruder returns. Denham is appalled by the intruders hideous (and wisely off-screen) appearance, and dies from exposure to radiation. The intruder escapes, and the sphere is stolen.

Shortly after this, a series of young girls go missing after answering an ad in a magazine. This link is made by Saxon when he talks to the parents of one of the missing girls (a wonderful cameo by Warren Mitchell as her father, concerned but vague). With help from Scotland Yard, the story unfolds; girls are invited for interview as models by a mysterious masked man. At the interview they are hypnotised, then given a strange picture that has a changing background. By night, this background re-awakens hypnotic suggestion, and they leave home to join the mysterious stranger, who is only ever seen at night (hence the title).

Haines is also pursuing a line of enquiry, and after Scotland Yard give her the address that the ads are delivered to – a sleazy Soho bookshop – she goes there to meet the stranger. She tries to convince him that she is a potential model, but he recognises and kills her. Her body is discovered by Saxon.

The film ends with a chase, in which one of the girls and the stranger are pursued. It ends with Saxon trying to reason with the stranger in a derelict house, but too late, the alien intruder reveals that he has come from a moon of Jupiter, seeking women to breed into his people, who are mutated. He reveals himself as half-man half-monster before disappearing with the girls in flash of smoke.

For all bar the last five minutes, this is a taut suspense movie, with excellent playing form the cast. Saxon and Haines are particularly good, sparking off each other with the suggestion of a relationship that goes deeper than just professional. Indeed, unlike most scream queens of the period, Haines is a cool and courageous heroine who has no fears when going to meet the alien. This makes her death all the more shocking, and gives Saxon a chance to emote excellently when he finds her. Dammit, you really believe he cares.

Filmed in black and white, with a lot of atmosphere and good point-of-view shots to add dynamics, the only thing that lets the film down is the rushed ending, where a rationalisation of the stranger's activities are hurried into the last two minutes. This does not spoil the rest of the film, however, and there is some excellent swinging organ playing on the soundtrack for those of us who like that sort of thing.

Two years before, Independent Artists had made *Unearthly Stranger* (1963), again handled by Albert Fennell along with Julian Wintle and Leslie Parkyn, and again with atmospheric photography from Reg Wyer. Directed by John Krish, with a script by Rex Carlton, the film was another tight B picture designed for a second slot, but with something that lifted it above that level.

Like *The Night Caller*, it was a sci-fi horror, and like all the IA movies, the low budget led to a lack of special effects (the night caller himself is a big mistake, looking silly rather than scary) and a reliance on brooding atmospheres and good acting. This was a peculiarly British approach to the art of horror, as the Americans would squeeze in a monster, no matter how cheesy it looked. The lack of money in this country, plus the years of heavy censorship developed a strain of restrained terror that really reached its apogee in movies like this.

John Neville stars as the scientist hero, who takes over his boss' job when that boss (a brief role by Warren Mitchell) is killed in his office by a mysterious heart attack – mysterious because a huge electric charge was recorded in the room, blowing out a lamp and burning papers in his hand.

The team of scientists are working on a method of transporting minds to other planets. Neville, ensconced in his boss' chair, is close to cracking the secret. The same secret that his boss had informed his secretary (the icy and efficient Jean Marsh) that he had just cracked, and was in the ashes he clutched in death.

Neville and his friend Phillip Stone are beset by a creepy security man, played with fake bonhomie by Patrick Newell (later cast as Steed's boss Mother in *The Avengers* by Wintle). When Neville starts to posit that perhaps – if we are after the secret – someone might have got there first, he and Stone suspect Newell; especially when a discrete look into Mitchell's coffin (for some unexplained reason in the basement of the building) reveals no body but a pile of bricks.

Newell is a red herring, and has his own suspicions: enemy agents. And Neville's new wife Julie, played by Gabriella Licudi, seems a likely target. After all, no-one knows anything about her, and as he recounts the story he was simply picked up on a deserted road by this beautiful stranger...

Neville is pursuing his alien theory, and notices that his wife sleeps with her eyes open, appearing not to breathe. Also, she never blinks. He tells Stone, who scoffs at him until, when invited for dinner, he accidentally catches sight of Julie taking a red hot casserole dish out of the oven with her bare hands.

Newell, too close to the truth, is killed, and when Neville reveals to Julie that he has cracked the secret, she begs him not to reveal it. She is an alien, here by sheer power of thought. And her compatriots will come and destroy her if she does not fulfil her mission, to kill him. He tells her that he loves her, even when she reveals that her real form is not female, nor even humanoid. Despite this, she has fallen in love with him.

The aliens come for her, a high pitched whining is the only sign of their presence, and Neville drags his alien bride to the attic, trying to hide. He clutches her to him, and the noise subsides. When he looks, her nightdress is empty.

The film began with Neville running along the Embankment of the Thames to his office, and beginning to breathlessly record the story for his friend Stone. It ends with Stone arriving to hear the conclusion. They decide that they must try and find the aliens – and the only way to do this is by anaesthetizing them. They will cease to breathe, and their eyes remain open. When secretary Jean Marsh enters, and reveals that she, too, is an alien, they attempt to subdue her. In the struggle, she plunges from a high window.

The film ends with the simplest and scariest of shots. Stone and Neville find an empty coat on the pavement, and as they crouch by it, a number of passers-by gather round and stare at them, unblinkingly. They are all women...

From the paranoid fear of the opening sequence, and the excellent tracking shots on the office building's incredible spiral staircase that induce vertigo, the film is kept taut as a bow throughout. Part of the horror is in the development of Julie into a being with emotions. She looks at babies (who cry) and playgrounds full of children (who go quiet and shy away from her) with longing, as despite her alienness, she longs to be part of the human race, even running home crying after her rejection by the children. But even this only proves her otherness, as the tears leave scar-tracks like streaks down her face.

All the aliens are women, and Marsh tells Neville and Stone that this is because women are an underclass, and the aliens can pass unnoticed. So is it a proto-feminist subtext, or a misogynist view of women as an outside threat? I suppose it depends on what mood you are in, and at different times I have seen it either way. What this does do is give the film another uneasy edge that makes it all the more creepy.

Over at Anglo, things had slowed down for the horror market – at least, in terms of production. True, they financed and handled *Carry On Screaming* in 1966, the cod-Hammer comedy from the Rogers/Thomas team, and they also part-financed and distributed a number of films by Harry Alan Towers, who usually scripted his films as Peter Welbeck as well as producing them.

Towers is a fascinating character, and one day someone will write a book about him. An Englishman who fled vice charges in the USA in 1961, he spent the next twenty years one step ahead of extradition whilst producing a string of strange low-budget movies across the world that usually had a crime or horror element. Some of his movies used English settings, like the crime melodrama *Circus Of Fear* (1967), English directors (like Don Sharp, who made some *Fu Manchu* movies for Towers), and English stars (like Christopher Lee, who played Fu Manchu five times, and was also in *Circus Of Fear*). Yet for all that his films are pan-European, and do not have the feel of English movies.

The closest to a totally English movie is the aforementioned *Circus Of Fear*, another alleged Edgar Wallace adaption. With Lee and a mostly English cast and crew, shot in London and the Home Counties, it qualifies on the British score, if not horror. Of his horror pictures, the five *Fu Manchu*'s are closest to British, three were directed by Don Sharp (the other two by Jess Franco), they all starred Lee as Fu Manchu, all had British stalwart Howard Marion Crawford as Dr Petrie, and two actors shared the role of Nayland Smith – Holmes to Petrie's Watson, both being English. One was Nigel Greene and the other ex-matinée idol Richard Greene (TV's original Robin Hood). Based on the pulp chillers of Sax Rohmer, they featured fog-bound London settings that were some in fact German back-lot, and soon travelled abroad to Spain or China (allegedly – looks like the Black Forest to me) for location shooting.

Towers eventually surrendered to American police in 1981, paid a nominal fine, and now produces movies from his Canadian home. However, while he was still on the run, he kept Anglo supplied with 1960's pulp horror on film.

Perhaps it was because of this that Anglo only produced one solo little horror B picture during the mid-1960's, but it turned out to be a gem ruined only by its budget.

The Earth Dies Screaming was released in 1964, and was a 60-minute sci-fi horror directed in black and white by Terence Fisher, taking a short break from his Hammer activities.

Willard Parker, a square-jawed American actor, plays the all-action hero who awakes to find that the small village in which he is staying is deserted. Out on the streets, it looks as though a plague has hit, wiping out people instantly. Driving around, he sees cars crashed on the road, front doors left wide open, and bicycles discarded.

Seeing some people, he hails them, and they attack. Their eyes are strangely empty, shining like lights. He fires on them (like all Americans in English movies, he always carries a gun) and makes his escape to a pub where he finds a few people holed up. Included amongst them are Thorley Walters and Dennis Price, performing their usual English gentlemen gone to seed acts, and heroine Virginia Field.

The Earth Dies Screaming

It transpires that they have all somehow missed an alien invasion, possibly escaping in the same way that the hero of the more overtly sci-fi The Day Of the Triffids (made the year before) was able to avoid blindness when the comet carrying the Triffid seeds arrived. In that movie, his temporary blindness through injury prevented the eye damage that blinded the world. In this case, all the people in the pub were locked away from the outside world when the aliens arrived (this idea was used in the US sci-fi cult hit *Night Of The Comet* in 1984, when the only people not reduced to vampiric zombies by the comet dust were those who were locked inside when the comet passed over).

The alien invaders are cardboard robots who look a little like clumsy Cybermen, and indeed one of them is definitely cardboard when Parker runs it over in a Landrover. For some reason never revealed, they have enslaved the human race into glowing eyed zombies... and while they try to escape, the small party must prevent themselves being taken over. Indeed, one of the scariest scenes in the movie is where Price is taken over by the aliens, and turns to reveal himself to Field, his eyes shining as white orbs in his blank face.

A strange movie to get a handle on, it is genuinely disquieting. Fisher was never one for pace (his Hammer *Dracula* being an exception) and this film certainly moves in fits and starts. However, he was always excellent at motivating his actors, and the cast are believable as outcasts in a nightmare situation. Despite the cheapness of the robots, the script by Henry Cross builds up a fine degree of paranoia, and the small village battleground on which the film is played out lends a claustrophobic edge to the proceedings. It seems as though this is the only place in the world, and nothing exists outside of it.

Given the merits of their respective movies, it is fitting that the last IA and Anglo horror movies of the 1960's should be a co-production, as was their first. *Invasion* was made in 1966, and is a fruition of all the merits that make their other movies so watchable.

Starring Edward Judd, who was also in the apocalyptic horror *The Day The Earth Caught Fire* (1963), this movie centres around a doctor in an English village. He accidentally knocks down a girl one night, and takes her to his home to give her treatment. Then another girl comes calling for her...

These are not Earth women, they are aliens. One is a prisoner, and the other her gaoler. Both were on their way to their home planet when their ship had to make an emergency landing, allowing the prisoner to escape.

Not really believing that they are aliens, Judd refuses to hand the girl over until she is well again. He does not realise that this will be the cue for an invasion of alien women, laying seige to the small village where he lives.

Good performances from Barrie Ingham and Arthur Sharp, with the aliens represented by Valerie Gearon, Lyndon Brook, Yoko Tani, and Tsai Chin (who was Fu Manchu's daughter in the Towers movies). Jack Greenwood produced for IA associates Merton Park, and Alan Bridges directed a script by Roger Marshall.

Marshall was a regular *Avengers* writer, and again the skill of handling wacky ideas and eccentric chills on a low budget proved good experience for this no-budget film, with Bridges excelling himself.

It might only have been 1966, but if Anglo and IA were to stop making horror – even the sci-fi horror hybrid that was so hard to get right – they could not have stopped with a better film.

There were plenty of other producers in their wake...

11. The American Invasion

In the 1960's, the Americans arrived in the shape of ex-AIP producer Herman Cohe
and the company themselves, with a UK base headed by Louis "Deke" Heyward. Bot
sensed that there was money in mixing the AIP style of horror with the mor
restrained English style – or even by aping Hammer directly and making Gothic movie!
While this was happening, Richard Gordon was still flying the flag for pulp horror vi.
his associations with the Gala and Planet distributors. Four films emerged from thes
partnerships, all of them interesting at the very least. Planet also had a double stab a
their own horrors.

As for Cohen and AIP, Cohen made five films in Britain, from 1959-73. AIP ·
ignoring their interference on Tigon product, which is dealt with separately – mad
ten. Nowhere near as prolific as Hammer or even Amicus, but still worth ar
independent look for their sometimes awkward transatlantic tone.

Herman Cohen was born in 1928, and produced his first successful horro
movie when he was twenty nine. *I Was A Teenage Werewolf* (1957) mixed US juvenile
delinquent styles with a traditional horror approach. Like Lon Chaney Jnr in higt
school, it touched a nerve with an audience that also felt like animal outcasts to thei
peers and elders as rock'n'roll invented the "teenager", and those awkward adolescent
years got recognised. Always quick to spot a trend, Cohen followed up with *I Was A
Teenage Frankenstein* (1958, GB title *Teenage Frankenstein*), and then *How To Make
A Monster* (1958), in which a movie-maker turns teens into monsters via his poisonous
make-up.

This was a theme that would not bare too much repeating, especially as other
AIP producers were getting in on the act with *Blood Of Dracula* (1957), which should
have been called *I Was A Teenage Vampire*... Cohen had an idea to wipe the floor with
everyone and make the ultimate teen monster movie, *I Was A Teenage Gorilla*. With
this in mind he set out for England in 1959, but before he could realise his ambition,
he put his name to one of the wildest horrors of that period.

Horrors Of The Black Museum was released in 1959, and directed by Arthur
Crabtree, who kept as tight a rein on pacing and suspense as he had with *Fiend
Without A Face* two years before. Cohen wrote the script with Aben Kandel, which
mixes police procedural with psychotic horror.

At this time, *Scotland Yard* was a popular TV series, a drama-documentary
narrated and introduced by novelist and criminologist Edgar Lustgarten. *Horrors Of
The Black Museum* is a strange mix of this series. Michael Gough, of the desiccated
looks and fruity accent, capable of superiority and sleaze in the same sentence, plays
Edmund Bancroft, a true crime writer who is immensely popular with the public and
loathed by Scotland Yard, of whom he is immensely critical.

A series of murders are committed in a variety of bizarre manners. The
opening scene features a flighty young woman who receives a pair of opera glasses
through the post. When she raises them to her eyes, spikes pop out and spear her
through to the brain. Another victim is the girlfriend of Bancroft, who he keeps hidden
away. After a row in which she condemns him for his lameness, sneering that he is not
a real man (and in truth he is not, his bitterness tainting him), she undresses in her
bedroom and lies down – only to have her head lopped off by a guillotine. Mind you,
the actress deserves it: June Cunningham was a model who was employed merely to
strip to her basque, her acting being non-existent.

The murders are being committed by mild-mannered Graham Curnow, who

Horrors Of The Black Museum

plays Gough's assistant. He is regularly hypnotised (the film originally went out in Hypnovision, with a 13-minute lecture tagged on the print) by Gough and injected with a serum that causes a green filter to be shone on his face, his lower jaw jutted out. The purpose of all this is for the ever-madder Gough to build his own black museum of murder, to rival that of Scotland Yard. Indeed, it was the Yard's gruesome exhibit that caused Cohen to come up with this idea.

Gough is wonderfully over-the-top, even murdering an old antique dealer who tries to blackmail him, by piercing her skull with ice tongs. His obvious enjoyment carries the film through the slightly dull patches in between killings. In glorious Eastmancolor, the blood is richly red, and Edmund is finally damned by his dying assistant in a fun fair – and the poor boy does not even get to kill his girlfriend (the irritating Shirley Anne Field, who got hers in *Peeping Tom*). Of course, the plodding boys of the Yard – personified by Geoffrey Keene – are on hand to make an arrest.

If you swapped Gough's assistant for a forty foot gorilla, then you would have a similar end for *Konga*, Cohen's 1960 picture and his stab at the "teenage gorilla" theme.

Horrors Of The Black Museum had met box office resistance because of the remnants of a local watch committee system that could veto BBFC decisions – indeed, I have an aunt who only got to see the film when on holiday in Sussex, and even now recalls the opening opera glass murder with relish! Cohen was unhappy at the way that his distributors handled this, and so switched to Anglo-Amalgamated for this movie. What Nat Cohen and Stuart Levy made of this I do not know – after all, they distributed the *Scotland Yard* TV series that *Horrors Of The Black Museum* slandered! However, business is business, and they were happy to get an experienced US producer on board for a horror flick.

Konga was originally written for US production, and it really shows. Produced at Merton Park, with little location shooting, the "London" that the giant ape devastates at the end of the picture is pretty paltry, a few back-lot streets and a phoney Big Ben that actually looks black on screen. The budget also runs only to a man in an ape suit and some rudimentary matte work. However, the truly scary part of the picture is Michael Gough's performance as a driven scientist, cold and calculating with his work until his lust for a young student drives him over the edge.

Gough, as usual, is suave and slimy in the space of a single sentence, and is capable of breathtaking feats of grand guignol. The plot centres around his character, Dr. Decker, who is a botany professor at the local college. One of his students is Jess Conrad, ex-pop singer turned tolerable actor. Another student is Claire Gordon, who is "going steady" with Conrad but is terribly studious, and interested in Decker's work. Decker is interested, as well... in her.

Back in his home lab, Decker is experimenting on growth serums for chimpanzees, with the idea of growing bigger people. His assistant (the downtrodden Margo Johns) is hopelessly in love with him, and he has promised to marry her in order to keep her quiet. He treats her like dirt, and she takes solace in the child-like affection of Konga, a chimpanzee Decker will be using.

Knowing that his serum has already worked on plants (he has a hot-house full of monster flowers to prove it), Decker tries it on Konga. Oh yes, the chimp grows... but, and here is the interesting side-effect that no-one seems to comment on, he changes species as well! From a small chimpanzee he becomes a large gorilla. Is this because the serum promotes growth through the genus ape as well as sheer size? Or is it – more prosaically – because no-one had a chimp suit for hire?

Decker uses the ape to extract his revenge, the college dean and Jess Conrad get theirs from Konga, and Decker also plots the end of his doormat mistress, lining up his prize student to replace her. But things do not go quite according to plan, and she screams the greenhouse down. Konga is freed, and goes on the rampage. PC Plod finally puts two and two together, and the forces of law and order are about to arrest Decker when Konga crushes him by Big Ben.

Not the most intellectual horror movie ever made, and certainly unsure of its continental pitch – Cohen and Aben Kandel's script is obviously US high school in tone, clumsily played by British actors, and John Lemont's direction is patchy – the whole affair is saved by the silliness of the ape-man, and the grandstanding of Gough.

When Cohen went back to the States for a few years, he took Gough with him, and they made some interesting pictures, including *Black Zoo* (1963), which is a semi-remake of the old *Murders At The Zoo* flick with Lionel Atwill. In this, Gough wears animal skins, is the head of an animal worshipping cult, and communes with beasts that he sends out to commit murders. With such things to keep him busy in the States, it is no wonder that Cohen did not return to the UK until 1967, when he made *Berserk!* aka *Circus Of Blood* aka *Circus Of Terror*.

Again, Cohen and Kandel wrote the script, with Michael Gough in the ranks of actors. Except this time around he is not the villain, and gets killed off early on. Gough is the partner of Joan Crawford's wonderfully over-the-top Monica Rivers, owner and ringmaster of a circus that is plagued by a series of extremely nasty and gory deaths. A cut wire means a quick trip to the ground for a high-wire artist, and Gough receives a close-up spike through the head after arguing with Crawford.

The object of Cohen's movies was shock and sleaze rather than horror through suggestion, and you certainly will not get the exposition of existential ideas espoused in movies like *Peeping Tom* in a Cohen extravaganza. The next murder features Ty Hardin, the circus' new high wire man, who performs his act over a bed of nails and comes to a gory end.

The publicity each murder attracts draws bigger audiences, and this disturbing facet of human nature is left unexplored in the search for more gore. Thanks to good work by director Jim O'Connolly and photographer Desmond Dickinson, this is a shocking rather than horrific movie. Although Crawford steals all honours in a series of ludicrously brief costumes that she was too old to really wear well (despite her own best efforts), the film has a cast of stalwart British talent that includes Philip Madoc,

Trog

Robert Hardy – a man for minor horror – he was in *Psychomania* (1972) and *Dark Places* (1973) in the early 1970's – Judy Geeson, and Diana Dors – later brilliant in *Nothing But The Night* (1972). Geoffrey Keen must have been Cohen's idea of the perfect policeman, as he pops up again here, as well.

I have a weakness for Circus thrillers and horrors, and this fits well between *Circus Of Horrors* and *Circus Of Fear* in any themed evening of video viewing. The same cannot be said for *Trog*, Cohen's next British foray, in 1970.

Switching from Columbia to Warner's for finance, Cohen kept a lot of his UK team together. Desmond Dickinson is behind the camera, Aben Kandel writes the script (on his own, this time), and Joan Crawford is teamed with Michael Gough again. In the director's chair is Freddie Francis, whose Hammer movies were so eye catching. However, there is little that even an eye like Francis' can do with a film so duff.

Basically, the plot concerns a lady scientist – Crawford – who discovers a pre-historic man-ape remnant in a pothole. She takes him back to civilization, trains him, and eventually he runs amok. And that, basically, is it. Not much of a plot for 91 minutes running time, although it is nice to see Crawford and Gough try and grandstand each other off the screen.

Trog is one of those movies that gets into the "so-bad-it's-good" type of movie book. But it does not have a sufficiently eccentric world view, or the technical ineptitude that usually makes such a film. Francis is a good director, Dickinson is a good cinematographer, Cohen produced films that were always entertaining if not intellectual, the actors are good (if a little hammy)...Let us just say everyone had a bad day, and leave it at that.

Cohen's last movie in the UK was made in 1973, and was again directed by Freddie Francis. *Craze* aka *The Infernal Idol*, produced in association with Harbour and distributed by EMI, was an attempt to emulate the latter day success of Amicus, who were using lots of star names in their anthology movies. Except that this was not an anthology, and the star turns showed up for the sole purpose of being killed. In this, it resembles AIP's *Dr Phibes* movies.

The first Cohen UK movie to be taken from a novel (Henry Seymour's *The Infernal Idol*), it saw Cohen co-write the script with Aben Kandel. The plot concerns the owner of an African idol which is accidentally involved in a death. Following this, the idol's owner comes into some money and gets it into his head that he can keep

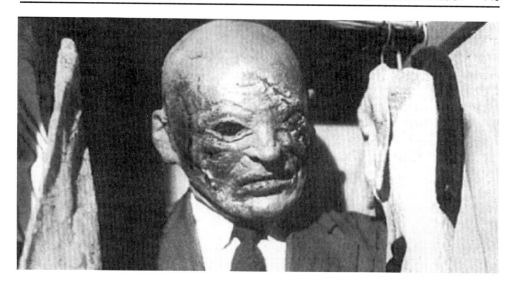

Craze

inheriting money and enjoying good fortune if he keeps on killing.

An uneasy alliance between the supernatural and the psychological, it is never too clear if the idol really works or if it is all in the crazed mind of the killer. I guess the title gives an indication of which way the viewer should take it, but then again, this is an exploitation movie.

Over ninety-five minutes, the stars and stalwart characters who do their bit in front of the camera are; Jack Palance (no stranger to British horror – he was excellent in Amicus' *Torture Garden* in 1967), Diana Dors, Julie Ege (a scream queen at this time), Edith Evans, Hugh Griffith (also a *Dr Phibes* regular), Trevor Howard, Michael Jayston, Suzy Kendall, and Kathleen Byron who, even approaching late middle-age was more beautiful than any other actress on show.

This film should not work; too many stars, hackneyed plot, clichéd script, etc. But, despite that, Francis handles it with aplomb, and the shocks keep coming. It does not suffer from the early 1970's malaise of British horror – the death of Gothic left producers casting around for a new direction, giving rise to ludicrous hybrid movies. Cohen, on the other hand, keeps to his guns. Plenty of blood and gore (or at least, as much as he could get away with), and solid direction and editing for shock value.

Cohen never made another British film, preferring to stay in the States until his death in 1985.

Gala are a distributor who have never particularly gone in for horror, although the ubiquitous Richard Gordon tempted them into three releases: *Devil Doll* (1963), *Curse Of The Voodoo* (1964), aka *Curse Of Simba* aka *Lion Man* aka *Voodoo Blood Death*, and the much later *The Cat And The Canary* (1979).

If Gordon had wished his name to be put on films throughout his career, more people would be aware of his portfolio. As it is, it was not until quite late in the day that I discovered some of the movies for which I held an affection were the results of his production skills. Having said that, the three Gala movies were not amongst his best.

Both *Devil Doll* and *Curse Of The Voodoo* were directed by Lindsay Shonteff and starred Bryant Halliday. Halliday was much better in *The Projected Man* (1967), for Compton, and Shonteff has always been uninspired. His penchant for endless James Bond/spy retreads has not endeared him to me, as I loathe that genre.

This is not to say that neither film is without its merits. *Devil Doll* reworks the theme that informed Michael Redgrave's role in *Dead Of Night* (1945) that later went belly up in *Magic* (1978); the idea of a ventriloquist's dummy that develops its own personality, slowly submerging that of the ventriloquist. The twist is that the dummy's personality is real – a human soul within a wooden shell.

Shonteff is not the world's best director – original choice Sidney J Furie would have been better, but his talents were already leading him on to bigger and better budgets. Even so, the sight of the dummy wandering around by itself is still a cause of unease. There is something frightening in the false, grinning face of a dummy that makes it – like a clown's make-up – a willing arbiter of evil.

Curse Of The Voodoo is a stranger film, Shonteff was surer of his skills, and Halliday more at home as a big game hunter returned to England with a curse hanging over him. Of course, using Hampstead Heath as a double for Africa was a bit of a mistake, but if the viewer can overlook this then there is still plenty to enjoy – particularly another piece of horror cameo from Dennis Price.

Gordon did not return to Gala until 1979, when they released his version of *The Cat And The Canary*. A hoary old comic melodrama, the most famous and popular version of which is the Bob Hope Paramount vehicle of 1939, Gordon's version was written and directed by Radley Metzger, an American who was more notable for his softcore porn than anything else.

The plot is a standard old dark house mystery, with an endangered heroine, a psychotic villain pretending to be a ghost, and lots of hidden passages. At the time of the Hope movie, it was old (that was at least the second version of the play) – by 1979 it had almost come full circle to becoming trendy again.

Honor Blackman, Edward Fox, Wendy Hiller, Beatrix Lehmann, Olivia Hussey, Peter McEnery, Daniel Massey and Wilfred Hyde-White are the family and staff drawn to the deserted house for the reading of the will. Some of them are going to die horribly in the shadows of the night, and one of them is a psychopath.

Metzger takes the comedy away from the movie, turning it into more of a straightforward chiller that owes something to the chain of psychological horrors concocted for Hammer by Jimmy Sangster. As a director, he moves his players like pieces on a chess board (an analogy helped by the parquet flooring of the stylish old house), each victim moving inexorably to their doom.

Perhaps more sombre than it should have been, the chills end up being spaced too few and far between. Not a bad film, but not wholly successful.

Gordon's last movie, *Inseminoid*, was made in 1980, and directed by old hand Norman J Warren. A good *Alien* (1979) rip-off that is not as heavy as the original, it had a strong UK cast, but was actually made outside the UK (putting it outside the scope of this book, unfortunately). Faster and more thrilling, it also had more gore than ever for Gordon, something he was not too keen on, and which presaged his retirement from production.

Still, if Gala were not lucky for Gordon, at least he made a gem of a movie for Planet in the 1960's...

Planet were another small independent distributor and occasional producer who scuffed around the edges of the British film industry. With Tom Blakeley producing they had already dipped their toe into the bloodied waters of horror via *Devils Of Darkness* (1964), an ultra-low budget vampire flick.

The first time I saw this, I thought it was crap, but each renewed viewing has led to a fascination with it. Is it really that bad, or are the actors supposed to be that stilted? Certainly, Hubert Noel as the vampiric French nobleman could be that wooden simply because he has been undead for over three hundred years. That could be why he always carries a silly cane around with him, a cane that has a golden bat on its handle. This is obviously supposed to be significant, as director Lance Comfort is forever zooming in on it – the only piece of dynamism his camera ever shows.

Not that there is that much to go on. Lyn Fairhurst's script is long-winded, and the 90-minute running time is at least a quarter of an hour too long. It takes ages to get going, as young honeymooners William Sylvester and Tracy Reed are accosted by the Frenchman while on honeymoon in France (actually a rather tatty bit of the Home Counties doubling as France). When it finally does get going, there are a few chills as Sylvester loses his bride and then has to defeat the Count. All told, it is a bit like an updated version of Hammer's *Kiss Of The Vampire* (1962), but without Don Sharp's pacing in the director's chair.

Having said all that, the fascination lies in its slow, dream-like quality and the brightness of the Eastmancolor, that makes the whole thing look like a slightly kinetic Pierre et Gilles postcard. Eerie rather than scary, and possibly unintentionally.

This is certainly not the case with Richard Gordon's *Island Of Terror*. A 1966 release, directed by Terence Fisher from a script which Gordon found ready to film, so good was it... Hmm, I'm not so sure about that. Perhaps it is Fisher's usual problem with pacing, but there are one or two scenes in the film that could have done with a bit of tightening. Produced nominally by Planet's Tom Blakeley, it was the first Gordon film to be in colour, and benefitted from the excellent camera work of Reg Wyer. To me, Wyer is one of the unsung heroes of British horror movies during this period, as his camera always responds to the atmosphere of a piece, no matter who the director may be.

Island Of Terror

Fisher's talent for motivating the actors is as strong as ever, as Peter Cushing gives his usual impeccable performance, supported by Edward Judd as the male lead, Carole Gray as his romantic interest. Judd is criminally under-rated as a solid action lead during this period, and action there certainly is in the Alan Ramsen and Edward Andrew Mann screenplay.

On a remote island, there are a series of strange deaths, the victims reduced almost to jelly as their bones disappear. The answer to this problem lies in a series of scientific experiments conducted at a remote house. The scientists have accidentally created a new form of life – small, non-vertebrate animals that feed on human and animal bone. And for most of the picture, there seems to be no way of stopping them as they decimate the island's population.

Ignoring the cheap models (the monsters look like rubber moulds and the boneless bodies are like deflated blow-ups), there are some incredibly tense moments as humans come up against the alien intelligence of the bone eaters (after all, there is no way to communicate with them). And when the pace flags, there are some good chase scenes, as a group led by Judd are forced to run through a wood with lots of little monsters falling on them from the trees.

Add to this good support from Niall MacGinnis, Sam Kydd, and Eddie Byrne, and you have an enjoyable and occasionally scary movie.

Planet were so pleased with this that they attempted a similar theme the next year with *Night Of The Big Heat* (1967, US title *Island Of The Burning Damned*), adapted from a pulp sci-fi thriller by John Lymington. Blakeley had Fisher back in the chair, and Cushing in the cast, this time playing opposite Christopher Lee, who traded brooding intensities with Patrick Allen.

Still set on an island, it was another "humans versus monsters in an enclosed space" movie. But even better, perhaps because of the familiar material, Fisher's customary lulls vanished, replaced by a pacing he had not given the audience since *Dracula* (1958).

Allen is a writer who also runs a pub with his wife Frankie (Sarah Lawson, who also did *The Devil Rides Out* for Hammer in this year). He has a new secretary sent up, played by sex bomb Jane Merrow, who has had an affair with him, and is keen to rekindle it. On top of this, the temperature seems to be running incredibly high for the time of year, and tempers are short. A tramp has been mysteriously killed in the woods – burned to death – and a stranger (Christopher Lee at his most foreboding) is striding around the woods and locking himself in his room with a ton of electrical equipment.

The local radio and satellite station is getting strange signals, and when TV and telephone start to go haywire, Lee knows what it is, aliens are using radio frequencies to beam themselves to earth, landing on this remote island. Taking time out from their love triangle, Allen and his women follow a light in the sky and find Lee striding across the fields. He has photographed the aliens, and is developing the photograph when Allen barges into his room demanding explanations, ruining the negative.

The horrific thing about this film is the way in which the tension builds, added to by the sheer sense of helplessness felt by the isolated humans. Unable to contact the mainland, and knowing nothing about these strange intruders except their need for heat, they are unable to fight back. Even the suave, cool and disbelieving local doctor – almost a cameo from Cushing – eventually succumbs to the heat, and is killed when attempting to help the others reach the local army base, and a way of contacting the mainland. When the end comes, it is not man's ingenuity that saves him, it is nature. A thunderstorm breaks over the aliens, earthing their electrical bodies.

A pulp horror worthy of Gordon, I am just surprised that he did not produce it. However, Ronald Liles' script, and the acting (Allen is particularly good as a man wrestling between lust for his secretary and love for his wife while trying to concentrate on the danger) lift it slightly above pulp. There is a feeling of paranoia and helplessness that other films of this type rarely attained.

In the 1960's, the Americans went film crazy in Britain. For a few years this country was the media capital of the world; an assumption based on Beatle haircuts and electric guitars, it was an artificiality that would not last for long.

While the major US companies made all kinds of movies here, American International concentrated on horror flicks; after all, you cannot make a beach movie in England. In the ten years between 1964 and 1974 they made a total of ten movies, the first two of which were additions to Roger Corman's Edgar Allen Poe cycle.

Although they were, strictly speaking, British horror movies, they were really little different from the earlier movies made in the USA. *The Masque Of The Red Death*

(1964) *The Tomb Of Ligeia* (1964) were both filmed using British crews and a largely British supporting cast. For instance, *Masque Of The Red Death* featured Hazel Court and Patrick Magee beside Vincent Price, and is an incredibly beautiful film photographed by Nic Roeg, with the usual baroque sets and surrealistic pacing expected from Corman's Poe films. A young Jane Asher makes an appearance, and the sets are wonderful. The story of the medieval prince holding a masque while plague rages outside his walls was scripted by Charles Beaumont and R Wright Campbell with little regard to anything Poe actually wrote (as usual).

Masque Of The Red Death

    The Tomb Of Ligeia on the other hand, is a bit of a lost film. Not seen for years, never shown on TV when the other Corman Poe movies are, and not available on video. Richard Johnson and Derek Francis are the familiar English faces alongside Price here, with Arthur Grant as the cameraman and Robert Towne as the scriptwriter. A simple story of a dead wife who metamorphoses into a cat and then into a woman again, the more intriguing element is simply why it has remained unshown for so long.
    So when is a British film not a British film? When everything about it except the supporting cast and the crew is American. That extends beyond these two movies and into a lot of product churned out by the US majors in this country during the 1960's.
    Beautiful as they were, the Corman Gothics had little to do with a British strain of horror, which AIP found more appealing when co-producing with the likes of Tigon. Indeed, their next stab at movie making in the UK, *City Under The Sea* (1965, US title *War Gods Of The Deep*), was another barely Anglicized production.
    Vincent Price again starred as the head of Victorian smugglers in Cornwall who have lived under the sea for a hundred years in their own city. Charles Bennett scripted this nonsense with Louis Heyward. Quite what a talent like Jacques Tourneur was doing here is anybody's guess, as the direction is perfunctory. Token American hunk is Tab Hunter, with English character acting from David Tomlinson and John Le Mesurier.

Despite the supernatural and semi-scientific premise, this is more a kids' movie than a horror film, and in truth, not even as much fun as the Jules Verne adaptions that the US majors poured out in the 1950's. Compared to Disney's *Twenty Thousand Leagues Under The Sea* (1954) with Kirk Douglas and James Mason, this is a wet weekend.

The Tomb Of Ligeia

The next AIP-produced British horror was nearer the mark. *Die, Monster, Die* (1967, US title *Monster Of Terror*) aka *The House At The End Of The World*, starred Boris Karloff in the Indian summer of his career, with pretty English actress Suzan Farmer as his daughter, and stolid Nick Adams as the hero. TV writer Jerry Sohl penned the screenplay, and Daniel Haller (usually a producer) took the director's chair.

Allegedly, this was an adaption of H P Lovecraft's novel *The Colour Out Of Space*, but like so many Lovecraft adaptions it has very little to do with the original source. In fact, in many ways it carries elements of *The Fall Of The House Of Usher* (1960, UK title *House Of Usher*) in it. One thing made it easier on the eye than other AIP attempts to fuse British and US horror – Lovecraft's New England settings translated well to a small English village.

Adams has arrived in England to see his love, who has returned home to her family from an American college. The first intimation that all is not well comes when Adams asks his way in the village, and the bucolic locals shun him... arriving at the house, he finds father Boris extremely hostile, a dodgy butler, and mother languishing in her room, unwilling to see anyone. In fact, Farmer is the only member of the family.

A little night exploration reveals all, a meteor had crashed on the estate several years before, leaving much of it barren. A brief chat with Patrick Magee – at his insouciant best – as the ex-doctor who attended dying family members and is now a shunned alcoholic, reveals that the family have all died horribly from some disease that he cannot name. Meanwhile, in the greenhouse, strange colours glow and pulse, while mutated plants and animals scream and twist in the night.

Mother goes mad, and runs around the estate screaming, the butler finally dies and dissolves to dust, and Boris goes too far with the remains of the meteor, turning a glowing silver and charging around the house, smashing anything that moves before Adams can finally destroy him.

In its brief 75-minute running time, this movie builds an atmosphere of brooding menace that manages to ignore the obvious fact that the frail Karloff is doubled at the end by a man in a painted silver Karloff mask. The suspense is well maintained, and the scene where Farmer is grasped by a mutated plant in the greenhouse really does make the viewer jump out of their seat.

A good mix of AIP showmanship and British restraint, it is well worth a look – just do not expect *The Colour Out Of Space*!

Die, Monster, Die

The Oblong Box (1969) was the last solely AIP-produced movie of the 1960's. Begun by Michael Reeves, it was taken over by Gordon Hessler when Reeves died half-way through production. Reeves is a fascinating figure whose career will be looked at in detail in the chapter about Tigon. This would have been his fourth film, and is a story of revenge. One of two brothers is disfigured and buried while still alive. Half-mad, he drags himself from his coffin and wreaks revenge. Ruined by bad make-up (the deformities look like boils and acne), and the break in directorial continuity, the film wastes Vincent Price, Christopher Lee, Hilary Dwyer, and a small cameo from Rupert Davis, who cameoed in a lot of horror movies in this period.

Hessler brought in writer Chris Wicking to help him try and salvage the script. It was too late, but it did establish Wicking as a writer to watch (he later went on to script several Amicus and Hammer movies). The only thing that did not need salvaging was John Coquillon's excellent photography, and if nothing else, it is beautiful to watch. It could have been better, but the disjointed nature of the project precluded any real chills.

Hessler and Wicking were behind the next year's *Cry Of The Banshee* (1970), with Tim Kelly's original script re-worked by Wicking, and John Coquillon back behind the camera. Another of Vincent Price's horror movies (did AIP ever let him rest during this period?), it again has Hilary Dwyer in the cast, as well as Hugh Griffith and Sally Geeson.

This was a comic book take on *Witchfinder General* (1968, US title *The Conqueror Worm*) and is pretty shoddy when compared to Tigon's own unofficial follow-up, *Blood On Satan's Claw* (1970) aka *Satan's Skin*. Once again, Price is a witchfinder, and one of his victims – the suitably irate Elizabeth Bergner – places a

The Oblong Box

curse on him as she is about to be killed. This curse takes the shape of Patrick Mower, a werewolf who follows Price around the country, cropping up at odd moments when he goes about his duties.

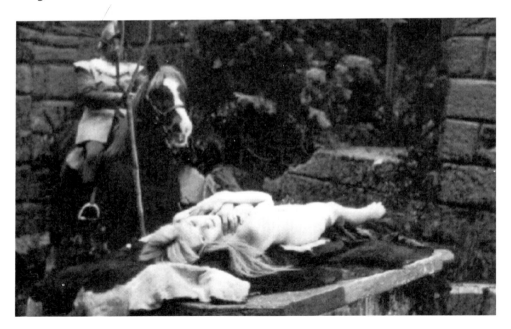

Cry Of The Banshee

Mower does his best with some appalling make-up, and Price returns to his hammier ways after *Witchfinder General*, but the kinetic use of camera by Hessler adds some dynamism to the movie, and allows for the liberal use of gore and nudity to provide some shocking cuts, if little else. The problem is that the script has little

The Abominable Dr Phibes

suspense or reason to it, and is not even surreal enough to be dreamlike. A noble failure – worth watching, but not a classic.

Something that could not be said of Price's next AIP outing in the UK. *The Abominable Dr Phibes* was made in 1971, and is one of the finest British horrors of its period. I was unsure about including it in the horror comedy section; certainly camp, and full of black humour, it has a nasty edge that stops it being a full-blown laugh-fest. Rather, it is a deeply ironic film.

Dr Anton Phibes is out for revenge. His wife died during a routine operation, and he intends to kill every one of the surgical team that performed the operation. To do this, he constructs a series of bizarre deaths based upon the curses on the Pharaoh. So we see a nurse having her head covered in liquified brussels sprouts, and locusts set upon her; a doctor attacked by rats (cute and cuddly rather than frightening, I'm afraid) in his aeroplane, another doctor attacked by vampire bats, and poor old Maurice Kaufman speared to a door by the golden horn of a unicorn – which has to be unscrewed counter-clockwise because of its thread, the poor corpse's legs turning circles for the camera.

The best death of all, however, is reserved for Terry-Thomas. While watching a naughty film, he is accosted by the Doctor's lovely assistant Vulnavia, who distracts his attention by belly-dancing while the good Dr Phibes attaches a drain to him... his blood is left on the mantle shelf in seven pint jars.

The police are represented by long suffering Peter Jeffrey, eager Neil Connery, and the irascible John Cater as their superintendent, who even accosts Jeffrey on his way to the toilet. The police's problem is that they know Phibes is behind the murders, but they also know that he died in a car crash several years before... not quite correct. Phibes is hideously scarred, with no features to speak of, and only becomes Price when he dons his rubber face mask. He also speaks through his throat and eats through a tube somewhere behind his neck.

The script – by James Whiton and William Goldstein – is suitably wacko for such a concept, and director Robert Fuest (an *Avengers* graduate) goes to town, squeezing as much as possible from the cheap art-deco sets. Basil Kirchin, an avant-garde composer and jazz musician, concocts a score that mixes weird noise with 1920's jazz and popular music. This is important, as Phibes is an organist who has a papier mâché band constructed in the ballroom of his house.

Stylish and witty as the movie is, it is the gravity of Joseph Cotten's performance as the surgeon who has to help the police find Phibes before his own son is killed that gives the film balance. Without this, it would descend into black farce. As it is, it maintains a fine balance, with genuine horrors shot through with gallows humour.

All this and Louis M Heyward produced it for AIP without interfering.

The Abominable Dr Phibes proved so popular that Fuest co-scripted (with Robert Blees) and directed a sequel in 1973. *Dr Phibes Rises Again* sees the doctor rise from his tomb (in which, self-embalmed, he placed himself at the conclusion of the first movie) in order to set off for Egypt in search of a hidden spring of ever-lasting life. Perhaps he should just ask his assistant Vulnavia, who is with him, though at the end of the previous movie, she was killed in a hail of acid.

But never mind such details. In this movie, Jeffrey and Cater follow Phibes to Egypt after he has left the usual trail of bodies in his wake. The irritable superintendent and the baffled inspector join forces with Robert Quarry, fresh from his US success as Count Yorga – in *Count Yorga Vampire* (1970) and *The Return Of Count Yorga* (1971) – and acting with a wonderful disinterest in the proceedings. Quarry is an Egyptologist who has stolen Phibes' map, and the good Dr is after him. In a sub-plot that is not fully developed, Quarry is down to his last few drops of "eternal life" elixir, and so needs the spring, as without it, he will age a hundred years and die.

Back in England, Terry-Thomas reprises as a murder victim, and Beryl Reid is his wonderfully vague sister, while Quarry's assistant is taunted by wind-up toy snakes, then impaled through the brain by a fake telephone receiver.

Once in Egypt, Gerald Sim is sandblasted to death, and John Thaw is squashed in a mechanical contraption. It all ends with Phibes eluding the police, and leaving a desperate Quarry pleading to be allowed through the gates that have opened to allow Phibes, his dead wife, and Vulnavia into the spring.

Full of thrills and sick laughs, it moves even faster than the first movie, but at the expense of genuine chills. Both films are packed full of character actors hamming and mugging, and glorious low-budget sets. Fuest directs with a sure hand, which makes you wonder why he messed up his version of Michael Moorcock's sci-fi masterpiece *The Final Programme* in the same year. Never mind, these were two of the early 1970's best horrors.

In between these, AIP gave us *Whoever Slew Auntie Roo?* (1972, US title *Who Slew Auntie Roo?*), aka *Gingerbread House*. Produced by John Pellat in a deal with Hemdale, it was written by Robert Blees and Jimmy Sangster, with direction from Curtis Harrington.

Shelley Winters, in the middle of her B-picture comeback, stars as a lunatic and psychotic woman who menaces two orphaned kids. A kind of Hansel And Gretel for grown-ups. Like all kids in movies, they were so bratty that you found yourself on her side, and wanted her to get them. It was a minor piece, with some chilling moments and a bravura performance from Winters. However, over the course of ninety minutes it becomes a bit of a chore, and is not one of Sangster's better efforts. It does have excellent photography from Desmond Dickinson, though.

I have to own up, the kids are played by Chloë Franks and Mark Lester, the latter on the downward slide from his *Oliver!* (1968) days. I saw this film as a kid, hated it, and have nursed a totally irrational dislike of Lester ever since. Even great cameos from Hugh Griffith, Ralph Richardson (was this his first horror since 1933's *The Ghoul*?), and Rosalie Crutchley cannot help me be objective.

As Hammer went into decline, and Amicus began to look around for co-productions to meet rising costs, it must have been obvious that the horror market was in decline. Post-*Exorcist* (1973), the trend was for big budget horror on both sides of the Atlantic. The smaller companies could not compete. AIP kept going longer in the States through sheer diversity, scoring sci-fi hits with *Westworld* (1974) and *Futureworld* (1976). So it was not surprising that Amicus turned to AIP for help.

Madhouse (1974) aka *The Revenge Of Dr Death*, directed by Jim Clark. Scripted by Greg Morrison and produced by Milton Subotsky, it was really an Amicus movie with a minimal AIP money-input. It will be discussed in the Amicus chapter.

Suffice to say that it was not a great success financially (although quite a good movie), and led to AIP finally withdrawing from a depressed British market.

12. Searching Through The Sixties

Hammer flourished during the 1960's, Amicus not far behind. Anglo-Amalgamated, Independent Artists, Herman Cohen and AIP all contributed to the genre. But there were also a string of horrors emanating from either low-budget independents or large American conglomerates that wanted to jump the bandwagon set rolling by James Carreras and oiled by Milton Subotsky.

It was a strange period for these film-makers. The necessary restraints of pre-Hammer British horror were evaporating but, as has been seen, the older producers had trouble coming to terms with their previous experience and the demands of the new audience. The censor was also extremely erratic: many Italian movies like *Black Sabbath* (1963) and *Bloody Sunday* – both English-titled and dubbed Mario Bava movies – gained legendary reputations on allegedly being cut to shreds by the censor. Ironically, for many of them false rumours of cut gore did little more than tarnish reputations when time – and permissiveness – allowed any cuts to be restored.

If the UK was bad, getting a movie to the States was worse. The iconography of horror in the US was based on the Universal model of the 1930's and 1940's, and the cheesy monster drive-in syndrome of AIP. Censorship was erratic from State to State, and there was a distinct antipathy to non home grown product (unless it was the Toho drive-in fodder of *Godzilla*, or the TV-fuelled Mexican horror industry).

As a result, many producers were caught in the middle, and while big studio movies still adhered to the old-fashioned models, giving us movies like MGM's *The Haunting* (1963) and 20th Century Fox's *The Innocents* (1961), the smaller and more desperate producers hit on a strange compromise whereby there was a build-up to a gore fest, then a quick cut. This may have fooled the censor, but ultimately caused the audience to go home thinking that they had seen more blood than was actually on screen. In the long run, the compromise forced producers to run against the censor in the gore war.

Was this a good thing? Perhaps; it seems a shame that many horror movies now aspire to gore where a more subtle approach would befit the story. The story of the 1960's shows that there is room for both.

The 1960's began with a burst of activity. In 1960 there were five horror movies produced outside of already mentioned companies. With these five, the great horror dichotomy that split the 1960's was spelled out.

Doctor Blood's Coffin (1960) was a collaboration between independent Caralan and America's United Artists company, keen to boost the British industry. A blatant attempt to steal a part of the Hammer market, it has motifs that re-echoed through Hammer movies down the years.

In a deep and disused Cornish tin mine, the good Doctor is working away at re-animating corpses and giving life to the dead and the undead: those he has built himself. An unholy amalgam of zombie story and Frankenstein mythos, it has a certain charm lent to it by the direction of Sidney J Furie, who was beginning to gain a reputation as a director with an imaginative eye through low-budget horror. In truth, he does not have that much to work with here, as Jerry Juran's script is at the level of a comic strip. Accordingly, the lighting and camera work (by Stephen Dade) reflect this, using the Eastmancolor stock to turn the movie into a bright farrago.

The acting is solid, Keiron Moore is a good romantic lead, capable also of the action man roles. Here he combines both, trying to save his girlfriend Hazel Court from the nefarious Doctor, who has designs on her. Court breezes through the film, adding

Doctor Blood's Coffin

a lightness of touch that the somewhat stolid supporting cast are unable to provide. The cheapness of budget is reflected in the lack of character actors doing their usual turns. By about an hour in, the viewer yearns for a Percy Herbert, or Michael Ripper – or even Miles Malleson, playing a bumbling vicar... comic book material of this sort needs stock characters to keep it ticking over, as there is not the depth of characterisation to hold the interest.

The climax, however, is filmed in kinetic style by Furie, aided by a good score from Buxton Orr (something of an unsung musical horror hero). With its use of the tin mines, it sets up resonances used by John Gilling to good effect in Hammer's *The Plague Of The Zombies* (1965) some six years later.

At the other end of the scale to *Doctor Blood's Coffin* is *The Innocents* (1961) aka *Suspense*, a 20th Century Fox-funded co-production with Achilles. Jack Clayton served as producer and director, working closely with a certain Freddie Francis, who was cinematographer. Both men turn in an excellent job, creating an atmospheric ghost story whose premise is only spoilt by the William Archibald and Truman Capote script. This insists on a psychological explanation for the ghosts seen by Deborah Kerr's repressed governess; a psychology/paranormal debate left open by Henry James, whose novel *The Turn Of The Screw* inspired this (fairly) close adaption.

Time to own up, as I find James – an American Anglophile who spent most of his life in England – dry and dull to read. He is also insufferably priggish and snobbish. So I never expected to like this movie. However, despite an ending which seems to negate the rest of the 99-minute running time, the film has a genuinely claustrophobic and paranoid air, mixed with the atmosphere of a fairy-tale gone wrong. It has been argued that the decision to film in Cinemascope negated the attempts to enclose the world that the film represents. This is true on the big screen, but as the film is mostly seen on TV these days, panning or letter-boxing the print tends to restore any lost atmosphere.

Ironic that one of the quintessential English ghost stories was written by an American... but James, for all his literary faults, knew his England and his time. Kerr is a sexually vibrant young woman, forced by circumstance to repress her ideas and emotions in order to earn a living as a governess, teaching other people's children. When she begins to see ghosts, and believes the malevolent spirits of dead servants to be possessing the young children in her charge, it pushes her already fragile mind

The Innocents

closer to the edge. Is it hysteria caused by her hemming in every thought, or is it a true case of possession where no-one will hear her cries?

The almost-empty house which she inhabits with the children is exploited to the full by Clayton's twisting and fluid camera. Jump cuts and good use of sound make it the sort of movie where, despite its lack of outright chills, you cannot help looking behind you. Excellent supporting work from Megs Jenkins, Michael Redgrave, and Peter Wyngarde give the film a patina of sophistication that lower-budgeted movies could only aspire to. Clayton uses the camera in a way that he could only dream of when he made *The Bespoke Overcoat* some four years before. Nonetheless, like the earlier film it is a simple tale told in a leisurely way, concentrating on atmosphere rather than plot development. The ending is a twentieth century cop-out, although James would no doubt have been aware when writing the novel that many mediums of the Victorian age were women. Later theory suggests that women became almost hysterical mediums, their repression forcing them to mediumship as a release from the chains of propriety. In becoming a medium, women were able to say and do things under the pretence of trance that would otherwise have scandalised society, and blackened their names.

In direct contrast, the King Brothers dusted down the plastic models and gave us Eugene Lourie's *Gorgo* (1960), a monster farrago almost as boring as his incredibly dull *Behemoth*.

It only runs for seventy-eight minutes, but this seems to be forever. A monster is decimating Irish fishing fleets, and a small boy helps heroes Bill Travers and William Sylvester trap the creature, which resembles some kind of aquatic dinosaur. Instead of studying it, or handing it over to the government, or whatever it is that usually happens in this kind of movie, they decide to show it as a fairground attraction at Battersea, in the heart of London.

By now, we are already leaving any ideas of horror behind, and moving off

Gorgo

into the realms of fantasy... for instance, how did they get a licence from the local authorities to show such a creature, eh? What about fire regulations, and the health and safety act, eh?

Okay, so I am being flippant, but believe me, you will be too when you sit through this. Travers and Sylvester row about the creature; one is in favour of milking it for big bucks, the other has a conscience and – pretty soon – a drink problem. Meanwhile, the boy wants to let the creature go. Why he is still with them I do not know – I would have given up by this point.

The alleged climax occurs when the creature's mother comes to get it... but the effects are so paltry, you just cannot get scared or even excited.

Writers John Loring and Daniel Hyatt should be ashamed of themselves. Oh, and there is even an ageing Bruce Seton in the cast, to show that working for Tod Slaughter only keeps you in the bargain basement.

Marginally better, but not by much, was *The Hands Of Orlac* (1960), a British/French co-production from Riviera/Pendennis. Made in the UK with a cast that included Christopher Lee and Donald Wolfit, with US star Mel Ferrer to give it US saleability, the script by John Baines and Edmund T Greville was flat, and Greville's direction even worse. Wolfit is as hammy as ever, and even Lee cannot resist the temptation to overplay. To make it worse, Ferrer is one of these deadly serious actors who believes in "art", and plays his role like a constipated seal.

However, the original story (from Maurice Renard's guignol novel) cannot be ruined. The love of a mad surgeon for another man's wife, and the way in which he grafts the hands of a murderer onto the pianist husband's stumps, is one of the original grand guignol shockers. Unfortunately, no-one can match Peter Lorre (who did it in 1935 as *Mad Love*), and the brave idea of mixing a Hammer star with the land of grand guignol – thus bringing together the disparate strands of UK horror – falls flat.

Never mind. MGM had a solid UK base at this time, with their own studios at Elstree, and were churning out B-programmers for the UK market. Quite why is a mystery, surely an attempt at A-production to get US bookings would have been an idea? For whatever reason, their UK films were more British than some UK producers' efforts. This showed through in the most subtle horror of 1960: *Village Of The Damned*.

Adapted from John Wyndham's classic sci-fi novel *The Midwich Cuckoos*, writers Stirling Silliphant, Wolf Rilla and Geoffrey Barclay cut out the verbiage and concentrated on the inter-personal relationships, turning it from a sci-fi into a creeping horror about paranoia and fear of the different and unknown.

Ultimately, fear is about that which we cannot understand, be it vampires, nuclear bombs, or a culture that is entirely alien. Xenophobia is at the root of most sci-fi horror, racism extrapolated into speciesism.

In many ways, that is what this movie is about. A strange pall falls over an English village. Soldiers who try to enter fall unconscious. Planes that pass over crash, their pilots asleep at the wheel. Then suddenly, all is restored to life. A strange and unexplained incident. Even more unexplained is that all the women in the village of a child-bearing age fall pregnant – even those who tearfully confess to the doctor that they are still virgins (remember, this was still important to a lot of people back then). Gradually it emerges that this has happened in towns and villages across the world.

The idea of this violation by an alien species or unknown force is down played in favour of what comes afterwards. It does, however, fuel the paranoia and mistrust between the men and women of the village. It is almost as if the men hold their women – victims of this violation – responsible for it. In a sense, this is one of the most horrific themes of the film.

When the children are born, they all have blonde hair and piercing blue eyes. They develop physically and mentally at a rapid rate. George Sanders, playing a doctor and scientist, is fascinated by them and tries to teach them. Soon he finds that they are out-stripping him mentally. He has government contacts, and soon finds that there is a fear about them that he does not share.

At home, he has his own problems. His son – long awaited – is one of these children (chillingly played by Martin Stephens, quite the best child actor in any horror movie), and his wife, in a tremendous performance from Barbara Shelley, cannot accept the fact that he is not "normal". Her attempts at maternal love are rebuffed, and she is falling apart.

Village Of The Damned

Eventually, after the children have caused accidents and ruthlessly caused the deaths of those who stand in their way, Sanders decides he has no option other than to kill them. He realises that they cannot be reasoned with, that they are the first of a colonisation, and have no emotions as we have them. He sacrifices himself, taking a bomb into the schoolhouse, struggling to keep his mind blank as he teaches, so they will not read it and see his intentions.

Rilla directs with an almost documentary feel, capturing the enclosed village and the strained tension brilliantly. The final scenes, with Sanders struggling against the minds of the children, are nail-biting.

MGM produced a semi-sequel in 1963. *Children Of The Damned* was written by John Briley and directed by Anton M Leader. It works as a suspense film, but has little of the tension and horror of the earlier film. Six children around the world are pinpointed as the next wave. They all have ESP powers, and the same detachment as their forebears, but do not share physical characteristics. In fact, they are of different nationalities and racial types.

Monitored by scientist Ian Hendry, who becomes emotionally involved with the older sister of the British child (Barbara Ferris as love interest), he finds himself at the centre of intrigue when the children are all gathered in London by the United Nations. Under the eye of security man Alfred Burke (a great performance, cold and hard), all the children escape their chaperons, and set up in a disused church. The army is sent in to worm them out as the world powers panic.

Hendry and Ferris are on the inside, and must try to stop the murder of the children... despite their best efforts, the likes of Burke have their way, and the children are destroyed in a downbeat ending that says a lot about mankind's fear of the different. The same fear that caused Jews and Gypsies, gays and the disabled to be gassed and shot by the Nazis.

Most horror movies do not have a point to make. They are entertainment playing on people's enjoyment of being scared. The contrast between the two was ably demonstrated by three films made in 1961.

The Anatomist was based on a James Bridie play and directed by Leonard William for British Independent Pictures. Basically, it was *The Flesh And The Fiends* all over again, only this time the good doctor in search of corpses was played by Alastair Sim. With George Cole and Michael Ripper in support, I expected this to be one for the chapter on comic horror.

Perhaps it is supposed to be, if so, then it just does not work. A comedy so black that it is almost tragedy, this is a stolid version of Burke and Hare, not helped by the appalling direction and low production values. Sim is, as ever, quite wonderful. His ability to dip from unction to low growling indignation, then to fey whimsy in the space of a single sentence is always breathtaking. And Cole, who made several films with Sim during this period, and was his unofficial "adopted" son, is true to the slightly cowardly form that made him a British comedy stalwart.

However, they are incongruous in such a setting, and the long wait for laughs that do not come puts the viewer off any chills there may be. Interesting, for Sim and Cole fans, or even Burke and Hare fiends (there are...?), but of little interest otherwise.

In a similar vein, BHP's *Shadow Of The Cat* (1961), produced by Jon Penington, is also lacklustre, which it should not be, seeing as it was written by George Baxt and directed by John Gilling, featuring in its cast André Morell, Conrad Phillips (excellent as the police inspector in *Circus Of Horrors*), Barbara Shelley, and William Lucas.

The problem lies in the premise, an old dark house mystery, the family have murdered the old woman who was head of the house in order to get their hands on her money. Now they all start to drop dead in a series of mysterious accidents. Shelley is the catalyst for this, returning home after a time away and taking in the old woman's cat. And it is the cat that is causing the deaths, acting as an animal avenger.

Morell and Phillips are suitably nasty, and the film is atmospherically shot (although the pacing is dreadful – not usually one of Gilling's faults). However, the thought of a domesticated, fat purring cat (as this one is) wreaking such havoc is laughable to cat owners like myself. Another problem is that a cat cannot be made to perform like a dog, only a happy cat will stay in front of a camera. And there is nothing frightening about a happy cat; this problem later nixed *The Uncanny* (1977), reducing a horror anthology to a farce.

Much more serious in intent and execution was Val Guest's *The Day The Earth Caught Fire* (1961), which was produced by Guest's Pax company in association with British Lion. Guest directed and co-wrote the script with Wolf Mankowitz, and it was a far cry from the comedies with which he made his name.

Edward Judd is a reporter on the skids, divorced and on the drink, his career is on the slide and the only thing keeping him in work is Leo McKern, a colleague who covers for him. Then there are sudden weather anomalies, and Judd stumbles on an incredible story; two atom bomb tests, carried out on opposite sides of the world at the same time, have sent the earth off its axis, spinning towards the sun. The only hope is another controlled blast to set it back.

Meanwhile, the heat gets worse, droughts and rationing begin, and a military state comes into play. But this – a whole film to lesser writers and directors – is only the sci-fi backdrop against which Guest and Mankowitz play out a drama of fear and relationships. Judd sobers, devoting what time there is to his son, to finding out the truth, and to the woman he meets when she is a Ministry receptionist (Janet Munro).

As London becomes deserted, law breaks down, and chaos ensues. Virtually the only people left are the reporters and print workers, with two front pages made and ready to roll: one giving the good news, one the bad. The film ends with the detonation, but not the result. A wonderful picture of hardened newsmen on the verge of breakdown, trying to keep their lives together in their beloved Fleet Street (an impression strengthened by then-editor of the Daily Express Arthur Christiansen playing himself); McKern almost steals the film from Judd, his playing so restrained as to be uncanny. The downbeat atmosphere of the movie, and underplaying all round drives the movie from the impossible to the possible, making it truly frightening.

Film train-spotters will notice Michael Caine in a brief extra role as a policeman, but in truth such minor points slip by as the narrative engrosses.

The Haunting

Just as engrossing in its own way was MGM's *The Haunting*, a 1963 version of Shirley Jackson's novel *The Haunting Of Hill House*. Although made in Britain, and featuring leading man Richard Johnson, it was basically an American venture, with director Robert Wise (a veteran of Val Lewton's RKO school of subtle terror) helming Claire Bloom and Julie Harris as the hard-bitten lesbian after the mediumistic neurotic (respectively), and Russ Tamblyn at the tail-end of his juvenile phase, as the nominal owner of the haunted house, visiting for the first time. Lois Maxwell and Valentine Dyall also appeared, sharpening their American accents.

Like Henry James, Shirley Jackson had more in common with the M R James school of ghost story than the American horror novel, so it makes spiritual sense for the film to be made here. Of course, tax incentives were the real reason, and US viewers would have had no idea why the leading man – a parapsychology professor – had an English accent when the film was set in America.

Wise learnt well from his mentor Lewton, and the strange rumbling noises and changes of perspective that could be the result of mental instability as much as spirits are all the more frightening for their lack of visible sense. Julie Harris is superb as the mousey woman who leaves her only home (with her domineering sister and brother-in-law) to take part in an investigation of the house, reputed to be a place of tragedy. Her performance is so on the edge of madness that the viewer is never quite sure if she is an unintentional poltergeist medium or is simply seeing ghosts.

As in *The Day The Earth Caught Fire*, much of the real fear comes from people trying to carry on an internal life with no normal base. In the former film, the earth is slowly crisping, in the latter, Bloom's lesbian is running away from her girlfriend, Harris is running away from everything, and Johnson is pursuing a goal which will justify his whole life, but is forever out of reach. Instead of a whole world off-balance, a series of personal worlds are off-balance. The result is the same.

A semi-successful attempt at the same subtext came a year later, with *The Caretaker* (1964), produced by Michael Birkett under the aegis of Caretaker Films. It took Harold Pinter's play and transferred it almost wholesale to celluloid, with minimal directorial involvement from Clive Donner, and excellent photography from Nicholas Roeg.

Alan Bates, Robert Shaw and Donald Pleasence were the players, with Pleasence as the tramp invited by two brothers to share their attic, and act as its caretaker.

It was wise for Pinter or Donner not to open out the play for the screen. Part of the power comes from its claustrophobic atmosphere. There is no plot development, or even character development. Pinter's world is a world of elliptical dialogue and non-sequiturs, where people let slip the truth about their fears and ambitions only by the odd accidental word. Within this claustrophobic nightmare, the only thing that matters is keeping your own internal life going when the world outside either crumbles or – in this case – stagnates. To do that requires an intensity that few can keep up for a long time – and these are people who have been doing it for a long time.

Like a suburban Beckett, Pinter's work is about the fear of letting loose, and the sick comedy of collapse. These people live in a perpetually tense state of flux, and it is pushing them towards madness.

In many ways this is more horrific than any monster movie, and it is no surprise that Amicus filmed Pinter's play *The Birthday Party* (1968), four years later. Both films ultimately fail because the kinetic nature of cinema demands more movement than these essentially stage-bound works can give.

In contrast, *Witchcraft* (1964) coming from 20th Century Fox in association with Lippert) was pure horror hokum, and none the worse for that.

Written by Harry Spaulding and given a strong direction by Don Sharp, the journeyman who helmed some interesting horrors, it took a torturous and twisting line through a series of revenge plots by a family of witches against long time enemies. A mix of contemporary gothic and grand guignol, it came closer than most to matching the two styles, but fell down on the episodic nature of the story. A stronger narrative would have made it a classic. As it is, the viewer can find their attention wandering over the short 79-minute running time. The strange casting does not help: Marie Ney and Jill Dixon are ineffectual, and leading man Jack Hedley is woefully out of place. Cast as an army officer or policeman and Hedley turns in a strong performance, but this is out of his league. Not that he is helped by Lon Chaney Jnr...

The younger Chaney by now had a severe drink problem, and was reduced to

Witchcraft

shuffling around in cameos and low budget duds. Even in his heyday he was buoyed more by Jack Pierce's Wolfman make-up than any real talent. In *Witchcraft*, every scene with him falls flat. It is both sad and painful to watch – but not as painful as Al Adamson's *Dracula vs Frankenstein*, Chaney's last movie some five years later, where he is so drink sodden and ill that he does not even get any lines...

The same team of Spaulding and Sharp had better luck the next year when Lippert teamed them again for *The Curse Of The Fly* (1965), with financing from 20th Century Fox. The only connection with the earlier *Fly* movies was the idea of a matter transporter in which a scientist gets parts of his – or any – body mixed with those of another creature. There were no flies at all in this movie.

Another imported hard-drinker takes centre stage with Brian Donlevy – best remembered as Hammer's Quatermass – starring as the scientist who is experimenting with people and animals, often leaving men with guinea pig feet and hands. There are also strange pulsing blobs of matter that may be people... or may not. Solid character support comes from George Baker as his son, who is himself harbouring a nasty secret.

Into the middle of all this comes heroine Carole Grey, who escapes from an asylum in the stunning opening sequence (a window shattering outwards in slow motion) and runs straight into another house of madness. Needless to say, it is difficult for the audience to find anyone to identify with, seeing as they are all mad... however, the twisting script has more of a narrative thrust than *Witchcraft*, and Sharp is an excellent director who brings his skills in adventure movies to bear on the pacing. Of the two, this is the better film.

Theatre Of Death (US title *The Blood Fiend*), aka *The Female Fiend*, was one of three low-budget horrors made in 1966, and was much the best of the bunch. Nominally, it starred Christopher Lee as the director of a grand guignol theatre in Paris who goes missing and is suspected of being the vampiric killer of women and old tramps – the wounds in their necks are caused by a rare style of dagger found at the theatre. However, Lee disappears less than half-way through, never to be seen again.

Julian Glover is the police surgeon whose girlfriend Leila Goldoni is an actress at the theatre. Her flatmate Jenny Till is also an actress, and seems to be under the hypnotic influence of Lee. At the behest of policeman Ivor Dean (at this time a popular TV policeman thanks to his role in *The Saint*), Glover is investigating the deaths, and keeping an eye on Till, who seems to see Lee everywhere.

The Curse Of The Fly

Sounds straightforward, right? Wrong. Scriptwriters Ellis Kadison and Roger Marshall (another graduate of *The Avengers* TV academy) are piling on the red herrings. Glover is off work with an injured hand, and is extremely twitchy. Goldoni is an ex-ballerina and former asylum inmate abused by Lee before he disappears. So are they the killers, and is Lee dead?

Although ninety-one minutes in length, the film actually seems much shorter as the twists and turns and red herrings are laid on thick, along with some nicely gory (for the period) deaths. There are also some great grand guignol shots taken before the theatre's audience.

The final twist comes with a guitar Till is always playing. On the back are inscribed her parents names... and just by chance the owner of the restaurant (a cameo by Steve Plytas, an unsung British support) travelled the same caravan from Romania after the war, and recalls the family being snowed in, the mother feeding the baby on her family's blood.

Glover stumbles on Till as she is about to kill his girlfriend. Lee was killed because he used hypnosis to probe her past and used her history as the missing last sketch for his show. A chase into the theatre sees Till killed somewhat ironically, when a spear used in a Voodoo sketch comes through a hidden trap-door and impales her as she tries to hide under the stage.

Theatre Of Death

Script and playing is fine, but Michael Smedley-Aston (who produced for Pennea) must have run out of budget when it came to a director, for Sam Gallu is appalling. Some of his shots are strange in a "what's that supposed to be?" way, and the camera forever goes in and out of focus. However, there is one way in which this works for him, the opening sequence, where Glover heads backstage after a performance, is shot by a hand-held camera that trembles continuously. In these days of camcorder culture, this gives the film an unintentional touch of vérité that adds to the chill factor.

The other two movies from this year emanated from the Goldstar stable, and seem to be the work of just one man, writer/producer/director Herbert J Leder. Although both use English settings, both have imported leads and in style are closer to cheap US exploitation than the general run of UK horror.

The Frozen Dead (1966), stars Dana Andrews, another hard-drinking American forced to find work in cheap British horrors. Now past the best that enlivened *Night Of The Demon* (1957), he plays a scientist who is working in a secluded English setting, his intention being to revive frozen Nazi leaders, on ice since the end of the war. There are some spectacularly silly scenes of freezers with fully-uniformed storm troopers in them, but little else to keep the viewer awake. Even Anna Palk, the beauty who enlivened British exploitation pictures at this time, can do little to draw the attention. Possibly the most boring film since *Gorgo*...

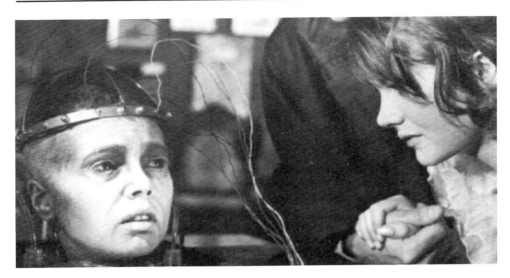

The Frozen Dead

Goldstar's other effort, *It* (1967) aka *The Curse Of The Golem* aka *Anger Of The Golem*, is better, but only just. An attempt to bring the Golem legend up to date, it did not quite work, but had more thought behind it.

Roddy McDowell – English, but long a US resident and a former child star yo-yoing between big-budget cameos and low-budget pulp – returned to his native land to star as Arthur Pimm, a museum curator who has the Golem made by Rabbi Judah Low in his collection. With his mummified mother propped up in bed, Arthur is not an everyday sort of chap, and he wants to bring the golem back to life.

The basic problem with the plot is that Rabbi Low's golem was a cipher, a strong clay man used by whoever was operating him. In this version, it seems to have a life of its own, and soon Arthur is powerless as the golem runs amok, destroying Hammersmith Bridge and killing another of the museum's curators. It even kidnaps Jill Haworth, the blonde who made a few dud movies more watchable during this period.

It

When the army are called into action, they decide to kill the golem with a small nuclear device. All this seems terribly irresponsible of them, as according to legend they have merely to remove the medallion around its neck. Even more irresponsible, they destroy Arthur with the device, leaving the golem to escape.

Quite enjoyable hokum, my only complaint is that the golem looks less like a man of clay than a tree trunk struck by lightning...

At least Goldstar had little in the way of pretension. MGM, in association with Filmways, had high hopes for *Eye Of The Devil*, aka *Thirteen*, released in 1967 and starring David Niven, Deborah Kerr, Emlyn Williams, Flora Robson, Donald Pleasence, David Hemmings, and Sharon Tate, with a nice cameo from John Le Mesurier.

Directed by J Lee-Thompson, a fine man for an action movie but out of his depth here, the film is about a French nobleman obsessed by pagan self-sacrifice. Set in the obligatory old dark house (or castle in this case), it would have been dated in the 1930's. The script is long winded and boring (by Robin Estridge and Dennis Murphy, from a novel titled *Day Of The Arrow* by Philip Lorraine), and the cast wander around wondering what to do.

A total waste of time and effort by all concerned; not scary, not even unintentionally funny, it has little to do with British horror – or any horror come to that. It was the type of movie beautifully parodied by Roman Polanski in *The Fearless Vampire Killers, or Pardon Me, Your Teeth Are In My Neck* (1967), a US production that utilised British talent like Jack MacGowran and Alfie Bass. Tate would have been better off in that movie.

Eye Of The Devil actually went through censor problems with the script, and had to be re-shot when Kim Novak blew out her role. Maybe the producers should have taken it as an omen.

The Shuttered Room

The Shuttered Room (1967), is a much better picture. Produced by Troy-Schenck for Warner's, it is based on stories by H P Lovecraft and August Derleth, and takes place in the sheltered environs of New England. As fans of *Die, Monster, Die* will attest, England and New England can easily be swapped, and one passes well for the other here. Gig Young and Carol Lynley move into her grandmother's old house, and are the subject of attacks by local youth. The house has a mysterious history, and there is something lurking upstairs.

Flora Robson and Oliver Reed skulk around being frightening and brooding respectively, and writers D B Ledrov and Nathaniel Tanchuck make a good job of adapting Lovecraft. Of course, the problem with Lovecraft is that his stories are always very static, and this does not translate well to the cinema. However, director David Greene and photographer Ken Hodges overcome this with kinetic camera work, aided by great music from Basil Kirchin.

Not a great movie, and more full of suspense that fear, it nonetheless is well worth watching. More than can be said for *The Vulture* (1967), a Lawrence Huntington production written and directed by that same man. Produced in Britain for financial reasons, it has no real UK input and looks like a low budget AIP movie (is such a thing possible?). Akim Tamiroff is the scientist who falls prey to an old family curse and is turned into half-man half bird, watched by on-lookers Broderick Crawford and Robert Hutton. To see three such talented actors struggle with such total rubbish is to marvel at what a pay-cheque will do. Not frightening, not funny, just foul (or should that be fowl?).

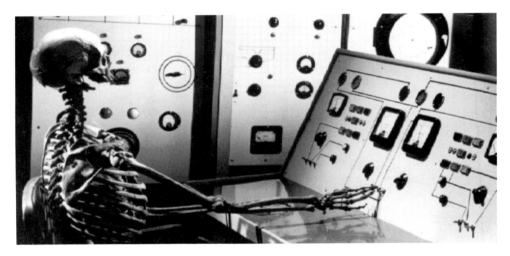

The Vulture

The last two films to be featured in this chapter are, in their ways, fine examples of off-centre British horror. The first, 1968's *Twisted Nerve*, gained a bad reputation because the central premise seemed to be that the families of Downs Syndrome children are apt to turn into vengeful killers.

Eh? Apparently, this was the popular assertion of the film's theme. A more than cursory watching of the film reveals more than this. It is true that Hywel Bennett's rich young man is a sick individual, especially if he believes that impersonating a person with Downs Syndrome, like his brother, will be a good alibi for murder. However, the point seems to be that his own psychopathic illness has driven him to the point where he is beyond any communication, and can identify with such a ludicrous idea.

Financed by British Lion and Charter Films (John Boulting), with direction by Roy Boulting, who wrote the script with Leo Marks, Bennett is a baby-faced killer who is adept at chilling the blood with his bland callousness. He terrorises Hayley Mills in a sufficiently nasty fashion that stops just short of being sexploitation of a nasty kind. Star turn is Barry Foster, supported by Phyllis Calvert, Billie Whitelaw and Frank Finlay in a bravura display of character acting. Essential because the characters and their inability to relate to each other is what makes such a situation possible, and that gives this film its edge.

It aspires to the psychological thriller that Hammer developed post-*Psycho*, but in fact goes off at a tangent and mixes kitchen sink drama with fear. Flawed but interesting, the idea that there are people like Bennett's character out there is not a pleasant one.

By contrast, 1969's *The Bed Sitting Room* is a horror by default. Adapted by John Antrobus from the play he penned with Spike Milligan, it is a savage portrayal of life after the atomic bomb, when all order is reduced to chaos, and all human pretension is reduced to a group of old tramps living out their fantasies and claiming to be turning from humans into objects of furniture. The players are a rag bag of comic talent; Peter Cook and Dudley Moore, Jimmy Edwards, Arthur Lowe, Marty Feldman, Harry Secombe; actors of the calibre of Michael Hordern, Mona Washbourne and Ralph Richardson also contribute.

Filmed almost entirely in a gravel pit by Richard Lester it flopped not so much through lack of quality as through its sheer darkness. People expect comedy from Milligan, who also stars, but there is a side to his absurd humour that takes that absurdity and takes it beyond laughs. This is the absurdity of Alfred Jarry and Samuel Beckett, where human frailties and pretensions are exposed for ridicule. Just as Michael Reeves reduced good and evil to two old people bickering in *The Sorcerers* (1967), so Milligan and Antrobus reduced great nations and great ideologies to what they really are; a bunch of raggedy-arsed idiots arguing about nothing while the world collapses around them.

Now that really is frightening.

13. The Terrors Of Tigon

When watching the output of a company like Tigon, the viewer is faced with that eternal question about bad film. Is it okay to like it? And what is it that makes some bad film so watchable, and others so boring?

In part, it is a question of what "bad" means in any given context. I always use the term "bad" to delineate that area where the technical side of the film is in some way deficient, or the script is disjointed, the direction, editing and acting below par, etc.

But, within that all-encompassing area there are movies that are deadly dull, and those that unintentionally tell us more about the times in which they are made than any blockbusting high grossing success story. The films produced by Tigon, and more particularly their horror output, fall into the latter category.

The genuine auteur, the true film visionary, is extremely rare. Someone with the vision of an Orson Welles or a John Waters, whatever extremes those visions may take, seldom gets the chance to express themselves on celluloid. Film is basically a collaborative process, partly defined by its finances and partly by its very nature. Anyone who puts money into a film wants to have their say in what goes on screen, and any group of people working together, regardless of under whose auspices, are going to produce a work that is in some way a consensus of ideas.

However, sometimes bad film can break out of this consensus and express something truly original, thanks to the technical incompetence of its makers, or their greed. A truly crazed auteur, working outside of normal boundaries, can impose his will on those he works with, particularly if they are technical incompetents, and come up with something that is remarkable. The perfect example of this is Ed Wood Jnr, the American film-maker best remembered for his 1950's movies *Glen Or Glenda* and *Plan Nine From Outer Space*. Wood had little technical talent but a driving vision, and worked with people whose own technical skills were too limited to detract from that vision. His films are technically awful, but strangely compelling, and can tell us a lot about the America he inhabited.

Tigon, on the other hand, are a perfect example of how a desire to make money can lead to interference on a movie, and the injection of exploitative ideas that say more about the mores of the time than was perhaps intended. The best example of this is what happened to Michael Armstrong's film *The Dark*, which became *The Haunted House Of Horror* for its 1969 release.

Armstrong was a wunderkind who had made a short movie with a friend of his, David Bowie. This was in the days of the Beckenham Arts Lab, and Bowie's Anthony Newley fetish. The film featured a paranoid Bowie characterisation, fresh from mime classes, prancing around an old dark house. Interesting at the time, it now looks sadly dated. However it was enough to persuade Tigon boss Tony Tenser that Armstrong was worth investment. The money was forwarded, and work began on *The Dark*.

Armstrong wanted Bowie in the movie, and with hindsight it would have given the company a strong piece of cult product to peddle over the next few decades. Unfortunately, this was in the days of *The Laughing Gnome*, not *Space Oddity*, and so Bowie was nixed in favour of Mark Wynter, a faded pop star who had turned to acting and was building a nice little niche for himself. Later to make a reasonable living in childrens' TV and theatre, Wynter was hardly the epitome of swinging London that Armstrong envisaged for his commentary on contemporary mores.

The Haunted House Of Horror

The story revolved around a group of young people who go to a deserted and allegedly haunted house after a party. They intend to stay the night as a dare, and then return home in the morning. Dirty raincoat viewers who might have expected an orgy from swinging teens are sorely disappointed as they listen to bad pop music on a tape recorder and then explore the house.

This is where things turn nasty, as Wynter is brutally murdered, his girlfriend discovering this when his blood drips onto her through a hole in the ceiling. The rest of the teens decide that, instead of reporting this to the police, they must hide the body and pretend that he has simply gone missing, after all, one of them must have killed him...

The rest of Armstrong's original film is lost in a welter of re-written and re-shot scenes. Tigon had a production tie-up with American International Pictures, the godfathers of grind-house and drive-in fodder. AIP's man in London, Louis M "Deke" Heyward, was not happy with the picture's potential for the US market, and insisted on changes. Although Armstrong still seems to be bitter about this, almost thirty years later, the viewer cannot help but feel that one man's portentous fable of the 1960's became an unintentional mirror of the times, and in many ways a more interesting film.

Heyward's first move was to bring in Frankie Avalon, another ex-pop star from an earlier age, as male lead. Avalon was wonderful in the AIP beach movies with Annette Funicello, but was floundering out of his depth in a strange country and a strange genre. Supposedly a sophisticated older roué who is a fairy godfather to the group of teenagers, he actually comes over as a horny old man trying to muscle in on some dolly birds. One of the most pleasing moments of the film is when he confronts the killer and is savagely stabbed in the groin: how appropriate.

Another horny old man is added in a sub-plot whereby the most sophisticated of the dolly birds is stalked by an older man with whom she has just broken a long affair. Played with genuine anguish by stalwart character actor George Sewell, he becomes a good red-herring for the killer until he, too, is stabbed in the old house.

Heyward's insistence that a part be written in for Boris Karloff led to Armstrong adding a police inspector who had little to do with the film but merely wandered in and out when first Wynter and then Sewell were reported as missing. Karloff did not play the part in the end, and a bemused Dennis Price sleep-walks his way through. Yet this quality of not understanding what on earth was going on perfectly mirrored the way that his generation viewed young people at that time.

On a minor note, a dreadful "song" sung by the boys in a pub was added, detailing the horrors of marriage and "responsibility". Pseudo-hip in sentiment, but about thirty years out of date in style, it contrasts with the other musical item, where a group whose bass drum proclaims them the "The Jazzmine Tea" look uncomfortable in supper-club psychedelic shirts and play a pretty flute-led tune over the questioning of Frankie by the police. If it was available on record, collectors would pay through the nose for it...

In retrospect, it is hard to take the group of teenagers seriously, as they consist in part of future soap and sit-com faces like Veronica Doran (*Coronation Street*), Richard O'Sullivan (*Man About The House*, etc) and Robin Stewart (*Bless This House*). For someone like me, who grew up in the 1970's with these people on TV, seeing them as a bunch of hip teenagers is a surreal experience. They do, however, turn in excellent performances, aided as they are by the baby-faced innocence of Julian Barnes, and the mini-skirted pulchritude of Jill Haworth, a blonde who seemed to spend the years 1966–69 populating a string of horror flicks.

In this collection of beautiful people, it is perhaps telling that the ugly O'Sullivan and the overweight Doran are the pair who form a couple, and seem to be the only ones with anything other than a superficial relationship. Not physically built for the "beautiful" 1960's they are forced to look deeper for comfort, and end up with stronger bonds. And it is the most beautiful of all – the Victorian-art beauty of Barnes, with his innocent face and blonde bob like something out of a Millais painting – who is the killer. His psyche as fragile as his physical beauty, he leads the group back to the house (it is his suggestion that initially takes them there) again and again in order to relive the trauma he suffered when he was locked in the old house by his brother as a child, an experience that has made him afraid of, and psychotic in, the dark.

Heyward's interference, and the re-shooting of director Gerry Levy, have given the film a disjointed feel. This makes Armstrong's lusty death scenes, where the blood flies with relish, all the more shocking for their sudden savagery. Although tame by modern gore standards, the restrained tone of the re-shot scenes and Armstrong's original pacing (stretched out to almost painful lengths by later inserts) produce a film that has an uneasy tone.

In their attempts to make the film more exploitative, Tigon added another layer of reality, in which their subconscious notions of youth and its desires clash and contrast wildly with Armstrong's, creating a dual idealism that more than makes up for the unintentional hilarities hidden amongst the shocks.

Exploitation...

Tigon's raison d'être was exploitation. A grind-house and double-bill distributor based in Soho, they specialised in importing and occasionally financing films that would play in the lesser houses. They, and others like them, would suffer from the cinema attendance slump in the 1970's and the birth of video; but for a short while, they took advantage of the opportunities placed before them and went into production.

Exploitation is all about taking advantage of markets that already exist, and seizing the opportunity to fill gaps. So it was no surprise that Tigon financed the comeback of Norman Wisdom in *What's Good For The Goose*, a dire 1968 sex comedy that was an embarrassment for both the ageing comic and co-star Sally Geeson, notable only for its excellent soundtrack featuring The Pretty Things. For, despite its interesting track record in horror, the roots of Tigon lay in sexploitation, a closely linked genre.

Tony Tenser, the head of Tigon, originally ran Compton-Cameo with his partner Michael Klinger. They made their money by distributing and occasionally making nudie cutie and sexploitation films, many of which were photographed by Stanley Long and featured the talents and charms of Pamela Green, Britain's first nude queen. Yet at the same time, thanks to Klinger's desire for mainstream success and art-house credibility, Compton were also the British distributors for art fodder like Alain Resnais' *Last Year In Marienbad* (1961). And it was Klinger who put up the money for Roman Polanski to make both *Repulsion* (1965) and *Cul De Sac* (1966).

While his partner opted for the odd chance, Tenser knew which side his bread was liberally buttered, and so stuck to financing sexploitation, with the odd foray into the horror field. It has been said time and again that horror and sex are closely linked in film-making, and this is undeniably true in the case of Tony Tenser, a man whose filmic legacy lies in his ability to spot a gap in the market.

Tenser and Klinger disbanded Compton in 1967. Tenser formed Tigon, and Klinger went off to make a string of big-budget pictures with Michael Caine, including *Get Carter* (1971) and *Pulp* (1972), and also blockbusters like *Gold* (1974) and *Shout At The Devil* (1976) before succumbing to a heart attack in 1989. Unable to resist his past forever, he had produced the *Confessions...* series in the late 1970's.

Tenser, on the other hand, had five glorious years at Tigon, with a string of wonderful horror movies, before deciding that the increasing trend for more gore was not to his taste. He resigned from the Tigon board in 1972, and spent several years importing wicker furniture in Southport, on the Lancashire coast, before moving into the leasing and renting of property. I, for one, sorely regret his retirement.

However, his legacy is worth a closer look. It is a legacy that dates back to pre-Tigon days.

Compton had three notable terror flicks in their output. The last, *The Projected Man*, came in 1967 via a deal with the Anglo-American producer Richard Gordon, whose speciality was low-budget sci-fi and horror that smeared the boundaries, and usually featured a minor American star to give it US sales-push. *The Projected Man* was different, featuring as it did Bryant Halliday as the lead and title character. Halliday was a fairly good-looking but unknown actor with a trace of a European accent (I always claim it is German, but another aficionado – my wife, actually – claims it is Scandinavian. Who knows?), and he brought a calm authority to this tale of a matter transference gone horribly wrong.

Halliday is an independent scientist working on the project. However, he is working under the auspices of a foundation, and the chief scientist at this mysterious organisation is collaborating with a Government minister to steal the project and sell it in order to pay someone who is blackmailing them... if all this sounds confusing, it is because the periphery of the plot is never adequately explained, and the central thrust of the story seems to exist within this nebulous framework. Despite this, the pace and direction of the main narrative is so strong that the viewer does not actually care, or even notice.

Initial experiments in transference produce animals who die when touched, their electrical fields reversed. Halliday is on the brink of being closed down, he thinks for failing, but in fact because his secret can be stolen more easily this way. Paranoid in the extreme, and sure that his assistant – romantic lead Ronald Allen (better known as a television soap star in *Compact* at this time, and later in *Crossroads*) – is against him.

Like all loony scientists in movies, Halliday arranges a private experiment at

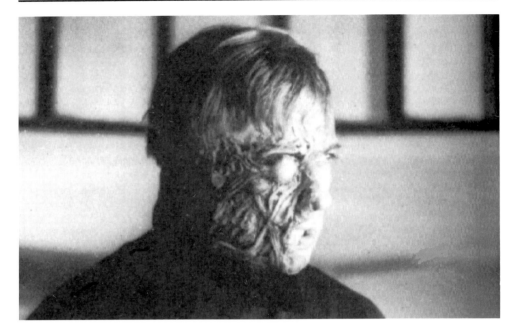

The Projected Man

night. He plans to project himself quite literally into the hands of the Minister and the head of the Institute, who are waiting for him to join them for dinner. He enlists the help of the obligatory dumb dolly bird secretary, who screws up... Halliday ends up interrupting a gang of robbers, hideously disfigured and burnt by his aborted transference and, crucially, with his electrical field reversed. He now burns everything, and kills everyone, he touches...

If this sounds like a throw-back to the Boris Karloff mad doctor movies of the 1930's and 1940's, do not be surprised: Gordon was a fan of uncomplicated pulp, and that is exactly what this is. Adapted from a pulp novel, and offered by Gordon's brother Alex, an AIP development executive, its locale was changed to London.

Director Ian Curtis seems to handle the pace and tension well, so it is somewhat of a surprise to learn that he was removed and the picture finished by long-time Gordon henchman John Reynolds. Fast, fun, and with that odd colour tint that all mid-1960's low-budget film stock seems to have, the only truly horrific element is Halliday's convincing burns make-up. Mad doctor devotees will not be surprised to learn that Halliday dies by his own hand when Ronald Allen attempts to help him reverse the process at the end of the picture. This fulfils another mad doctor movie premise in enabling Allen to walk off into the sunset with the pulchritudinous female scientist they spent the first reel fighting over.

Much darker than this pulp runaround were the first two Compton forays into terror...

The Black Torment was a sophisticated take on the *Rebecca/Jane Eyre* myth, made in 1964 by director Robert Hartford-Davis, and written by Derek and Donald Ford. All three were experienced sexploitation pioneers, producing *The Yellow Teddybears* the year before, also for Tenser. In the latter, sexploitation was given a serious social edge by the Fords, who wrote a hard-edged drama about schoolgirls who show their loss of virginity by the wearing of teddy bear badges. Derek was a cinema enthusiast and writer who worked in all branches of the business, while brother

Donald later became a justice of the peace. As for Hartford-Davis, he was a talented, if erratic director, who was also responsible for the flop pop movie *Gonks Go Beat*, in 1965.

The Black Torment, however, shows all parties at their best. A period piece in which the second wife of an eighteenth century Baronet investigates hauntings that have apparently followed the suicide of his first wife, the Ford's only fault is to give the viewer a rational explanation at the end, rather than leave this complex tale open. Hartford-Davis also directs with a brooding intensity that adds atmosphere to the necessarily cheap sets. Leads Heather Sears, John Turner and Ann Lynne are competent, but the thunder is stolen by stalwart supports Raymond Huntley and Joseph Tomelty, men incapable of turning in a poor performance. A quietly compelling piece, it is spoilt only by the resort to rationalising at the end.

The Fords returned to horror the next year, with a film directed by James Hill and under the aegis of Tony Tenser Films rather than Compton (a financial rather than artistic move). Taking a novel by Ellery Queen (actually a pseudonym for two American writers) and removing the framing device of the arch and irritating "author"/detective, they fashioned a chilling horror whodunit in *A Study In Terror* (1965).

Like 1979's *Murder By Decree*, this pits Sherlock Holmes up against the originator of the slasher genre, Jack The Ripper. Unlike the latter film, the Fords are not concerned with grinding an axe against the Masons, however justified that may be, and as a result does not suffer from the moralising that sometimes mars the later picture. Instead, the Fords take as their subtext the social conditions that breed prostitution, and the difficulties in escaping the poverty trap. As they are better writers than *Murder By Decree*'s John Hopkins, their point is never hammered home at the expense of pace or suspense.

John Neville plays Holmes with panache and a sense of adventure, with Donald Houston producing a variation on the usual bumbling Watson characterisation. Houston's Watson is every bit the ex-Army man, only too keen to get into a fight. The great detective is investigating the disappearance of a baronet's son, and this seems to tie-in with the Whitechapel murders. Included amongst the dead are the likes of Barbara Windsor and Georgia Brown, which ensures a surfeit of local character, if little else.

Holmes and Watson encounter Anthony Quayle, turning in a fine performance as a drily humorous doctor who has devoted his life to helping the poor and saving prostitutes. His daughter, Judi Dench, is romantically involved with the missing man's brother, who has also been searching. Just to round off a fine cast, Frank Finlay plays Inspector Lestrade, a role he would reprise in *Murder By Decree*...

Quayle's doctor is set up as the killer, and the missing heir is believed to be dead, as blood flows on the streets of London and Holmes and Watson get embroiled in a seedy world of prostitution and a drunken underclass with no hope. The sets and copious fog are atmospheric, and taut direction keeps the viewer on the edge of their seat. Art director Alex Vetchinsky had been working in British movies virtually since they started, and knew how to make the most of a shoe-string budget.

The dénouement comes when Holmes discovers the missing man; having married a prostitute who was after his money, he was then beaten and left for dead. Now little more than a shambling idiot, he is looked after by Quayle, who was his tutor when he was a medical student. And it is one of his set of surgical instruments that is being used by the Ripper...

The unmasking of the murderer is genuinely shocking. John Fraser, in a wonderful piece of casting against type (usually the genial friend or cousin in light comedies like the *Doctor* films), turns from the concerned aristocrat working with the poor into a vengeful animal whose only desire is to kill prostitutes, the very women his fiancée is trying to help her father save...

A Study In Terror

A tight, thrilling film that also has a depth rare in exploitation fodder, it was not perhaps a true indication of the future for Tigon: this film told you something by design, rather than by accident. However, as entertainment it was a sign of good things to come.

1967 was the year that London was swinging. Everything was beautiful in the garden, the Beatles were the British hope in a world-wide TV satellite link-up, and peace and love were the buzz words of the age.

In the centre of all this activity, in London's film capital, Wardour Street in Soho, Tony Tenser had split from Michael Klinger and started Tigon. In the year of love and peace they produced three horror movies, two of which were total negations of the times.

The odd film out was *The Blood Beast Terror* (1967, US title *The Vampire Beast Craves Blood*) aka *Blood Beast From Hell* aka *The Deathshead Vampire*, which was a piece of grand guignol Hammer gothic that actually stands up a little less stiffly than its role models. An obvious attempt to crash into a good solid market, it went out on the usual double-bills, and is not as well remembered as the year's other movies. Nonetheless, there are things to both admire and smirk at in its eighty-eighty minutes.

Set in late Victorian England, it begins with a beautiful and peaceful shot of a man collecting butterflies and insects by a river. Filmed almost through a gauze, it looks like the beginning of a nature documentary. Come to think of it, director Vernon Sewell must have made a few of those in his time. A veteran writer and director, he numbers several intriguing movies in his portfolio, as well as some extremely perfunctory work. Often dismissed as a hack who made a career out of one vehicle (*The Medium*, something he bought the rights to and first filmed some thirty years before), this does not quite give the viewer the whole picture. Sewell is competent if uninspired, and soon graduated in the 1950's to the treadmill of television. Some of the techniques used there to hook the viewer and sustain interest over a commercial break were carried over to his cinema work, most notably here and in his 1960 film *House Of Mystery*, made for Independent Artists and discussed elsewhere.

The Blood Beast Terror

Because of his high work rate, Sewell only really shines on those projects he was particularly interested in, such as those he scripted himself. But although the script for *Blood Beast Terror* was written by Peter Bryan, Sewell must have really liked it, as the film flies by in a series of climaxes that – along with the film stock quality – make it look like a superior episode in an ITC series. Filmed by Stanley Long and paced with small screen ideals in mind, it looks great on late night TV, unlike the more stately fables of the Hammer stable it so obviously tried to imitate.

The plot, such as it is, concerns entomologist Robert Flemyng, a suave scientist who teaches groups of rowdy young students about moths. He lives with his supposed daughter, Wanda Ventham, who seduces some of these young men and turns into a death's head moth, draining them of blood.

This is where the budget lets everything down; as far as I am aware, death's head moths – even giant ones – do not have a pair of black opaque tights over their head, and the halves of a red-painted tennis ball stuck where their eyes may be...

But if the viewer can ignore this – or just chuckle indulgently – there is much to enjoy, particularly in the usual superb performance from Peter Cushing as a police inspector and friend of the mad scientist, who traces the murders to his door and uncovers his gruesome secret, that the beautiful Wanda Ventham is no mere human, but the result of an experiment to cross-breed moth and human... and what is more, there is a mate pupating for her in the basement.

Overall, there is little suspense, and the film moves by more like a thriller than a chiller. However, it is still worth a look, if only for the wonderful cameo by comedian Roy Hudd as a mortuary attendant who devours his lunch with relish while showing Cushing's prim inspector the mutilated victims of the moth-woman.

Incidentally, Cushing once described this as one of his worst movies... a bit harsh, in my view, unless he was thinking of the black tights and the tennis ball.

Of a much more serious tone was *Corruption* (1967), Cushing's other vehicle for Tigon in the summer of love. Love was only to be twisted into cruelty in this version of reality. In some ways a steal from *Les Yeux Sans Visage* (1959) – released in the UK as the literal *Eyes Without A Face* and in the US as the more explicit *The Horror Chamber Of Dr Faustus* – no prizes for guessing which Tony Tenser would have used..., the Tigon entry was harder-edged than Georges Franju's elegiac and suspense-filled vehicle, developing some of the latter film's ideas.

Like Franju's cult movie, *Corruption* takes as its basic plot the idea of a doctor whose fiancée is badly scarred in an accident. In an attempt to give her back her beauty, he embarks on a campaign of murder and mayhem, using the pituitary glands of beautiful young women to win back his love's looks through the glories of science.

Franju may have had more overt gore and the beautiful sense of framing and art direction that many Euro horror movies have, but the British film had the writing talents of the Fords reunited with Robert Hartford Davis.

It is often said that British films have suffered visually because they are stage bound, and sunk in a theatrical, literary tradition, rather than the visual richness of a purely filmic culture. There is a certain truth in this, however, the logic and imagination of good writing is a necessity when dealing with the ultra-low budgets that a company like Tigon had – of necessity – to place upon its product. That skill, combined with a sure directorial touch, can be more truly frightening than a bucket of gore and a gauze on the lens.

This is where *Corruption* scores. Cushing is excellent – this writer cannot recall a single bad performance from the actor – and the supporting cast is also superb, especially Sue Lloyd, an ex-model who later proved herself a versatile actress in TV series ranging from *The Baron* to *Crossroads*. Hartford-Davis directs with the sureness of touch he brought to *The Black Torment*, and although producer/photographer Peter Newbrook disdains the overt use of gore, the film is always remembered with more blood than actually appears on screen. Excellent editing and the hard-nosed amorality of the Ford's script, which examines the mental disintegration of Cushing as much as his deeds, give the film a much harder edge than most horror seen in the UK up until this point.

If *Corruption* seemed to be a negation by default of the summer of love, then a more overt disgust could be seen in the movies of Michael Reeves.

Reeves is a director around whom a sizeable cult and an almost mystic reputation has arisen. After hustling his way into films, he landed the post of assistant director on an Italian movie called *Il Castello Dei Morti Vivi* (1963, UK and US title *Castle Of The Living Dead*) aka *Crypt Of Horror*. Following the usual Italian industry disagreements between producer and director, Reeves found himself finishing the film, as a result of which he was offered the chance to direct another routine horror vehicle called *La Sorella Di Satana* (1966, UK and US title *The Revenge Of The Blood Beast*), aka *The She Beast* aka *Satan's Sister*. Somehow he managed to turn a cheapjack Barbara Steele vehicle into a watchable movie, with some witty touches equating communism and vampirism.

Returning to England, he hooked up with writer Tom Baker, and between them they adapted two books for filming. One was a novel, the other a slice of dramatised history. Both had a cynical and distinctly misanthropic view of the world. Both were made under the auspices of Tigon, who Reeves browbeat into financing his projects. Both were amongst the best horror movies ever made: it is as simple as that. They are horrific because they show how the petty jealousies and rancours of humankind can evolve into malicious vendettas and violence when fed with a little power.

Reeves began work on *The Oblong Box* for AIP in 1969, and was shortly

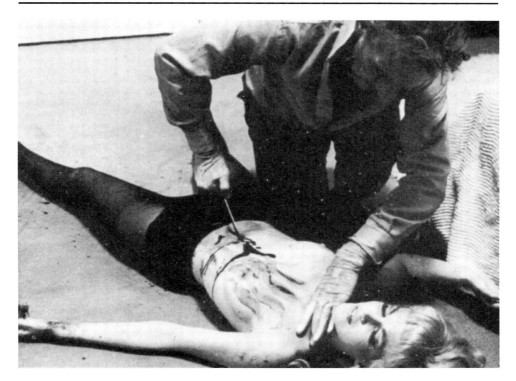

Corruption

afterwards found dead from a barbiturate overdose. He was twenty-five. No one knows if it was accident or suicide.

From such things are myths made. Many critics build a nest of motives around Reeves' work and sudden death that are no more than speculation. For every critic who eulogises Reeves' aversion to gore in his movies at the expense of thoughtful pessimism, there are people who worked with him like photographer Stanley Long (who filmed *The Sorcerers*) recalling the glee with which he flung buckets of blood and gore around the set.

Over a quarter of a century later, what does it matter what Reeves was like? The viewer will never know and instead, we can only judge him on the films. Certainly, he was a director who gained inspired performances from his cast, and had a unique eye. His scripts were, with the assistance of Baker, literate and witty in a mordant manner, issuing their message without once obscuring plot or pace.

But, in the final analysis, it has to be said that half of Reeves' reputation is based on his ability to pick a winner in terms of source material.

The Sorcerers was the antithesis of the summer of love. Ian Ogilvy is Mike, a bored post-teen who works in an antiques shop and is tired of his friends. He is looking for a new kick when he is accosted by kindly old Boris Karloff, who offers him an experience beyond his dreams...

After persuading Mike that he is not an ageing cottager, Karloff leads Mike back to his seedy lodgings, where he introduces him to his wife, played as a fluttery old lady by Catherine Lacey. It transpires that Boris is a Doctor – an expert in hypnosis who has been drummed out of his profession, and earns a few pennies helping people to stop smoking and lose weight whilst working on his master plan; he has a machine which will take Mike wonderful places. And in a wonderfully psychedelic kaleidoscope,

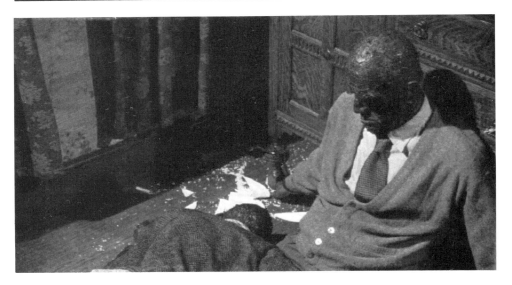

The Sorcerers

it does. Up until now, the film has seemed like a variant on the old mad doctor themes. This is about to change.

Mike begins to suffer blackouts. In these, he is under the control of Karloff and Lacey, who can vicariously live with the younger generation. They feel him as he breaks into a swimming pool and plunges into the waters before making love. They feel the excitement as he beats up people in dark alleys... and they feel the thrill and lust as he rapes and murders a singer.

Yet all this is blandly conveyed; the real drama is going on in one room, as good and evil, personified by Karloff (who wants to make his discovery public and regain his reputation) and Lacey (who gradually becomes an evil old witch, jagged on the thrills she can experience), are reduced to two bickering old people in a seedy back room.

The dénouement comes when Karloff, after a car chase when Mike's crimes are discovered, forces him to crash. The fire which consumes Mike also blows back to burn both good and evil, and no-one wins.

The film is an adaption of a book by John Burke, an excellent suspense novelist whose original work has been ignored over the years. He has spent most of his time writing TV and film tie-ins, including two volumes of Hammer film adaptions (three novellas per volume), the novelisation of Amicus' *Dr Terror's House Of Horrors*, and such unrelated projects as television sit-coms *Till Death Us Do Part* and *Dad's Army*. In recent years, he has been responsible for several volumes of *The Bill*, the police soap opera.

Around this time, Burke also wrote *The Weekend Girls*, an original novel in which a young girl is plunged into a paranoid world of half-truth and layered realities when her flat-mate goes missing. With a totally unexpected ending, it would have been another excellent pessimistic vehicle for Reeves, or even a Hammer psychological thriller. Unfortunately, it was never filmed.

Instead, Reeves turned away from the present to make *Witchfinder General* (1968), sometimes better remembered by its US title of *The Conqueror Worm*. In this, Reeves and Baker presented a stark and sombre picture of the witchfinder Matthew Hopkins who, like many of his ilk, used spurious "powers" of devil-finding to bring

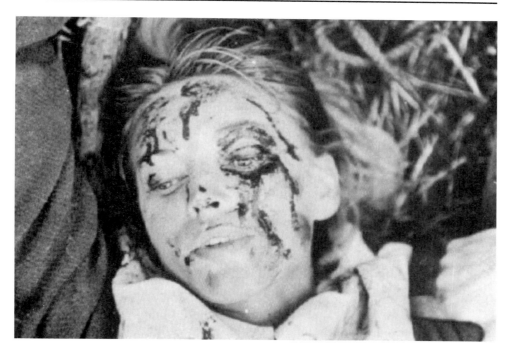

Witchfinder General

themselves wealth and power; none would oppose the man who could have them condemned as a witch, and killed. On a pedantic note, it was the most historically correct of British witchfinder films. No witches were burned in this movie, just as none were ever actually burned in this country, as that was a European prerogative. The kindly British preferred to hang or drown their witches...

Ronald Bassett's turgid book was turned into a stately drama with an icy performance from Vincent Price, possibly his best ever, as Hopkins. Interestingly, Price supposedly argued with Reeves over the portrayal, which differs wildly from his usual hammy grand guignol (somewhat like an American Tod Slaughter – but with more talent). Allegedly he claimed to have made over eighty horror films – so what had Reeves done to enable him to dictate Price's performance?

"I've made one good one," is the reply which is possibly apocryphal. Be that as it may, something made Price restrain himself, and give a performance that suggested a man with no emotional attachment to reality, only to his own avarice.

The plot, such as it is, concerns Ian Ogilvy's roundhead soldier, whose girlfriend is taken as a witch and her priest uncle tortured and killed simply because the girl will not let Price sleep with her. In search for her, Ogilvy deserts, and eventually tracks them down as Hopkins and his chief torturer are laying waste to the poor girl's back with a red-hot poker, in search of "devil marks" (of the "oh look, your skin is blistered and covered with sores now, so you must be a witch" variety).

The films ends with the girl (Hilary Dwyer, who puts in a good performance despite having little to do except scream a lot) completely insane, and Ogilvy standing over Hopkins' corpse, repeatedly battering it with an axe, his eyes dull with madness.

On one level a melodrama, the subtext of the movie is that man is an animal, never happier than when he is perpetrating acts of wanton violence for nothing more than his own gratification. Not a view with which I can whole-heartedly concur, but one which is forcibly and cogently argued. If only for this, it is one of the few horror films that is in any way truly horrific.

One of the incongruities that adds to the power of the film is its beautifully photographed English countryside. This was by John Coquillon, who also worked on one of the two other Tigon movies made in 1968. These were both lightweight in comparison, but not without their own value as entertainment.

Coquillon's photography greatly enhanced *The Curse Of The Crimson Altar* (US title *The Crimson Cult*) aka *The Crimson Altar* aka *The Reincarnation* aka *Spirit Of The Dead*, which was a strange concoction of cod-H P Lovecraft and M R James, dressed up in psychedelic clothes. Mark Eden plays the personable hero in search of his missing brother. Unfortunately, the brother had been on an antiques gathering expedition in their home village (what is this thing that Tigon scriptwriters had about antique dealers?) and has run into the gaunt and serious figure of Christopher Lee, out to avenge the death of his ancestress, burned at the stake as a witch (note the lack of historical accuracy here).

The first thing Eden does is run full pelt into a psychedelic party, complete with groovy music, body painting, and an attempted seduction. As a side issue, it is worth noting that Tigon had groovier soundtrack music than any other British horror producer during this period, and one of the joys of watching a Tigon movie with a contemporaneous setting is to look forward to someone at some point whizzing along the keyboard of a Hammond organ.

A co-production with AIP, like *Witchfinder General*, it not only brought Louis M Heyward into the fold for the first time, as co-producer, but also gave Tigon access to AIP stars. Whereas Karloff had agreed to play in *The Sorcerers* as a favour to Michael Reeves, here he found himself being written in simply because he is around. And Barbara Steele parades around in a strangely horned headpiece and green body paint as the spirit of the dead witch Lavinia, with a rather odd echo on her voice.

As the confused plot evolves, Eden falls in love with Lee's niece (Tigon starlet Virginia Wetherall), and also finds himself being shot at in the woods by Basil, the mute and strangely attired manservant of Karloff's professor, who is an excellent red-herring as the baddie – at one point he even shows our hero, with a glorious relish, his collection of torture implements.

Vernon Sewell returned to Tigon to direct the torturous Mervyn Haisman and Henry Lincoln script. There are vague references at the beginning to psychedelic drugs – which is interesting, as all the effects of mind control in the film are produced by Christopher Lee's skill at hypnosis. Far be it from me to suggest the text at the beginning was added to cash-in on the post summer of love LSD scares, but... the knowledgable viewer can no doubt detect the hand of Deke Hayward here, just as the insertion of "orgy" party scenes seem to be an attempt to exploit the older generations view of depraved youth – and so pull them into the theatre as well as the depraved youths themselves, who want to see what they are supposed to be getting up to.

Thoroughly enjoyable hokum if you check your brain at the door before viewing, it moves at a rapid pace, with a nice cameo from English sleaze/horror king Michael Gough as a butler with a severe twitch. Most notable are the hallucination scenes, where green and red filters and lighting are used to suggest that Eden is being held in some kind of star chamber while a variety of animal gods and Pan (or is it Herne?) – represented by a burly wrestler with a leather apron and horns on his head – try to force our hero to sign a "confession" while Lavinia looks on.

The film ends with Lee being burnt alive, and a sudden cut and fade between Lee and Lavinia that suggests he was not so much insane as possessed.

On a practical note, the film realistically treats the disability of Karloff's character, perhaps because the actor was by this time also a wheelchair user. During the final climactic escape from the house, it is heartening to see Eden stop in mid-

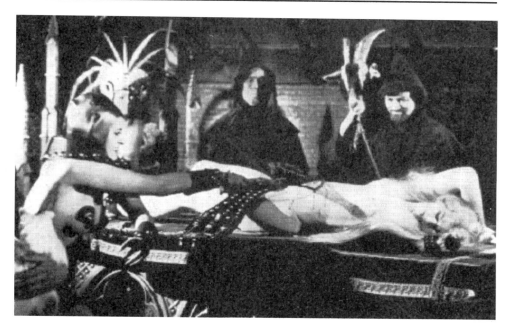

Curse Of The Crimson Altar

flight and help Basil lift Karloff's chair down the steps that every Tudor house is beset by... only a small thing, but somehow it gives the film a vérité it otherwise lacks.

Even the slightest degree of vérité cannot be credited to the final Tigon film of the year, which actually gained release in 1969. *The Body Stealers* is more than hokum, it is one of those films that you end up wondering why you watched, yet find yourself drawn to again and again in an attempt to understand what on earth has been going on.

One of those sci-fi/horror crossovers beloved of small-time producers (more promotion potential, perhaps – if it flops as a horror, re-promote it as sci-fi), it was directed by Gerry Levy with the same level of disinterest that marked his sections of *The Haunted House Of Horror*. In the latter film, this worked for the overall feel. Here, it has the reverse effect.

Patrick Allen is the investigator called in by army chief George Sanders when a group of airmen testing a new parachute go missing in mid-air after being engulfed by a red mist. Allen teams up with parachute engineer Neil Connery (who has the accent, but not the talent or looks of brother Sean – not that this stopped him starring in a string of Italian Bond rip-offs), and the pair of them search for a resolution to the mystery.

What it is all about is the abduction of the airmen by a group of aliens, who need to take the airmen back to their planet in order to undertake vital physical work that they cannot perform. They have chosen the parachutists because they were all astronaut trained. One of the aliens appears to Allen as a beautiful woman who tries to seduce him throughout the film, and always disappears into thin air at crucial moments. The other cunningly disguises himself as a fellow scientist, working at the test centre, having first killed the unfortunate human.

As always happens in tenth rate sci-fi movies (especially Amicus' *They Came From Beyond Space*), the human hero says "but why didn't you just ask? Of course we'll help," and everything ends on a happy note, regardless of the mayhem and death that has occurred in the preceding eighty minutes.

In truth, the only thing worthy of note in this film is the repressed sexual tension that Allen seems to bring to all roles of this nature, he was the same in *Night Of The Big Heat* (1967). Every woman he comes across seems a target for him to leap on top of... during one viewing of the movie, myself and my wife began to run a book on when he would leap into bed with the landlady of the grotty hotel in which he is billeted. She seems to be flirting – heavily – with Allen throughout, and the sexual tension between them seems not so much drawn as heavily etched.

The fact that their sexual tensions are kept tightly drawn and not consummated seems, in a perversely funny way, says a lot about the film.

Perhaps it was the fact that this stiffed at the box office (no Tigon film was ever a success as such, but to get the money back you have to at least get bookings), or perhaps it was their tie-up with AIP, who had a brief period of activity in UK studio space, but there was no Tigon product on the market for the rest of 1969. Instead, the turn of a new decade saw the release of their strongest films besides Reeves' classics.

Blood On Satan's Claw (1970) was a concerted effort to recapture the glories of *Witchfinder General*. Another seventeenth century witchfinder melodrama with plenty of torture and death, it had a downbeat feel that was depressing without having the reasoned misanthropy of the Reeves film.

The plot is a little stronger, centring upon the discovery of a strange set of bones in a ploughed field. The bones are taken to the house of Simon Williams, about to get married and inherit a goodly amount of real estate. His wife-to-be becomes possessed, he becomes haunted, and ends up chopping off his own hand.

Meanwhile, amongst the peasants, the sulky Linda Hayden is starting a little back to nature movement of her own, influenced by the malevolent power of the bones. And everywhere, people are beginning to grow patches of fur, the Satan skin that gave the film its US title.

Into the middle of this rides Patrick Wymark, no stranger to low budget horror (as a quick look at the chapter on Amicus will show), as a travelling magistrate. He is at first dismissive of notions concerning witchcraft, and is more concerned at lack of morality, roundly berating the local priest. He also dismisses Williams' loss of a hand as the result of mere insanity. However, the plough-boy who found the bones (Barry Andrews, one of Tigon's crossover sex comedy/horror leads) is insistent, and Wymark broods on the matter when at home, finally electing to return when hearing of more deaths. This time, he will be prepared...

Linda Hayden by now has all of the local children in her grasp, and is growing hairier by the frame. Even the poor old plough-boy starts to sprout fur as he follows his girlfriend, seduced into the coven.

All this may sound straight forward, but the direction and cutting give the film an unsettling, disorienting feel. There is a chase scene through the woods, in which the possessed children taunt and torment Andrews, stoning and injuring him in the same way they have picked off other adults throughout the picture. This is genuinely bewildering because of the rapid cutting and excellent camera work.

Wymark arrives as Hayden, now covered in fur and audibly growling, leads the children through an invocation in a ruined church, conjuring up their master... a cheesy monster. However, the director knows the first rule of low-budget horror (if you've got a terrible monster, then keep it in shot as little as possible), and Wymark uses a holy trident to spear the creature and destroy it in flame, all in a gloriously gauzed slow-motion.

Director Piers Haggard is no Reeves, but he brings a strong sense of pace and tension to the sometimes confusing script. He also coaxes good performances from Andrews and the pouting Hayden, a protégé of Michael Klinger who appeared in several horror films during the early 1970's. Wymark is one of those actors who never

Blood On Satan's Claw

turns in a bad performance, and brings a tetchy disbelief to his reluctant witch-hunter; a disbelief that slowly dawns into fear. The finale is frightening not because of the cheesy monster, but because Wymark makes you believe that, although he must kill the creature, he is absolutely terrified of it.

Photographer Dick Bush films the story in glorious autumnal colours, and this lushness contrasts nicely with the darkness of the tale.

The Beast In The Cellar (1970), was a horror of a different kind. Writer and director James Kelly secured the services of Beryl Reid and Flora Robson to play two sweet and dotty old spinsters with a terrible secret.

The Beast In The Cellar

Ostensibly, the simple plot was about their brother, who had been drugged and kept in the cellar by Flora – the dominant sister – to prevent him going off to war. Afraid to let him out, they had kept him down there ever since, and he was now quite mad. Flora keeps him in line by pretending to be their father, an old military man. So when the beast in the cellar does escape, who does he kill? Army men from the nearby camp...

The police, represented by T P McKenna, are after the murderer, and wonder why dotty and worried Beryl keeps pestering them... why, simply because she knows her brother is getting out, and finding his escape route leads to an accident which sees Flora bed-ridden and nursed by a young Tessa Wyatt, who falls in love with soldier John Hamill (another Tigon sex comedy star moonlighting in horror). Of course, no prizes for guessing who will be the next targets of the beast...

Kelly deals with the eventual chase and capture of the killer in a perfunctory manner, glossing over such details as how can a man who must be nearing old age have the kind of strength that mutilated trained soldiers and survived being shot at. And in a sense he is right to be so off-hand with genre details. The real action is not happening here; it is happening on one set, in a genteel and slightly faded parlour.

The real horror is in the characters of Reid and Robson, who have tortured themselves for over thirty years about their brother; should they have locked him up, should they have let him out, should they kill him now that he is completely insane? The real fear and loathing is in their relationship to each other, a pretence of everything being alright while all the time they hate each other, each blaming the other for what happened, and trapped by their own fear and unwillingness to attract scandal into keeping someone they love chained up in the cellar. The fear and loathing has eaten into them like a canker, so that the brittle and charged performances are like watching two women walking on egg shells.

The set pieces of the film are the long discussions in the parlour, where time flashes back and forth into the past as the sisters share a last meal with their brother before chaining him up, then snapping back to a present where they skirt around the real subject in small talk. Filmed in long takes that quite exhausted Beryl Reid (as she confesses in her autobiography), the clipped and elliptical dialogue approaches Pinter at his most charged.

The outside sequences are sometimes clumsy in contrast, so this is a flawed film, but one worth treasuring for its eccentric attempt to present a different face to horror. If Pinter had attempted a take on *Whatever Happened To Baby Jane?* (1962), it may have been a little like this.

The Beast In The Cellar was not a success, and there was a gap of a year before the final horrors emerged under the Tigon banner. One of these was a TV spin-off, and the other had the most overt blood and gore seen in a Tigon movie to date. It was the move towards this kind of film that forced Tony Tenser to sell up his interest in Tigon and retire, as he had no desire to make this type of movie. His decision to quit coincided with (and may have been partly spurred by) a downturn in trade for double-bill and B-movies, as the big studios returned to blockbusters and gimmicks in an attempt to win back TV audiences. In the pre-video age, there was no room for low-budget fodder during this period, and Tigon reverted to distribution over production.

Doomwatch

Ironically, it was the pre-video age that gave the company a chance to cash-in on a TV hit. *Doomwatch* (1972) had been a successful TV series that dealt with environmental issues in a semi-sci-fi format. The title of the show was the name of a government agency run by a maverick scientist whose team investigated environmental problems. Created by Dr Kit Pedlar and writer Gerry Davis, the series starred John Paul, Simon Oates, and Robert Powell. In the screen version, Powell does not appear, and Paul and Oates are reduced to small roles. Instead, the action centres around a Doomwatch scientist played by Ian Bannen, and is set far away from London on a small Cornish island.

The plot is simple; sent to investigate the results of an oil spill, Bannen stumbles into a situation where illegally dumped chemicals have leaked into the local water and fish, giving the inhabitants of the island the bone distorting disease acromegaly, and symptoms of severe mental illness. The islanders are trying to hide it, believing it to be in-breeding and a vengeance from God.

Having such a simple framework allows writer Clive Exton to explore the tensions on the island and the characters of Bannen, local teacher and fellow outsider Judy Geeson, and the locals that are still relatively unaffected by the disease. The latter include Percy Herbert, with an effective make-up that just coarsens and widens his brow, as the mildly afflicted and very twitchy local constable. Even the local priest is hostile, superbly played by Joseph O'Conor. His anguish is caused by his daughter, who gives birth to a dead child in the presence of Bannen. The daughter has the disease, and the unseen child is presented as being distorted at birth by the overdose of artificial pituitary hormone that is leaking into the seas.

In many ways, this is more of a suspense movie than an outright horror vehicle. The unease of the local atmosphere, and the repressed fear, is used as a counterpoint to tension as Bannen tires to unravel the mystery of the island. This is possibly because writer Clive Exton went on to become a best-selling thriller and espionage writer, as his talents certainly seem better geared to thrills than chills.

The director was Peter Sasdy, who had graduated from poorer Hammer efforts like *Countess Dracula* (1971) to suspense/fear pictures like this and the same year's *Nothing But The Night* (1972) – which, curiously enough, is also set mostly on an island off of mainland Britain. It was rapidly becoming apparent that Sasdy was a director whose expertise was better exercised in thrillers rather than horror. Having said all this, the movie is still highly watchable, being a noble failure rather than a total dud.

The Creeping Flesh

The final Tigon horror was one last barnstorming effort to capture the Hammer audience. It was directed by Freddie Francis, starred Christopher Lee and Peter Cushing, had bit-parts for Michael Ripper and Duncan Lamont, and was a Victorian period piece. *The Creeping Flesh* (1972) is about the discovery of a skeleton, the remains of a Neanderthal man. Scientist and archaeologist Cushing accidentally discovers that water can make the flesh regenerate on the skeleton, which promptly runs amok.

Yet another of those enjoyable "leave your brain at home" horror romps that Hammer had forgotten how to make, it was perhaps a little out of time to be a success. Certainly, there was more excess blood than Hammer had ever used, and Francis upped the pace from his usual stately approach to period pieces. The script, however (by Peter Spenceley and Jonathan Rumbold), was full of non-sequiturs, and did not really hang together. Despite this, Cushing and Lee are as enjoyable as ever, in the same year that they reprised Dracula and Van Helsing for Hammer (*Dracula AD 1972*) and rode the *Horror Express* for Benmar.

For me, the regeneration of the flesh was a little too close to the plot device used in *Carry On Screaming* to be taken with any degree of seriousness, but having said that the movie is still a hundred times pacier and more thrilling than Tyburn's attempts to resuscitate the genre a few years later.

It is ironic that Tigon, who seemed to have moved English horror away from the Hammer pattern with the films of Michael Reeves and oddities like *The Beast In The Cellar*, should close their account with a blatant attempt to copy a well-worn formula. Times were changing, and the values of the British horror film – always, in many ways, in conflict with the idea of change – had to adapt and change with them. *The Creeping Flesh* was a desperate attempt to rake in a few pounds at the box office, taking no account of the exploitation formula that had made Tigon shine so brightly for a while, and their was no connection with either the mood or the peccadilloes of the day. Instead of moulding history to a morality, as Reeves and Baker had done, Spencely and Rumbold had produced a time capsule script that impoverished the film, and spelt the end of a film-making adventure.

14. Amicus: Fairytales With Menace

If Hammer defines the British horror movie for the casual viewer, then Amicus is the name that runs second. Often seen as a "poor relation" to the larger company, Amicus was a two-man show; whereas James Carreras had an army of relatives and long time staff under his command at Bray, Amicus was simply Max Rosenberg handling the money, and Milton Subotsky dealing with the creative side. Although other talent was brought in – most notably Robert Bloch, who scripted several movies – Subotsky's tastes defined the Amicus output.

Hammer and Amicus shared a lot of talent in the 1960's; Peter Cushing and Christopher Lee were regulars for both companies, and Freddie Francis directed several Amicus movies during those periods when Hammer would let him out of the Bray dungeons. This crossing over of talent is probably the main reason why the companies are seen as similar. In fact, when their respective movies are looked at in detail, there is little similarity beyond the superficial.

Once again it is a great irony that some of the most representative of British horror movies were scripted and produced by an American. Like Henry James, Subotsky was an Anglophile who loved traditional ghost stories. Many of the Amicus movies are much more gentle in style and effect than Hammer. Whereas the Bray company was concerned with titanic struggles between good and evil played out on a large canvas (budget permitting), Subotsky was more concerned with the small things; little gestures and madnesses, usually played out in a suburban setting. Sometimes the budget let down their intent, but the fables of (usually) revenge were different in tone to Hammer.

Subotsky came to Britain and horror movies by a roundabout route. Born in New York, he served as a cameraman in World War II and worked in the army film unit, making training movies. Not exactly creative, it was nonetheless a good grounding in basic techniques. After the war he settled to an editing job, where he had to take old movies and edit them down to half-hour slots for TV showing. Through this, he claimed to learn a lot about story construction, claiming that he could chop a good half of any Hammer film and no-one would notice the difference. In fact, he claimed he could improve them...

Given that there was always an enmity between Carreras and Subotsky, it seemed likely that he would never get the chance. However, it does explain his penchant for anthology movies. The most remembered of any Amicus movies are their portmanteau collections, the format taken from the *Dead Of Night* (1945) blueprint. Each story is between fifteen and twenty minutes, linked by a framing device. Amicus movies that are full-length stories can tend to flag, or be padded out. *The Skull* (1965) is a good example of the latter, as will be seen.

Subotsky got into making movies almost by accident. Settled as an editor and distributor of these truncated B-pictures, he was approached by a group of film students who had a documentary about kites which they had not the money to finish. Subotsky approached Rosenberg, one of his regular clients, for the backing, and finished the film himself. It was acclaimed in documentary circles, and Rosenberg put up the money for Subotsky to write and produce a series of educational children's programmes. The buyer wanted a second series... Subotsky and Rosenberg were now a fully-fledged production company, taking the name Amicus, derived from the Latin for friends.

Subotsky was an Anglophile with a love of fairy stories and ghost stories, so it was hardly surprising that he settled in Britain after making a movie here, and wanted to make horror pictures. Rosenberg was strictly the money man, and stayed in the US, arranging financing and distribution deals. As a working relationship, it worked just fine.

Early Amicus pictures were bandwagon jumpers like *Rock, Rock, Rock* (1957), *Jamboree* (1958), *It's Trad Dad* (1961) and *Just For Fun* (1961) – rock'n'roll, Brylcreem and twanging guitars with zilch storyline. But in an era before MTV or even *Top Of The Pops*, British youth were starved of rock'n'roll, so these pictures made money. There were also dramas like *The Last Mile* (1959) and *The Lost Lagoon* (1959). These kept the pennies rolling in, but were not a true reflection of Subotsky's ambition.

In 1956, in the wake of Hammer's success with *The Quatermass X-periment* and *X – The Unknown*, Subotsky had approached Hammer with a treatment of *Frankenstein*, which incorporated more of the book than the eventual Hammer version. James Carreras rejected it, and promptly put his own version into production. For many years Subotsky felt a little cheated by this, and also by the constant sniping by Michael Carreras that the Subotsky Frankenstein would have been a dull movie.

As all three men are now dead, the real truth will never be known. However, I have little doubt that the Hammer and Amicus approaches would never have been compatible. Subotsky was always keen to cut away from blood, and leave it to suggestion, whereas Carreras wanted the obvious, knowing it drew the crowds and got the press interested.

Given this essential difference, it is no surprise that the initial Amicus horror was a much more subtle affair.

Subotsky was not credited on *City Of The Dead* (1960, US title *Horror Hotel*), except as author of the story. Instead, Donald Taylor got the credit, as it was a co-production with his Vulcan/Trans-Lux company, which was staffed by people responsible for TV series like *Robin Hood*. Amicus were invited to co-produce, and Subotsky – still living in the USA at this point – flew over to find that they had a 60-minute script and a budget too high to recoup on a mere B-slot. So he performed the reverse of his usual training and added twenty minutes to the picture.

George Baxt incorporated this well into his script, and director John Moxey gave the picture some beautiful atmospherics, with more dry ice and mist-shrouded woods than any other picture of the time. Perhaps this was to hide the lack of sets, but it nonetheless gave the film a fine atmosphere in which to work.

Yet another of those movies that is set in the US despite being made in the UK (at Walton, previously doubling for Canada in *Fiend Without A Face*), it stars Venetia Stevenson as a student of Christopher Lee's classes in the occult. To further her studies, he advises her to carry on her research in the town of Whitewood, Massachusetts. Despite Lee's excellent accent, any student of British horror movies would already be screaming at her not to go, but she does, picking up a hitch-hiker on the way. This is Valentine Dyall at his sepulchral best, archly dropping hints about witchcraft.

Once in town, she books in at the hotel, run by Betta St John. There is a strange atmosphere about the whole place, and the maid tries to warn her about something, but is cut short before she can unfold her tale. Meanwhile, back in civilization, the concerned boyfriend (a good performance from Dennis Lotis, a big band singer turned actor, and better than that would suggest) is questioning Lee's twitchy professor. He gets no change from him, but as soon as he leaves, Lee reveals by his actions that he does more than just study the occult...

Back in ghost town central, our heroine discovers that the inn where she is staying (the *Horror Hotel* of the US title) was once run by a witch who was burnt in 1692, and who bears a striking resemblance to the current owner. After a confusing encounter with a priest who is scared to leave his house while the sullen residents

City Of The Dead

troop about town (actually a two-street set, but claustrophobic for all that), she returns to her room and hears strange noises under the floor. Discovering a trap-door, she creeps through an ancient passage to come upon a ritual...

The smiling St John and Dyall, resurrected from their burnt state for one night a year, have their sacrifice. And who is that with them? The good professor, no less.

Remembering that this was a year before *Psycho* was released, the idea of the heroine being killed before the end of the picture must have stunned a few audiences. It does, however, add suspense to the end, when Lotis arrives in town, bent on finding his girlfriend. There are attempts to kill him, but he shows incredible determination as he intrudes on their rites in the graveyard. In a wonderful ending (helped by lashings of dry ice and a good score from Douglas Gamley, as well as good use of lighting), he hoists a cross into the air, the shadow falling upon the coven, scattering them.

Perhaps this was Subotsky's subtle dig at Hammer, mirroring as it does the ending of *Dracula*. It is quite the best finale to a horror movie made in the UK up to this point. The final shot shows St John sitting in her robes behind the hotel reception desk. When the hood falls back, she is nothing but a charred corpse, returned to her undead state...

Despite the success of this film, it was another five years before Amicus began to make horror on a full-time basis. In the meantime, dramas and juvenile movies helped the company to its feet. Subotsky planned his emigration, and was resident in Britain with his English wife by the time the next horror emerged. This time it was in colour, and used the two great icons of British horror; Cushing and Lee.

Dr Terror's House Of Horrors (1965) is a bit of a misnomer, as the framing action actually takes place in a train. Dr Schreck (Cushing) is on a train with Alan Freeman (a rare acting turn for the DJ, and he is surprisingly competent), Neil McCallum, Donald Sutherland, Roy Castle and Christopher Lee. As the train speeds along, he reads them their future from Tarot cards. Somebody points out that Schreck means death in German – what a giveaway! As each card is turned, a supposed future event is unveiled. In each one, death is the end result.

Dr Terror's House Of Horrors

Subotsky's training editing down movies comes into play here, as each story is tightly structured in his original script. Eschewing outright gore in favour of suggestion and whimsy, Freeman finds his family at the mercy of a killer vine that begins to grow and respond to speech, gradually enveloping the house. It kills his pet dog, and strangles botanist Jeremy Kemp when he stumbles on its origins. Even hard man Bernard Lee cannot burn his way out...

Neil McCallum is an architect who travels to his own ancestral home on a remote Scottish island to work on conversion plans for the new owner. She is the widow of an archaeologist, and strange things populate the house. There is also the mysterious coffin in the cellar, and the old family retainer who uncovers the family curse. Just when you think a werewolf is going to spring from the coffin, sweet widow Ursula Howells begins to change – shape-shifters can change sex, too...

Roy Castle gets a chance to act and blow a mean trumpet as a musician who, while working in the West Indies, steals the melody from a Haitian voodoo ceremony. When his group (actually the post-bop group of the late Tubby Hayes, and a fine chance to see some British jazzers blowing on film) play his new composition, then strange things happen, and he finds himself pursued by the god Damballah.

Christopher Lee is haunted by the disembodied hand of lunatic artist Michael Gough (as always wonderful), who loses it in an accident caused by Lee, the art critic who has always hated him. The disembodied hand is a bit silly (and was used again by Amicus), but the story is strong.

The weakest story stars Sutherland as a doctor who has several cases of anaemia brought to him. This ties in with his own uneasy feelings about his new wife. Urged on by his partner, he stakes his wife after she flies home one evening from a search for blood. The twist being that he is arrested for murder, set up by his partner, who is also a vampire. It is when this character turns and talks into camera that the story collapses. A wry ending it may be, but it jars with the sombre tone of the rest of the film.

Freddie Francis directs with a rapid pace and a sure eye, echoing the rhythms of the train. Each story gets faster as the train nears the end of the track. Of course, these future events have already happened, and the men are on a train to limbo, the halt at which they alight is quiet and mist-shrouded, Schreck turning into the grim reaper.

If this is the best of the portmanteau movies, it is simply because it is the first. The tricks and construction of the movies are set up and blueprinted in this, and the framing device – where the participants are on their way to the graveyard or some kind of limbo without realising they are actually dead – is never quite as surprising. Other movies may have stronger individual stories, but none has the overall impact.

In the same year, Subotsky took a Robert Bloch short story and concocted a surreal little film called The Skull (1965) which has four reels of hallucinogenic surrealism tagged on to it. This and another Bloch story – The Psychopath (1966) – the following year also showed the producer's ability to reconstruct his films at the last minute.

The Skull concerns two collectors of antique occult artifacts – played by those British horror icons Christopher Lee and Peter Cushing. In this movie, Cushing is named Maitland, this was a favourite name of Subotsky's, and train-spotter viewers should try and catch how many of his movies have a character with that name.

Lee has the skull of the Marquis De Sade, and Cushing covets it. Lee, however, warns his friend about it, claiming that it has a certain power. He begins to do strange things, like out-bidding even himself at auctions, seemingly in a trance, in an effort to obtain small stone gargoyles.

Enter the wonderfully slimy Patrick Wymark as a crooked dealer, who lives in a grotty flat and sells Cushing the stolen skull. He first appears bearing a book bound in human skin, and the way he gloats over it is genuinely creepy. With the skull in his possession, Cushing starts to behave oddly, and breaks into Lee's house in search of the gargoyles. In a struggle, Lee is killed, and Wymark attempts to blackmail the hapless and possessed Maitland. This is a bad move, as he dies spectacularly, plunging through a patterned stained glass skylight in his lodgings.

Suddenly, a slightly sinister film takes a dive into the unknown, as Cushing is grabbed from his house by a couple of policemen and deposited at a judge's house, where he encounters a number of strange and surreal trials, including rooms filled with gas and psychedelic lights.

This section was added by Subotsky when he realised that the story would not last feature length. Teased into the narrative with pieces of other footage, it turns a routine chiller into a surreal nightmare. The end of the film – where Cushing is killed by the spirit of the skull before policeman Nigel Greene can catch up with him – comes almost as an anti-climax.

Freddie Francis is in the chair, and he handles the strangeness with aplomb.

The Skull

The editing is also good, adding pace where necessary in the surreal sequences. My only problem with the movie is Francis' decision to shoot through the eyes of the skull as it moves around the room. This looks silly, as the inside of the eye sockets that cover the camera are palpably cardboard. It was a technique he used again in Tigon's *The Creeping Flesh*, eight years later... where it looked just as ridiculous.

The Subotsky ability to re-create a movie as he went along (a skill which mirrors horror/crime king Edgar Wallace's ability with novel writing) went into action on Bloch with 1966's *The Psychopath*, with Bloch adapting his own story and Francis in the chair again. Wymark played Inspector Holloway – a character resurrected by Bloch for *The House That Dripped Blood* (1970) four years later, where he was played

The Psychopath

by John Bennett – on the trail of a series of murders. At the scene of each killing, a doll of the victim is left by the body. The only link is that all four victims were on a tribunal that convicted a German industrialist of using slave labour during World War II. Holloway pays the man's widow a visit...

Skirting the borders of psychological horror, this is more of a police procedural with some skilful deaths – the cut from a man squashed beneath chains to a fork twirling spaghetti is particularly well-judged. The true horror lies in the paranoia that Holloway begins to feel as he approaches the killer – a paranoia built mostly by judicious re-editing. Subotsky found that everyone who previewed the picture guessed the killer, so he re-cut the dialogue, cutting vision away from Wymark as he questioned suspects, and cutting to him when they replied. With re-dubbed dialogue, he was able to create a whole new killer.

Audacious – yes. Desperate? Maybe... but it worked.

Bloch stayed around long enough to script *The Deadly Bees* (1966) with Anthony Marriott from the novel *A Taste Of Honey* by H F Heard. Another Freddie Francis picture (did they chain him to the directors chair that year?), it featured Suzanna Leigh as a burnt-out pop singer who travels to a remote island in order to get some rest and recuperation. Unfortunately, she has picked an island where one of the locals is developing a nice line in killer bees, some of which get out and start to terrorise the neighbourhood.

Subotsky obviously saw this as a good chance to muscle in on *The Birds* (1963) territory, but although there are plenty of picturesque shots of the countryside, and train-spotters can get to glimpse a very young pre-Rolling Stones Ronnie Wood in his band The Birds, there is little to get excited about. The bees look unthreatening, and the only repulsive thing about them is the make-up they force their "victims" to wear. This is actually quite good and rather stomach churning for insectophobes.

Guy Doleman and Frank Finlay are on hand to provide some "quality" acting (behaving as though they are on a stage and have to emote loudly), and all in all it is a bit of a disaster area. Having said that, it is still better than Irwin Allen's 1970's débâcle *The Swarm*, which only goes to show that bees en masse are not horrific – at least, not on screen.

Much better are two sci-fi horrors made in the same year. Amicus always had a bit of a problem with sci-fi, responsible for the two cinema versions of Doctor Who – *Dr Who And The Daleks* (1965) and *Daleks: Invasion Of The Earth 2150 AD* (1966) – made as Aaru Productions, which turned the Daleks into cuddly toys rather than evil tin cans, they also tried the whimsical approach with 1968's *The Mind Of Mr Soames*, from Charles Eric Maine's novel about a man who has been in coma since birth and has to discover the world. All three were fine in their way, but showed that the latter – with its lack of special effects – was easier for them to handle on the sort of budgets they were using.

This lack of money is at the route of the problem with the two movies from 1966. *The Terrornauts* and *They Came From Beyond Space* are both scuppered from being top class by the lack of special effects, although both feature good playing and scripts.

The Terrornauts was scripted by sci-fi writer John Brunner from *The Wailing Asteroid*, a Murray Leinster novel. Simon Oates, later to feature in the *Doomwatch* series, is in excellent form as an astronomer who establishes contact with an alien race. Both he and his laboratory are beamed across space to the alien planet, where he discovers that the race he has contacted are not as civilized as they may seem, and in fact, they are on the descent into savagery.

Brief at seventy-five minutes, the film manages to keep a fast pace despite some leaden-footed direction from Montgomery Tully, and the paucity of effects sometimes lets down the acting. Worth noting is Charles Hawtrey, quite astonishing

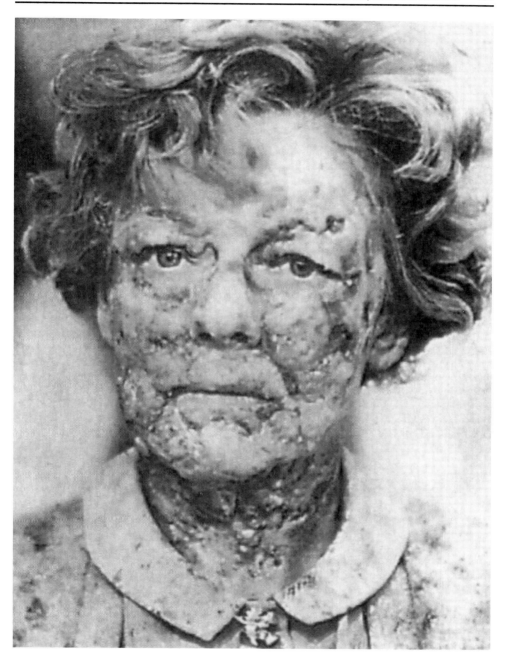

The Deadly Bees

in a non-comic role which reminds the film buff that he was not always purely a caricaturist.

They Came From Outer Space is ten minutes longer, and benefits from Freddie Francis' pacey direction and eye for making the most of the no-budget sets. Robert Hutton stars as an American scientist working in Britain. When an asteroid fall occurs in Devon, he sends his assistant and girlfriend Jennifer Jayne down to investigate. She and her team are inhabited by energy creatures from within the asteroids, and set up a camp on the site. With the help of others who are occupied by the energy forms, they amass enough money to build rockets to the moon, at the same time causing an outbreak of a plague that appears to kill people, but in fact only suspends animation. These supposedly dead people are then shipped to the moon in order to repair the aliens spacecraft.

Taken from a dreadful pulp novel by Joseph Millard called *The Gods Hate Kansas* (spot the original location!), Subotsky's script strips away excess. Hutton is on his own against the creatures because a silver plate in his head prevents the energy gaining access. He enlists the help of physicist Zia Moyahaddein, who has to spend most of the film with a silly helmet that looks like a steel colander perched on his head. Despite this, he is the best actor on show, and easily outstrips the wooden Hutton.

The ending is dreadful, when Hutton persuades the entities that they only had to ask for help, and after all their storm-trooper behaviour they acquiesce, releasing their "leader" (Michael Gough, who is starred but is only on screen for a few minutes). Despite this, however, and some truly awful matte work (Hutton's car actually bleeding the back projection onto it during some shots), Subotsky and Francis manage to infuse an atmosphere of fright and despair into the main body of the film.

It was back to the anthology format for 1967's *Torture Garden*, which had Burgess Meredith as the framing device, enticing passers-by into his tatty carnival side-show. The fact that his name is Dr Diabolo should be a giveaway, but it does not stop his sidekick Michael Ripper from getting everyone's attention by pretending to see his future and then dropping dead (in a nice sequence, they chat amiably about it at the end of the movie).

Robert Bloch lines up four suckers who want to see their future, and the stories unfold. Michael Bryant is after money, and feeds heads to a cat that promises to lead him to buried treasure. All it leads to is premature burial. A rising movie actress accepts the offer of a fellow star (Robert Hutton) whose perpetual good looks she admires. When she finds out the methods he uses to stay so young she soon regrets it... Hutton is a robot, and the only way for her to keep her youth is to be substituted for one as well. The third story must have looked good on paper, and almost works. A beautiful young reporter falls in love with a classical pianist (John Standing) whom she interviews. He falls for her, but there is a third party to the triangle, the piano that has been his only love to this point. It starts to move in on her, nudging, creating noises while she is in another room, enticing him away.

On paper, it must have seemed creepy, and in many ways it still is. But come to the crunch, and the moving piano looks a little absurd chasing her towards an open window. Her husband cries and laughs in total insanity as his beloved piano pushes his beloved wife to her death.

The final story is the gem. Jack Palance is a collector of Edgar Allen Poe memorabilia and manuscripts, and is bewildered when fellow collector Peter Cushing has manuscripts that seem to be unpublished. He is curious, and without malice asks Cushing where they have come from. Cushing shows him, a desiccated and undead Poe lurks in the basement, still writing. Palance must have the ultimate collectors piece – the man himself – and tries to break into Cushing's house, the episode ending in death by fire.

Not overall as impressive as *Dr Terror's House Of Horrors*, this second anthology is still highly watchable, with some chilling moments.

The years of 1968 and 1969 were difficult for Subotsky. Before returning to his macabre fairytales in the early 1970's, he tried two differing and partially successful approaches to horror that were not really in tune with his tastes.

Torture Garden

The Birthday Party (1968) was Harold Pinter's version of his own play, directed by future big budget man William Friedkin – whose *The Exorcist* (1973) changed the face of cinema horror and hastened the demise of companies like Amicus. It starred Robert Shaw as Stanley, a broken-down pianist who has been secreting himself in Dandy Nichol's boarding house. Suddenly, two friends turn up to celebrate his birthday – mobsters Patrick Magee and Sidney Tafler, quiet menace and undertones of sadism included. Only one thing – it is not Stanley's birthday.

What I said about *The Caretaker* applies to this. Pinter writes about the horror of the human condition under pressure, and you either tune into it or not. This film is inferior to *The Caretaker* because the insufferable claustrophobia of the stage set is lost. Otherwise, it is still a chilling piece of terribly British terror.

At the other end of the scale stands *Scream And Scream Again* (1969), which is a Wicking and Gordon Hessler vehicle that adapts Peter Saxon's novel *The Disorientated Man*. Saxon was a name which hid a number of writers from W Howard Baker's Sexton Blake stable, including Baker himself. So God alone knows who actually wrote this, but the Saxon name was also used for a series of occult thrillers featuring a group called the Guardians, which are like pulp horror movies in print, and should be looked out for.

Scream And Scream Again is about a man who is inventing a race of super-humans with no morality. One of them is sex-crazed Michael Gothard, who commits a series of sex crimes and is chased by police after evading capture by ripping off his own hand before throwing himself into a bath of acid. In a parallel development, a sportsman keeps waking from drugged sleep to find a separate limb amputated on each occasion. When he tries to escape, his super-strong nurse treats him like a rag doll. Alfred Marks is superb as a sarcastic policeman who cannot quite believe what is happening, while Peter Cushing makes an appearance as a scientist. Vincent Price is the loony doctor – in truth an alien trying to create an army to annex earth, while Christopher Lee is another alien, this one a sleeper who works as a spy.

Scream And Scream Again

Wicking's script always gets praise, but in truth he just copies the book scene for scene. The true star is Hessler, whose kinetic direction, matched with the screaming psychedelic soundtrack, turns this into a roller coaster that succeeds despite Subotsky's tinkering. He changed the end of the movie, re-cut it, and could never understand why it was a success. All this does is underline his fairy tale roots in fantasy, where this is a callous horror of the scientific age.

Subotsky was happy to return to the classics and his anthologies with the two movies that he made in 1970. *I, Monster* is a curiously flat version of *The Strange Case Of Dr Jekyll And Mr Hyde* story, with Christopher Lee as Dr Marlowe, whose

I, Monster

experiments turn him into the ugly and depraved Mr Blake. Not that there is much depravity around, as he seems to spend all his time as Blake skulking in corners. Subotsky's script goes nowhere, and wastes Lee and also Cushing, who appears as a friend of Marlowe's who wants to help him.

Subotsky wanted to film a faithful version of the book, but on celluloid it needs more, and this film seems twice as long as its seventy-five minutes, not helped by poor direction from Stephen Weeks and a well-cured piece of ham from Mike Raven, a disc-jockey who wanted to be a horror star. His terrible acting suited the lunatic sculptor he played in *Crucible Of Terror* (1972), but here it is ludicrously out of place.

Much better was *The House That Dripped Blood* (1970), a Bloch script that centred around Inspector Holloway investigating the disappearance of horror star Jon Pertwee. Talking to the estate agent involved in renting the house where Pertwee was living, Holloway finds out it has a history...

Christopher Lee lives there with his daughter. The new nanny wonders why he does not allow her any toys, and furtively buys some. Then we notice the daughter taking some of daddy's beard shavings from his electric razor. When he reveals to the nanny that his wife was a witch, and he is afraid that his daughter has inherited her powers, he is scoffed at – something that sticks in the nanny's throat as young Chloë Franks (sinister and sweet at the same time) flings a voodoo doll of daddy into the fire...

More wax is involved in the story of Peter Cushing and Joss Ackland, two old friends who meet for the first time in many years. Both loved the same woman, and both lost her. Yet Cushing has found her likeness in the local waxworks. The sinister curator reveals that she was his wife, killed because she had a lover, her body encased in wax. She has a magical power to drive men wild, imagining her to be their own lost loves, and Ackland and Cushing, despite themselves, fight to the death over her. The story ends with a newcomer being entranced by the wax figure.

Denholm Elliott is a writer who keeps seeing one of his own creations – a lunatic killer – lurking by the house. He consults a psychiatrist, and eventually succumbs to the killer, who is no figment of his imagination but his wife's lover, disguised as the fictional character. The only trouble is, he really believes he is the character, and strangles her as well.

Finally, Jon Pertwee takes up residence. He is a horror actor, and in search of a new cape for his vampire role, stumbles on a rundown shop run by Geoffrey Bayldon, who sells him a genuine vampire's cloak. How genuine he finds out when his co-star and lover Ingrid Pitt dons it and bites him... Holloway finds them both in the basement, and is bitten by Pitt as he stakes Pertwee.

Peter Duffell, then a new director, gives everything, and the film is stylishly comic-book, befitting Bloch's black fables, shot through with wry humour. Bloch would script *Asylum* (1972) aka *House Of Crazies*, but in between Subotsky made *What Became Of Jack And Jill?* (1971), a stylish and dark story scripted by *Avengers* man Roger Marshall and directed with a light touch by Bill Bain.

Again, Subotsky could not quite come to terms with the story, which concerns the efforts of Paul Nicholas (pre-pop star and sit-com fame) and Vanessa Howard to kill off her grandmother (Mona Washbourne) by natural causes in order to get their hands on her money. A large part of their plan consists of convincing her that all the old people in Britain have agreed to voluntary euthanasia by the young. She then dies of fright when they re-route a demonstration past her house. Of course, they did not ask her what she had done with the money...

Full of wry twists and dark humour, this is a subtle film about the terror of growing old, the fear of death, and the dangers of greed. Morally more ambivalent than the usual Amicus films, it is one to watch in a thoughtful mood.

The House That Dripped Blood

Asylum, on the other hand, is more of the same from Bloch. And when it is this good, who needs anything else? Robert Powell arrives for a job interview, and has to decide which of the inmates is his predecessor. If he passes, then he has the job. The candidates are...

Barry Morse as a tailor who produces a suit to order for Peter Cushing. It is supposed to restore his son to life, but when Cushing cannot pay there is a struggle, and he dies. The suit is put on a shop dummy, which then comes to life...

Richard Todd, who gets sick of his wife and kills her, chopping up the pieces. Unfortunately, they come back to life...

Charlotte Rampling, home from a breakdown and told to avoid her evil friend, who has led her astray. But the friend – Britt Ekland – turns up and convinces her to rebel against nurse Megs Jenkins and husband James Villiers. It is only when Britt has killed Villiers that the truth is revealed in the mirror, that Ekland and Rampling share the same body...

Finally, Herbert Lom is the madman who builds little ·homunculi with which to kill his enemies. Powell does not believe him, but one is set loose and kills head of the asylum Patrick Magee as he interviews Powell. When the distraught Powell goes to confront Lom, he finds that the real lunatic is none other than nurse Geoffrey Bayldon, who kills him as another interviewee arrives...

Directed with pace and aplomb by Roy Ward Baker, it settled Amicus into a run of anthologies: *Tales From The Crypt* (1972) and *Vault Of Horror* (1973) aka *Further Tales From The Crypt*, were adapted from the EC horror comic stories by William Gaines and Al Feldstein that lent their names to the films. Freddie Francis directed the former, with Ralph Richardson as the Crypt Keeper, linking the stories together. This is the movie with the classic Peter Cushing performance as the old man hounded to death by his landlord, who returns from beyond the grave to gain his revenge. Nigel Patrick is the sadistic head of a home for visually impaired people, whose sadism is turned back on him when he is blinded and forced to feel his way down a passage lined with razor blades. Richard Greene is wished back to life by his grieving family – the only problem is he has just been embalmed. Ian Hendry dreams he dies – and then he does. Finally, Joan Collins is chased around her house by a homicidal Santa Claus.

Scripted with ease by Subotsky, and moving quickly, it was the most successful of the Amicus anthologies, yet somehow lacks the depth of others: perhaps the number of stories here is just one too many for the running time. The same can be said of *Vault Of Horror*, which is played for laughs and falls flat, although the story of Tom Baker as the voodoo-practising artist who plans the perfect murder then leaves his Dorian Grey-style portrait behind to get burned along with his victim is nicely done. Michael Craig is a horror writer who plans to be buried alive for the insurance, but is let down by his partner, who leaves him (this features a dated cameo from Robin Nedwell and Geoffrey Davies as two grave robbing doctors – nonsensical now, it was a reference to their success in the *Doctor...* television sit-coms, based on the movies and Richard Gordon books). Daniel Massey tries to murder his sister for money (played by real life sister Anna), without realising that she is a vampire, and so is everyone else in the town. He soon finds himself on the menu at the local restaurant.

Curt Jurgens tries to buy the Indian rope trick and loses his wife, while Terry Thomas is the too neat prig who pushes his wife too far – so far that she chops him up and bottles the pieces in a neat reverse of a story in *Tales From The Crypt*.

The owners of EC were not happy with the tone, and so scuppered any ideas of a third film, leaving Subotsky with a Raymond Christodoulou script for *From Beyond The Grave* (1974) aka *The Undead* aka *Tales From Beyond The Grave* aka *Tales From The Beyond* aka *The Creatures*, an adaption of R Chetwynd-Hayes' novel *The Unbidden*. Written with grace, and directed with a good eye by Kevin Connor on a low budget, it is a treat after the EC movies, as each story has time to develop. Centred around Peter Cushing's antique shop, the stories concern the come-uppance meted out to those who try to rip-off our kindly shopkeeper.

Ian Carmichael has an invisible entity on his shoulder, and a visit to medium Margaret Leighton only makes things worse. David Warner falls under the spell of a mirror. Ian Ogilvy and Lesley Anne-Downe discover a gateway to hell in their cellar. Ian Bannen decides to kill his wife (Diana Dors) and gets involved with lunatic Donald

Tales From The Crypt

Pleasence and his equally barmy screen and real-life daughter Angela. A chilling little film, with a lot of atmosphere, it emerged after the release of *The Exorcist*, when low-budget horror just could not get the bookings, and so went unnoticed.

The writing had been on the wall since the year before. *And Now The Screaming Starts* (1973) aka *Fengriffen* aka *I Have No Mouth But I Must Scream* aka *Bride Of Fengriffen* aka *The Screaming Starts*, was a Gothic horror – rare for Subotsky – with Roy Ward Baker directing a Roger Marshall script. Based on the novel *The Curse Of Fengriffen* by David Case, it is the tale of newly-wed Stephanie Beacham, returning to her new home with husband Ian Ogilvy. It is the late seventeenth century, and ancestor Herbert Lom has abused the locals, raping a farmers wife and drawing down a curse upon the family. Now that curse is out to get Stephanie as a disembodied hand scuttles after her. The same hand from *Dr Terrors House Of Horrors* and *Tales From The Crypt*, it seemed a trifle out of place, as Marshall's script seemed to dwell more on the psychological damage inflicted on Beacham than on the ghost.

Ian Ogilvy is in fine form as the bewildered husband, and Peter Cushing is his usual professional self as the doctor who investigates the affair. Add the very physical menace of the farmer's descendant, out for revenge, and you have an interesting mix of a film.

However, it did not do as well as it should. Neither did *The Beast Must Die*

Vault Of Horror

(1974), which casts solid actors Cushing and Calvin Lockhart adrift in a terrible attempt to update the werewolf myth. On a remote estate, a big game hunter invites a group of people to stay. One of them he knows to be a werewolf, and he hunts them down one by one until he finds the true lycanthrope. So cheap that it uses real wolves and no transformations, the script by Michael Winder is padded out and dull, and the direction by Paul Annett is flat and lifeless. Even a most uncharacteristic "werewolf-break" of thirty seconds in which to guess the lycanthrope's identity does not help. I guess it shows how desperate Subotsky was...

Desperate enough for the last Amicus movie to be a co-production with AIP. *Madhouse* (1974) was written by Greg Morrison and Ken Levison, adapted from Angus Hall's novel *Devilday*. It was directed by Jim Clark, who had made a couple of thrillers for Richard Gordon but was more at home in the world of sit-com. As a result, a good little movie goes to waste.

And Now The Screaming Starts

Madhouse

Vincent Price is Paul Tombs, famous as Dr Death, a horror character with a silly make-up. After a break-down when his girlfriend loses her head – literally – in front of him, Tombs makes a come-back at the behest of old rival Robert Quarry, now a TV producer. Quarry has employed Peter Cushing, the writer and actor who created Dr Death, to make a new series of TV movies.

On the boat across the Atlantic, Tombs is accosted by Linda Hayden, intent on using him to further her career. He rebuffs her, but she is not put off. Later, when she is found dead, her parents try to blackmail Tombs. They too meet sticky ends. A set catches fire, a trick bed squashes a producer, and a researcher who finds the identity of the murderer also meets a messy end.

Is Tombs the killer? Is he really insane? Or is it Quarry, the lover of Tombs' headless wife?

Neither, in fact it is Cushing, permanently miffed at Tombs getting the role he wrote for himself. In his contract as writer, he gets to take over the role if anything happens to Tombs. So now he wants to kill him or frame him...

Let down by poor production values (Quarry's office door has letraset instead of a brass plate) and some strange direction (the aimless sequence where Tombs is interviewed on a chat show is particularly clueless), the film does nonetheless have some wonderful surreal touches. Cushing's wife (played by Adrienne Corri) is bald and scarred after a car crash. Now permanently mad, she lives in the cellar with her spiders. Cushing makes himself up as Tombs and takes his place, the final shot – after the decayed corpse in amongst the spiders – being of a Cushing/Price hybrid braying maniacally at the dinner table.

In places, this is a truly unsettling movie, but it still was not enough to save Amicus. Subotsky and Rosenberg parted company, and although Subotsky regained the name in the 1980's, he made no more films under that banner before his death in 1991. Having bought the rights to several Stephen King stories, he was unable to get them made. Eventually, he sold the rights on to Dino De Laurentis, gaining name-only producer credits on *Cats Eye* (1983) and *Maximum Overdrive* (1985). His last project was

The Uncanny

a series of fairy stories for children, a return to his roots.

Between this, he made two final films. *The Monster Club* was another Chetwynd-Hayes collection, made for ITC in 1980, and will be discussed in the section on ITC. Three years before, he made the English-Canadian co-production *The Uncanny* (1977) for Tor.

This anthology is based around the idea that cats are evil. As already stated, the idea of unhappy cats appearing on screen is a non-starter, so any such film is hindered by lots of happy, purring pussies who look anything but frightening. The framing device is that of the twitchy Peter Cushing trying to convince publisher Ray Milland that his book on the evils of cats must be published. Milland has a hypnotic white tomcat that influences him into putting the manuscript on the fire after Cushing departs to be killed by a gaggle of strays.

In between, writer Michael Parry supplies three stories: Cushing's case histories. The first is a Victorian piece, with Susan Penhaligon the wayward maid convinced by wicked nephew Simon Williams into getting a copy of Joan Greenwood's new will. When he finds he is not in it, he wants the old lady killed. This Penhaligon does when Greenwood tries to ring the police. Unfortunately, the old lady had hundreds of cats, and these turn on Penhaligon, trapping her in the larder and forcing her to eat cat food before she makes a break for it. In the meantime they have eaten the corpse, and proceed to scratch her to death.

The last is a wonderful parody with Donald Pleasence as a vain actor who "accidentally" kills off his wife so that he can marry bimbo Samantha Eggar, he also tries to get rid of his wife's cat. A big mistake, as it comes after him, finally tricking him into killing Eggar...

The middle story is the worst. A dreadful child inherits her mother's cat and her mother's books of spells, when she goes to stay with her aunt after her parents' death. The aunt has a bratty daughter who tries to make life hard for the girl and the cat, and eventually gets subjected to a spell that shrinks her so that the cat can play with her like a mouse. This would not be so bad if the matte work and models were good, but the fake cats paw is like a lump of wood with fur stuck on, and the scale is all over the place – the girl seems to veer between two foot and six inches in height.

Director Denis Héroux is leaden, and producers Claude Héroux and René Dupont really scrape the barrel. Subotsky's contributions are obvious in the first and last stories, which have a certain tongue-in-cheek charm, but the middle story really is a disgrace.

Some of the later Amicus movies look rushed and tawdry: in this they are comparable with the decline of Hammer. But between 1965 and 1972 they were a worthy companion to Hammer as the company that did most to promote a most British kind of horror. Their fairytales which concentrated on the dark corners of the imagination were a fine counterpoint to the outright blood and sex of their counterpart.

Though it is still strange that one of the most typical British horror producers was an American...

15.   Independent Contrasts

If the early to mid-1970's was a time of fruitful flux for the British horror movie, it was naturally a time when the strangest contrasts made themselves apparent. A horror fan going to a double bill of Peter Walker and Tyburn movies would find themselves bewildered by approaches that seemed totally contrary.

As the fairy tale and Gothic approaches of the better known companies slowly began to fade, they looked for different ideas. In the case of Amicus, a sideways move into Gothic and gimmicks proved short-lived and disastrous, their last few movies being Edgar Rice Burroughs sci-fi productions that owed little – if anything – to horror. As for Hammer – the attempts to make Dracula hip and bring in kung-fu action may be fun in retrospect, but they confused viewers who did not know what to make of this distortion of Gothic. Where a totally new approach was needed, Hammer merely tinkered.

So it was left to independents to find new directions, and there were plenty, sone of them interesting, some of them just plain weird. But the contrast between the films of Peter Walker and Antony Balch, and those of Tyburn, are so great as to warrant a chapter to themselves.

Tyburn opted for the higher budget, returning to Gothic days, and an attempt to resurrect a genre not yet buried. Walker and Balch went for the grotty, blood-soaked end of the market. In many ways, their films presaged the American domination of the market in the late 1970's and 1980's, covering many of the same themes with an English irony that did not translate to box office.

Both approaches failed, for varying and vastly differing reasons. But one thing remains, a clutch of interesting pictures.

Tyburn was a company formed by Kevin Francis, son of Freddie. A horror fan since youth, he had worked for Hammer in a variety of capacities, and had received advice on business from Sir James Carreras. By the time he got the company up and running, he knew exactly the sort of film he wanted to make – the sort that Hammer had just stopped making...

Although Tyburn still exists, they now make a variety of programming, mostly for TV. In recent years they have produced documentaries on Peter Cushing, some *Sherlock Holmes* TV movies, and a variety of drama series. A long way from their first three features, which were old-style horror movies. Francis had, from the beginning, avowed that he would make the kind of horror movie he liked, which eschewed a more obvious gore and sex content in favour of an almost Victorian restraint.

The first three Tyburn productions were old-style horrors. They flopped, and nearly killed the company. Part of the problem was that Francis was no iconoclast, and approached the style with a reverence and respect that almost smothered any life. At a time when horror audiences needed something different, this was box office poison. Looked at twenty years or so down the line, the films are beautiful homages to a dying style, and probably seem better now than they did at the time...

Persecution (1974) was the first off the blocks. The script, written by Rosemary Wootten and Robert B Hutton, was in the style of the old Hammer psychological thrillers – not the more kitchen sink *Straight On Till Morning* (1972), but the grand dame theatrics of *Maniac* (1963). And just as those decade old Sangster vehicles had an ageing Hollywood queen wheeled out for a few bucks, so this picture had Lana Turner as the ogre-like mother of Ralph Bates, with Patrick Allen and Trevor Howard as her ex-lovers. Suzan Farmer played the woman who was unlucky enough to marry young Ralph.

The script is actually quite tight, a catalogue of mental cruelty against Bates by his mother, who blames his birth for her illness and ability to lounge on a chaise longue all day. Played with waspish venom by Turner, mother is able to twist her milksop boy around her little finger by all manner of wheedling and mental cruelty. There is a distinct Oedipal element to the film, as he seems to both adore and despise her at the same time, torn internally by his conflicting emotions.

Following a series of scenes taking the viewer through little cruelties in his childhood – the rejection of a present, the love lavished on her succession of cats while she is cruel to her son – we eventually arrive at adulthood, with Bates burying yet another cat beneath a massive monument. He is now married, and his wife is pregnant. Mother is distinctly offhand, despite the best efforts of Farmer to placate her, and it is no surprise that she can hardly conceal her glee when her cat accidentally suffocates the infant. Farmer goes into an understandable decline, and mother hires a nurse – who she pays to seduce Bates...

All these years, Bates has thought that it was his long absent father (Allen) who threw his mother down the stairs and caused her injuries before disappearing into the night. Then he discovers that it was her other lover (Howard) who was responsible, and that his father lies buried under one of the cats' headstones.

This causes him to snap. A descent into madness follows, with Bates wrecking the house and torturing his mother, forcing her to drink milk from the cat's bowl before drowning her in it. Only Bates was able to act insanity with a simper, and the film is all the more effective for his bravura performance.

In many ways disturbing and repulsive, mostly in undertone, the film is really let down by Don Chaffey's stately direction, which allows things to unwind at a leisurely pace and does not really exploit the shocks and nastiness lurking in the script. The viewer can only presume that Francis so wanted to pay homage to the genre that he was unable to approach it with the necessary dynamic, and push his director into a bit more action. Still, for all that a fascinating movie.

From here, Francis moved directly into old Hammer territory with *The Ghoul* (1975). Nothing to do with the 1933 Karloff movie, this was written by Anthony Hinds under his John Elder pseudonym, and directed by Freddie Francis. At the time it seemed like a revival of classic mid-1960's Hammer; at this remove, the only palpable difference is the quality of the film stock. Time can play strange tricks, and instead of aping a form, this now seems to fit in a linear descent.

Francis gives this film the pace that *Persecution* sorely lacked, and it develops a simple story extremely well. Peter Cushing lives in the middle of nowhere, playing violin and weeping over the son he keeps in the back room. There is an Indian woman in attendance (played by the very English Gwen Watford, blacked up in a move that leaves a nasty taste for this viewer), and John Hurt lurks around the grounds and surrounding bog-strewn countryside in an old army greatcoat, being twitchy and menacing to all and sundry.

In truth, the bulk of the scares fall on him, because the title character – Don Henderson in a loin cloth and green face paint, a devotee of Kali and feeder on human flesh – is little seen until Cushing finally ends their family misery by shooting him at the end of the last reel. Despite this, the pace and quality of Cushing and Hurt's performances carry a slim story. It is the 1920's, and after a car crash a group of young things find their way to Cushing's house. Little do they realise that they are to be sacrificed to Kali for his son's nourishment. Picked off one by one, the film becomes a series of animal hunts, directed with elan through swirling fog-enshrouded moors. It is only when a young man comes looking for his friends that all is revealed. Cushing's anguish over his son, and his conscience over the deaths he has assisted being exacerbated by his status as an ex-Vicar.

The Ghoul

Elder eschews a strong plot-line in favour of a number of set-pieces that are a good excuse for some frightening jump cuts and atmospheric horror from Francis. This is two old stagers working together with a strong cast and thoroughly enjoying themselves. It harks back to their golden days at Hammer, and while adding little to the genre is a good example of how to get this type of film right.

The only wrong note for me is the performance of Alexandra Bastedo, still trading on her 1960's starring role in the ITC television series *The Champions*. She could not act then, and she seemed to actually get worse as the years rolled by. Being a beautiful blonde is no excuse for being duff. Well, alright, it was for Jill Haworth...

With his first two productions not performing well at the box office, it was up to Francis to really pull out the stops... instead, he made the worst of the three horrors, and condemned himself to a career of making other programming.

This is not to say that *The Legend Of The Werewolf* (1976) is a bad movie per se: it does, however, suffer from a somewhat bloated running time and a script from Elder that is little more than a retread of the Hammer *Curse Of The Werewolf* movie with the setting switched to France.

The main body of the film is fine: where it really suffers is the voice-over narration at the beginning which implies that this is a great legend about to unfold...no, this is another guy in hairy make-up movie, better than the average but not that spectacular.

Hugh Griffith is the owner of a tin-pot one-caravan carnival show who shoots a werewolf and adopts the child it leaves. As the boy grows up, he becomes part of the show and looks on Griffith and his wife as his parents. This comes to an end when the strongman of the act tries to kill some wildlife on the full moon, and the boy goes into a rage after a transformation...

Making his way to Paris, and now the adult David Rintoul, he finds work at a grotty zoo run by Ron Moody, who turns in a glorious comic grotesque performance

Legend Of The Werewolf

complete with false teeth. Rintoul has an affinity with the animals, and keeps himself to himself until falling in love with one of three prostitutes who visit the zoo each day for lunch.

Of course, he soon finds out what she does for a living, and when the full moon comes he starts to wreak revenge on the brothel's clientele.

Enter Peter Cushing, immaculate as always and playing the local pathologist as a Sherlock Holmes figure, helping the police with their mysteries and generally taking relish in cutting up corpses. He is the only one to take seriously the idea of a werewolf, and eventually pinpoints Rintoul as his man.

The climax is a chase through the sewers of Paris, Rintoul trying to retain the awareness of his human side as Cushing offers to help him. It is only when the blundering gendarmerie stumble on them and start shooting that things go wrong, and Rintoul is killed.

Freddie Francis directs with a good pace once we get past the pompous introduction and the boring scenes with Griffith's character. Elder develops the characters well, and Rintoul (at this time a classical actor, now a TV drama stalwart) gives a convincing performance. It also helps that Lynn Dalby, as the love interest, can actually act.

The main problem with the film is that it is not terribly frightening. As an understanding drama on the plight of the werewolf it is fine, but as horror it really goes nowhere. Still worth watching for Cushing and Moody trying to out act each other, the cheap-looking sets condemn this as a lower budget movie that the other two, as do the skimpy transformation shots. In the post-*Exorcist* world of horror, low budget was box office anathema for a while, and this movie suffered accordingly.

If Kevin Francis was no iconoclast, then Antony Balch certainly was. A childhood spent discovering the joys of old horror movies – one of his later passions was to screen his own print of the b & w classic *The Devil Bat* (1941) for friends – was followed by a career in TV (his first film was a Kit-Kat advert) and then in cinema working for a distributor.

His first real movie was made in 1963, after he met writer William Burroughs while bumming around Paris. *Towers Open Fire* is the best of all Burroughs' cut-up movies, with the stock exchange crumbling, whirling hypnotic kinescopes, and Burroughs with a machine gun in the BFI boardroom. Of course, because it was the great beat god Burroughs, all acclaim went to him; however, none of his other films have been anywhere near as fascinating.

Following this, Balch became film programmer at the Times cinema in Baker Street, London, programming and re-titling European movies with a sense of humour that bordered on the surreal; at one time he re-named Alain Jessua's art-house movie *Traitment Du Choc* as *Doctor In The Nude*. When enraged cinéastes cornered him, he mildly replied that ten thousand people had seen the movie who would not otherwise have bothered...

Given this attitude, it is no surprise that his two features are strange amalgams of art-house and schlock, mixing sex and horror in blood-curdling doses.

Secrets Of Sex (1970), aka *Bizarre*, is an anthology movie that would have made Milton Subotsky faint. Linked by the voice of doom, Valentine Dyall, in a mummy-wrap that may not actually be Dyall at all (it could just be a post-dubbing job), it collects together a series of vignettes that are distinctly more sadistic and stomach churning than the average 1970 horror flick.

Following a montage of sexual imagery, a female photographer is taking pictures on the history of torture. Her male model does not look pained enough, so he is forced onto the Spanish Horse – a knife edge which he has to straddle, with weights tied to his feet. He is left there while the photographer goes to lunch...

A young female scientist is having an affair with an elderly business man whom she despises. To gain revenge, she bears him a monster as a son. This is followed by a piece of sexual blackmail as a female burglar uses her charms to dissuade her victim from calling the police. A light episode, it is followed by nude model Maria Frost as a spy who attempts to steal papers from a diplomat by seducing him, but he locks her in his safe, where he keeps her predecessors. A surreal episode follows with a call girl having sex in front of a cold-eyed lizard. Finally, an old lady reveals to her valet how she has trapped the souls of her lovers in the flowers in her greenhouse, he replies by admonishing her before strangling her...

Too brief to have any real development, their strength lies in their bizarre imagery and flat appropriation of erotic images for horrific purposes. The fact that all the "villains" are women could be taken as misogyny; there is, however, a strain of irony that suggests this is merely a commentary on the way women are viewed in movies – and, by extension, life.

It was three years before Balch made his next feature, and this time it was a continuous narrative titled *Horror Hospital* (1973), aka *Computer Killers*. Interestingly, it was partly produced by Richard Gordon, who had promoted the 1951 tour of *Dracula* by Bela Lugosi, when Balch had got to meet his idol for the only time.

Way outside Gordon's usual league, *Horror Hospital* starred Michael Gough as the extremely hammy Dr Storm, who has a hospital where he operates on patients to turn them into brain-dead zombies. He wants to do this to Vanessa Shaw and Robin Askwith (hey, sounds like a good idea). Amongst his side-kicks are a dwarf and an ex-brothel madam, as well as a number of motorcycle thugs with opaque helmets, one of whom was Balch himself.

It transpires that the good doctor is wearing a face mask as he has face burns of Dr Phibes proportions. His motive for performing the operations is so that the women will have sex with him...

Blood-soaked and grotty, it send up pictures like *Circus Of Horrors* with a wry smile while also managing to be a good chiller in its own right. Dennis Price, fresh from his stint with Jess Franco – *Dracula Contra Frankenstein* (1972) aka *Dracula Against Frankenstein* aka *Dracula In Frankenstein's Castle* – the most impenetrable

Horror Hospital

horror ever made, wanders into the action and out again, playing a gay travel agent who wants to get laid with Askwith, and there is also a neat line in Rolls-Royce's that have wheel blades fitted to decapitate escapees.

Again, there could be said to be a misogynistic sub-text to the film, but I would put this down to a critique of the genre rather than any personal view.

Balch did not make another feature, as the mid- to late-1970's were a hard time for all independent film-makers in Britain, and someone who straddled both art-house and exploitation was in line to get the worst of both worlds. Any chance to see what Balch had in his boiling brain disappeared in 1980, when he died from cancer.

Kevin Francis never realised his potential because of money and being a man out of time. Balch, a far greater talent, was denied by the grim reaper.

But what of Peter Walker?

Peter Walker is something of an enigma; is he really the auteur behind a string of low-budget horrors that mixed suburban Gothic and grand guignol in a bloodthirsty brew with such aplomb? Or is he a talentless idiot who somehow struck a vein of terror that was, if not unique, original?

The answer probably lies somewhere between the two. Walker was a failed comic (his father was Syd Walker, whose monologues were popular on *Bandwagon*, the BBC radio sit-com that gave the world Arthur Askey and Richard Murdoch) who turned to bit part acting.

After deciding that he was a failed bit part actor as well, he stumbled into movie-making by reeling off hundreds of super-8 styled cheesecake and glamour films for the home soft-core market. Moving amongst men like Harrison Marks and Stanley Long, it would not be long before Walker, too, ended up in features. *I Like Birds* (1966) and *School For Sex* (1968) are self explanatory titles. By 1971, his *Cool It, Carol* was actually attracting serious attention from the movie press.

Moving amongst other men – like Tony Tenser, whose soft-core Compton had become horror loving Tigon – it was not really surprising that Walker would look towards horror when it came to broadening his palette.

Die Screaming, Marianne (1971) was written by Murray Smith, who had scripted *Cool It Carol*, and was a Hitchcock-inspired psychological chiller centring around Marianne (Susan George) and her boyfriend Barry Evans (a British sex movie lead who later graduated to sit-coms). Marianne's dad is a judge who has left £70,000 and some incriminating documents in dead wife's Swiss bank account. Only Marianne can get at them, and he tries to intimidate her at long distance using a couple of heavies. In the film's high-spot, Evans is locked in a dingy Soho cellar with them as they try to extract information. He thinks they are police, and the viewer knows they are not. The frisson is palpable, and Walker's still somewhat haphazard "point a camera and pray" approach gives it a cinema vérité feel that adds to the downbeat noir atmosphere.

A quite amazing film considering its antecedents, it is comparable with Edward G Ulmer's cult noir classic *Detour* (1945) in that everything works when you know it should not.

To prove it was not just a flash in the pan, Walker followed this with *The Flesh And Blood Show* (1972), a whodunit scripted by Alfred Shaughnessy that echoed Agatha Christie, but added a darker and more menacing atmosphere. Previously, he had made *The Four Dimensions Of Greta*, a 3D sexploitation movie, after finding a 3D camera secreted in an old studio. He used the camera again for the climax of this movie. Those viewers who paid attention would have gleaned the plot from a brief black and white sequence near the beginning where it was revealed who was the killer of a group of out of work thespians gathered to make a sex comedy.

Such obvious self-parody, and the tongue in cheek atmosphere of the movie as a whole, marked Walker as running a little apart from other horror and sex-ploitation film-makers at the time. Like Balch, he was aware of the implications of his material, and if he did not have Balch's instinctive eye for a camera, at least he had the self-awareness to guy this trait.

Both films were interesting, with a few chilling moments. However, they were just the hors d'oeuvres for Walker's next attack on the bloating corpse of British horror... but first, another quick sex comedy, *Tiffany Jones* looks like a movie made to fill in time. An exploitation piece based on a newspaper strip cartoon, it has nothing to recommend it, not even Bill Kerr and Anouska Hempel in the almost-nude. And how did Ray Brooks end up in this? Never mind, Walker was working on his first masterpiece, *House Of Whipcord*.

Released in 1974, *House Of Whipcord* was scripted by film critic David McGillivray from a story and original treatment by Shaugnessy. It told the sordid story of a mad woman named Mrs Wokehurst, who runs an unofficial house of correction for bad girls from her home in the Forest Of Dean (although the interiors were shot at a disused asylum in South London). Her ageing and blind husband is a justice of the peace, and he unwittingly feeds her the victims. Of course, the inmates are all so bad that they are condemned to death by hanging... thus ensuring that no-one escapes to tell the tale. In fact, the film was written around Walker's poster concept of a girl with her head in a noose.

Between capture and death, the non-plot offers us solitary confinement, flogging, and a number of other vile punishments meted out by Warden Walker, played with hard-nosed fury by Sheila Keith. An inspired piece of casting, Keith is a nice little old lady with a sweet Scots accent who usually plays grannies and aunties in sit-coms. The incongruity and sheer joy of her performance is chilling to watch.

The protagonist is nude model Anne-Marie (played by Penny Irving, a 1970's sit-com dolly bird), and the audience is encouraged to sympathize with her. Not me – I was too busy shivering at Keith's performance.

Walker obviously agreed – Keith was back in the next movie, *Frightmare* (1974), originally called *Nightmare Farm*, in which she plays Dorothy Yates, who was committed to an asylum in 1957 for cannibal acts, but was then certified sane and returned to her husband Edmund (a wonderful performance of impotence and despair

House Of Whipcord

from horror stand-by Rupert Davies). Despite her daughter's attempts to feed her animal organs and offal, Dorothy craves human brains, and organises home tarot readings that end with the death card being drawn... To be frank, the plot is nothing more than an excuse for atrocity after atrocity, delivered by Keith with spine-bending glee as the gore drips down her face. Even the heroine gets it, watching her boyfriend have his brains removed with a Black and Decker drill before mother and daughter descend on her with meat cleavers at the ready.

Frightmare

An impossible film to quantify or qualify on any level except sheer visceral horror, it is nonetheless compelling both in its downbeat – and probably quite realistic in that sense – ending, and the mode of filming.

Everything about this film is grotty, everyone involved lives drab little lives, and the chintz of suburbia is barely rattled by the thrum of the power drill. Poor sound quality and dark lighting make it look like a home movie of someone's unholy barbecue.

If that was bad enough, *House Of Mortal Sin* (1975) aka *The Confessional*, was worse, enough to drive a religious person over the brink with anger, I found it a black comedy of acidic proportions. Sheila Keith is back again as the one-eyed housekeeper to priest Xavier Meldrum (Anthony Sharp), who has sublimated his desires to the Catholic church for thirty years only by breaking the rules of confession and torturing his flock with moral blackmail. If anyone objects, they end up dead... This even applies to Meldrum's own mother, who he kills by giving her a poisoned sacrament on her sickbed – a sacrilegious stroke designed to offend and gain publicity. Ironically, everyone ignored this attention grabbing device and instead concentrated on the rumour that blood used in the film was real!

The film ends with both Meldrum and his housekeeper (who has kept secret her love for decades) committing suicide; the ultimate sin.

Another grotty suburban horror masterpiece, it was about as far as Walker could go without being banned, and from here there was bound to be a drop in atrocity level.

Schizo (1976) was a poor script by Murray Smith re-written by Francis Megahy and Bernie Cooper, and finally polished by McGillivray. An attempt to move sideways

House Of Mortal Sin

into Hitchcock territory (Walker never recovered from *Die Screaming, Marianne* being compared to Hitchcock), it was unfortunate that another Hitchcock-influenced director, Brian De Palma, had already covered the same territory with *Sisters* (1972) aka *Blood Sisters*, a couple of years before. And he had a better budget and higher production standards...

All Walker was left with was a second-rate project that misfired on all levels. Lynne Frederick put in a good performance as the newly-wed wife who was being threatened from an unknown source, and John Leyton was having a severe off-day as her husband. The only trouble with Frederick was that, despite the twists and turns injected into the storyline, it was blatantly obvious what was going on, and she looked histrionic instead of convincing.

Despite a few interesting deaths, the film needed Sheila Keith to buoy it up. Without her, it was sinking fast.

However, she was back the next year for *The Comeback* (1977), as a loopy mother whose groupie daughter died as a result of her association with pop singer Jack Jones, now attempting to make a – surprise, surprise – comeback. Keith keeps her daughter's mummified body in the attic, and as the daughter committed suicide when Jones retired she (perhaps rightly) feels that he should pay for having the audacity to make a comeback.

In this film, the whodunit formula was mixed with the grotty suburban Gothic elements of the early movies, and Jones was always a good bet for the chop. Walker

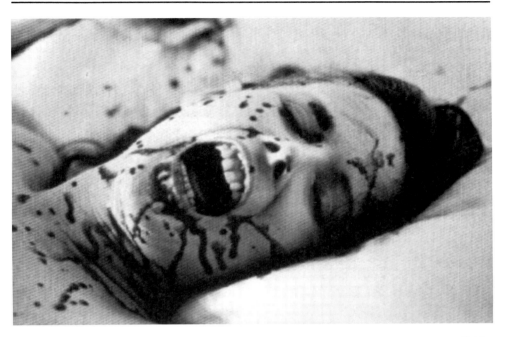

Schizo

chose him for the role because he was American, and the name could – in theory – help a US sale. Ringo Starr and Cat Stevens had also been in the running for the role.

Murray Smith wrote the script, which was his best yet, and it went through a series of title changes, from *I Wake Up Screaming* to *The Sixth Gate Of Hell* to *The Day The Screaming Stopped* before Walker decided *The Comeback* was a classier title. Maybe, but no-one knew what it was about under this name, and the film did not live up to expectations. This was a great pity, as it was the most accomplished – if not the most outrageous – of Walker's oeuvre.

The Comeback

Walker was by now investing his cash in property, and was becoming wealthy enough not to depend on making movies for a living. Discouraged by the lack of recognition for his last movie, he temporarily retired during a period when the abolishing of the Eady Levy meant that there was less financial incentive to film in England, and British producers had a hard time of getting backing.

In his brief retirement, Walker wrote a script with Michael Armstrong (writer/director of *Haunted House Of Horror* and sexploitation script writer) called *Deliver Us From Evil* which was never made. He also followed Russ Meyer for a brief spell in the director's chair on *Who Killed Bambi*, the original version of the Sex Pistols' *The Great Rock'n'Roll Swindle*.

It took the Go-Go twins of Canon, Golan and Globus, to drag him back to production in 1983, when he directed the Armstrong scripted *House Of The Long Shadows*. Looking for a director and vehicle to encompass Vincent Price, Christopher Lee, John Carradine and Peter Cushing, the Go-Go twins approached Walker, who wanted to make a new version of *Seven Keys To Baldpate* (1935), an old dark house mystery that was a creaky stage play and one of his favourite movies. Originally written by Earl Derr Biggers, the creator of Charlie Chan, it was a nice period piece but totally out of time for the 1980's.

Desi Arnez Jnr, Sheila Keith, and Richard Todd played support in a mystery that saw Chris Lee get axed in the chest and people run down atmospherically dark hidden passages as writer Arnez agrees to a bet in which he must spend a night in the supposedly haunted house.

Looked at now, the film does have some inspired self-parodic moments, but overall it falls flat as there are not enough chills to justify the budget or the wonderful old horror stars who just go to waste. In a *Halloween* (1978 etc) and *A Nightmare On Elm Street* (1984 etc) climate, this was not enough. However, it would be unfair to blame Walker alone, as the Go-Go twins did have a habit of screwing up every film with which they were ever involved.

Walker retired from the film industry to lick his wounds, taking solace in his fortunes amassed from property. Every now and then he makes noises about returning, but perhaps it would be best for him to leave his legacy well alone, as his time has gone, and the type of film he was able to make would seem out of time in the 1990's.

If Balch was prevented by fate from making more movies, and Kevin Francis diverted by a poor box office, then Peter Walker was diverted by both the times in which he lived and his own ambivalence about his talents. His self-parodic tendencies would jar with the more pompous excesses of modern horror, and who is to say that his "talent" was nothing more than a happy series of accidents?

16. Sucking In The Seventies

It is strange how patterns can repeat themselves, often for entirely different reasons. The beginning of the 1960's was echoed in the 1970's, and there was an initial rush of independent horror film production in Britain, mirrored by a sudden decline. There the similarity ends, and unlike the previous decade, there was no upturn in production towards the end of the 1970's, in fact quite the opposite. By the start of the 1980's, horror movie production in Britain was in a terminal decline – as was all low-budget movie-making – and the beast known as the British horror film was dead.

There are really two distinct reasons for this. The first is that Hammer and Amicus died out partly because their product began to get stale. Having exhausted their Gothic mine, and then the psychological thrillers master-minded by Jimmy Sangster, Hammer were reduced to desperate variations on the *Dracula* and *Frankenstein* series. Attempts to go mainstream with non-horror were also desperate back-tracking moves; in the late 1950's and early 1960's, Hammer were still an all-purpose studio. By the mid-1970's they were typecast.

Amicus, too, were hit by the law of diminishing returns, both creatively and at the box office. With anthologies becoming clichés, and the relaxation of censorship, there was a harder edge to horror that did not suit the fairy tale mind of Milton Subotsky. He was much more at home producing his Edgar Rice Burroughs movies like *The Land That Time Forgot* (1974), a fairy tale of a different sort. Horror had moved on, he had not. In the late 1970's he reluctantly left it behind.

With the two big-name horror producers out of business, and in decline for most of the decade, the smaller producers entered the picture, keen on finding new gimmicks. This could mean anything from zombie motorbike gangs – *Psychomania* (1972) – to cannibalism on the underground – *Death Line* (1972). It gave a certain spice to 1970's horror, but did not open up any areas that could be used to build a studio or producer up into a big name.

So if this sudden lack of an identifiable name to draw punters into the theatre, and the desperate search for new sensation was one factor, then the other had to be money. It always is; many film critics forget that pictures are money-making concerns (although more often than not the more you put in the more you lose!), and it was this that spelled the end of British horror.

In the end, it was down to the Americans. First there was George Romero's *Night Of The Living Dead* (1968), a cold and callous and quite brilliant film, more explicit than anything before it, that sounded a warning bell as its popularity grew throughout the early 1970's (released in 1968 in the States, it was a word-of-mouth phenomena in the UK). Then came a double-whammy in 1973 that killed off – slowly at first – home-grown horror.

The Exorcist (1973) was the first mega-budget horror. Taking a popular novel and translating it to the screen, it had effects that looked expensive, excellent camera-work, a big name cast – and hype, and there is nothing a big budget can buy like hype. Although it is an excellent film, the publicity machine brought it to an audience that usually would not watch horror. It was the movie that whole families (age permitting) went to see. There were also faked "controversies" about young actress Linda Blair being allowed to see her own work (she was under the certification age) and curses on the cast. No-one ever made a fuss about kids in low budget horror, and the "curse on the cast" trick had been played before – but not with so much money and hype behind it.

From now on, audiences wanted more gore and more effects. If they were not there, the non-horror lovers in the audience were disappointed by the lack of spectacle. Fair enough for them, but hard for horror producers who did not have such a big budget. It got so that bookers would not take a movie unless it had a big effects budget. Which meant that a lot of producers looked to Europe and America for funding. Some movies got made, but the tone changed, and they were no longer creepy or suggestive of terror in the traditional way. Instead, they adopted the shock approach of quick cutting and sudden horror with plenty of gore.

The last nail in British horror as a flourishing genre was *The Texas Chainsaw Massacre* (1974), a film banned in many places and shown fitfully in London thanks to the Greater London Council passing the film when it had been refused certification (I can remember the ads in the film pages of the London *Evening Standard* when I was too young to get into an "X" film, and how exotic it seemed). If possible, this film was even harder and more callous than the Romero movie. It also had a sense of sick humour that Romero's movie lacked, and colour... very important when blood began to flow.

Although US gore-hounds like Herschell Gordon Lewis had been making gore for a decade before this – starting with *Blood Feast* (1963) – Hammer were the ones to be hoist by their own petard, as their twist on the British horror ideal, and the gimmick which made them world-famous, was that they had more blood and sex than any other horror producer. The sex angle was a non-starter in the world of hard-core cinema clubs and European sex'n'horror kings like Jess Franco and Jean Rollin. And now they were out-done on the gore front. Hammer's – and by extension British horror's – problem was that more sex and gore was outside the formula, so they had to find a new one. And once they did, they had to get it past the censor. Without the possibility of a certificate and a showing in its own country, who was gong to help pick up the tab?

It was a corner from which no producer found an escape. The suspension and eventual abolition of the Eady Levy in 1979 – the tax relief and semi-funding of British productions that was a jobs drive and hangover from the quota system – was the last straw. It actually became cheaper to make movies abroad. So whereas a few European directors and producers had used England as a backdrop – the Italian *No Profanar El Sueño De Los Muertos* (1974) aka *The Living Dead At The Manchester Morgue* springs to mind, the reverse now became true.

Despite this, there were still some excellent films made in this diverse decade; some extolling the traditional virtues of British horror, others looking for a new context in which to place that feeling of fear, and the rest just plain odd.

And Soon The Darkness was made by Associated British in 1970, and welcomed the new decade with a bang for *Avengers* creators Brian Clemens and Albert Fennell. If *The Avengers* had been quintessentially 1960's in its colour (having ended in 1969, as befits a series which defines a decade on TV), then this movie presaged a move towards the downbeat terrors that Clemens would use in his under-rated television *Thriller* series (one-off plays using a subtle terror theme). It certainly had little in common with the two kinetic horror comics he wrote and produced for Hammer the next year.

Written by Clemens and Terry Nation (an occasional collaborator and full-time TV fantasy guru, best remembered as the creator of the Daleks), the film was directed by Robert Fuest, another *Avengers* graduate who had started as set designer and ended up a stylish director. Again, this movie is untypical of the man behind the *Dr Phibes* films. And just to keep the incongruity going, Laurie Johnson contributed a score that was the opposite of his playful *Avengers* themes.

Knowing of their pasts, it is almost as if the creative team on this picture wanted to get away from the 1960's and redefine their art for the new decade. For all the action on this movie takes place on a couple of miles of road in France, as two nurses on a cycling holiday get sucked into world of a sexually motivated killer. One of the two is killed, the other is stalked. Yet the second nurse is, for some while, unaware of what is going on and is blithely searching for her friend, who she thinks has just been separated from her. The identity of the killer is hidden, and it could be any of the young men she comes across.

A simple plot, with a cross-weave of bluff and double-bluff, the muted tone of the picture reflects accurately the dullness of such a situation in reality. Of course, I can only speculate as it has never happened to me, but it would seem that nothing would appear odd to someone who did not actually know a murder had been committed. This is conveyed well, and the conflicting tones of differing scenes – switching between killer and potential victim – are well-presented.

A deliberately minor-key film, it has good performances from Pamela Franklin and Michele Dotrice as the nurses, and Sandor Eles – an under-rated supporting and character actor who ended up in the television soap *Crossroads* for his pains – as a possible murderer. Not a classic, but an essay in uneasy fright.

The same year also saw a film that painted fear on a far wider canvas. *No Blade Of Grass* (1970) was produced for MGM's British unit by Cornel Wilde, who also directed a strong cast including Nigel Davenport, Jean Wallace, Patrick Holt and sex comedy star John Hamill, who was still trying to escape his typecasting. The screenplay was written by Sean Forestal and Jefferson Pascal, taken from a sci-fi novel *The Death Of Grass* by John Christopher.

This was one of those borderline sci-fi/horror cross-overs that had a lot of themes in common with *Doomwatch*, which was just beginning a TV run. In *No Blade Of Grass* a virus caused by industrial pollution has run through the crops of the world, destroying them and leaving vast tracts of land unfarmable. In the face of this, economic systems crumble, and governments collapse. A global catastrophe is eventually reduced to the plight of one family who take to the hills in the Lake District, hoping to escape the worst of the "anarchy" (we'll use the common term for disorder, though it rankles anyone who knows anything about the precepts behind anarchist philosophies of any hue).

There are some scenes that suggest the scope of the carnage, but in the end it is only when the film settles to concentrate on the plight of the one family that it gains any power. The wide sweep of issues only really make sense in an everyday sense when reduced to the circumstances of living, and to see people like oneself struggling against not only the lack of food but also the fear of a disordered society intruding upon its attempts to survive has a poignancy that no rhetoric, platitude or wide-screen effects can equal.

Committed acting to a tight script lift this a notch above other attempts at such a theme (too numerous to mention – the low budget possibilities of a group of remote survivors after some kind of apocalypse have always held appeal for low-rent auteurs; Ray Milland and Roger Corman spring to mind). Another low-key movie, but another that is worth a look.

The first year of the decade passed with only two independent films. The next year saw a sudden upturn in production, with a more variable quality.

Not content with writing two movies for Hammer, and even directing one of them, Brian Clemens tried to make a bid for writer of the most horror movies in one year by scripting *Blind Terror* (1971, US title *See No Evil*), directed by American Richard Fleischer and produced by Basil Appleby for Genesis Productions, in conjunction with Columbia/Filmways. Mia Farrow was the token imported star, with sound support from British TV faces like Norman Eshley and Robin Bailey.

Following a massacre on a lonely estate, only one girl is left alive. She is blind

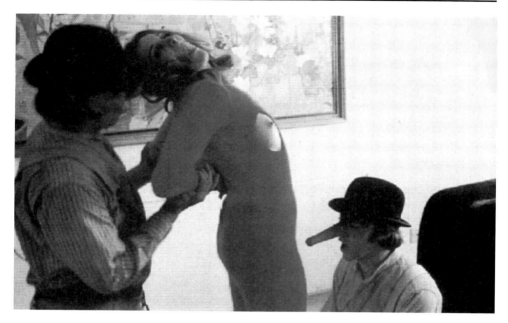

A Clockwork Orange

(as the title proclaims), and could only possibly identify her killer (well, she didn't *see* him, did she?). Back in society, she believes she is being stalked by this man, and that she knows who he is. Of course, no-one believes her, as she is blind, and she didn't *see* him, did she? Etc...

Clemens developed this theme to a much more subtle and aware degree in an episode of his *Thriller* series, where a killer takes refuge in a home for the blind, and finds himself outwitted by the residents. In this version, however, Farrow is as appalling as Dorothy McGuire was in *The Spiral Staircase* (1945), from which this is fairly obviously derived. Instead of mobsters after the blind girl, we have a lone maniac. Otherwise, the theme of pretty blind girl (being sight impaired and female obviously making her doubly vulnerable) being chased is very much the same.

The frights and terrors of being stalked are brought well to the fore by the script and Fleischer's handling, but the main theme is repulsive to anyone with any sensibility – sight impairment does not make you stupid, for God's sake! – and the alleged acting of Mia Farrow is enough to make you change channels when this crops up on TV.

Equally repulsive, but for different reasons, is Stanley Kubrick's *A Clockwork Orange* (1971), which Kubrick's Polaris company made in conjunction with Warner's. In much the same way that he gutted Stephen King's *The Shining* (1980) some nine years later and made a wonderful film that missed the point of the book totally, so Kubrick's script changed several themes of Burgess' seminal novel, and missing the point of what the writer was trying to say.

I confess to being no Burgess fan, but feel that he was trying to say something important about social conditioning and the deadening effects of violence with this book. It was also an attempt to come to terms with the death of his first wife, who was raped and murdered by on-leave soldiers during World War II, and it seems to me that Burgess felt that the senses-dulling effect of front-line action had altered the perception of these men about what was socially acceptable and also intrinsically correct about violent and sexual behaviour.

In Kubrick's hands, this was turned into a horror comic full of visual gimmicks and well-staged violence that seemed to lose its way about half-way through. It is also far too long at two and a quarter hours, and perhaps this realisation of its lengthy failure made Kubrick withdraw all prints after an initial controversy. Certainly, the film is not legally available in Britain, and the only chance I have ever had to see it was on bootlegged videos emanating from Holland.

Malcolm McDowell made a legend out of Alex, the violence and Beethoven loving malchick who gets caught and reconditioned by the state before finally breaking out in a return to his violent ways by the end. Not much plot for that much film, and the original short novel distils this into a series of events that prove nothing if not that violence comes from within, and the attempt to right by outside means (ie the reconditioning) will ultimately be counter-productive. Kubrick, on the other end appears (if not intentionally) to revel in his violent set pieces and seems to suggest that sterner measures are necessary.

Ironic, then, that this authoritarian version of a feasibly libertarian text should be the very tool with which other authoritarians raised a censorship rumpus.

In the midst of all this, it is easy to forget that McDowell is brilliant, and Warren Clarke is also pretty damned good as the sidekick who assumes leadership of the droogs when Alex is caught. Adrienne Corri and Miriam Karlin are sexually assaulted and murdered in performances that are amongst the most powerful up to this time, and some indication of the true horror of rape is at least implied by their performances. Patrick Magee is excellent as a victim of the droogs, and Michael Bates also turns in a good performance a long way away from his sit-com roots.

In the face of two large studios screwing up so badly, it is nice to see that the tiny producers were at least doing something interesting. *The Corpse* (1969, US title *Crucible Of Horror*) aka *The Velvet House*, was produced and directed by Viktors Ritelis, and featured Michael Gough as a man who returns from the dead to haunt his family, responsible for driving him there. While the script was nothing to write home about, the performances from Gough, Sharon Gurney, and Yvonne Mitchell are all strong, and the director shows some imagination in the handling of the subject, with good use of unusual angles.

Not to be confused with the US titled version of *The Corpse*, *Crucible Of Terror* (1971) stars James Bolam as an art gallery owner who is not doing so well. The only things he is selling are the works of an obscure artist supplied to him by his drunken friend Ronald Lacey, the artist's son. Bolam's backer is also the middle-aged woman to whom he is a gigolo, and her husband is getting suspicious about where the money is going.

The first intimation that something is wrong is when the husband gets suffocated in a plastic sculpture after recognising a die-cast bronze of a nude model. Following this, Bolam and his girlfriend (the one he lives with, not the older woman – with me so far?) join Lacey and his other half for a trip to Cornwall to see daddy... who turns out to be none other than fruity-voiced and palpably mad ex-DJ Mike Raven.

From here, very little happens that makes any sense. Lacey's mother is quite mad, and talks to her dolls like she was seven years old. There is a military type who fires the furnaces for Raven and dotes on the dotty mother. And there is a live-in model who gets a bit miffed when Raven decides he wants to paint and sculpt (terms also used with a heavy hint of euphemism) Bolam's girlfriend.

Lacey gets bumped off on a beach by someone he obviously knows throwing rocks at him (a subjective camera masking the identity of the killer), and there are some really odd sequences where people are chased through old tin mines, with a suspicion that there is something supernatural in the air.

Disciple Of Death

In the climax, the ghost of the model fired in bronze at the beginning of the film comes back to kill Raven, and Bill (the military type) whips out a quick twenty second plot explanation to a bemused Bolam. It still does not explain the other deaths, and the viewer is left suspecting some judicious re-editing to make a film out of a mess.

Bolam was at that odd period in his career, post-*Likely Lads* television stardom but before *When The Boat Comes In* established him as more than a comedy actor. He seems bemused through the whole film. Lacey is wild and brilliant (he is best remembered as the coat hanger-wielding SS man in *Raiders Of The Lost Ark*) – but he did not know how to play any other way. Betty Alberge is the dotty wife, Me Me Lay is the ghostly model, and Melissa Stribling is token pulchritude with only a few lines. Speaking of which, the script was written by producer Tom Parkinson and director Ted Hooker. Their lack of writing skill is reflected in some weird shots and some odd production values: for instance, photographer Peter Newbrook is a skilled man, but the quality of film stock he gets looks like super-8 blown up at times. Yet perversely this only adds to the strange feel of a film that seems to work by default.

Disciple Of Death (1971) is even more confusing. I once saw it and thought I had hallucinated. A devil-worshipping cult gets mixed up with what looks like a satire on kitchen sink drama. I have never seen it anywhere else, and if not for reading about it elsewhere would genuinely believe that I had dreamt it. It is beyond criticism in that same way of strange movies like *Reefer Madness*.

Fright (1971) was a Fantale production, produced by Harry Fine and Michael Style, and written by the third member of the company, Tudor Gates. Fantale had already produced three Gothic sex-horrors for Hammer, and I would guess that this was originally offered to that company as a psychological-styled thriller, as it has much in common with that strain of movie. Obviously not enough, as it ended up being financed by British Lion.

Peter Collinson directed Susan George as a baby-sitter who is menaced by a

Burke And Hare

psychotic intent on killing her. It starts with a screaming fit, and keeps up that pitch of hysteria. Moving at an incredibly fast pace, it features a young(ish) Dennis Waterman as the anti-hero, and good supporting roles from Ian Bannen, John Gregson and Honor Blackman.

While the suspense is tight, and the whole film has that necessary "don't look behind you" air that such a story must maintain to work, the pace is just that bit too frantic. There is not any chance to build George's character, with the result that the viewer tends not to care what happens to her. It is also just that bit too obvious, something that Jimmy Sangster always managed to avoid (at last until the last reel).

The last movie of 1971 was yet another re-telling of the *Burke And Hare* mythos, taking their names as the title. Produced by Guido Coen for Armitage, with monetary input from UA, it saw Coen return to horror after several years break.

While he was aware that times had changed, he still believed in the old qualities, so Vernon Sewell was back in the director's chair, working on a script by Ernie Bradford. The photographer was Desmond Dickinson, which at least ensured a wonderful clarity to the finished product.

As a matter of fact, this is my favourite Burke and Hare movie, partly because the duo of Glynn Edwards and Derren Nesbitt are so gleeful about their task, and start bumping off hookers from the local brothel run by Edwards' then-wife Yootha Joyce. Later a television sit-com queen in series such as *Man About The House*, Joyce is here a stunning mix of ugliness and sensuality that has rarely been equalled on film – at least, non-hardcore film.

Harry Andrews, on his way to a career fag-end in exploitation after big-budgets and theatre stardom, plays Dr Knox as a leering anatomist who takes delight in the bodies of young ladies that are delivered to him – and is it me, or is there an almost parodic feel to the piece?

Sordid it most certainly is, but only in the sense that it joyfully revels in the sleaziness of the subject. Which is probably closer to the truth than anything Tod Slaughter or Baker and Berman could get away with. A strange horror, with a minimal restraint that leads to unease rather than outright terror, it was certainly one of the more interesting movies of the year.

The following year was a year of more interesting small productions. Apart from the Scotia-Barker strangeness of *Disciple Of Death* (1972) there was a movie from Christopher Lee's production company, and two diverting movies from Benmar.

Charlemagne Productions was a project put together by Christopher Lee and Anthony Nelson Keys, a line producer of immense experience whose entire family had worked in movies (one of his brothers being director and novelist John Paddy Carstairs). Keys had, for many years, worked for Hammer as well as freelancing, and Charlemagne was supposed to be the opportunity for himself and Lee to escape the sinking ship of Hammer.

The company had options on three Dennis Wheatley novels, and an obscure horror thriller by John Blackburn. The package was offered to Rank, who for obtuse reasons entirely their own insisted that the Blackburn novel be filmed first. *Nothing But The Night* (1972) was the result, but the returns and reviews were poor, and Rank pulled the plug on Charlemagne. Hammer optioned the Wheatley projects with the proviso that Keys work on them. However, when the only one to reach filming was completed – *To The Devil... A Daughter* (1976), the last Hammer horror – Keys was nowhere to be seen.

Quite why *Nothing But The Night* flopped is somewhat of a mystery. While no stone cold classic, it is certainly no worse than many films that were thrown into the British horror melting pot during that period. In many ways, it is a tightly constructed thriller with moments that are genuinely chilling.

The ageing trustees of a remote orphanage are dying in mysterious circumstances. Because some of them have military connections, Christopher Lee enters the scene as a security officer. Parallel with this is the story of Diana Dors, who is a psychotic ex-prostitute in search of her child. The young girl is under the psychiatric care of Keith Barron, a doctor who is trying to get to the root of her strange fear of fire. She has been at the orphanage.

Dors turns up at the hospital, and goes berserk, claiming that the child is not hers... restrained by police, she vows revenge, and contacts journalist Georgia Brown. Brown (a wonderful singer and part-time actress who enlivened a few horrors during this period) believes Dors despite her better judgement, and visits Barron. A relationship starts to develop. Meanwhile the child is shipped back to the orphanage, which is on a remote Scottish island. Dors follows, and there are deaths.

Lee believes that Dors is a psychopath, extracting her revenge. But there are hints that something else is going on, why are certain of the children dressed for a ritual bonfire night in the manner of the trustees who are dead? And why are these children the beneficiaries of the dead trustees' wills?

The truth lies in a strange form of reincarnation, where the souls of the trustees are finding new youth by taking over the children's bodies. This is revealed to a trussed Lee shortly before he is to be the guy on the bonfire, a fate that has already befallen Dors.

As the police roll up, the children/trustees realise that they cannot go on, and throw themselves off a cliff to avoid discovery and freak-show status.

A strange anti-climax of an ending, it rather negates the tension built before. There are some good downbeat moments in the lives of Barron and Brown that contrast with the unease whenever the children enter the picture. Peter Sasdy (the same year as *Doomwatch* and with three Hammers behind him) presents it as much as a thriller as a horror, thus (like *Doomwatch*) presaging his move away from horror and into TV drama. Brian Hayles' script is occasionally clumsy, but the performances are all

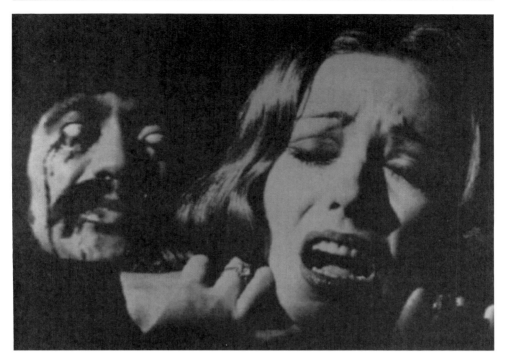

Horror Express

good (particularly Diana Dors), and the film is not without some extremely interesting moments.

The first of the two Benmar movies, *Horror Express* (1972), is much more straightforward. Made with Spanish input, it manages to mix the bloodletting of a Paul Naschy movie with the Gothic gallop of a Hammer. Set on a train rolling through China and Russia in 1906, it is the story of a fossilised primitive man discovered by scientist Peter Cushing. Inside this shell is the spark of an alien life, trapped by the cold of thousands of years. As it comes to life, it animates the corpse, and at first it appears that the prehistoric man is rampaging through the train. Christopher Lee, a colleague of Cushing's, is at first sceptical, but the appearance of a terrible monster suit soon convinces him otherwise.

Telly Savalas interrupts the train as a Cossack major with a platoon of men. Supposedly investigating one of the deaths on board, he merely wreaks havoc after being possessed. Also possessed is Jorge Rigaud, wonderful as a Rasputin-styled monk who believes the alien is the devil, and invites him into his body.

With a semi-literate script by Arnaud D'Usseau and Julian Halevy, this has the usual problems of a pan-Europe production. However, Spanish director Eugenio Martin keeps it going at a rapid pace, so the holes in the plot and some dodgy dubbing are not too noticeable. The odd scary moment, and a lot of fun if you have nothing else to do.

Benmar's other short-lived contribution to British horror is quite another matter...

Psychomania (1972) is one of those movies that you cannot quite believe you have seen. Don Sharp, a director who has dabbled in horror but is also at home with musicals and action thrillers, directs an Armand D'Usseau script that he tinkered with, and handles it with a commendable straight-faced attitude.

Psychomania

The plot concerns Nicky Henson, leather-clad leader of a motorcycle gang. His father mysteriously disappeared in a locked room in his mother's large house. Mother, played by Beryl Reid, is a medium, and gives sittings for people, assisted by her suave and sinister butler George Sanders. When Henson goes into the locked room, he discovers that his mother devoted him to the devil at a ring of standing stones. He also discovers that – if you truly believe – you can come back from the dead.

He tries this, and is buried upright on his bike by the rest of the gang (maybe it's me, but it looks like his head is actually two feet above ground level!). He then comes roaring back, convincing the rest of the gang to do the same. They all do this with the exception of Abby, his girlfriend, who is such a wimp that she cannot make it. She is then used by policeman Robert Hardy (sporting the worst Birmingham accent I've ever heard) to trap the gang.

Seeing as this is England, the bikes are more like mopeds, and the gang's nasty ways consist mostly of skidding around shopping precincts upsetting shopping trolleys. However, there are some imaginative suicides and some sick humour to make up for the lack of atrocity. Sanders is suavely menacing, and at the end reveals himself to be a messenger from the devil, turning Beryl Reid into a frog and stopping the gang in their tracks by turning them into standing stones.

Apart from a drippy song at Henson's funeral by Harvey Andrews (a folkie wimp-rocker of little success), the rest of the soundtrack is wah-wah heaven, and just adds to the period feel. Henson seems to know that it is a ridiculous movie, and plays throughout with a barely suppressed smile that – perversely – adds to the character he is playing.

Great fun, and nowhere near as bad as Sanders' subsequent actions would suggest – he returned to his Spanish villa and committed suicide.

If 1973 was the year of *The Exorcist* and the tolling of the death bell for low-budget horror in Britain, it was also the best year for independent production (as always, in this context that is independent of Hammer or Amicus – some large studios pumped money into some of these pictures). Eight pictures of varying quality, starting with another Don Sharp movie with Robert Hardy – thankfully minus the accent.

Dark Places (1973) was produced by Embassy films, and had the feel of a latter-day Amicus. This may be because it is set in a mental hospital, which immediately brought to mind the previous year's *Asylum*. Hardy is the administrator who is left a large estate. On this estate is a fortune, hidden of course.

While Hardy is searching, he is unaware that Christopher Lee also has designs on the money. Being a doctor at the asylum, he is naturally as loopy as most of his patients and has an over-sexed sister in Joan Collins, who can help him get the money out of Hardy.

However, not content with a mere psycho-horror, we also have a vengeful spirit stalking the house, and when this latches on to Hardy, then things really begin to go haywire. A taut film is suddenly dragged down in pace by too many flashbacks, and the linear plot goes flying out of the window, ending in confusion. In the end, the film is a swirl of plot strands that are never satisfactorily resolved.

Unsatisfactory is also a term that could be applied to *Tales That Witness Madness* (1973) a film that is so much of an Amicus rip-off that Halliwell's Film Guide attributes it to Milton Subotsky. In fact, it was an independent production by Norman Priggen that was financed by Paramount, keen to grab some of the Amicus box-office.

Directed by Freddie Francis and written by Jay Fairbank (a nom de plume for actress Jennifer Jayne), it is set in an asylum (hey, just like *Asylum*) where Jack Hawkins and Donald Pleasence discuss the latter's theories about the psychoses of four patients. Are they real or imagined?

In a ragbag of stories, Peter McEnery is possessed by the portrait and old penny-farthing bike of his great-Uncle Albert, flung from his antique shop into the Victorian past where he must relive Albert's fiery death, culminating in a fire at the shop and some good poltergeist effects. Michael Petrovich is an unlikely Hawaiian (even more unlikely is his secretary Leon Lissek, usually found playing East Europeans!) writer whose publisher – Kim Novak – lusts after him. But he has his eye on Mary Tamm, her daughter. Not for anything sexual, he must eat her as a sacrifice to the God MamaLu.

Joan Collins is at the mercy of a tree trunk shaped like a woman that Michael Jayston brings home. It starts to take over their lives, and even shares the bed with him. In this extremely kinky triangle, it is poor Joanie who gets the axe. More death is on the cards for Georgia Brown and Donald Houston, rowing parents whose small son claims there is a tiger in the bedroom...

The story about Uncle Albert is told with style both visually and in the script. The tiger episode also has some chilling atmosphere. But the other two just do not cut it. And it is sad to see Jack Hawkins – in one of his last movies – being so obviously dubbed and looking so ill because of his throat cancer. He died shortly afterwards.

A strange compendium that looks like a lot was done in the editing room, it really is quite poor, with only two stories (and McEnery's performance in one of them) to recommend it.

Much better was *Death Line* (1973) aka *Deadline* aka *Raw Meat*, a Probe release through Jay Kantner and Alan Ladd Jnr. Another Ladd – David – plays the spiky anti-hero in this tale of terror on the London Underground. When Ladd (Alex) and girlfriend Sharon Gurney (Patricia) find VIP James Cossins on the stairs of a tube station after the last train has left, they attract the attention of a guard and the police. However, when they return, he is gone. Suspected of hoaxing, it is only because he is a VIP that police inspector Donald Pleasence gets interested. Soon he connects this to a series of disappearances, and when two cleaners are killed (gorily) and one goes missing, forensic evidence shows that there was a fourth person on the platform – one with a rare plague, and anaemia caused by lack of light and vitamins.

With the help of Clive Swift, a London Transport man with a map listing all the disused tunnels and stations built under the capital, Pleasence realises that there

Death Line

is someone living down there. What he does not know is that a group of male and female navvies trapped in a cave-in in 1892 have bred and inter-bred until only two descendants are left alive. One of these is a pregnant woman who has just died, and the other is her distressed mate. Inarticulate, disease riddled and close to death, they have kept alive by eating meat – human meat snatched from the platforms.

Patricia is caught by the sole survivor, and dragged off to the charnel house that serves as a store cupboard. She escapes and is found by Alex, who has ventured into the tunnels just ahead of the police. The inbred cannibal dies screaming the only words he ever knew – "Minadoors", as in "Mind the doors" – in the mausoleum in which successive generations are laid-out.

Written by Ceri Jones from a story by director Gary Sherman, the film is relentlessly downbeat and grainy. It is impossible for a plot synopsis to really give the reader a feel of the film, as the accent is on the excellent use of darkness and tunnel sets. Christopher Lee contributes a pointless cameo as an MI5 man, but the real talent lies with Pleasence and his sidekick Norman Rossington. Rossington, usually found in comedy, is a cultured sidekick to Pleasence's moaning, drily comic policeman who seems as concerned with the fact that he has lost his football pools and that his tea is made with tea bags not leaves, as he is with solving crime. Yet he is sharp enough to put together what is going on.

The film is packed with incongruities like a pub scene where Pleasence and Rossington get drunk – nothing to do with the plot, but good character stuff, filmed in a way that gives a vérité feel to the piece.

Ladd and Gurney are also excellent – why Sharon Gurney, already having appeared in *The Corpse*, did not become a scream-queen is beyond me. Also worthy of note is Hugh Armstrong, who is superb as the tunnel dweller. When his mate dies, there is genuine pathos and poignancy in his performance, and his attempts to communicate with Gurney make his outbursts of violence all the more shocking.

Music train-spotters will be disappointed to find nothing more than a title piece and one lousy synth line in the whole picture. A shame, as the music was by Jeremy Rose and Will Malone – Malone was an ex-member of psych legends The Smoke and The Orange Bicycle, later engineer and producer at Morgan studios where he was

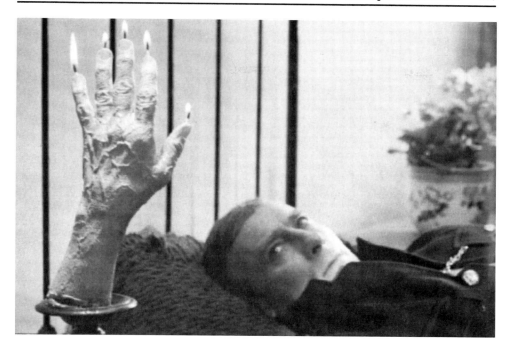

The Wicker Man

at the same time a Radio 2 act with the Wilson Malone Voiceband and a progressive legend with Motherlight. He later produced the first Iron Maiden LP. It is also worth noting that Ladd and Gurney are so switched on that they listen to progressive rock legends Secondhand on their record player.

More music comes in *The Wicker Man* (1973), a British Lion production that features folk singer Alex Campbell contributing a pagan hymn in this tale of strange goings-on the Scottish island of Summerisle.

Quite the best film of the 1970's, and by far the most chilling, it was also the culmination of many British horror themes. The idea of the outsider intruding on a culture that is entirely alien, and stirring up nothing but trouble is a xenophobic trait that seems in many ways to be peculiarly British.

Written by Anthony Shaffer and directed by Robin Hardy, it tells of staunch Protestant Edward Woodward, a policeman who comes to the island in order to search for a missing girl. Prim and pompous, he disapproves of the publican's daughter (a dubbed Britt Ekland) and the easy sexual ways of the island. He also disapproves of the lack of Christian teaching. So it is somewhat of a shock to discover that the laird of the island (Christopher Lee, relishing a role that really gives him a chance to stretch out) is behind this revival of the old ways, following the example of his father and grandfather.

It is when Woodward notices that the annual harvest photographs are missing for 1972 that he realises what is wrong, a sacrifice is to be made to the pagan gods, and the missing girl is to be the subject.

Already outraged by the burial of a hare in her grave, and the distinctly ragged state of the church, he is further tormented by Britt Ekland making moves on him with a pagan dance (a stand-in – the naked bottom we see on screen is too large for the bony Ms Ekland). He resists with prayer, in scenes cut by the distributor to make it fit a double bill, and which are now lost, we should have seen examples of his fierce religion and his implied virginity before marrying his fiancée.

Taking the place of the fool in the summer procession (led by Lee in symbolic drag as a Goddess), Woodward attempts to save the girl, only to realise too late that she is leading him to his fate, and he is to be burnt in a giant wicker man, along with animals and birds, as a sacrifice to the gods. He has come willingly as the fool, to be king for a day. As Lee smilingly tells him: "we are offering you a rare thing for your faith – a martyr's death".

Superbly directed, it is truly frightening as Woodward is consumed by smoke and flame, still yelling prayers and hymns as he chokes. Even more terrifying is the bland acceptance of this by Lee and the islanders, their perverted version of paganism allowing them to kill without conscience.

All concerned are wonderful, Woodward and Lee make fine sparring partners, one apoplectic and the other implacable, both as bigoted in their religious views. The script tackles the subtext without it intruding on the plot, and the film moves quickly, leaving the viewer little idea of what will happen next.

From the sublime to the ridiculous, *Theatre Of Blood* (1973) aka *Much Ado About Murder*, was produced for UA by John Kohn and Stanley Mann, with Vincent Price revelling in the role of a ham actor-manager (shades of Wolfit) who is denied an award by the Critic's Circle. Intruding on their meeting, he takes the award and throws himself into the Thames.

A short while after, critics start dying Shakespearean deaths. Michael Hordern is first, a death of a thousand cuts in a deserted warehouse being his fate. Robert Morley is forced to eat his poodles – his "babies" – in a pie, and is force-fed to death. Coral Browne is fried under a hair-dryer. Arthur Lowe has his head cut off and replaced on his body so that his wife will knock it off in the morning. Harry Andrews is lured away by a sexy young actress and ends up having his heart cut out as Price (in best Shylock guise) gets his pound of flesh. Drinker Robert Coote is drowned in a butt of malmsey and dragged through the cemetery by wild horses. Jack Hawkins strangles Diana Dors, the wife he suspects of infidelity after a Price set-up, thus condemning himself to prison.

The only critic to survive is Ian Hendry. Wounded in a fencing match with Price, he is warned that he will be last. With comic relief coppers Milo O'Shea and Eric Sykes as his only defence, he tries to find out where Price is, starting with his daughter, a make-up artist played by Diana Rigg. She is little help, not surprising as she is in league with her father (wonderfully named Richard Lionheart), who was saved by a group of winos with whom he has set up his theatre of death.

It is here that Rigg brings Hendry, cheating death thanks to a defective prop intended to put out his eyes, the winos set fire to the theatre, and he escapes while Rigg and Price perform their last Shakespearean scene on the roof before being consumed by flames.

Really little more than an excuse for a series of horrific deaths à la *The Abominable Dr Phibes*, Price is at his hammiest best, and Rigg is a superb foil. Hendry is fine as a protagonist, and the comic relief is sure. Anthony Greville-Bell's script crams in so much Shakespeare that even a philistine like myself can appreciate it, and Douglas Hickox keeps it moving at a fast pace. A sick humour horror comic, but with enough drama and tension to stop it falling into pure comedy, it is an extremely entertaining and sometimes chilling movie.

Also chilling, but totally sombre, is *The Asphyx* (1973), a little seen but compelling Victorian piece starring Robert Stephens and Robert Powell. Produced for Glendale by John Brittany, it was written by Brian Comport and directed by Peter Newbrook, the former photographer.

Slow and sombre, it tells the story of Stephens' Victorian scientist, who is convinced that there is a force in the body that is aroused when the subject is near

Theatre Of Blood

death. If the force can be somehow contained, then death can be averted. With the help of Powell he builds a machine to photograph this essence or force, and they eventually try to capture it at a public hanging. The eerie blue creature trapped in their machine's rays as it tries to take the life of the hanging man is truly frightening.

Leading on from this, Stephens is determined to bottle and trap his own force, which he terms the Asphyx after mythology – the Asphyx being the spirit that comes to claim the dead, each person having their own Asphyx. His wife, Jane Lapotaire (slumming it in horror, frankly), is unwilling, and the experiment, though a success, brings about the destruction of their house, and the death of herself and Powell.

The strange opening shot of a tramp being knocked over in contemporary London is made clear when the film ends; the tramp is Stephens, still alive and unable to die, his only companion the white rat whose Asphyx was his first success.

An even, unspectacular picture, there are some uneasy chills in here, and the acting draws you into the characters.

The opposite of this low-budget gem was *Night Watch* (1973), an Avco-Brut production in which Elizabeth Taylor plays a widow recovering from a nervous breakdown. The recovery is somewhat hindered by the fact that she keeps seeing dead bodies in incongruous places. Is she still in need of psychiatric help, or are her seemingly nice friends in fact in league to hasten her downfall into insanity? Certainly, her riches and some hidden family secrets are a possible reason.

Based on a play by Lucille Fletcher, this plot was old even when movies started to talk, and although Tony Williamson (an ITC graduate scriptwriter used to tough thrillers) does his best to keep the shocks coming with mechanical regularity, the direction by Brian G Hutton does little to aid this, uneven as it is. The gore seems strangely out of place in the lavish sets, and Taylor overacts as only Liz Taylor can. Can someone explain to me why this overweight old ham was ever a star?

Toiling in the background, Billie Whitelaw is immaculate, and even Laurence Harvey turns in a good performance in a genre that was alien to his urbane persona. Stalwart British character actors Tony Britton and Bill Dean also turn in solid performances. But at the end of the day, the ancient plot and Taylor's side of ham ruin the best efforts of all concerned.

The last film of 1973 was one that could – shock for shock – rival *The Exorcist*. The only thing letting it down was the budget – not because of the actual production quality, but simply because it could not be hyped.

The Legend Of Hell House (1973) was scripted by Richard Matheson from his own novel, and is like an up-tempo gory version of *The Haunting* (1963). Four people visit a haunted house where psychic investigators have died. Nasty things happen to them. That, basically, is that…

The skill lies in the way that Matheson builds his tension and suspense through a series of extremely nasty happenings, where gory things of a supernatural nature happen. Nothing more or less than a series of climaxes, director John Hough handles the script with aplomb, drawing good performances from his cast (which includes Clive Revill, Michael Gough, Gayle Hunnicutt, Roddy McDowell, Pamela Franklin, Roland Culver and Peter Bowles) and pacing the shocks and terror with a steady hand and a sure eye.

This is the type of horror movie which it is impossible to do justice in print. Kinetic and visually stunning, it is a superb piece of craft that needs to be seen to be appreciated. The good production values were ensured by the presence of Albert Fennell as co-producer.

How ironic, therefore, that the movie that ended 1973 on a high note should be the last truly shocking film of the decade rather than the harbinger of more terror.

The post-*Exorcist* horror industry in Britain got off to a less than wonderful start with *Vampira* (US title *Old Dracula*), aka *Vampirella* aka *Vampir*, the first of three independent movies in 1974. Financed by Columbia, with Jack H Wiener producing for WFS (World Film Services), it featured a tired and disinterested David Niven hamming his way through the role of a semi-Dracula character who lures the winners of beauty contests to his remote castle in order to use their blood and revive his undead wife.

Flatly directed by Clive Donner, from a script by Jeremy Lloyd that cannot make up its mind whether to be flip or deadpan, the film falls uncomfortably between parody and an attempt at a Dracula revival. Lloyd is better known as the English "chinless wonder" who graced *Rowan & Martin's Laugh-In* for a season or two, and as the writer of television sit-coms *Are You Being Served?* and *Allo, Allo*. Given his obvious predilection for comedy, I suspect that this was supposed to be a parody, however, it is so feeble, with the odd dramatic moment, that I was unsure whether or not to include it with the horror comedies.

The sets are quite nice – a mix of Gothic and art-deco revival – but the acting is abysmal, and even a smirking Nicky Henson cannot pull this one around. Bernard Bresslaw lurks, and the pulchritude is well represented by Linda Hayden, Veronica Carlson, and Jennie Linden – horror starlets all.

Of a much better hue was *Ghost Story* (1974), which was produced and directed by Stephen Weeks, from a script by himself and Rosemary Sutcliff. Sutcliff is better known as a historical romance (in both the modern and old sense) writer, and she brought the sweep of dynamics needed for such a form to a tight little ghost story that is very M R James in its subtlety. Weeks was briefly an enfant terrible of the horror cinema following his *I, Monster* for Amicus a few years before. Fortunately, *Ghost Story* suffers none of the drag and lack of pace or depth of that movie. Quite the opposite.

Larry Dann is an Oxbridge scholarship boy who has been invited for a weekend to the country house of an old acquaintance. On the way there he meets the superior and snotty Vivian Mackerall, an upper-class ex-fellow who palpably looks down his nose at Dann. When they reach the secluded halt where they must alight, they are met by the wonderful Murray Melvin, camp and twitchy, trying to pretend that everything is alright.

The Legend Of Hell House

But it isn't, the house is deserted, and shows every sign of being closed-up for several years. After some character sketching (the two upper-class chaps gang up on Dann, laughing at his comics and dirty postcards), Dann goes to bed. Strange noises in the pipes, and a doll that moves from out of a cupboard, just a dream?

While all is made clear down below – Mackerall is an amateur psychic investigator, who has brought all sorts of devices to see ghosts – Dann is whisked into a dream-like world, where the parallel plot develops. Leigh Lawson is having his sister Marianne Faithfull confined to an asylum. She harbours unnatural lusts for him, and he thinks she is mad – more to the point, he is guilty as he shares her feelings. Asylum head Anthony Bate whisks her away to his snake pit, where nurse Barbara Shelley is his only aide. Between them, they keep the patients quiet by brutalising them. Only Penelope Keith, as Faithfull's old governess (harbouring some lesbian lusts by subtle implication) can save her – but before this happens, a rapidly bankrupting Bate sets fire to the asylum.

Inter-cut with this story, the chaps stride the grounds, and Dann goes to a local pub, where he is spooked by the same actors as in his visions, but all assuming everyday roles as barmaid and customers.

Every night, and in the day, the dreams come back. Ironic that Mackerall – who so badly wants to see – remains blind to this, while Dann is sucked in further and further by the animated doll. At the end, he and Melvin try to make an escape, Mackerall having departed in a huff, but the doll will not let Dann go, cutting his throat before secreting itself behind Melvin in his old tourer.

Marvellous restrained acting, a disorienting direction style whereby Dan slips into the past without any dissolves or effects, and atmospheric camera work by Peter Hurst make this a joy. Partly filmed in India, it does not notice as all seems terribly

British. A perfect evocation of a lost form of ghost story, special mention must go to Ron Geesin's soundtrack, which mixes period music with avant-garde atmospherics in a manner that only the enigmatic Mr Geesin can manage.

More in-your-face but equally as strong was *The Mutations* (1974), produced by Robert D Weinbach for J Ronald Getty. This was another movie with a great soundtrack, parts of Basil Kirchin's *Worlds Within Worlds* was used for numerous sequences, and the shifting sound collage fitted the beautiful lapsed-time photography of developing plants that formed a tranquil backdrop to the evolving story.

Donald Pleasence plays a loony doctor, who lectured in biology. He has a theory about reversing decay and also – more importantly – about fusing man and plant. Scott Antony is Tony, an American student who thinks the doc is mad, but fellow students Julie Ege and Jill Haworth think he is fascinating. Tony places his faith in biologist Brad Harris, who is flying from the States to hear the doc's wild ravings.

Meanwhile, Tom Baker and Michael Dunn are running a freak show in Battersea Park. Dunn is a person of restricted growth best remembered as a super-villain in the western/sci-fi series The *Wild, Wild West*, while Baker labours pre-*Doctor Who* under heavy make-up as a hideously mutilated or deformed man. He has a chip on his shoulder about being "different", and while the other freaks (all real sideshow veterans like the bearded lady, "pop-eye" whose eyes come out of their sockets, the lizard-lady, and a couple of chaps with unusual bone problems) revel in their "otherness", Baker plots and plans. Keeping Dunn under his thumb by blackmail, he kidnaps girls for Pleasence to experiment on – the doc has promised a "cure" – and the failures are exhibited in the side-show before they die.

This happens to Haworth, and Tony recognises her by the medallion Dunn has stolen from her. Determined to find out what is going on, he breaks into the side-show and is over-powered by Baker, who takes him to Pleasence.

Mildly discoursing on plants and man while stroking a rabbit, he idly tosses it into the maw of an animal-plant hybrid before operating on Tony, who turns into a plant-man, devouring tramps for food while searching for help.

Ege and Harris trace him to Pleasence's establishment, where a fight ensues. The freaks come after Baker, sick of his behaviour, and he is eaten by Pleasence's guard dogs. The lab goes up in flames, and Harris rescues Ege. It is only in the last shot, where Ege embraces Harris and starts to mutate, that the viewer realises she was operated on before she could be saved.

A film of uneven tone, it veers between a slow documentary approach, a fine reading of the freak-show inhabitants as an oppressed minority who finally turn on their oppressor (Baker), and a fast-moving pulp mad-doctor movie. Director Jack Cardiff somehow manages to pull all the different strands of the screenplay (by Weinbach and Edward Mann) together into a coherent whole. Fascinating, and by turns chilling and genuinely repulsive, this is a lost classic. The only minus is for the appallingly wooden Harris – was he Getty's cousin or something?

If 1974 had represented a downturn in production, then the next four years were even worse, only one film a year, and only one of them even mildly interesting...

The worst shall come first. 1975's *I Don't Want To Be Born* (US title *The Devil Within Her*), aka *The Monster* aka *The Baby* aka *Sharon's Baby*, is a truly terrible picture, worth watching only to gawp in sheer disbelief. Peter Sasdy must have been short of cash to accept the job of directing the atrocious Stanley Price script. And speaking of shortage of cash, the only prints I have ever seen have been murky, with sets that look like the inside of someone's house, and production standards that are appalling for a film that was eventually handled by Rank, although produced by Norma Corney for Unicapital.

Joan Collins is a stripper married to Ralph Bates. When she is about to quit her job, she is accosted by a person of restricted growth (not as good an actor as Michael

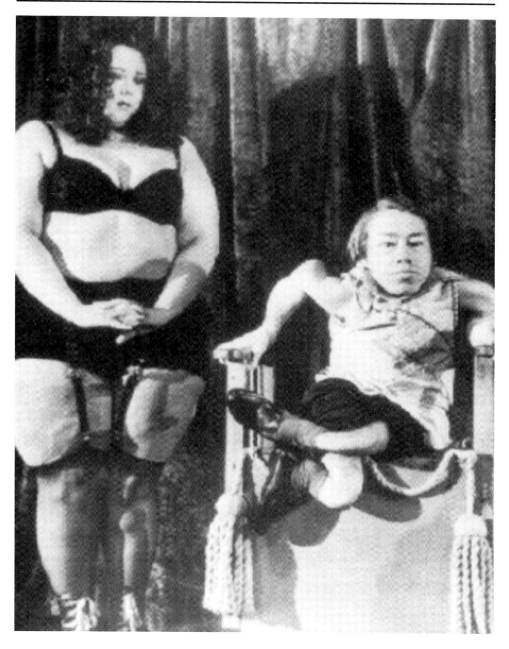

The Mutations

Dunn, by the way) who wants to get laid. Joan goes way over the top in her rejection, and the small chap curses her. Excuse me, but are we back in the sixteenth century or something? Dwarves cursing thee, and all that? No, it is contemporary London, and Ralph Bates walks about with a puzzled expression – so would I if I had to wear those flares. He gets Joanie pregnant, and her bouncing baby is a killer, seeing off all those who get in its way as it seeks to drive Joanie mad.

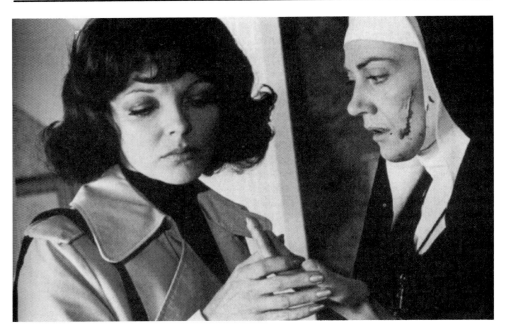

I Don't Want To Be Born

The only good performance comes from Eileen Atkins, an elderly British character actress who is the housekeeper (how can they afford a housekeeper – she was only a stripper, and Bates does not seem to do any work!?). She is wonderful, and it is genuinely shocking when the baby kills her. Donald Pleasence walks on and off as a psychiatrist.

A shoddy mess, good only for laughing at, the premise of a killer baby might have worked if Sasdy had not insisted on showing the gurgling infant in its pram. It just looks sweet. The US title, *The Devil Within Her*, sounds like a hardcore/horror cross-over. That might have been more interesting.

Full Circle was marginally better. A British and Canadian co-production from 1976, it was based on Peter Straub's novel *Julia*, with a literate script by Dave Humphries and competent direction by Richard Loncraine. Mia Farrow played the lead, a woman whose child has just died. She leaves her home and moves to a house that has a reputation as being haunted. So it is, by the spirit of another dead child. Mia takes comfort in this to begin with, but the spirit is malevolent and slowly begins to take over her life, twisting her to its own ends.

A subtle film, about grief as much as haunting, the support playing from the likes of Tom Conti, Keir Dullea, Jill Bennett and Edward Hardwicke is strong and sympathetic. Farrow surprised me by being good as the lead, and the film – although breaking out into a few token "horror" moments (post-*Exorcist* effects that look clichéd now, but were de rigueur at the time) keeps its subtly sad tone throughout.

Not a classic, but definitely worth more than a cursory look.

The Black Panther (1977), was a harder-edged horror, all the more terrible for being real. Written by Michael Armstrong, directed and produced by Ian Merrick for Impis productions, the movie was a straight re-telling of the facts surrounding the exploits of Donald Nielsen, an ex-army man who terrorised the lowlands of Britain in the mid-1970's as The Black Panther, carrying out raids on post-offices and kidnapping Lesley Whittle, whose family were wealthy. Nielsen had an underground base, and seemed to truly believe he was at war. A psychosis taken too far, he had Whittle strung up to the ceiling, virtually immobile. The unfortunate girl ended up being hung by her bonds, and when her body was discovered the search for Nielsen became a murder hunt.

All this is carefully represented by Armstrong, who wisely opts for a down-played approach. This makes Nielsen's actions and motivations all the more horrific, and the death of Lesley Whittle is truly harrowing. Armstrong approached the family when writing the screenplay, as he did not want to cause them distress, and this care in approach is what makes it a truly horrifying film.

Debbie Farrington conveys Whittle's fear and terror superbly, and Donald Sumpter is excellent as the detached, sociopathic Nielsen. Good strong support from David Swift and Marjorie Yates. An exploitation film that transcends that tag through the quality of writing and becomes a study of one man's disease, it sits uneasily with the horror genre, but is in actual fact far more horrific than anything else in this book.

From the sublime to the ridiculous; *The Legacy* (1978) was a fairly large-budget picture made by Columbia. Katherine Ross and Sam Elliott are two interior designers who are employed by an Englishman to come and work on his mansion. By coincidence, they crash near the house, and are picked up by their employer (John Standing), who seems to be taken suddenly ill when they arrive. Next thing you know, he is in an oxygen tent, shrouded for the rest of the movie, and a group of international jet-setters are arriving for a weekend party.

They include Roger Daltrey, Charles Gray (always a good bet for something sinister), Hildegard Neil and Lee Montague. They talk to Ross as though she is in on their private party, and ignore Elliott. Problem is, despite their hints of something odd going on and the portrait that looks like Ross in the study, she does not know what they are talking about.

Daltrey dies after choking on a chicken bone ("but he'd only had fish", as nurse Margaret Tyzack remarks after a late attempt at a tracheotomy), which could account for his singing over the years; Hildegard Neil drowns in the swimming pool; Elliott and Ross try to escape but find that every road leads back to the mansion...

Just what is going on here? Every film needs to drop some clues, but this one seems to have had them all edited out. Even at the end, where Ross takes over the head of some sort of cult from the dying Standing (now reduced to a gauze curtain and a fake claw) and the servants applaud, nothing is made clear. Elliott seems quite happy, whereas in the shot before he was the absolute opposite...

I suspect this was not a happy production. David Foster, the producer, managed to get through two cameramen (Dick Bush and Alan Hume), which suggests re-shooting. Richard Marquand helmed the whole project, but there were three scriptwriters: Patrick Tilley, Paul Wheeler, and... Jimmy Sangster. Now then, Sangster never works in a team, and had been writing horror for twenty-two years by this point. He may have stretched logic in some of his movies, but he never dispensed with the clues for the audience – he is too good a craftsman for that. So I suspect his original script was heavily doctored, resulting in this appalling mess.

Not even as funny as *I Don't Want To Be Born*, this is some kind of nadir... which is okay, as 1979 brought three varied movies proving that horror could still be interesting and find new variations.

Dracula (1979) was a Universal/Mirisch production, with Marvin Mirisch and Tom Pevsner producing. W D Richter wrote a screenplay that went back on the bloodletting and concentrated on the Gothic romance of an undead Count in search of a bride. Frank Langella had the matinée idol looks to carry off such a portrayal, and he was well-supported by Laurence Olivier as a slightly eccentric Van Helsing. Donald Pleasence and Trevor Eve also lend solid English character support to John Badham's stolid and stately direction.

Like the much maligned Coppola version of the early 1990's, this *Dracula* is not really a horror in the sense that we tend to think of Dracula – it is much more of a tragic love-story with some horrific edges, and to approach it expecting Lugosi or Lee would be a mistake. Taken on its own terms, it is an extremely solid picture which showed the Count in a different light to the increasingly hiss-and-yell Hammer movies that were still fresh in the memory.

Much more dynamic and exciting was *Murder By Decree* (1979) aka *Sherlock Holmes And Saucy Jack* aka *Sherlock Holmes: Murder By Decree*, produced by Robert A Goldstone for Saucy Jack/Decree/Avco. Written by John Hopkins and directed with an surprising elan by schlock horror Canadian director Bob Clark, it makes the most of its fog-bound London sets with Christopher Plummer relishing his role as Sherlock Holmes, chasing Jack The Ripper. Frank Finlay plays Inspector Lestrade, as he did in the Tony Tenser-produced *A Study In Terror* (1965), and James Mason is a game but ageing Watson, who near the end of the film takes a knife in the arm to defend his friend Holmes – the interplay between the two men, at such a high-tension moment, is a wonderful study in character.

In this version of the story – loosely based on Stephen Knight's *The Final Solution* book – the Ripper is surgeon William Gull, quite mad and also a Mason, operating independently in an attempt to hush up a Royal scandal about the bastard child of Royalty and a prostitute.

In many ways, the gore of the killings is not where the horror lies, although there is much tension in the stalking of the killer by Holmes and Watson. It is the incidentals that are horrific; the filthy asylum in which one prostitute is incarcerated, the way in which Anthony Quayle's idiotic and pompous police chief covers up Masonic evidence to protect a fellow, and the manner in which John Gielgud's suave prime-minister covers up the matter despite the protestations of Holmes.

Donald Sutherland contributes a fine performance as psychic Robert Lees, and David Hemmings is suitably conniving as Inspector Foxburgh, an undercover anarchist who is subverting the killings and furore surrounding them to his own political ends.

A triumph of a pulp horror/thriller, it contrasts with the quiet despair of the 1970's parting shot...

Film (1979) was produced by the British Film Institute, and runs for just under half an hour. It is also one of the most harrowing half-hours you could wish to spend. Samuel Beckett's script was originally written for Buster Keaton, but after Keaton died Max Wall took over this mantle. Wall is the man in this movie, and Patricia Hayes plays the old woman glimpsed briefly.

Director David Rayner Clark follows Beckett's meticulous directions to the letter, and designer Ariane Gastambide builds a suitable atmosphere. As with all Beckett, nothing much happens. Wall is pursued by the camera, which pokes and pries at him, rooting at some secret terror which leaks out on his face. It follows him into his home, where it reflects the despair of a wasted life, waiting for death to relieve the pain of existence.

Interesting that Beckett always loved old comics in his plays. Like his suburban counterpart Harold Pinter, Beckett is representing the elliptical fear and terror that lie behind the everyday smile, the loathing of life that can make a man frightened to move. Wall represents this perfectly, his own inner torments coming out on screen.

Obtuse, but quite frightening, it was a suitably off-key note on which to end a decade that saw the life of British horror slowly bleed away.

17.   The Eighties: End Of A Nightmare

If the 1970's, post-*Exorcist*, had been a difficult time for the British horror movie, the 1980's saw its death knell. Stretching beyond, into the 1990's, there were only a couple of movies that really fitted the genre, and both of these were more transatlantic in tone.

By the late 1970's, Hammer were reduced to tenth rate TV, and Amicus were little more than a series of fading movie posters. The avalanche of 1970's independent horror had slowed to a trickle, most of it with one eye firmly on the US market. As such, these movies tended to be very American in approach, and although some of them were fine movies, they were lacking that piece of something extra that defined a British horror flick.

The Gothic tradition died, replaced by the stalk and slash movie. This was no bad thing, as Gothic had reached a plateau, and producers were repeating themselves. Everyone needed a break, and they got it in the form of John Carpenter and Sean Cunningham, whose *Halloween* (1978 etc) and *Friday 13th* (1980 etc) series dominated the tail end of 1970's horror. The low-key, kitchen sink approach welded to a high gore content set the tone for a decade in which horror was the lunatic lurking in the shadows rather than a grand fable à la Hammer.

Although many of these films were extremely good, and opened the door for an on-rush of European product that included as many Italian gialli and zombie movies as you could shake a severed arm at, they spelt the end for British horror. Censorship problems and the lack of financial return led to less production overall, and when there was a revival in British production over the next fifteen years, it was always with "quality" productions such as *Chariots Of Fire* (1981) or anything based on an E M Forster novel. The problem being that such movies needed a large cash injection to get going, and as Margaret Thatcher's pseudo-fascist state swung into action, the money was drained from Britain into overseas affairs.

The very same brand of "nanny knows best" was responsible for the other crunching blow to the head of British horror; the video nasty scare of the early 1980's. Just when home video was becoming a reality, and presenting another way of viewing product, the Tory government cracked down against horror, labelling certain films as "depraved and likely to corrupt". The only thing wrong with many of the movies they banned – like *Driller Killer* (1979) the best known example – was that they were so poorly made as to be offensive in their dull-wittedness. Many interesting Italian directors like Lucio Fulci and Dario Argento found themselves on the nasty list, and everyone was supposed to watch *Bambi* (in which the mother of an infant is ruthlessly killed, etc – the argument can be reduced ad infinitum).

With the prospect of little money coming in from British-oriented production, most British-produced horror was aimed directly at the States or – in the case of Palace – at the art house. The latter move did see a brief and interesting flowering of a new Gothic, the tone of which was not really taken up until the current wave of Gothic romances emanating from America – Coppola's *Dracula* (1992) and Neil Jordan's *Interview With The Vampire* (1994) being the most obvious examples; despite this, by the 1990's British horror production was almost dead on a professional level (some amateurs and semi-pro's try to keep the flag flying).

The final nail – so far – was the murder of Jamie Bulger, a Liverpool infant, which was allegedly inspired by a viewing of *Child's Play 3* (1991) a somewhat less than thrilling potboiler from Charles Band, the low-budget US horror supremo. The murderers – themselves only pre-pubescent – allegedly killed the child in a manner copying the film. This opened the old debate about violence in movies affecting children, there is nothing to add either way to this debate, except to say that there have always been child killers. Mary Bell did not watch horror movies... could it be that the solicitors acting for the killers just sought an excuse?

Whatever the reason, it brought down a wave of censorship fever, and even as this is written there are still moves to ban certain films – including the black comedies of Frank Hennenlotter, which have a morality and comic-book humour lifting them beyond movies like *Death Wish* and any Bruce Willis action spectacular, in which there is no point to violence except spectacle. I have no view either way on these type of movies, but would just note that there are no attempts to ban them...

At the end of any working day, the final decision is financial. Horror in Britain is not kept at bay by the censorship lobby per se, but by the difficulty they cause producers in getting bookings and releases. If the picture cannot make money, then it will not get made.

Midway through the 1990's, Hammer announced a comeback, with remakes of some of their greatest hits, such as *The Quatermass X-periment*. With a huge US cash injection, some of these will reportedly be made in the States. Norman J Warren, a director of long standing in British exploitation, is re-making *Fiend Without A Face*, aided by overseas money. Clive Barker is making movies, aided by Hollywood cash... There will always be British horror talent out there making movies – remember, Universal's first *Frankenstein* (1931), and its sequel, *The Bride Of Frankenstein* (1935), were helmed by Englishman James Whale – but whether they will be British horror movies as we know them remains to be seen.

Meanwhile, back at the turn of the 1980's...

Lord Lew Grade, former world Charleston champion, media mogul, and owner of Midlands TV franchise holder ATV, had plans for his ITC company. Not content with some of the best fantasy and thriller TV ever seen (from *The Saint* to *Thunderbirds* via *The Prisoner* and *Jason King*), he still nursed an ambition to make movies. Like most UK media men of his generation, he wanted to have a studio like the old Hollywood combines, something not possible in the 1970's and 1980's. Still, he persevered until the abominable *Raise The Titanic* (1980) sank his company in a welter of bad reviews and too-expensive effects. Along the way, however, there were a few attempts at bringing British horror into the 1980's.

Perhaps the first ITC attempt was the psycho-thriller *The Medusa Touch*, a 1978 picture that starred Richard Burton at his drunken hammy worst. A writer with the psychic ability to alter events and cause planes to crash, buildings to collapse, he spends the second half of the film mute and swathed in bandages in a hospital bed. One problem, the obvious stand-in was about three stone lighter and a head taller than Burton. No matter, as the film cannot make up its mind whether to be a thriller or opt for horror, bungling both. Jack Gold has a surprising off-day in the directors chair, and John Briley's script makes no sense.

Hardly auspicious, it set the tone for the three ITC horrors that started the decade. All in 1980, they virtually killed off any hopes of a British horror revival before the decade was a year old.

Dark Water (1980) was a low-budget attempt to create a horror short. Possibly an attempt to second bill to a bigger ITC movie, it was co-produced by Dragonfly, the company of director Andrew Bogle, who co-wrote the script with Tony Grisoni. The three cast members – Gwyneth Strong, Phil Davis and David Beames – centre the action around a swimming pool, where a girl locked in is terrorised by a maniac whose only intent is to frighten her to death.

Even in half an hour, some kind of plot is required; although the direction is full of long shadows, and the tension is kept up, the lack of story leads to clock-watching before the end. A noble failure. Which is more than can be said of...

Saturn 3 (1980) is a sci-fi horror scripted by Eng. Lit. enfant terrible Martin Amis. Not the kind of thing he probably puts on his CV, but it does pay the rent. Based on a story by John Barry, it is not the script that lets this down, but rather the direction. Stanley Donen is in the chair, and he also co-produced this for his Transcontinental company.

The plot is simple. Kirk Douglas and Farrah Fawcett are running the space station of the title, having an idyllic time and running around nude (that's pretty horrific in itself). Saturn 3 is an attempt to re-create a garden of Eden above a polluted world. Shades of the superior sci-fi flick Silent Running (1971) here. However, all similarity ends with the entrance of Harvey Keitel, doing his patented twitchy and intense shtick as a madman who is a bit annoyed with the bliss of Kirk and Farrah. So he builds a robot, directing it to stalk and destroy.

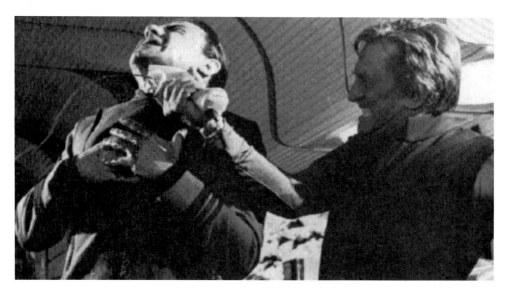

Saturn 3

The main problem with the film is that the viewer is supposed to identify with Kirk and Farrah, but they are so nauseating that you actually want Keitel to sic 'em. Having thus subverted the original premise unintentionally, Donen then lets great stretches of the film wander by with nothing happening, and concentrates some quite frightening moments into a few scenes.

A salutary lesson in how not to make horror, it has a good Elmer Bernstein score, and an appearance from ITC sci-fi veteran Ed Bishop (Commander Straker in UFO and voice man for Gerry Anderson). Even this cannot redeem it.

The final movie of the trio was Milton Subotsky's swan song. The Monster Club (1980) another anthology, based on an R Chetwynd-Hayes collection. Edward and Valerie Abraham fiddle with the stories until they bear no resemblance to the book (actually, in some ways they're better!), and have the nice conceit of John Carradine playing the author R Chetwynd-Hayes in the framing story. Accosted by vampire Vincent Price, he refuses to be bitten. When Price recognises his favourite author, he takes him to the club of the title, where they watch some execrable music from B A Robertson and the Pretty Things (in one of their less appetizing incarnations), see a striptease that is down to the bone (tacky), and get introduced to some monsters in make-up that looks like a kids party. The end, however – where Hayes is elected to the club, as humans are the biggest monsters due to their catalogue of atrocities – is a serious point humorously presented.

In many ways, that is the biggest problem of the film. The framing device is full of juvenile humour, yet the episodes within are two parts straight to one part parody. The parody is Richard Johnson as a vampire, forced to trawl the underground for a quick nip and suck here and there, coming home to mother Britt Ekland and young son, who is pursued by vampire hunters Donald Pleasence and Anthony Valentine. Witty and daft, it fits well with the tenor of the frame.

The two straight stories, however, would not be out of place in an earlier Amicus anthology. James Laurenson is a 'shadmock', whose whistle can disfigure and kill. The centre of a plot to gain his money, he is wooed by an attractive girl, but when he discovers the real plot, he sends her back to her boyfriend in a less than attractive state... The second story is about Stuart Whitman, trapped in a village of ghouls when his car breaks down. Befriended by Patrick Magee's daughter Lesley Dunlop (a 'humgoo' – her mother was human, before the villagers ate her), he tries to escape, only to run into a police escort bringing the village elders home.

Director Roy Ward Baker handles the serious stories with aplomb, and they look good, but the frame and parody, however, are beyond him and these look forced and trite. If the film could make up its mind which way it wanted to fall, then it would be a better viewing experience. As it is, it does not stand as a testimony to Subotsky.

ITC had one last fling at the great British horror in 1984. This was a co-production with Palace pictures, a company originally set up Nik Powell and Al Clarke, who were ex-Virgin employees. The company itself, although part-owned by Virgin, was separate.

The Company Of Wolves (1984) was produced by Chris Brown and Stephen Woolley, with a script by Angela Carter and Neil Jordan taken mainly from two stories by Carter, *Wolf Alice* and *The Company Of Wolves*.

This was my first introduction to Angela Carter, whose surreal and fantastic fables are often mixed with a subtle polemic and shot through with wry, dark humour. Before her death in 1992 she was producing the best fiction of anyone over the last fifty years. So I am going to be biased about this film, right?

Right. Taking an allegorical look at the trip through adolescence of one girl, in the space of one strange night, it tells of werewolves and men who are "hairy on the inside", with a farrago of audacious and startling images that bring out the Gothic horror of most fairytales and match them to the modern myths of pulp fiction and the media. An intensely personal journey and vision, it is to the credit of Jordan that he not only helped Carter translate her prose into a screenplay (no easy task, as should be obvious to anyone who has read her work), but directed with a stunning breadth of vision. Jordan returned to horror and Gothic fantasy with 1994's *Interview With A Vampire*.

Included in the cast – all of whom play up to the script's exacting standard – are Graham Crowden, Sarah Patterson (the adolescent around who events revolve), David Warner (as her father), and Stephen Rea (who loses his head in a spectacular slow motion sequence, turning from wolf to man). The real star is Angela Lansbury, as the lycanthropic grandmother who is the fount of all wisdom – a wisdom that the young girl realises is false by the end of the picture.

The beauty of this film is that it is scary, enthralling and a terror story on many levels. The traditional terror of monsters, and the terrors of growing up and discovering sexuality are mixed in a heady brew.

That is how I see it, the allegory is so loose that other viewers may find something else in there. Whatever, it is always a visual feast.

Keen to keep their Gothic revival going, Palace made *Gothic* (1986) the next

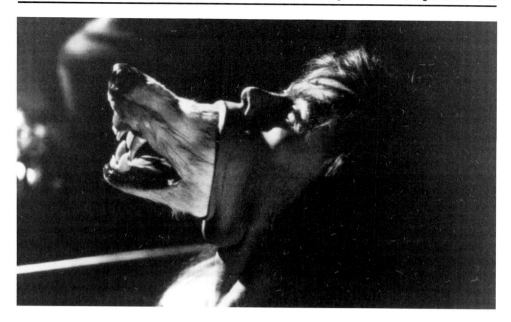

The Company Of Wolves

year, with Ken Russell directing a Stephen Volk screenplay that Al Clarke immediately optioned. This is not so much a horror movie as a movie about horror, but is worth mentioning as it covers the infamous Villa Diodati party where Mary Shelley wrote *Frankenstein* and physician John Polidori wrote *The Vampyre*.

Byron is played by Gabriel Byrne, Shelley by Julian Sands, Mary by the wimpish Natasha Richardson (not like the real Mary – daughter of anarchist philosopher Thomas Godwin and feminist Mary Wollstonecraft – at all). The star turn, however, is the unctuous and creepy Timothy Spall, who plays Polidori as a leering pervert.

As the laudanum starts to flow, the nightmares begin, and the film is one long series of hallucinogenic sequences. An interesting take on Gothic, it is not so much horror as an historical fantasy, and worth a look.

Encouraged by the success of this, Russell returned to Gothic horror for *The Lair Of The White Worm* (1988), another Palace attempt to resurrect British horror, in 1989. Starring Amanda Donohoe as Lady Sylvia Marsh, the film centres around a Scottish archaeologist who unearths a worm-like skull in the wilds of Derbyshire. This immediately attracts the attention of Lady Sylvia, who moves in on the nervous Scot with a sexuality that causes him to go weak at the knees.

She is interested in the skull because she has a white worm in her cellar, to which she feeds the corpses of passing men whose blood she has sucked. Our archaeologist is about to go the same way.

Not really frightening, this is a Ken Russell erotic romp through the outer reaches of surreal grand guignol. I do not think it is possible for Russell to make a truly frightening film as his impish sense of humour always intrudes. However, the author of the original book – Bram Stoker – probably never expected to see the sexual connotations of this story brought out in such a blatant manner, as Lady Sylvia comes on like Hammer's *The Reptile* with added Janet Reger lingerie and a leather fetish. Not terribly British in a horrific manner, Russell's sexual peccadilloes are nonetheless very British in their way. The S&M undertones of a vampiric/sexual relationship are intriguingly skirted in a tease of a film.

The Lair Of The White Worm

Paperhouse

Much more dour was Bernard Rose's *Paperhouse* (1988) a Palace production from the year before. Based on a children's novel by Catherine Starr called *Marianna Dreams*, it tells of a girl whose drawings appear to influence reality. During a long stay in bed due to illness, Marianna does an awful lot of drawing, and finds her world becoming lop-sided and dream-like. For an unknown reason it begins to mirror her drawings. Thus her father – the ever-absent Ben Cross – is drawn with a hideous grin that makes him look angry. So when he does turn up again, he is no longer a distant relation so much as a looming threat.

Charlotte Burke is annoying as the child – but then again, I hate most child actors. Pure prejudice, I admit. However, the character develops well as she begins to come to terms with the looming emotional shadows and very real physical threats. Genuinely scary, this straddles the divide between supernatural horror (or should that be preternatural?) and emotional terror as Marianna faces up to the fact that her inner fears are being reflected by her drawings and thus – by inference – the outside world.

While Palace were forging an answer to British horror in the 1980's, Canon were producing pure pulp for now people. The story of Golan and Globus – the Go-Go twins – is infamous: Israeli entrepreneurs buy cinema chains and start production company, let the cinemas go to waste and fritter big money on blockbusters that flop, then go bust. Along the way, they attempted to muscle in on the horror market with a wildly profligate and haphazard approach to film-making that is breathtaking in its stupidity.

Their first effort at British horror was *House Of The Long Shadows*, the long awaited and totally duff comeback from low-budget Brit-horror guru Peter Walker. Made in 1983, this remake of the old film *Seven Keys To Baldpate* (1935) has already been discussed. It could have – should have – been better.

Life Force

Two years later, Canon employed Tobe Hooper to make *Life Force* (1985), with a script from Dan O'Bannon and Don Jakoby. Based on Colin Wilson's novel *The Space Vampires*, it stripped away the philosophy and theorising of the original, then got down to some serious pulp action.

In many ways, this was an impossible book to film, as Wilson is a psychic investigator and philosopher with a strong interest in criminology. His non-fiction books are amongst the most fascinating and important of our times. However, his few novels have usually been vehicles for his H P Lovecraft obsession and his ideas, with the result that great gobs of static text proselytise ideas before a quick action sequence tries to keep things moving. In *The Space Vampires*, a space craft is found to contain aliens who – when bought to earth – turn out to be bloodsucking fiends who also drain vital life energies from the mind. It is Wilson's best novel as it moves relatively quickly – but there are still those great static passages to overcome.

O'Bannon and Jakoby turn it into a romp around London, with Peter Firth, Frank Finlay and Patrick Stewart looking grim and muttering lines of serious import. Enjoyable as a pulp horror, the true worth is in the way Hooper keeps it moving and manages to inject shocks and atmosphere into a script that seems strangely dated.

It was certainly better than the same year's *Déjà Vu* (1985), in which a couple discover each other and fall in love before realising that they are the re-incarnation of lovers who died in a fire during World War II. Jaclyn Smith is terrible as the token US star, her performance shown up all the more by the excellent Nigel Terry, always a good actor no matter what the circumstances.

Directed by Anthony Richmond, who also wrote the script with Ezra D Rappaport, the action is static. This is what ruins the movie. Apart from Smith, the rest of the cast (including Clare Bloom and Shelley Winters) are solid. Although excessively talky, with little in the way of outright horror, the performances of the actors as they realise what has happened imparts a creepy atmosphere to the piece. It falls down simply because it is cinema, and there is always a need for kinetics of some sort.

Perhaps this would have worked better as a play: it was based on a book by Trevor Meldal-Johnsen, and is perhaps suited to the written medium more than the visual.

Something that could not be said of 1990's *I Bought A Vampire Motorcycle*, mentioned in the horror-comedy chapter. With little input from Golan and Globus, this was one of Canon's best horrors – what does that tell us?

In between, Canon financed the initial flowering of Clive Barker on film – for which any British horror fan should be thankful. Barker – a former stage manager and actor turned writer – burst on the scene in a bucket of blood in 1983, when his *Books Of Blood* were published in three volumes by Sphere. Short story collections, they had the splatter of a Shaun Hutson mixed with the subtlety of a Ramsey Campbell, and a rare talent that needed nurturing. Since then, Barker has broadened his canvas to encompass all forms of fantasy, and has taken his visual flair to its natural conclusion in the cinema.

After scripting director George Pavlou's *Underworld* in 1985, Barker saw the same man make a mess of his *Rawhead Rex* the next year. The story of a ten foot cannibalistic monster unearthed in a Irish field, the film is as raw as the title character, with some bad sound recording and some nice locations mixed with a monster suit that would shame AIP. The basic story is a bit thin; unearthed, the monster wreaks havoc by ripping open courting couples and urinating on passing vicars. As monsters go, a bit of a juvenile delinquent. Having said that, Pavlou does manage to get a few shocks into the cutting, and the monster's table manners really are revolting.

Canon financed Barker's next script, *Hellraiser* (1987), and allowed him to be director. This was a wise move, as Barker knew exactly what he wanted from his script and his actors. The story of a puzzle box that unlocks the secrets to the world of the Cenobites, almost elementals whose stock in trade is fear and pain, it was handled with skilful direction and lighting. The special effects were good for the obviously tight budget, and Claire Higgins turned in a wonderful performance as the girlfriend of the box's owner, luring men back to her flat to feed him their blood and flesh.

The film was also notable for creating a new horror icon in Doug Bradley's Pinhead, one of the Cenobites. If nothing else, Barker and his make-up men created an enduring British horror image for the 1980's and 1990's.

Interestingly, Canon insisted on the minor characters being dubbed with American accents, which seems a little incongruous when the action takes place in Hampstead. The Cenobites, with their deformities and self-imposed tortures (a throat held open by surgical clamps and sewn shut eyelids amongst them) reflect a fear of technology – less organic than other monsters, much more mechanical, they seem to reflect a modern view of hell; man overcome by machinery. But at the root there are still the same old desires.

Barker and Higgins moved to America for *Hellbound: Hellraiser II* (1988), and the third *Hellraiser III: Hell On Earth* (1992) movies, both scripted by horror novelist Pete Atkins, whose friendship with Barker meant that the men's views on the project were attuned. Barker's production company struck a deal with New World, the US company, to make the movies as no British company had the money to afford Barker's effects and dark visions. Barker's *Nightbreed* (1990) has a similar history, and his story *Candyman* (1992) had its locale switched from Liverpool to Chicago for the movie version starring Tony Todd.

So when is a British horror movie not a British horror movie? Answer: when it is Clive Barker's perspectives filtered through a Hollywood money machine that thinks the world revolves around the USA. And I suppose it does in that sense... At least the British horror lives on in spirit, if not in the traditional sense.

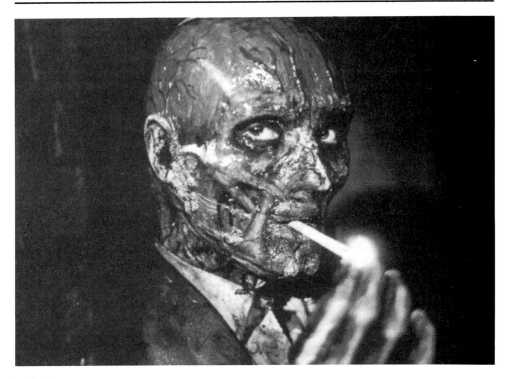

Hellraiser

Meanwhile, outside of the larger companies already mentioned, there were a few attempts in the 1980's and early 1990's to make a British horror movie. Some of them even worked – a rare thing in the compromising search to recoup costs.

If ITC made three movies with a horrific theme in 1980, they were not alone in taking the last gasp of British horror as a chance to make a quick buck. There were four other horror movies from that year, one of which was a fine short, three of which were features perhaps best forgotten.

The Awakening (1980) was produced by EMI and Orion, with Mike Newell helming a feature that was overly long at one hundred and five minutes. Based on Bram Stoker's novel *The Jewel Of The Seven Stars*, it had all of that unfortunate writer's long-winded banality, and few of the ideas that Hammer distilled into the far more effective *Blood From The Mummy's Tomb* (1971) some nine years earlier.

Stoker is a writer served well by movie-makers: *Dracula*, *The Jewel Of The Seven Stars*, and *The Lair Of The White Worm* have all made better movies than the original books would suggest, and contemporary artists have managed to realise more fully the sexual imagery that Stoker almost subconsciously buried under his stilted prose.

But not here! Like the Hammer version, this updates the story to the present day. Scriptwriters Allan Scott, Chris Bryant and Clive Exton then proceed to bleed any pace out of the film, and the presence of three writers on the credit, one of whom (Exton) usually works alone suggests that there were numerous re-writes. This would account for the fragmented nature of the narrative, which jumps from the birth of a daughter as archaeologist Charlton Heston uncovers an Egyptian tomb through to the grown-up girl (Stephanie Zimbalist in her pre-*Remington Steele* and stardom days) beginning to act a little strangely with little mention or reference to passing time.

Indeed, Heston appears to have got younger during the passing years.

British in name only, the mostly American cast (Susannah York being the sole starring British name) pay little but lip service to the English setting. Newell attempts to inject some pace and atmosphere into the proceedings, but is let down by poor work from cameraman Jack Cardiff, who films the whole thing in washed out tones and flat focusing that robs it of any visual character. For all the money spent on it, it comes over as little more than an overlong TV episode, and by the time Heston tumbles to what is happening, his attempts to set things aright by behaving just like Moses coming down from the mountain are little short of ludicrous.

A more ludicrous movie that actually works is *Holocaust 2000* (1977) aka *The Chosen*, an Italian/British co-production between Rank subsidiary Aston and Embassy, produced by Italian Edmonto Amati. Despite the European locations and the dubbing, a strong British flavour of repressed religiosity helps to quell the usual Italian submersion into the paranormal, making the extremely bizarre storyline that bit more believable.

Set in the Middle east (but certainly not filmed there), it is a semi-plagiaristic take on *The Omen* (1976), with the executive in charge of a nuclear plant discovering an ancient legend relating to the rebirth of the anti-Christ. At first he dismisses this as nonsense, but gradually it begins to dawn on him that the legend is referring to his own son. Given his position, and the influence his son is beginning to exert as he discovers his powers, the viewer is in for a series of spectacular deaths and a race against time to prevent the plant being blown up and presaging the coming of judgement day.

With an almost obligatory stirring soundtrack from Ennio Morricone and whiplash direction from Alberto de Martino, the script by Sergio Donati, Michael Robson and director de Martino is taken along at a lightning pace. Kirk Douglas is believable (more than he was in *Saturn 3*), and Anthony Quayle and Simon Ward provide good old fashioned British gravitas and character acting, with stern support from Adolfo Celi and Virginia McKenna.

But by far the best horror of 1980 was *The Appointment*, written directed and produced by Lindsay Vickers. Although in some ways it looked like a short project that had been expanded to feature length (it runs for ninety minutes), this went in its favour as it is a good old fashioned flick in the Amicus or Hammer tradition.

Samantha Weysom – a surprisingly un-bratty child actress is the daughter of Edward Woodward. In the one big effects sequence of the movie she is captured by a supernatural force while walking through the woods. It seems that this is to be the end of her... until she arrives home quite happily.

Having been jolted to attention in this manner, the viewer is then kept on the edge of their seat by a series of subtle mishaps and building paranoias as Woodward starts to realise that his daughter has, in some way changed. Very cleverly, this physical change is tied in with the subtle psychology of realising that his daughter is growing up. It is only when he fails to do something as trivial as turn up to hear her play violin in the school concert that things really begin to go awry, and the girl decides to make his life a hell on earth, culminating in a slow-motion car wreck.

Vickers may have graduated from advertising, but there are none of the flash visuals and shallowness that some TV ad directors have brought to the screen. Instead, he concentrates on building up an atmosphere through the use of pace and framing, drawing great performances from Woodward and Weysom, and also from his supporting cast, which includes John Judd and Jane Merrow, familiar TV faces.

Perhaps a little out of time, and ultimately failing through being over-stretched, it did not fare well at the box office, and soon made it onto video – which, in the very early 1980's, was usually taken as a sign of poor quality in low budget movies... how times change.

The last horror of the year was a short support feature produced by Picture Partnership, entitled *Cry Wolf* (1980). In half an hour, and on a budget of less than the average sit-com, it managed to be both a thrilling little picture in its own right and a homage to the low-budget shockers of the 1950's and 1960's which it sets out to pastiche.

The plot is simple: a scientists invents a serum which will turn him into a werewolf, and tests it on himself. Then, having changed, he sets out to terrorise the local town. In a rather fey touch, he becomes friendly with a Jack Russell terrier by the end of the film, and even raises the hackles of the local police.

Because the budget is low, the most that is ever really seen of the monster is a shadow – but this works both on the level of making the viewer do the work and also in pastiching the unwillingness of old movies to reveal their sticky-tape monsters.

Written by Stan Hey and directed by Leszek Burzynski, the film features Paul Maxwell as the scientist, Rosalind Ayres, and Stephen Greif. Coming over rather like a local village production of *The Wolfman* (1940), it was tremendous fun and even managed to raise a few chills with some atmospheric camera-work.

Perhaps unintentionally, it was a commentary on the dying British horror tradition: in the days of Jason and Michael the Shape, with Freddy Krueger just around the corner, blood needed to be seen. Although not necessarily a good thing, it was important that horror movies pushed the boundaries of what was permissable on screen. Only if this was explored could the older methods of restraint be revitalised and re-explored.

Interestingly, *Cry Wolf* went on release with a picture that managed to approach the subject from both angles, and also combine an incredibly English approach with a American grasp of market forces: *An American Werewolf In London* (1981).

Written and directed by Jon Landis, with a score that used every kind of musical joke imaginable (from Creedence Clearwater's *Bad Moon Rising* to Warren Zevon's *Werewolves Of London*), the film now looks terribly dated and nowhere near as good as it did at the time. Perhaps this is because, although it captured a moment in time for British horror, it was an eclipse that had no real life to it, a compromise that worked for a brief second then dissipated.

David Naughton and Griffin Dunne are American hitchhikers who are traversing the Yorkshire Moors. In a spoofy scene they enter the local village pub to be greeted with dead silence, a parody of every horror scene like this there has ever been, they are warned not to go out alone after dark. And of course they do. Dunne is ripped to pieces, and Naughton injured by a wild animal that is not caught, and that the local police are understandably evasive about.

Naughton falls in love with the nurse who looks after him (played by Jenny Agutter), and moves in with her on his return to London. Soon the full moon comes around, and he feels decidedly odd... in a sequence by make-up wizard Rick Baker that looks dated only because it was the blueprint for countless other movies, Naughton turns into a werewolf and goes on the hunt.

From this point, a drama with spoof undertones takes on a decidedly blacker edge. Dunne turns up in strange places to talk to Naughton – like behind him in the bathroom, or beside him at the cinema. At first, Naughton believes he is going mad as Dunne explains that he is now a werewolf, and he has got to die before causing too much harm. At each appearance, the corpse of Dunne degenerates, and soon he starts to bring Naughton's victims with him...

Turning to despair, Naughton thinks at first that Dunne is an illusion, and that he is going mad. Then he realises the truth – and everyone else thinks that he is going mad when he tells them...

The film can only end in tragedy, and Naughton is cornered and killed in

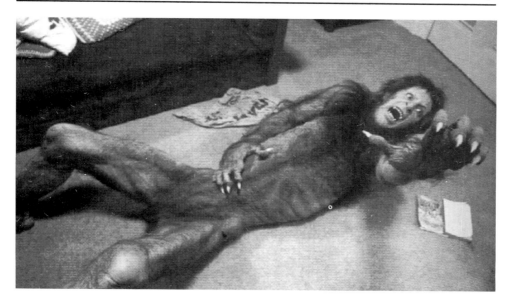

An American Werewolf In London

central London, with Agutter weeping over the corpse. Moving from humour to horror to almost romantic drama in rapid succession, this is an uneven movie that is still worth a look, and was a brave attempt to meld two styles of horror film-making together.

It was two years before another British produced horror movie hit the screens, and in the wake of the first video nasty swoop it could not have been more poorly timed. In a climate where horror was becoming the scapegoat for society's ills (much better to look to fiction than harsh reality for blame, after all), *Don't Open Till Christmas* (1983) was exactly what the censor ordered.

Starring and directed by Edmund Purdom for 21st Century, it was a British hack and slash movie. In setting alone it differed from the American movies littering the shelves, and was frankly poor quality compared to even the worst of these. The problem seems to be that British film-makers, still obsessed with "quality", could not get their heads around churning out a quickie slasher film. In a climate where British movie buffs and critics are always looking back to past glories (by now, Hammer were being praised where they were cursed when actively producing), the old traditions have a golden glow. Let us be honest, this book is a little like that – although I hope that I can also look to the future...

So this was a bit of a disappointment on all counts. It could not live up to the old ways, and was not so hot in competition with the Americans. Old stager Derek Ford (a sexploitation and horror script writer in the 1960's) wrote the script with Al McGoohan, and it was relatively imaginative. Especially nice was the idea that all the victims would not be scantily dressed young girls, but Father Christmases... as someone who has always felt uneasy with the slasher ethos of cutting up girls, and has always hated Christmas, this seemed like a fine idea.

There are a few witty lines, and a surprisingly good performance from Alan Lake, a bit-part actor most noted for being Diana Dors' last husband and sharing a bed with Mary Millington in *The David Galaxy Affair* (not that he was alone in that film!). The editing is also strong, adding a few genuinely shocking moments. But at the end of the day, Purdom's direction is sloppy, and he seems to sleepwalk his way through the film. Which is a shame, as if it had been well-made it could have competed with the Americans.

Instead, it was two years before another British horror, one that harked back to the golden days and tried to enshrine the style in aspic. All it succeeded in doing was killing it stone dead.

The Doctor And The Devils (1985) was produced by Mel Brooks' Brooksfilm company, which had previously strayed into Victorian grotesque with David Lynch's *The Elephant Man* (1980). A serious film on a serious subject that had met with acclaim. Perhaps Brooks felt that getting his hands on the Dylan Thomas screenplay refused a certificate by the censor nearly forty years before – and as a result never made – and having it polished by award-winning playwright Ronald Harwood would give him a similarly prestigious vehicle. Getting Freddie Francis in to direct suggested that he intended to invoke the spirit of Hammer.

The end result was a stilted, dull mess. Francis tried hard, but the cast – including Timothy Spall, Julian Sands, Twiggy, the insufferable Jonathan Pryce, and Stephen Rea – played the vehicle like it was high art. As a result there was little dynamism, and no way to inject the tension necessary for horror or terror of any kind. They stand around mouthing their lines as though they are great poetry – and one thing you can say about Dylan Thomas, he may have been a poet, but he was no Jimmy Sangster.

Ludicrously out of its time, awfully overplayed, and pompously boring, this Burke and Hare resurrection shuffle was proof that the Gothic genre was dead and buried – and certainly did not need digging up.

In contrast, Terry Gilliam made *Brazil* (1985) in the same year. Also starring Jonathan Pryce, who was not as irritating in this movie, it had a pointed and terrifying script brainstormed by Gilliam, Tom Stoppard and Charles McKeown.

Produced by Arnon Milchan, it is perhaps a little long at one hundred and forty-two minutes, and does owe a lot to George Orwell's novel *1984*. However, the bleak and pessimistic eye that Gilliam casts over the future is far more terrifying that anything in Room 101.

Pryce is a bureaucrat who quite cheerfully accepts the world of forms, rules, and conformity that runs his life for him in a nightmare landscape where there are hissing pipes and broken machinery around every corner. Everything is permanently dark and enshrouded in a chemical haze. You get the idea that just breathing could kill you – or get you killed, if you do it wrong.

Things really start to go wrong when Pryce is taken ill, and something goes wrong at work. This starts off a chain of events that includes household breakdowns and the entrance of Robert de Niro – the scariest repair man you would ever wish to meet. Pryce finds himself questioning what is going on, sucked into a world of guerilla warfare, and fingered by his bosses as a subversive when all he is trying to do is stay alive.

Taking great chunks of paranoia and nightmare from Kafka's novel *The Trial*, *Brazil* is a movie about losing control and the nanny state turning on the "ungrateful" child – highly pertinent when you consider it was made at the height of Margaret Thatcher's pernicious term of office, and Gilliam – another Anglophile American – is just that bit removed from England, enough to see our follies when we are too close.

There are some great performances from Michael Palin, Bob Hoskins, and Peter Vaughan (always a good bet as a villain or copper), and a killer of a false ending, Pryce is being tortured in a steel and glass dome when he sees his friends from the guerilla movement crash through the roof and descend for him... until the camera pulls back to show nothing more than the poor, broken fool smiling madly to himself, his interrogator dismissing him as totally lost in his insanity.

Okay, so it mirrors the end of Virgin's *1984* (1984) – but that film was flaccid sci-fi, missing the point of Orwell. Gilliam adds his own paranoia and fear of authority

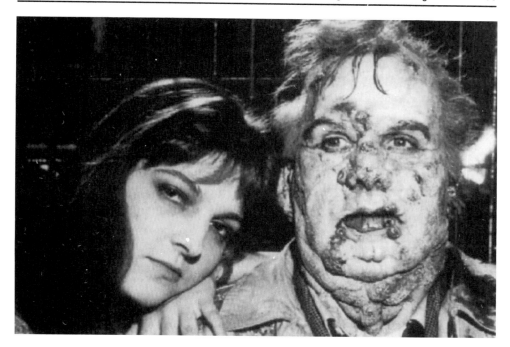

Dream Demon

to the mix, making for a strong brew where the occasional laugh is more of hysterical fear than comedy.

Dream Demon (1987) was an attempt to weld an American sensibility to a British approach that very nearly worked. Made by Harley Cokliss for the Cotillion company, it was a film about nightmares that leap from the world of sleep and into reality. Timothy Spall played well, but I have to be honest and say that it actually sent me to sleep... that is not terribly "critic" of me, I know, but it may say something about the picture.

Better by far was *Split Second*, produced for Challenge by Susan Nicoletti and Laura Gregory. Gregory was head of Challenge, an ad agency who wanted to get into features, and Nicoletti was an American producer who bought the project to her, with a screenplay by Gary Scott Thompson, set in LA.

Changing locale to London, and fast forwarding to 2008, Gregory turned a serial-killer movie into a film about a technological near future in which belief in the occult triggers a series of killings – mostly of police officers.

Thompson's script is fast, witty and frightening, mixing near-death fright with creeping tension. This is fully brought out by Tony Maylam's excellent direction and the playing of Rutger Hauer as cop Harley Stone, saddled with hard-man Scots actor Neil Duncan as Durkin, the partner Stone does not want.

The claustrophobia of this industrial wasteland near future is fuelled by Chris Edwards' great sets, for which he took over two derelict factories in London's East End. The dinginess of the locales infuses its way into the set, giving the film a marvellous downbeat feel.

British in its dour approach, this is one of the few movies to match the two styles with anything approaching real success. Americans Michael J Pollard and Kim Cattrall join Ian Dury as supporting cast, with Hauer trying to out-intense everyone else on screen and succeeding.

Split Second

Exciting and frightening at the same time, its success artistically was not been matched at the box office. Yet it is not a ghetto "British" film: perhaps the true demise of British horror can be laid firmly at the door of the money-men. Unless it fits the "national heritage" view of Britain, like the big-budget E M Forster and *Chariots Of*

Fire-styled movies, then it just can not get the necessary overseas business to recoup costs.

In the light of this, it is all the more remarkable that *Funnyman* got made. A 1994 movie with a brief Christopher Lee cameo as the owner of a house in which a group of people are gathered, only to be picked off at random by the malevolent jester/elemental of the title, it is an intriguing mix of "old dark house" mystery and slasher tactics.

Not great art, and with more in common with US pictures than old British horror, it perhaps proves that there is life in the twitching corpse yet.

Ultimately, the British horror movie was a beast dependant on time and circumstance to shape it. It flowered, and then it died. No amount of Hammer "comebacks" will change that. However, there are elements of that style that are worth preserving, and carrying forward to meld with the kind of horror that is being made in the US and Italy today. Despite their own industry's problems, they have kept going, and why should not UK film-makers, even if they have to look further afield for finance?

People may tire of gore, and effects and make-up become the preserve of the train-spotter, but everyone is still scared by a ghost story, and their own nightmares. The unknown and the unseen, the essence of the British horror movie, and well worth preserving.

Appendix

The joy of watching old horror movies is that you discover new things about them all the time, and the more you watch the more links you make. I guess the same applies to any other genre (one day I will write a book about British film comedies, and that really will be a train-spotter's paradise), but as we are talking about horrors made in Britain, or by British production companies, then I will keep it simple...

Since finishing the main body of the text, I have found out that a couple of the Larraz movies made in the UK were actually produced by British financed companies – yet the most typically English (and the least typical of Larraz) was actually a Spanish production! I have also discovered that *Incense For The Damned* (1970) aka *Bloodsuckers*, which I thought was actually Greek funded, was financed by a British producer. This is possibly not good for the reader, as I shall proceed to bore everyone with how badly it has been butchered over the years...

But before I get on to those topics, there is a couple of things to add to the main text. Firstly, there is the matter of Jeremy Burnham, a scriptwriter whose sole horror credit I was less than enthusiastic over, and I described him as primarily a sit-com writer. This would be reasonably accurate for his post-1970's credits, but a recent avid viewing of *The Avengers* on cable has revealed to me that he also penned a fair number of Tara King-era *Avengers* episodes. Unfortunately, they also tend to be the most flaccid... Faring better in the matter of *Avengers* credits is Sidney Hayers, a director whose work on 1961's *Night Of The Eagle* I praised, but who made such a lumpen job of the otherwise enjoyable *Circus Of Horrors* from the year previous.

The disjointed feel of *Circus Of Horrors* can only be put down to production interference, as Hayers directed a number of Emma Peel-era colour *Avengers* episodes, and also a couple of *New Avengers* episodes. All of these were stylish in the extreme and showed continuity with *Night Of The Eagle* in pacing and framing.

Is it me, or does this look like turning into a paean of praise to *The Avengers*? Certainly, a number of talents involved with that show made interesting contributions to British horror in the 1960's and 1970's.

Interesting is a word that could also be applied to *Disciples Of Darkness*, the Scotia Barker movie from 1973. This was mentioned briefly in the chapter on the 1970's as being even more incomprehensible than *Crucible Of Terror*, the previous year's movie from Tom Parkinson and actor/DJ Mike Raven. Both also featured Ronald Lacey.

I recently had the chance to catch *Disciples Of Terror* again, and still find it disjointed. The grainy photography was explained when I learnt that it was made for £50,000 out of Raven and Parkinson's own pocket, and actually shot on 16mm rather than 35mm. Certainly, the confused story of a mysterious man brought back from the dead by an infusion of blood is just as surreal as ever – although I suspect this is low-budget non-continuity surreal rather than an intended effect. Co-producer Charles Fairman and co-script writer Churton Fairman are both Raven, using parts of his real name. He desperately wanted to write, direct and act in his own horror movies... how do you break it to a guy that dedicated that he has no talent? You do not go to see his movies, he is now a sheep farmer.

Now we come to the additions to the story of British horror. The first is *Incense For The Damned*, more commonly known these days as *Bloodsuckers*. This was the title I saw it under on late-night TV in a severely butchered print. It was incomprehensible, and a waste of the talent involved. This may, however, not be entirely disconnected to the fact that it was squeezed into a 60-minute slot.

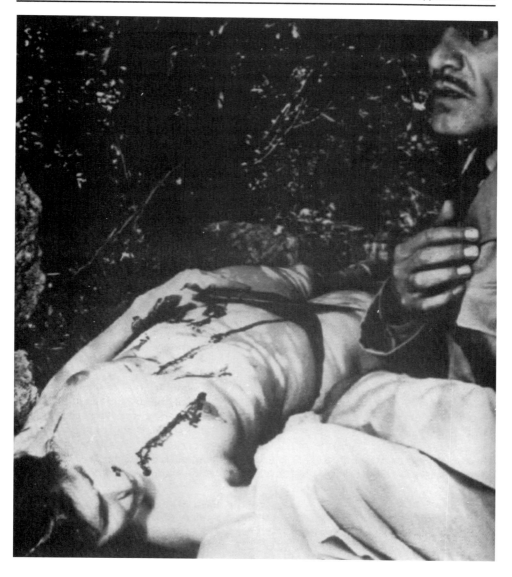

Incense For The Damned

Directed by Graham Harris and directed by the under-rated Robert Hartford-Davis, it was adapted by Julian More from Simon Raven's novel *Doctors Wear Scarlet*. Raven is not a genre writer, preferring to range his talents over a wide area, but he does excel at a distant irony and sense of paranoia that can infuse his work with uneasiness. *Doctors Wear Scarlet* is a good example of this, although my personal preference is for the amoral thriller *Brother Cain*, where the sense of a world with all moral moorings ripped away is truly chilling and disorienting, particularly in a Kafka-esque finale.

The plot of *Doctors Wear Scarlet* concerns a young Oxbridge professor who is set to marry the Master's daughter and continue a glittering career. There are, however, hints of a homosexual relationship with a negro friend, and when they return from Greece the young professor is strangely distant. Eventually he runs away, and the Master sends an ex-student – now in the services – to locate him.

Our nominal hero, who in truth is little more than a cypher for the reader to use as a window on the plot, discovers when he reaches Greece that the professor is under the influence of Chriesis, a vampire woman. This is no supernatural vampire, but rather a perverted sex maniac who is draining him of his life. The wooden narrator and the negro friend join forces with other acquaintances to save the professor. Chriesis is routed, but a final twist comes when, on the first night of his marriage, the young professor kills his bride by ripping put her throat with his teeth.

I have provided a synopsis of the novel because some, if not all, of this is in the movie. However, butcher-handed editing has reduced the remaining print to little more than a series of snapshots. I find it terribly frustrating, as you can see that there is a good movie in there waiting to get out, but it is constantly denied by the choppy edit.

Patrick Mower contributes a vulnerable performance as the young professor, with Patrick MacNee in a post-*Avengers* (what was I saying earlier?) role as a British attaché caught up in events. Imogen Hassall is wonderful as the succubus, and even Edward Woodward crops up as a plot device – a psychologist proclaiming "of course, you know that vampirism is a sexual perversion..."

Add to this Peter Cushing as a ruthless and mean-minded Master (a nice cameo), as well as good, swift direction on those parts that remain relatively unaffected, and it is easy to see that this may once have been a cracking movie. It is still entertaining, with nice travelogue shots of Greece, but ultimately a let-down. One interesting aside is that, unlike most movies from its era (it was shot over 1969-70), there is little in the fashions or trappings to date the film. Maybe this was the idea of the editing...

Someone who did not suffer this indignity – at least, not on the two movies under discussion – is José Larraz. Beginning as an artist and photographer, the Anglophile film-maker ended up living in Kent and making sexploitation movies for English producers, either comedies or thrillers. Later, although living still in England he worked in his native country, directing some horrors on the basis of his UK reputation, but mostly comedies for which he discovered he had a flair. Like latter-day Bunuel, he takes the everyday and subverts it to the surreal. However, constrained by producers and budgets he has never made anything that is free from some kind of exploitation tinge.

Symptoms (1974) aka *The Blood Virgin*, and *Vampyres* (1974) aka *Daughters Of Dracula* aka *Vampyres – Daughters Of Darkness* aka *The Vampyre Orgy*, were produced by Brian Smedley-Aston, film editor and sometimes producer who was the man behind Pennea's *Theatre Of Blood* in 1966. His father was a respected film-maker, and he just loves movies and he will make them, even if it means tossing in exploitation elements.

Symptoms has the feel of M R James, and is so terribly English it is hard to believe that a Spaniard made it. Angela Pleasence is Helen Ramsay, a slightly dotty woman who writes things in her diary about "them" coming to visit her, and invites an old friend to her rotting country home. The old house is full of dark shadows, sighs and whispers. Intercut are some suitably bucolic country scenes.

The odd-job man finds the body of the previous guest in the river, more people start to die, and Helen descends in a spiral of homicidal madness. Yet still, at the heart of the film, there is a strange calm.

Good support comes from Michael Grady (usually a sit-com or sex comedy support) and Peter Vaughan (a menacing British character actor). Larraz helms this one in like Arthur Machen making a movie, and it has the rambling, elusive and allusive feel of that writer's best work. Totally English, yet not in the filmic sense, this has none

Symptoms

of the blatancy seen in most British horror during the 1970's.

Symptoms won some awards, and seemed to be a good sign for Larraz. So what did he and Smedley-Aston do in 1975? Make *Vampyres*, which puts the likes of Jean Rollin and Jess Franco to shame for naked vampire wantons, and has zilch plot. However, for sheer bravado and naked flesh, it beats the Fantale/Hammer soft-core horrors at their own game.

It may have killed his chances of being anything but a cult, but it was a genuinely scary and erotic movie, with Anulka and Marianne Morris as a pair of nubile vampires on the road in England. Again, lots of countryside and British sex comedy character actors populate the frame, but the real action begins when the vampire women seduce their prey, taking great gouges from their bodies in sex acts, blood emerging in huge gouts.

So visual that you really have to see it to understand the feel, it was a most un-English horror movie, but one which drew a good box-office. I have to confess that I can get bored with it if not in the right mood – but then I am unrepentant about my love of plot, and this film does not have that. Hell, with ex-model Anulka and sex comedy actress Morris it does not *need* a plot.

Interestingly, Larraz returned to rustic horror with *Black Candles*, a Spanish movie he managed to relocate to England in 1981. This follows a similar course to *Symptoms*, with a couple visiting the husband's sister in a quiet village. The sister also happens to be leader of the local coven, and much murder, mayhem and Satanic sex ensue. Larraz actually hated the way the movie turned out, but his love for the English countryside lingers on in some of the settings. Ironically, its blundering use of gore to substitute for suspense is symptomatic of latter-day British horror, when the unique elements of that strain began to fade. In this sense, it is far more typical of British movie-making that either of the films actually financed in this country.

Black Candles is symptomatic of the problems that I, as compiler, faced with this book. Like *Living Dead At The Manchester Morgue*, it is a European movie made in England, with European perspectives. The difference with Larraz is that, although

Vampyres

his Spanish sensibility throws a different perspective, even on his UK-produced horror movies, his love of England transcends this, and he manages to pick up strains in the English horror movie that perhaps most English directors miss.

Much to my horror, and even closer to deadline date, I find yet another movie that has been missed, and even worse, this is a Tigon movie, that much-beloved (by me) home of terrible English tat. The movie in question is *Virgin Witch* (1972), directed by English sex movie man Ray Austin from a script by Klaus Vogel. Vogel even got to write a tie-in novel for Corgi that had a photo insert... this was a big deal, right? Well, it should have been, the only problem was that the novel and film were authored in 1970, and Tigon did not actually get the film into theatres until two years later.

An attempt to marry the horror and soft-core strains that were keeping Tony Tenser's little company afloat, it is marginally more successful than the Hammer attempts at such things. This is partly because it has a contemporary setting, and has acquired a kitsch period feel a quarter of a century later, and partly because it makes no pretence to be anything other than what it is – pure exploitation.

Provincial sisters Ann and Vicky Michelle are models who are, to put it bluntly, incredibly stupid. A pseudo-lesbian agent gets them a modelling assignment in the country that turns out to be little more than an excuse to get them in an out of the way place so that they can be used in a ritual sacrifice by a coven. However, Ann proves to have genuine psychic powers, and embarks on a battle to the death with Sybil, the lesbian agent who is also part of the coven.

So much for the plot. Not frightening, and with a leaden-footed direction that nonetheless throws up some accidentally beautiful images, the film is redeemed in many ways by the sisters Michelle, who run around in various states of undress in best British sex-comedy style.

This sits uneasily with the cheapo-horror plotting, and produces an unexpected frisson that actually holds the attention. The pull of tension between the need for atmosphere and the need for well-lit nudity says a lot about the desperate state of the British exploitation industry at the time.

Vicki Michelle, who is less impressive than her sister, later went on to fame as

Virgin Witch

Yvette in *Allo, Allo*, the TV sit-com – while Ann seemed to vanish... funny old business, showbiz.

To bring us right up to date, there has been one horror movie produced in Britain over the last year or so. *Shallow Grave* débuted in early 1995 to rave reviews from the critics and a good audience reaction (in other words, it got a few bums on seats). So this is a good thing, right?

Wrong. *Shallow Grave* is one of those typical products of the 90's British film industry – worthy and dull. Bad news for a horror movie, right? In fact, whether or not it actually is horror is a moot point.

The plot revolves around three nondescript people looking for a fourth flatmate. Enter someone with a lot of stolen dosh to hide, a convenient murder, and the breakdown of morality as some spotty herbert of an accountant metamorphoses into a killer of loopy proportions.

The cast is as nondescript as the characters, and despite a few nice noir-ish camera tricks they get little assistance from a plodding script.

So this is what it takes to make a horror movie in the UK these days?

In contrast, 1995 saw both the BBC and independent television producer Yorkshire produce horror series that were networked in prime-time slots. *Ghosts* was a good series, without the usual BBC standard of writing and acting, and had some genuinely scary moments. It managed to keep the British tradition of restrained horror and at the same time add a judicious helping of gore – certainly as much as it could get away with on Saturday night prime-time (which isn't much, but certainly more that *Shallow Grave*!).

Yorkshire's *Chillers*, on the other hand, was of a variable quality – but even at its worst it was still as much fun as a ropey 70's indie flick.

So is this the way ahead for people who want to produce low-budget horror

Shallow Grave

in Britain? Despite their relative successes, neither the BBC nor Yorkshire plan to follow up their series. But there is still more hope there than in a moribund British movie industry that now (big generalisation coming up) produces middle-class fodder for dwindling UK audiences and PBO cable sales in the US.

Appendix Two... The Return

Just when you thought it was safe to go back into the bookshop, we get you with a second appendix. Now, for all those critics who couldn't figure out why an appendix had to have recently discovered movies at the end of the book, here's a little lesson in economics. Those lovely chaps at Creation have given me a little extra space in the new edition by squeezing out all the ads that appeared in the first. This way they don't have to spend money on re-setting the type – something they can't actually afford. This way, you get extra information without them going bust – we're not a multinational conglom publisher, after all.

The point of this appendix is to cover Norman J. Warren, who I unforgivably left out of the first edition. Oddly, Norman was the only one who didn't get severely peeved about this, and I have to say that he's one of the nicest people I've met in a long time. Through him I've come into contact with Richard Gordon, who has also been a great help.

I met Norman via Darrell Buxton, film writer, film fan, and Creation Records enthusiast. Darrell has been an immense help in supplying me with details about obscure movies. If nothing else came out of this book, it introduced me to a man who I'm glad to call a friend. This edition is for you.

Before I get on with it, I'd also like to thank David Slater for contacting me with more movie details. The Frankie Howerd fanclub is alive and well...

Okay, on with the show.

The British film director is a much maligned breed. Unless they make their home (spiritual or physical) in Hollywood, then work is going to be sparse. Harder still for those directors who want to make movies in the UK, with English actors and settings, and don't wish to make their base overseas. Harder yet for those who just want to do what they want, and haven't the time or inclination to play silly games.

Such a director is Norman J. Warren. In a 30-year career as a film director he has made a total of nine features, the last one in 1986. After the production problems that beset *Bloody New Year*, Warren decided that he would rather go his own way than work on another low-budget horror movie with a producer who didn't understand the genre. With *Beyond Terror*, a self-penned script, he started to knock on doors for financing. The general indecision of the British film industry eventually forced him back to that work which pays the rent: he has directed around 40 documentaries for the BBC, and nearly 140 documentaries, adverts and pop promos in total (including Gary Numan and The Fixx), as well as an hour long drama – *Person To Person* – for the BBC. At the moment, he is stuck in Hollywood development hell with a remake of producer Richard Gordon's 1958 sci-fi terror *Fiend Without A Face*. Warren and Gordon last worked together in 1980, on *Inseminoid*, and the prospect of the *Fiend* project has spurred both men into active film production once more.

Always interested in film – from such an early age that he can't even remember a time when he wasn't – Warren joined amateur film societies and was soon making first attempts at film. By this time he was hitting his teenage years, and although he hadn't decided on being a director, he was adamant that he wanted to work in movies. Particularly sci-fi and horror movies, which had already seized his imagination.

This was still at a time when the school leaving age was fifteen, and when he heard that a company called Screenspace had a vacancy for a teaboy, he snatched at the chance. It was a small beginning – but nonetheless, a break into the world of celluloid.

The next step was for Warren to make his own film: a showreel of quality. Of course, there were the amateur movies he had made – but so much had been learnt since then. There was no way he could afford to make a feature, but by borrowing some money, getting a few credit accounts with labs, and using all he had stashed away for such a purpose, Norman Warren was able to make his first professional film as a director.

When the film – knowingly titled *Fragment* – was completed, he hawked it around distributors, trying to get it shown. This was far from easy, as its length militated against its showing – often, distributors just didn't know what to do with it. Eventually, a distributor named Charles Cooper, who ran Contemporary Films, took it on – on the condition that Warren try to get it shown himself, as they had little chance in placing it in this country! However, Cooper did manage to get it shown in Holland and Germany, and got it college and university distribution in this country.

It may not have seemed much of a deal, but at least Norman Warren now had a film with a legitimate distributor. It was 1964, and there were still a number of independent cinemas around the country that didn't have the block-booking policies and restrictions of today's big chains. Norman began the thankless task of ringing around to try and get it shown – even offering it free of charge.

Fortune truly does sometimes favour the brave. Eventually, the manager of the Paris Pulman theatre in South Kensington agreed to show the film. Richard Schulman, the Pulman's manager, was thinking of going into production. At a time when, with Eady Levy money and audiences still strong for exploitation movies, there was money to be made for independent producers who could get it right. Schulman's partner was businessman Bachoo Sen, who was later to make a name – and fortune – as a producer of soft-core sex movies which were comic (sometimes unintentionally).

The idea was to make low-budget movies, with directors whose relative inexperience would make them both cheap and liable to be undemanding. As they discussed their plans, *Fragment* played on the screen behind them...

"I had a call from Bachoo Sen asking me if I'd like to meet with him about directing a film. I couldn't believe it, as it was the call I'd always been waiting for. Actually, I had a job not being there two minutes after I'd put the phone down, and somehow managed to last out the few days until he offered me the film.

The 1967-released film was *Her Private Hell*, a sexploitation flick about an Italian girl imported by a naughty photos syndicate who fronted as a model agency and doctored said naughty photos to make them pornographic.

Her Private Hell was a commercial success, even though Norman considers it "rather dull". It made a fortune, playing on the Cameo and Classic circuits – doyens of exploitation movies – as well as the West End of London for over a year. It had a full theatrical release in the UK and was exported around the world. A palpable difference from *Fragment*... As a result Norman was asked to direct a second such film. Released in 1969, *Loving Feeling* has – if anything – even less of a plot than the first movie, and features the troublesome Francoise Pascal, an actress who has made more of a career out of controversy than her actual work.

Unlike *Her Private Hell*, *Loving Feeling* was shot in colour, and the budget was stretched to allow Norman to realise a personal ambition and shoot in Cinemascope.

As with the first movie, *Loving Feeling* made a lot of money. And so Norman was offered another movie: *The Wife Swappers*. At this point, he decided to step back from softcore skin flicks.

"It wasn't that I had any great insight into the fact that these were a limited market that was going to collapse – it was simply that I didn't enjoy making them very much. Not in a moral sense: they just get boring after a while. There's only so many

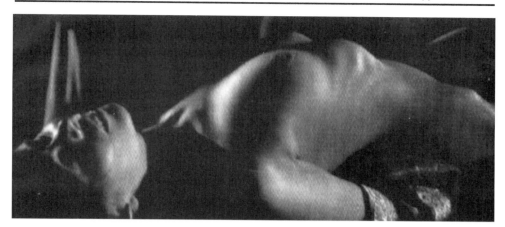

Satan's Slave

ways you can shoot people taking off their clothes and getting into bed without repeating yourself."

But a man with a name in sexploitation who wants to go his own way isn't always going to find it easy to get financing: it took 6 years before *Satan's Slave* was ready to roll. Producer Les Young had the script, and numerous offers of finance that suddenly dried up when it came time to write the cheques. Eventually, Young got tired of waiting: he mortgaged his home, added this to money that others involved in the production could raise, and the film went into production. For the tiny sum of £30,000 – small, even by the standards of 20 years ago – Warren was able to direct a tight, literate and scary film that raised the spectre of Satanism in the suburbs. An almost dreamlike surrealism imbues the twists in David McGillivray's script (which had more lyrical imagination than Peter Walker allowed him on their pictures together). Besides which, any film that has Michael Gough in the vanguard as a smooth arbiter of evil has got to get my vote. Interestingly, there is one scene in the film that only appears in the overseas prints – having been replaced in the UK by a much milder version. Near the beginning of the film, a young man (played by Martin Potter, a fixture in British exploitation movies at this time, and a fine actor) attempts to sexually assault a woman, shredding her clothes with a pair of scissors. He then draws them over her body, threatening to – but never actually managing to – cut her with them.

Anyone who has ever seen this scene finds it deeply disturbing – but not /as disturbing as it was to film, the entire cast and crew having to take a break when it was completed.

Satan's Slave made money. A lot of money. Not that Les Young saw that much of it – in fact, he was forced by financial straits to sell out his share in the film as producer. But the distributors made so much money that they were clamouring for a second film – and so *Terror* followed in 1978. But in between was *Prey*.

The year after *Satan's Slave*, Norman was approached by Terry Marcel, a former first assistant director whom he had known for some time. Marcel had ambitions to get into production and also to direct – something he later achieved – but at the moment was looking for someone to helm a small picture he was getting together. Marcel had been working on Blake Edwards' *Pink Panther* pictures, and a number of technicians working on those had agreed to work for nothing upfront as long as it was a quick shoot. He also managed to get Shepperton Studios – at this time going through one of their sloughs – to let him have the use of certain sets and soundstages for a week free of charge, as long as there were no prior bookings.

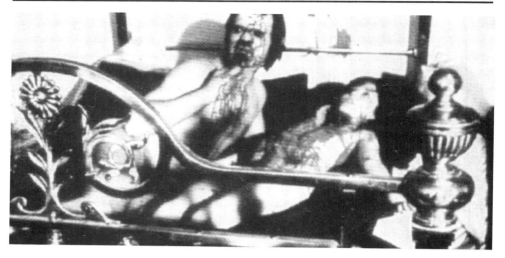

Prey

When Norman was contacted, Marcel outlined the story over the phone and asked if he'd be interested. If so, then they had to begin shooting in 3 weeks.

It was only after Norman had agreed, and things were formalised, that he realised the outline was all that existed. With three weeks to go, there was no actual script.

"It was quite an interesting film to do, as the script wasn't finished when we began shooting. It was a 10-day shoot, so we had to work harder every day. *Satan's Slave* and *Terror* were 3-week shoots, which is tight, but 10 days is quite a reduction from that. It's tough, but it is possible – you just have to keep on running!

"But somehow it all worked. I was pleased with the film when it was finished, and it's gone on to be quite a favourite with fans."

And why not? *Prey* is the tale of an alien who stumbles upon two young girls who live alone in the country. It has a brooding intensity as the three form a bizarre *menage-a-trois*, with emotions and paranoia running rampant. The alien is in search of a new food source for his race, and it's not until the end that you realise that source is humanity – revealed in a gory cannibalistic scene that is all the more shocking for coming as a complete surprise.

Basically a 3-hander, the acting is superb, helped by the fact that Warren was able to rehearse the actors and take them through the scenes carefully. The reason for the small cast was partly budgetary – less actors, less money – and partly the dictates of a quickly written script.

Terror – another slice of suburban terror – did so well on its release that it was, for one week, the top grossing box office film in the UK. Made with Martin Potter from *Satan's Slave* but an otherwise different cast (including Glynis Barber in her first British film), and a slightly larger budget, it saw Warren stretching out as a director. Given the luxury of a little more time and the opportunity to take actors through rehearsals, *Terror* was even more accomplished than *Satan's Slave*. Opening in Chicago and Oaklahoma, it went to number one regionally, wiping the floor with big-budget opposition. In fact, this low-budget English movie finished nineteenth in the year's *Variety* Top 50 grossers.

Interestingly enough, there was only one real censorship problem with *Terror*... in one scene, a woman is stabbed on a flight of stairs. What did the censor want to cut? Her feet... so perhaps the truth about the BBFC is that they are comprised

Terror

of foot fetishists. Whatever...

So how come Norman Warren didn't have a glittering career in horror and science-fiction? How come he made a few more low-budget movies and now spends his days on more mundane – if lucrative – work?

Norman himself believes the answer is simple: "I didn't move to America. When I was doing promotion for *Inseminoid*, in the US, I had several people approach me with offers that would have meant relocating to the States. I had affairs to settle in the UK, so had to return for a couple of months. Unfortunately, it was 'out of sight, out of mind', and when I was ready to move the offers had gone. I like living here, and I like working here. But at the same time, I've always loved America – it's a wonderful and exciting place. Ideally I'd like to make movies in both countries, but it just hasn't worked that way... yet."

The problem now was that Warren was typed as a man who could work wonders on a small budget, with the result that the British offers were for very small budgeted pictures: "They seemed to think 'he's done well on that amount, so let's see what he can do on even less...'"

And none of these offers were for films that interested him. He even tried writing his own scripts, but still couldn't find the right project. A couple of deals fell through, and then with income running low he was approached to direct a film called *Outer Touch*.

It was 1979, and someone wanted to make a sci-fi sex comedy... I always think of it as a cross between a *Carry On* film and *Fire Maidens From Outer Space*. It's very British, as the sex is coy and almost non-existent. And it wasn't terribly funny. We went through re-writes on the script, but it was still very corny. I look back on it as fun now – especially if you've had a few drinks. The problems weren't really in the production values, but in the script."

From here it was back into development hell with projects that didn't work out, one of which was *Gargoyles*, to be co-financed and co-produced by Richard Gordon. Gordon is a horror buff and producer whose credits include *Island Of Terror*,

Horror Hospital, and *Fiend Without A Face*. An admirer of Warren, whom he knew from the intermingled film-fan and film-maker circle of horror buffs, Gordon approached him with a script which had been given to him by a pair of shady characters, in search of a co-producer, who had agreed to finance the other two-thirds. A shaky script, it was re-worked by Richard and Norman... and then came the time for signing cheques.

Suddenly, the two men disappeared. Totally. Home phones disconnected. Office phone disconnected. Office empty. Never to be seen again.

Leaving Gordon and Warren with a script they couldn't use because it wasn't their copyright, and one-third of a movie financed and ready to roll. Still keen for them to work together, Gordon invited Warren to come up with a project. Providentially, Norman attended the anniversary meal of Nick and Gloria Male, the make-up man and an actress who had met and married working on *Satan's Slave*. Having mentioned the project casually, Norman was pleasantly surprised to get a call about a week later from Nick, telling him that the couple had drafted a script for him. Called *Doom Seed*, Norman was impressed and sent the script to Richard Gordon, who agreed that it was a good script that needed a few changes, and said "Let's go".

This was the birth of 1980's *Inseminoid*. Re-worked by Nick, Gloria and Norman, the producers of *Outer Touch* were approached, as were the Shaw Brothers of Hong Kong. Under Gordon's expert guidance, financing was set up in just six weeks from the time the script landed on his desk.

The film is a tight, literate movie that has a true sense of terror in its tale of an alien attempting to impregnate the member of a space exploration team. The final title was Peter Schlesinger's (he was also Executive Producer), and the movie was shot in Chiselhurst Caves in Kent. It was damp and cold, but cut down the need for expensive sets as it came, so to speak, ready-made as an alien environment. The feeling amongst cast and crew was such that Judy Geeson even volunteered to come in on her one day off and make tea and coffee for the equally cold, damp crew.

Strange things happened in the caves – things that wouldn't have been out of place in the film itself. The oddest was that the batteries on the cameras and lights would run down within minutes when their charge was usually good for several hours. And there was a definite atmosphere about the place... in the shape of a strange but indefinable smell. Rushes were flown to the Shaw Brothers in Hong Kong at the end of each week, and the only comment they had to make was "more blood": they had no problems with anything in the shoot except that they wanted gallons of gore splashed around. A simple enough request, I suppose...

One of the first films to get a sell-through release on video in the UK, back in 1982, it managed to shift over 40,000 copies, which is a phenomenal number for the early days of video. It has been re-released twice – once by Allied Vision, and then in 1992 by Vipco in a widescreen edition. Successful across the world, it has also had a laser disc edition – and Norman remembers one late night in Italy where he turned on the TV to find it coming out of the screen in a dubbed version... a surreal experience.

Perhaps it should have been the start of a beautiful relationship, but sadly for Norman, Richard Gordon was about to retire from active production. Citing the changes in the industry that made self-finance and distribution more and more difficult, Gordon found life was easier if he concentrated on exploiting his old movies, and spent time on his business distributing others' films in the USA.

When Norman was given the opportunity to make another feature – 1984's *Gunpowder* – it wasn't without misgivings. An action-adventure picture centred around the buddy-buddy teaming of an American action man and a suave English spy, it seemed that there wasn't enough money to go round.

Between them, Norman, art director Hayden Pearce and the two leading men (one of them being Martin Potter) came up with a way to overcome the cheapness and make the film work as a comic strip. Linking scenes would be comic-strip panels that would dissolve into the actual scene. It would have worked... but they were all over-ruled on grounds of money.

Gunpowder had a patchy release, did little business, and occasionally crops up on TV in a few territories.

"Foolishly, both myself and the crew from *Gunpowder* decided to do another film with the same producer – Maxine Julius. I asked if she felt she had learned anything, and she told me she had.

"She hadn't... we persuaded her to do a horror movie as she didn't have enough of a budget for action-adventure. She presented us with a lot of scripts that weren't quite right. So myself and Hayden Pearce, who had been promoted to line producer, did one of our own. She liked – or rather, she accepted – it, as she admitted she knew nothing about horror – and that's how *Bloody New Year* was born.

"It could have been good. The effects we needed could have been done on the budget, as they weren't that different from what had been done on *Terror*, but she was always moving us on, not allowing time for the right thing. She rushed through the sound mix and music – and that's so important. For the music, she'd done a deal with two guys who provided songs, and some of the material was supposed to be late '50s – Jerry Lee Lewis, Little Richard-type hard rock'n'roll – and these songs... they were okay, but they weren't right. It's sad, as these compromised the film. Take away a good soundtrack and you take away half a horror film.

"Hayden worked miracles for no money. He found a deserted hotel on the Welsh coast that he managed to persuade the local council – who owned it – to let us use for nothing. We had a fairground for peanuts. And one part of the film centres around a '50s flashback ballroom scene. Somehow, he managed to secure the services of the Rock'n'roll Preservation Society, who turned up for nothing more than coffee and sandwiches and danced all day.

"Unfortunately, all the main actors were young and inexperienced, and there wasn't enough time to really coach them. The film could have been so much better..."

And so he trails off with a wistful tone. *Bloody New Year* (aka *Timewarp Terror*) is perhaps not as bad as some commentators claim, but was certainly not the sort of film that Norman J. Warren wanted to put his name to: so he returned to the long route of finding financing himself. As for Maxine Julius: she made one more movie (not horror), then disappeared.

As I write this, Norman has several projects in development – including his re-make of *Fiend Without A Face*, produced by Richard Gordon – all of which are stuck in development hell. It would be nice to think that if this book goes to a third edition, I'll be able to write that one of these projects is at least in the can...

Filmography

The following films were discussed in the text. Some may only have been mentioned in passing, while others were discussed in detail. This list is by no means a complete archive of British Horror, but does represent several decades of dedicated film viewing, scouring of second hand video stalls in dodgy markets, and late-night channel surfing. Having said that, a few of the films are mentioned because of their historical importance, even though I have never managed to see them. This is particularly true of some of the films made in the 1930's, many of which do not even exist anyway, as the nitrate stock has dissolved before they could be saved.

Any omissions will be gratefully received by myself, c/o the publishers, and may be included in future editions.

Other films mentioned in the text that do not fit the criteria of "horror", but were germane to a particular chapter, have not been included in this list.

The Abominable Doctor Phibes (AIP 1971)
The Abominable Snowman (Hammer 1957)
The Abominable Snowman Of The Himalayas *see* The Abominable Snowman
An American Werewolf In London (Polygram/Lycanthrope 1981)
The Anatomist (BIP 1961)
And Now The Screaming Starts (Amicus 1973)
And Soon The Darkness (Associated British 1970)
Anger Of The Golem *see* It
The Anniversary (Hammer 1968)
Are You Dying Young Man? *see* The Beast In The Cellar
The Asphyx (Glendale 1973)
Asylum (Amicus 1972)
Asylum Of Blood *see* Ghost Story
The Awakening (EMI 1980)
The Baby *see* I Don't Want To Be Born
Back Room Boy (Gainsborough 1942)
The Beast In The Cellar (Tigon 1970)
The Beast Must Die (Amicus 1974)
The Bed Sitting Room (UA 1969)
Behemoth The Sea Monster *see* The Giant Behemoth
Berserk (Columbia/Herman Cohen 1967)
The Bespoke Overcoat (Remus 1956)
Birth Of Frankenstein *see* The Curse Of Frankenstein
The Birthday Party (Amicus/Palomar 1968)
Bizarre *see* Secrets Of Sex
The Black Panther (Impis 1977)
The Black Torment (Compton-Tekli 1964)
Blind Terror (Columbia/Filmways/Genesis 1971)
Blood Beast From Hell *see* The Blood Beast Terror
Blood Beast From Outer Space *see* The Night Caller
The Blood Beast Terror (Tigon 1967)
The Blood Fiend *see* Theatre Of Death
Blood From The Mummy's Tomb (Hammer 1971)
Blood Of The Vampire (Berman/Baker/Alliance 1958)
The Blood On Satan's Claw (Tigon 1970)
The Blood Virgin *see* Symptoms

Blood Will Have Blood *see* Demons Of The Mind
Bloodbath At The House Of Death (EMI/Wildwood 1983)
Bloodsuckers *see* Incense For The Damned
The Bloody Scream Of Dracula *see* Dracula, Prince Of Darkness
The Body Stealers (Tigon 1968)
Brazil (Arnold Milchin 1985)
Bride Of Fengriffen *see* And Now The Screaming Starts
Brides Of Dracula (Hammer 1960)
Burke And Hare (UA 1971)
Burn, Witch, Burn *see* Night Of The Eagle
Captain Kronos – Vampire Hunter (Hammer 1971)
Captain Kronus, Vampire Hunter *see* Captain Kronos – Vampire Hunter
The Caretaker (Caretaker Films 1964)
Carnage *see* Corruption
Carry On Screaming (Anglo-Amalgamated 1966)
Carry On Vampire *see* Carry On Screaming
Castle Sinister (Delta 1932)
The Cat And The Canary (Gala 1979)
The Cat Girl (Insignia 1957)
The Cat Woman *see* The Cat Girl
Children Of The Damned (MGM 1964)
The Chosen *see* Holocaust 2000
Circus Of Blood *see* Berserk
Circus Of Horrors (Anglo-Amalgamated 1960)
Circus Of Terror *see* Berserk
City Of The Dead (Valear/Amicus 1960)
City Under The Sea (Burton/AIP 1965)
A Clockwork Orange (Warner/Polaris 1971)
The Comeback (Walker 1977)
Company Of Wolves (ITC/Palace 1984)
Computer Killers *see* Horror Hospital
The Confessional *see* House Of Mortal Sin
The Conqueror Worm *see* Witchfinder General
The Corpse (Riklis 1971)
Corridors Of Blood (Producers Associates 1958)
Corruption (Tigon 1967)
Count Dracula And His Vampire Bride *see* The Satanic Rites Of Dracula
Countess Dracula (Hammer 1970)
The Crawling Eye *see* The Trollenberg Terror
Craze (Harbour 1973)
The Creatures *see* From Beyond The Grave
The Creeping Flesh (Tigon 1972)
The Creeping Unknown *see* The Quatermass X-periment
Crescendo (Hammer 1969)
Crimes At The Dark House (Pennant/George King 1939)
The Crimes Of Stephen Hawke (George King/EMI 1936)
The Crimson Altar *see* The Curse Of The Crimson Altar
The Crimson Cult *see* The Curse Of The Crimson Altar
Crucible Of Horror *see* The Corpse
Crucible Of Terror (Scotia Barker 1972)
Cry Of The Banshee (AIP 1970)
Cry Wolf (Picture Partnership 1980)
The Curse Of Frankenstein (Hammer 1957)
Curse Of Simba *see* The Curse Of The Voodoo
The Curse Of The Crimson Altar (Tigon 1968)

Curse Of The Demon *see* Night Of The Demon
The Curse Of The Fly (Lippert 1965)
The Curse Of The Golem *see* It
The Curse Of The Mummy's Tomb (Hammer 1962)
The Curse Of The Voodoo (Gala 1965)
The Curse Of The Werewolf (Hammer 1962)
The Curse Of The Wraydons (Bushey 1946)
The Damned (Hammer 1963)
The Dark *see* The Haunted House Of Horror
Dark Eyes Of London (Pathe/Argyle 1939)
Dark Water (Dragonfly/ITC 1980)
Daughters Of Dracula *see* Vampyres
The Day The Earth Caught Fire (British Lion/Pax 1961)
Dead Of Night (Ealing 1945)
Deadline *see* Death Line
The Deadly Bees (Amicus 1966)
The Deathshead Vampire *see* The Blood Beast Terror
Death Line (Probe 1973)
Déjà Vu (Canon 1985)
Demons Of The Mind (Hammer 1971)
Devil Doll (Gala 1963)
Devil Girl From Mars (The Danzingers 1954)
The Devil Rides Out (Hammer 1967)
The Devil Within Her *see* I Don't Want To Be Born
The Devil's Bride *see* The Devil Rides Out
Devils Of Darkness (Planet 1964)
The Devil's Own *see* The Witches
Die! Die! My Darling *see* Fanatic
Die, Monster, Die (AIP 1967)
Die Screaming, Marianne (Walker 1973)
Disciple Of Dracula *see* Dracula, Prince Of Darkness
Disciples Of Death (Scotia Barker 1971)
The Doctor And The Devils (Brooksfilms 1985)
Doctor Blood's Coffin (UA/Caralan 1960)
Doctor From Seven Dials *see* Corridors Of Blood
Dr Jekyll And Sister Hyde (Hammer 1971)
Dr Phibes Rises Again (AIP 1973)
Dr Terror's House Of Horrors (Amicus 1965)
Don't Open Till Christmas (21st Century 1983)
Doomwatch (Tigon 1972)
Dracula (Hammer 1958)
Dracula (Universal 1979)
Dracula AD 1972 (Hammer 1972)
Dracula And The Seven Golden Vampires *see* The Legend Of The Seven
    Golden Vampires
Dracula Chases The Mini Girls *see* Dracula AD 1972
Dracula Chelsea 72 *see* Dracula AD 1972
Dracula Has Risen From The Grave (Hammer 1968)
Dracula Is Dead...And Well And Living In London *see* The Satanic Rites Of
    Dracula
Dracula, Prince Of Darkness (Hammer 1965)
Dracula Today *see* Dracula AD 1972
Dracula's Desire *see* Mother Riley Meets The Vampire
Dracula's Revenge *see* Dracula Has Risen From The Grave
Dream Demon (Cotillion 1987)

The Earth Dies Screaming (Anglo-Amalgamated 1964)
Enemy From Space *see* Quatermass II
The Evil Of Frankenstein (Hammer 1964)
Eye Of The Devil (MGM 1967)
The Face At The Window (Hiscott 1932)
The Fall Of The House Of Usher (Valiant 1949)
Fanatic (Hammer 1965)
Fear In The Night (Hammer 1972)
The Female Fiend *see* Theatre Of Death
Fengriffen *see* And Now The Screaming Starts
Fiend Without A Face (Eros/Producers Associates 1957)
The Fiendish Ghouls *see* The Flesh And The Fiends
Film (BFI 1979)
Fire Maidens From Outer Space (Criterion/Eros 1956)
First Man Into Space (Producers Associates 1958)
Five Million Years To Earth *see* Quatermass And The Pit
The Flesh And Blood Show (Walker 1972)
The Flesh And The Fiends (Regal/Triad/Baker & Berman 1959)
Frankenstein And The Monster From Hell (Hammer 1973)
Frankenstein Created Woman (Hammer 1967)
Frankenstein Made Woman *see* Frankenstein Created Woman
Frankenstein Must Be Destroyed (Hammer 1969)
Fright (Fantale 1971)
Frightmare (Walker 1974)
From Beyond The Grave (Amicus 1973)
The Frozen Dead (Goldwater 1966)
Full Circle (Paramount 1976)
Further Tales From the Crypt *see* Vault Of Horror
The Gemini Twins *see* Twins Of Evil
The Ghost Of Rashomon Hall (Highgate 1949)
The Ghost Of St Michael's (Ealing 1941)
The Ghost Ship (Anglo-Amalgamated 1952)
Ghost Story (Weeks 1974)
The Ghost Train (Gainsborough 1931)
The Ghost Train (Gainsborough 1941)
The Ghoul (Gaumont 1933)
The Ghoul (Tyburn 1975)
The Giant Behemoth (Artists Alliance 1959)
Gingerbread House *see* Who Slew Auntie Roo?
Gorgo (King Brothers 1960)
The Gorgon (Hammer 1964)
The Greed Of William Hart (Bushey 1948)
Grip Of The Strangler (Producers Associates 1958)
The Guest *see* The Caretaker
Halfway House (Ealing 1944)
Hands Of A Strangler *see* Hands Of Orlac
Hands Of Orlac (Riviera/Pendennis 1960)
Hands Of The Ripper (Hammer 1971)
The Haunted *see* Night Of The Demon
The Haunted House Of Horror (Tigon 1969)
The Haunted Strangler *see* Grip Of The Strangler
The Haunting (MGM 1963)
The Haunting Of Julia *see* Full Circle
Hellraiser (Canon 1988)
Holocaust 2000 (Aston/Embassy 1980)

Horror Express (Benmar 1972)
Horror Hospital (Balch 1973)
Horror Hotel *see* City Of The Dead
Horror House *see* The Haunted House Of Horror
Horror Of Dracula *see* Dracula
The Horror Of Frankenstein (Hammer 1970)
Horrors Of The Black Museum (Cohen 1959)
The Hound Of The Baskervilles (Hammer 1959)
The House At The End Of The World *see* Die, Monster, Die
The House In Nightmare Park (EMI/Associated London 1973)
House Of Crazies *see* Asylum
House Of Fright *see* The Two Faces Of Doctor Jekyll
House Of Mortal Sin (Walker 1975)
House Of Mystery (Independent Artists 1960)
House Of The Long Shadows (Canon 1983)
House Of Whipcord (Walker 1974)
House That Dripped Blood (Amicus 1970)
The Human Monster *see* The Dark Eyes Of London
Hysteria (Hammer 1964)
I Bought A Vampire Motorcycle (Canon 1990)
I Don't Want To Be Born (Unicapital 1975)
I Have No Mouth But I Must Scream *see* And Now The Screaming Starts
I, Monster (Amicus 1970)
Idols In The Dust *see* Saturn 3
Incense For The Damned (Chevron 1970)
The Infernal Idol *see* Craze
The Innocents (TCF/Achilles 1960)
Inseminoid (Jupiter 1980)
Invasion (AA/Merton Park 1966)
Island Of The Burning Damned *see* Night Of The Big Heat
Island Of Terror (Planet 1966)
It (Goldstar 1966)
Jack The Ripper (Midcentury/Baker-Berman 1958)
Jekyll's Inferno *see* The Two Faces Of Doctor Jekyll
Juggernaut (Ambassador 1937)
King Robot *see* Mother Riley Meets The Vampire
Kiss Of Evil *see* Kiss Of The Vampire
Kiss Of The Vampire (Hammer 1962)
Konga (Cohen 1960)
Kronos *see* Captain Kronos – Vampire Hunter
The Lair Of The White Worm (Palace 1989)
The Legacy (Columbia 1978)
The Legend Of Hell House (TCF/Academy 1973)
The Legacy Of Maggie Walsh *see* The Legacy
The Legend Of The Seven Golden Vampires (Hammer/Shaw 1974)
The Legend Of The Werewolf (Tyburn 1976)
Life Force (Canon 1985)
Lion Man *see* The Curse Of The Voodoo
The Lodger (Gaumont 1926)
The Lodger (Twickenham 1932)
Lust For A Vampire (Hammer 1970)
Madhouse (AIP/Amicus 1974)
The Man Behind The Mask (Joe Rock 1936)
The Man Who Changed His Mind (Gainsborough 1936)
The Man Who Could Cheat Death (Hammer 1959)

The Man Who Lived Again *see* The Man Who Changed His Mind
The Man Without A Body (Eros 1957)
Mania *see* The Flesh And The Fiends
Maniac (Hammer 1963)
Manutara *see* The Vulture
Maria Marten, Or Murder In The Red Barn (George King 1935)
The Masque Of The Red Death (AIP 1964)
The Medium (Delta 1934)
The Monster *see* I Don't Want To Be Born
The Monster Club (ITC 1980)
The Monster Of Terror *see* Die, Monster, Die
Mother Riley Meets The Vampire (Renown 1952)
Mother Riley Runs Riot *see* Mother Riley Meets The Vampire
Much Ado About Murder *see* Theatre Of Blood
The Mummy (Hammer 1959)
The Mummy's Shroud (Hammer 1966)
Murder By Decree (Avco/Decree/Saucy Jack 1979)
Mutations (Getty 1974)
My Learned Friend (Ealing 1943)
My Son The Vampire *see* Mother Riley Meets The Vampire
Mystery Of The Marie Celeste (Hammer 1935)
The Nanny (Hammer 1965)
The Night Caller (New Art/Armitage/Independent Artists 1965)
Night Of The Big Heat (Planet 1967)
Night Of The Demon (Columbia 1957)
Night Of The Eagle (Independent Artists 1961)
Night Watch (Avco/Brut 1973)
Nightmare (Hammer 1964)
Nightmare Park *see* The House In Nightmare Park
No Place Like Homicide *see* What A Carve-Up!
No Blade Of Grass (MGM 1970)
Nothing But The Night (Charlemagne 1972)
The Oblong Box (AIP 1969)
The Old Dark House (Hammer 1962)
Old Dracula *see* Vampira
Old Mother Riley Meets The Vampire *see* Mother Riley Meets The Vampire
Paperhouse (Palace 1988)
Paranoiac (Hammer 1963)
Peeping Tom (Anglo-Amalgamated 1959)
Persecution (Tyburn 1974)
The Phantom Fiend *see* The Lodger
Phantom Of The Opera (Hammer 1962)
Phantom Ship *see* Mystery Of The Marie Celeste
Plague Of The Zombies (Hammer 1966)
Prey (Tymar 1978)
The Projected Man (Compton Cameo 1967)
Psycho Killers *see* The Flesh And The Fiends
Psychomania (Benmar 1972)
Psychopath (Amicus 1966)
Quatermass II (Hammer 1957)
Quatermass And The Pit (Hammer 1967)
The Quatermass X-periment (Hammer 1955)
Raw Meat *see* Death Line
Rawhead Rex (Canon 1986)
The Reincarnation *see* The Curse Of The Crimson Altar

The Reptile (Hammer 1966)
The Resurrection Syndicate *see* Nothing But The Night
The Return Of Jack The Ripper *see* Jack The Ripper
The Revenge Of Dr Death *see* Madhouse
Revenge Of Dracula *see* Dracula, Prince Of Darkness
The Revenge Of Frankenstein (Hammer 1958)
Room To Let (Hammer 1949)
The Satanic Rites Of Dracula (Hammer 1973)
Satan's Skin *see* The Blood On Satan's Claw
Satan's Slave (Monumental 1976)
Saturn 3 (ITC 1980)
Scars Of Dracula (Hammer 1970)
Schizo (Walker 1976)
Schizoid *see* Psychopath
Scream And Scream Again (Amicus 1969)
Scream Of Fear *see* Taste Of Fear
Screamer *see* Scream And Scream Again
The Screaming Starts *see* And Now The Screaming Starts
See No Evil *see* Blind Terror
Secrets Of Sex (Balch 1970)
The Seven Brothers Meet Dracula *see* The Legend Of The Seven Golden Vampires
Sexton Blake And The Hooded Terror (George King 1938)
Shadow Of The Cat (BHP 1961)
Shallow Grave
Sharon's Baby *see* I Don't Want To Be Born
The Shuttered Room (Troy/Schenk 1967)
The Skull (Amicus 1965)
The Sorcerers (Tigon 1967)
Spirit Of The Dead *see* The Curse Of The Crimson Altar
Split Second (Challenge 1992)
Stolen Face (Exclusive, 1952)
Straight On Till Morning (Hammer 1972)
The Strangler Of Bombay *see* The Stranglers Of Bombay
The Stranglers Of Bombay (Hammer 1959)
A Study In Terror (Compton 1965)
Suspense *see* The Innocents
Sweeney Todd, Demon Barber Of Fleet Street (George King 1936)
Symptoms (Cambist 1974)
Tales From Beyond The Grave *see* From Beyond The Grave
Tales From The Beyond *see* From Beyond The Grave
Tales From The Crypt (Amicus 1972)
Tales That Witness Madness (Paramount 1973)
Taste Of Fear (Hammer 1961)
Taste The Blood Of Dracula (Hammer 1969)
The Tell-Tale Heart (Gaumont 1934)
Terror (Crystal 1979)
The Terror (Gaumont 1936)
The Terror Of Sheba *see* Persecution
Terror Of The Mummy *see* The Mummy
The Terror Of The Tongs (Hammer 1960)
The Terrornauts (Amicus 1966)
Theatre Of Blood (UA 1973)
Theatre Of Death (Pennea 1966)
These Are The Damned *see* The Damned
They Came From Beyond Space (Amicus 1966)

The Thing In The Attic *see* The Ghoul
Thirteen *see* Eye Of The Devil
To Love A Vampire *see* Lust For A Vampire
To The Devil A Daughter (Hammer 1975)
The Tomb Of Ligeia (AIP 1964)
Torture Garden (Amicus 1967)
Trog (Cohen 1970)
The Trollenberg Terror (Eros 1958)
Twins Of Dracula *see* Twins Of Evil
Twins Of Evil (Hammer 1971)
Twisted Nerve (British Lion 1968)
The Two Faces Of Doctor Jekyll (Hammer 1960)
The Uncanny (Tor 1977)
The Undead *see* From Beyond The Grave
The Unearthly Stranger (Independent Artists 1963)
The Unholy Quest (Adney 1934)
Vampir *see* Vampira
Vampira (WFS 1974)
The Vampire Beast Craves Blood *see* The Blood Beast Terror
Vampire Circus (Hammer 1971)
Vampire Castle *see* Captain Kronos – Vampire Hunter
The Vampire Lovers (Hammer 1971)
Vampire Over London *see* Mother Riley Meets The Vampire
Vampirella *see* Vampira
The Vampyre Orgy *see* Vampyres
Vampyres (Cambist 1975)
Vampyres – Daughters Of Darkness *see* Vampyres
Vault Of Horror (Amicus 1973)
Village Of The Damned (MGM 1960)
Virgin Vampires *see* Twins Of Evil
Virgin Witch (Tigon 1970)
Voodoo Blood Death *see* The Curse Of The Voodoo
The Vulture (Huntington 1967)
War Gods Of The Deep *see* City Under The Sea
What A Carve-Up! (Baker-Berman 1961)
What Became Of Jack And Jill (Amicus 1971)
Who Slew Auntie Roo? (AIP 1972)
Whoever Slew Auntie Roo? *see* Who Slew Auntie Roo?
The Wicker Man (British Lion 1973)
Witch And Warlock *see* Witchcraft
Witchcraft (TCF 1964)
The Witches (Hammer 1966)
Witchfinder General (Tigon 1968)
The Wolfman *see* The Curse Of The Werewolf
X – The Unknown (Hammer 1956)
Young Man I Think You're Dying *see* The Beast In The Cellar
The Zombie *see* Plague Of The Zombies
The Zombies *see* Plague Of The Zombies

Index

Page number in bold indicates an illustration

W

X

www.creationbooks.com